# the automobile

enzo angelucci & alberto bellucci

# the automobile
## from steam to gasoline

McGRAW-HILL BOOK COMPANY

New York • St. Louis • San Francisco • Toronto

Originally published in Italian under the title
LE AUTOMOBILI


Library of Congress Cataloging in Publication Data

Angelucci, Enzo.
The automobile.
1. Automobiles—History. I. Bellucci, Alberto, joint author. II. Title.
TL15.A497 1976 629.22′22′09 75-19486
ISBN 0-07-001870-7

First published in America by
McGraw-Hill Book Company, 1976

Printed and bound in Italy by Arnoldo Mondadori Editore, Verona

# contents


preface vii

1 when the automobile had sails 9

2 steam comes of age 21

3 the automobile is born 31

4 la belle époque 45

5 a new century 61

6 dust and glory 77

7 ford's revolution 107

8 the war is on 117

9 the golden age 137

10 the automobile in the army 181

11 rebirth of the automobile 197

acknowledgments 241

appendix 243

index 273

# PREFACE

The history of humanity is more than heroic deeds and important dates. In fact, the advance of civilization owes much to man's creativeness in devising and constantly improving various forms of transportation, for free and rapid mobility makes possible the interchange of ideas and the meeting and merging of contrasting cultures. The automobile is an example of one means of transportation which occupies a crucial place in the dramatic story of man. However, the automobile was not the result of a single invention. Rather, it came into being through a centuries-long process and the combined efforts and experiments of many skilled and talented men—men who often worked alone in different countries and at different times.

War and peace, work and leisure, have had a significant part in the growth of the automobile. In turn, the automobile has had a tremendous influence on the manners and social customs of people, the development of entire countries, and the relations among nations (for instance, the role it has played in making the world less provincial, in uniting town and country, and in bringing diverse societies together).

Our book attempts to trace the evolution of the automobile and to show how the contributions of pioneer inventors and engineers—all endeavoring to fulfill the dream of a self-propelled vehicle—eventually culminated in the motor car as we know it today.

THE AUTHORS

CVRRVS VELIFERI Ill.mi Pr. MAVRITII NASSOVII.

# When the automobile had sails

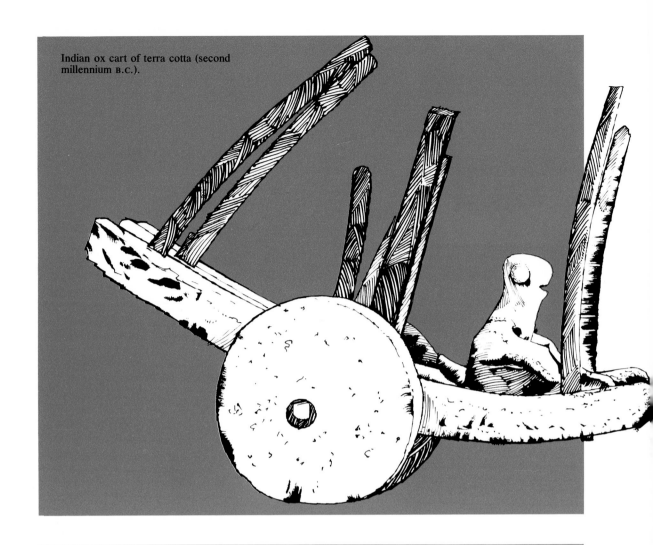

Indian ox cart of terra cotta (second millennium B.C.).

The **banner of Ur** (3000 B.C.), now in the British Museum, shows the first Sumerian wagons. They had wooden wheels and two axles and were drawn by wild asses.

Right: A cart shown in a Chinese print from the second century B.C.

# When the automobile had sails

"Automobile: a vehicle that moves under its own power." This is the brief dictionary definition of the result of centuries of effort by hundreds of brilliant inventors. The outcome of all that effort is worthy of respect: 250 million cars circulate in the world today!

Just who invented the automobile? It's not an easy question to answer; let's just say no one and everyone. The truth is that the story of the automobile can be compared to a mosaic to which many inventors contributed over the course of the centuries. But although it took about 6000 years to start this mosaic, only about 100 were needed to finish it. Now let's try to see the connection between the first cart and the automobile of today.

The desire to use something besides his own legs in moving from one place to another is as old as man himself. Can't we really consider as an automobile—since it was an animal vehicle moved by its own power—the ancestor of the present-day horse, which man surely made use of, riding it or making it pull a sled, even before the wheel was invented?

The wheel—certainly the neolithic age's most important invention. Ever since time began, men have used tree trunks for moving heavy objects; that is surely the way the immense stones used in erecting the megalithic monuments were transported to their sites. Man moved by degrees from the trunk to the wheel. First he carved out the center of the trunk, and made a kind of axle with two rough wheels at each end, to which he tried to give equal width. He then got the idea of strapping, onto this axle with wheels, a wooden floor with two shafts to which a horse—or, more probably, a mule or an ox—was tied.

So the animal-drawn cart was born. It's hard to establish the exact date of this fundamental event in history. One thing is sure, however: as far back as about 4000 B.C., one-axle carts were in use. And in 3000 B.C., the Sumerians already had two-axle carts. These carts had wheels made out of the half-circles of wood joined together, in the center of which there was a disk with a hole through which the axle passed. This axle end was almost surely not attached to the wheel itself, so that there would be less friction on curves. The Sumerians also thought up the scythed chariot, which had deadly sharp blades attached to the wheels and the tiller and was the real prototype of the modern armored tank. The first great pitched battle that history records was fought at Fiadesh in 1296 B.C.: the light war chariots of Egyptian Pharaoh Rameses II faced the heavy chariots of Hittite King

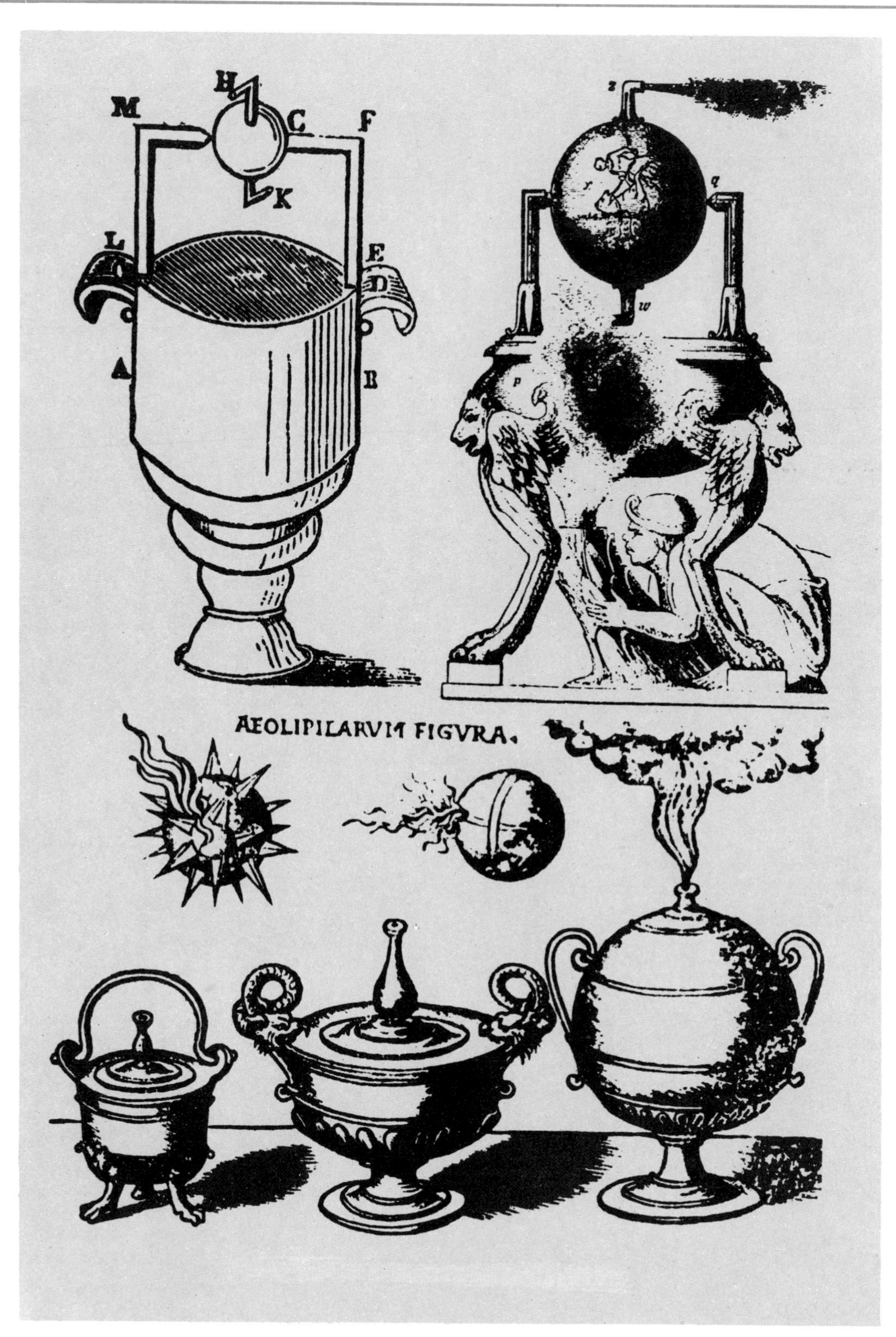


Various types of **eolipilas** designed by Hero of Alexandria in the second or first century B.C.: the first rudimentary example of a steam turbine.

Muvetahi in what is considered the first battle between "armored" vehicles.

The Romans made an extremely important contribution to the evolution of transportation. Among other things, they invented the front steering axle on two-axle carts. Roman, too, is the creation of organized transportation—slow as it seems to us—between important cities; this was done with covered wagons with two axles. These wagons contained beds and were therefore called "*carruca dormitoria.*" But the main contribution of the Romans was the building of an efficient road network from one end of their empire to another, a network still in use today. These roads gave wheeled transportation the stimulus it needed to progress.

Still despite such progress, Caesar's legions went on foot when they traveled and, at best, employed small squadrons of cavalry. Each soldier carried on his person all that he needed in the way of arms, food, and clothing—a weight that often reached a hefty 50 kilograms. The reason for this was the extreme slowness and great instability of the carts of that time, which could only be used safely for short distances. If the trip was a long one, much time was lost in the frequent halts for sudden breakdowns. We know that the Romans preferred to travel in litters on long trips; it is true that this required many changes of porters, who were distributed along the route, but it was also much faster, not as rough, and much more trustworthy and comfortable than the animal-drawn wagon—even if infinitely more expensive.

The automobile, born 2000 years later, met with much the same fate. For the same reasons the Romans preferred the litter to the wagon, plus the noise factor, people preferred to travel in carriages for some decades after the birth of the car. In ancient times, we know that Hero of Alexandria invented the first rudimentary kind of steam turbine, called an "*eolipila,*" but did not conceive of its practical use and abandoned it in the experimental stage. Hero's *eolipila* was probably created around the first century B.C. Nor were the Romans idle in that period: in fact, we owe to them the invention of the ball bearing (unfortunately not used on vehicles) as well as a war chariot moved by the human strength inside the chariot itself and used by Caesar in Gaul in 52 B.C.

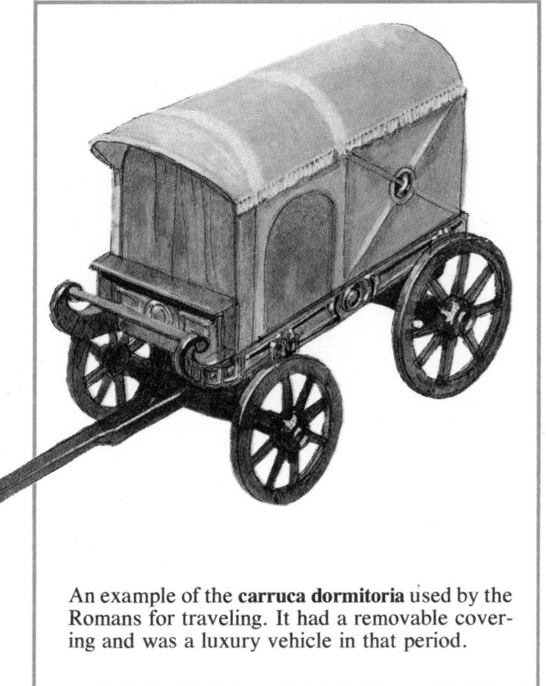

An example of the **carruca dormitoria** used by the Romans for traveling. It had a removable covering and was a luxury vehicle in that period.

Even before that time the Chinese had studied steam, the power of which was well known to them, and imagined its practical uses. As far back as 800 B.C., in the Chu Dynasty (1125–255 B.C.), they experimented with machines "worked by fire"; many voyagers in later centuries mention these machines, including English monk Roger Bacon (who invented gunpowder, also known to the Chinese, and who lived from 1214 to 1284). And it was probably by making use of the Chinese knowledge of steam, plus his own mechanical skill, that Father Ferdinand Verbiest was able to complete his work for the Emperor Khang Hsi; around 1665–1680 Verbiest created a self-propelled, five-wheeled vehicle driven by a turbine engine. This may have been the first automobile in history—*may,* because, apart from Emperor Khang Hsi and his courtiers, no one else ever saw it. However, Father Verbiest left us such an accurate description of his invention that

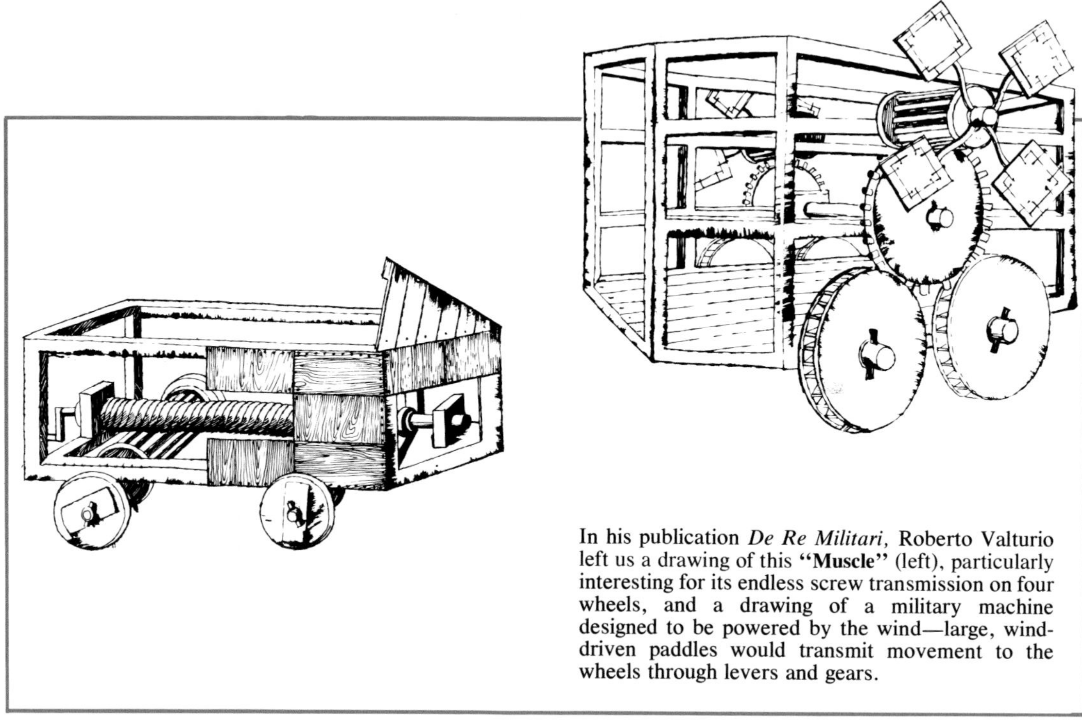

In his publication *De Re Militari,* Roberto Valturio left us a drawing of this **"Muscle"** (left), particularly interesting for its endless screw transmission on four wheels, and a drawing of a military machine designed to be powered by the wind—large, wind-driven paddles would transmit movement to the wheels through levers and gears.

more than one working model has been built from it.

In Europe, no one had ever thought of steam as a means of self-propulsion. All movement of vehicles was dependent on animals or man. And all studies and practical realizations that might have changed things—especially those of the Romans—literally slumbered all through the long stretch of the Middle Ages. Unfortunately, the roads too were left to fall to pieces, so that the only means of transportation ended up being what it had been thousands of years before the horse.

We must wait for the Renaissance, and especially for the plans of Leonardo da Vinci and Roberto Valturio, to see the automobile—a vehicle not relying on animal strength—make its reappearance. Leonardo applied himself intensely to the study of the differential gear, to the transmission of motion, and to a project for a spring automobile (but was never interested in the practical realization of his plans). We find an accurate description of these projects in the *Codex Atlanticus*.

The studies of Roberto Valturio (1413–1483) were equally astonishing; especially

Belgian missionary Ferdinand **Verbiest** used steam in 1672 to power a vehicle he designed and which he left thoroughly described. This machine—even if extremely limited, especially in its fuel distance—was important because it helped to develop the use of steam as a driving force.

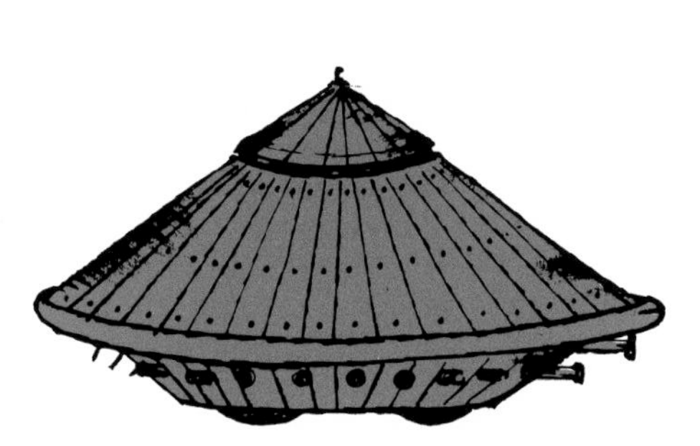

This armored tank or **testudo** by Leonardo da Vinci had four wheels for movement and steering. Eight men were to supply power for the vehicle.

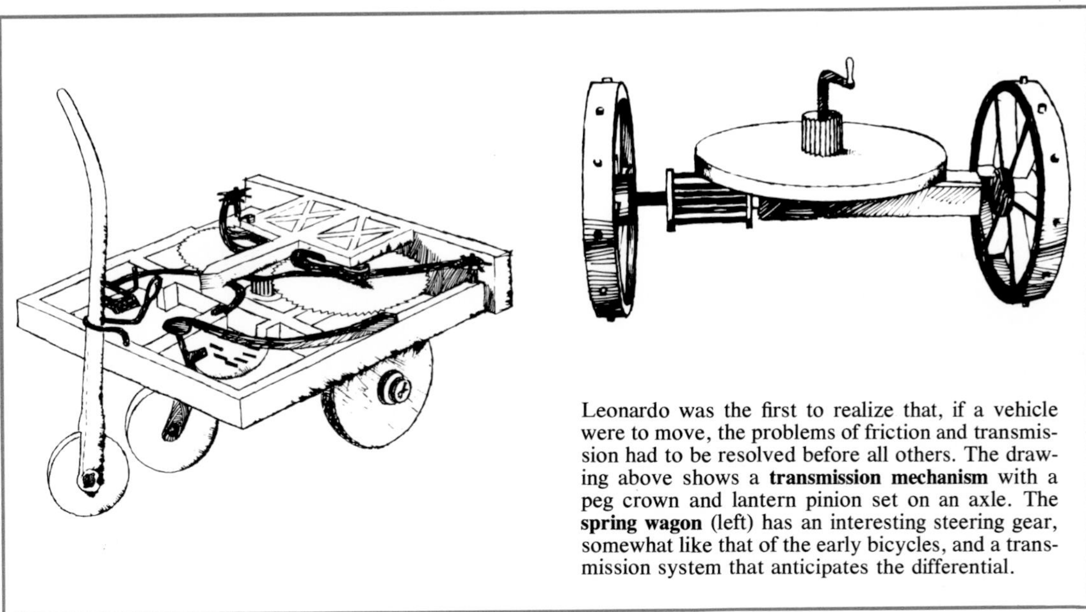

Leonardo was the first to realize that, if a vehicle were to move, the problems of friction and transmission had to be resolved before all others. The drawing above shows a **transmission mechanism** with a peg crown and lantern pinion set on an axle. The **spring wagon** (left) has an interesting steering gear, somewhat like that of the early bicycles, and a transmission system that anticipates the differential.

interesting are those for a cart propelled by the wind through the rotation of blades, which was never achieved. Valturio also prepared a project (which may even have been produced for Sigismondo Pandolfo Malatesta, lord of Rimini) for a war machine—a self-propelled vehicle to use in battle, a kind of tank *ante litteram*. Valturio's vehicle may be the first example of transmission through an endless screw, with two axles as a chassis. Naturally, at that time any "motor force" could only be assured by the strength of a man who turned the screw with a handle.

Around 1510, the great German Renaissance painter and etcher Albrecht Dürer planned a self-propelled car using arm power for Maximilian I and left a precise drawing of it. A few years later another German, Mathesius, tried to use steam as the driving force of a cart. Even earlier, a Spaniard, Blasco de Garag, made experiments in the same direction in 1543, without ever attaining practical results.

Europe waited for steam, and was thus filled with projects and studies involving the automobile: with springs, with wind, run by arms or feet, but without the horse. Watchmaking technique had reached such a high technical level at the end of the sixteenth century that more than one spring-driven car was produced. We have certain information about at least one, which was produced in Nuremberg, cradle of watchmaking, in 1649 by Johann Hautsch. It must indeed have been harder to wind than a watch, and had an extremely limited range of action: 250 meters! The maximum speed was 3 kilometers an

This **amphibious armored car** is one of the two hundred drawings used by Ramelli to illustrate, in 1588, his book *Various and Artful Machines*. It was driven by paddlewheels with the tiller in the rear. Above: An endless screw **transmission system** with crown and pinion, also by Ramelli.

# THE CART BECOMES A CARRIAGE

It was no small matter to travel in a wagon before the sixteenth century. The extremely bad state of the roads—practically those inherited from the Romans and ruined by time and weather—was heightened by the lack of suspension in the wagons—a fatal combination. So the horse—or the litter drawn by two horses—was preferred to the discomfort and danger of the wagon. The latter, in fact, moved at half the speed of the horse and litter, since it barely managed to exceed walking pace.

A splendid ceremonial carriage (1690)

# CARRIAGE

Royal conveyance (c. 1280)

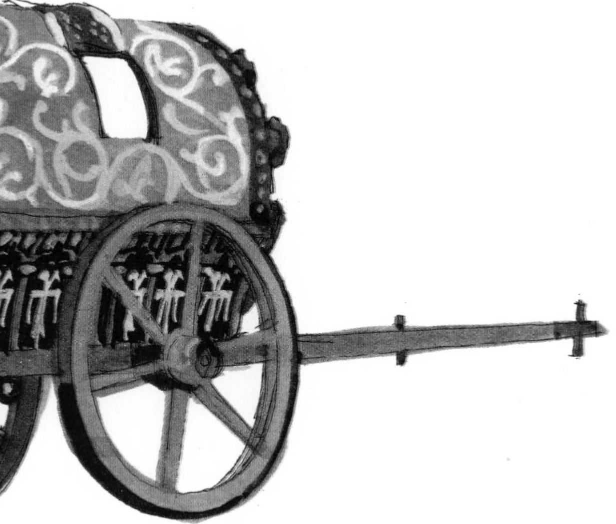

About the middle of the fifteenth century, the wagon was revolutionized by the invention of suspension: it became a carriage. The Hungarians get credit for this idea, which soon made them the official suppliers of all of Europe in the field. An increase in demand favored technological evolution, and the primitive strap or chain suspension which linked the body to the wheels was quickly replaced by one-leaf springs, then, in later centuries, by multileaved springs.

Italy was, with Germany, one of the first countries to see a widespread use of the carriage, largely due to its craftsmen, who made an important contribution to the refinement of building techniques, especially that of the springs.

As far back as 1534, a carriage repair-shop was opened in Ferrara. An Italian, Caterina de' Medici, took the first carriage to Paris in 1550. But this type of vehicle was not popular in France, and a few decades after Caterina de' Medici's arrival there were still very few carriages in the French capital—about ten in all, of which only one was owned by the King of France. In the same period in Germany, the Elector of Brandenburg alone had thirty-six, and in Milan an attempt was made to limit the use of the carriage by forbidding women to ride in them (the first recorded example of a traffic neurosis). In those years, in Rome, Pope Sixtus V tried in vain to keep the cardinals out of carriages; his effort met with such resistance from the "drivers" of the time that he had to content himself with limiting the number of carriages in circulation. Despite all restrictions, though, the carriage continued to spread throughout Italy: there were more than 1500 in Milan at the end of the seventeenth century.

The carriage was introduced to England only in 1580. In the centuries that followed—and especially during the eighteenth and nineteenth—it was steadily improved. Among the new additions were multileaved steel springs, brakes, bodies with windows that could be opened, and, above all, wheels with positive inclination (camber angle), convergent so as to better the vehicle's balance, as well as to avoid the wheel's slipping off the pivot. At that point, the carriage was ready to become the car: only the engine was missing.

Phaeton or tonneau (1860)

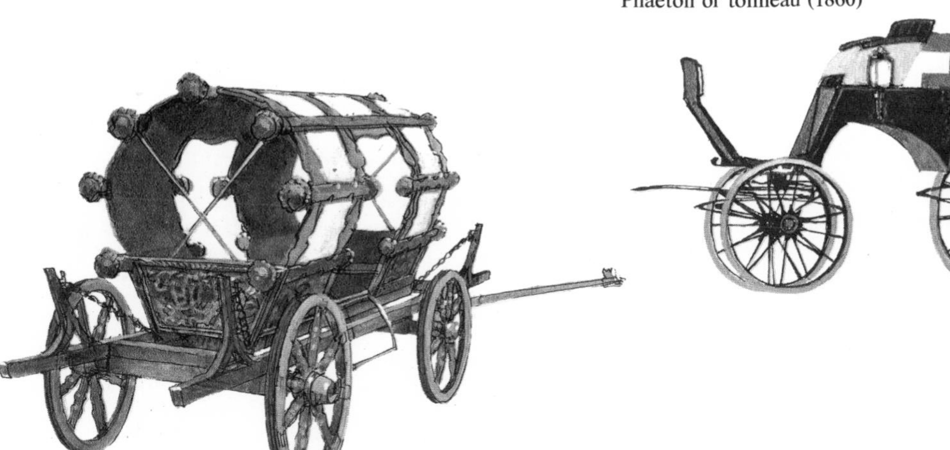

Char branlant (c. 1520)

Panel sedan (1780)

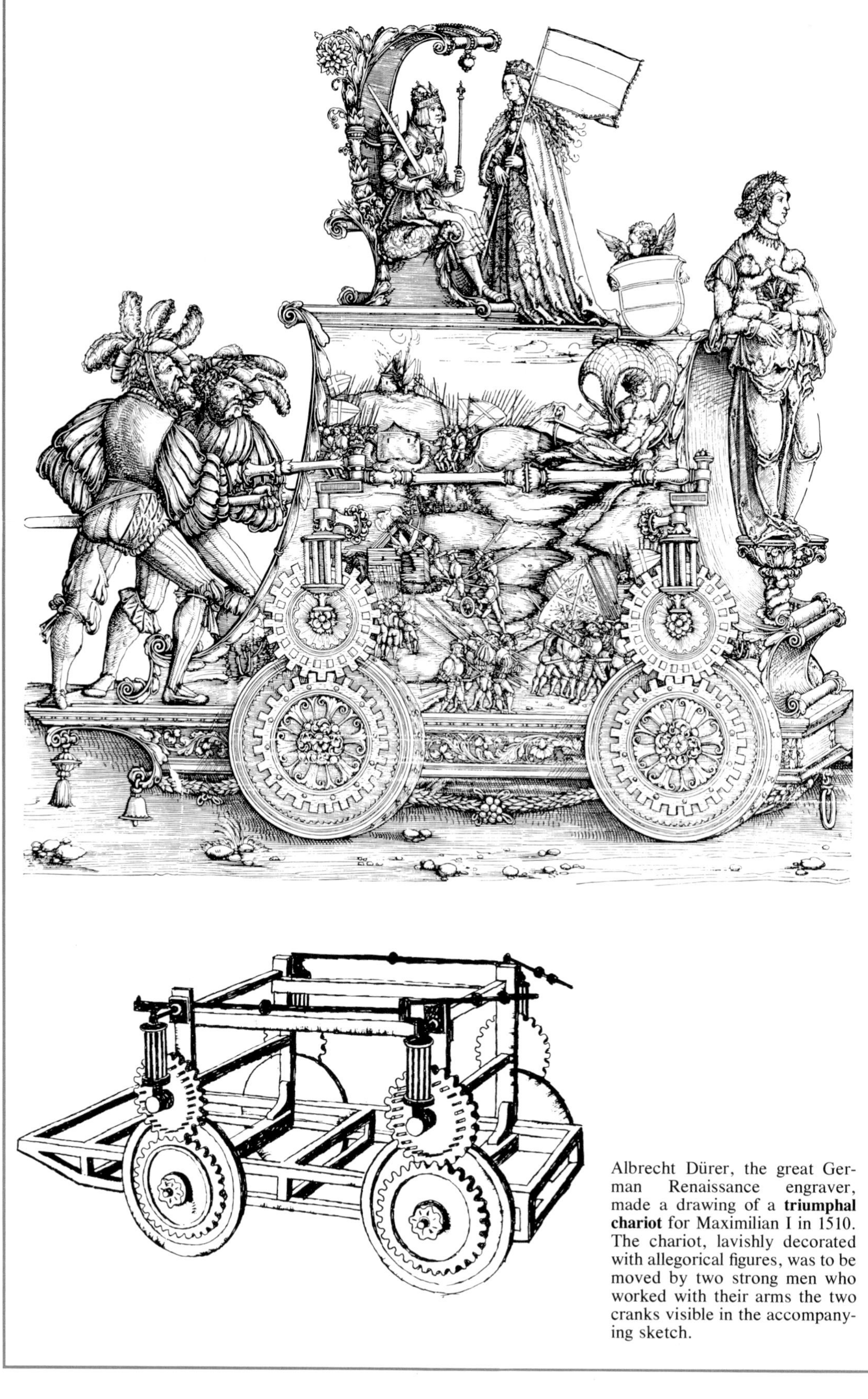

Albrecht Dürer, the great German Renaissance engraver, made a drawing of a **triumphal chariot** for Maximilian I in 1510. The chariot, lavishly decorated with allegorical figures, was to be moved by two strong men who worked with their arms the two cranks visible in the accompanying sketch.

hour and the driver had to stop and wind up the springs every five minutes. And yet . . . it moved.

Automobiles pushed by the wind were even harder to make function—even if some said that, if a ship moved on the sea that way, a car with wheels should be able to do the same on land. But in spite of the wheels, there was more resistance on land than at sea, for on land one had to stay on the road without being able to follow the whims of the wind. Besides, roads occasionally went uphill! Despite all this, some vehicles were made, especially in Holland, where the ground was perfectly flat; these heavy landships had little effect on the history of the automobile, however.

In the meantime, studies on steam and its applications, and on the carriage, continued in Europe. In the first field, the Italian Giovanni Branca (1571–1645) planned some interesting steam turbines, even before the studies of Isaac Newton and Denis Papin. As for carriages, credit for them must go to Hungary, which produced around the middle of the fifteenth century very efficient springs, first with straps and then with metal. The cart then became a carriage and spread quickly throughout Europe.

But not until the eighteenth century does the first automobile, driven by a steam engine, make its first timid move over the ground. Just as the day Christopher Columbus landed on the shores of the New World ended the Middle Ages and opened the modern era, so the unsteady advance of the wheels of Nicolas Joseph Cugnot's vehicle represents the first paragraph in the history of the automobile. But just when did this history begin? We aren't sure of the precise date, and historical

In 1680, English scientist Isaac Newton made a model of a **reaction vehicle** to be driven by steam issuing from a boiler. This model had two great weaknesses, however: first, the steam hit those passing by, and second, the absence of a steering mechanism made the vehicle extremely hard to drive.

sources are often contradictory on the matter. One thing is sure, however: Cugnot's car was the first vehicle to move by itself or, rather, to be free from the force of man, animal, or wind. It is, in fact, the first "auto-mobile" on record, with definite documentation—absolutely definite, because an example from the year 1770 (unfortunately incomplete) still exists and can be seen in the Conservatoire National des Arts et Métiers in Paris. Let's take a close look at this famous car.

As it survives, this three-wheeled vehicle (a faithful, full-scale model is in the Turin Automobile Museum) cannot function because some of its parts are missing, mainly in the transmission. Driving power went directly to the single front wheel; thus, among

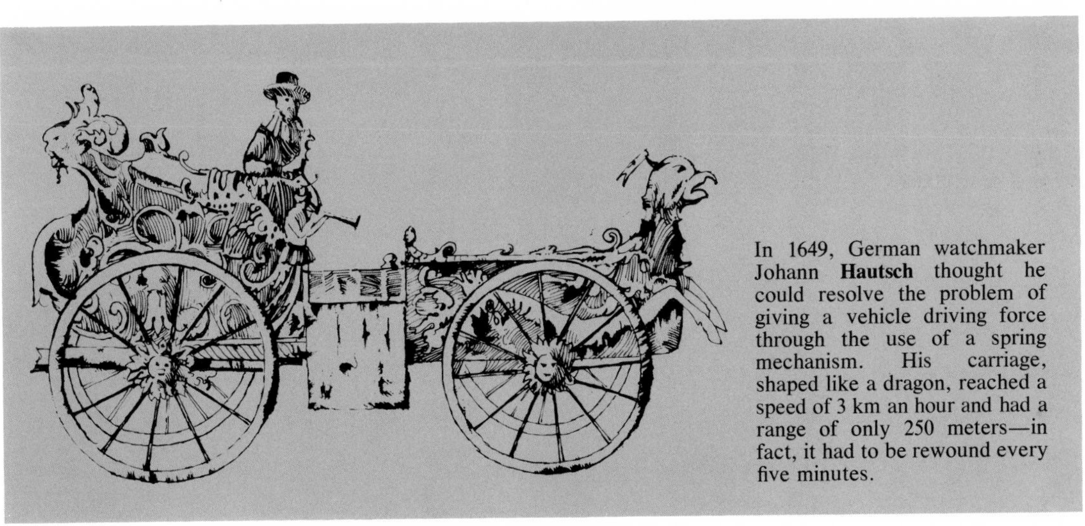

In 1649, German watchmaker Johann **Hautsch** thought he could resolve the problem of giving a vehicle driving force through the use of a spring mechanism. His carriage, shaped like a dragon, reached a speed of 3 km an hour and had a range of only 250 meters—in fact, it had to be rewound every five minutes.

# Steam comes of age

Nicolas Joseph **Cugnot** got a grant from the French War Ministry in 1769, for building the prototype of a steam vehicle to be used for pulling artillery pieces. Thus the first "auto-mobile" vehicle was created. It was a three-wheeled wooden cart moved by steam energy released from a boiler set in front of the rear wheel. After an unfortunate test demonstration, during which the cart—hard to steer—was damaged when it hit a wall, the funds were withdrawn. The cart remained in the prototype stage, and Cugnot died poor and forgotten in 1804.

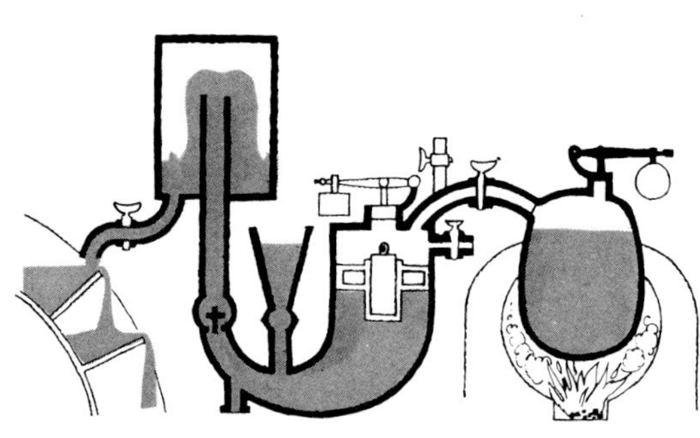

Research into the use of steam as a driving force was carried ahead in the second half of the seventeenth century by many investigators. In 1690, **Papin** built a machine made up of a cylinder in which a piston moved and of a moving furnace. When the fire came close to the cylinder, the water boiled and steam pressure pushed up the piston; when the furnace was moved away, the steam condensed, the internal pressure diminished and the piston moved down again under the thrust of atmospheric pressure.

This atmospheric steam machine, built by the English blacksmith **Newcomen,** worked a pump. Basing his machine on Papin's machine—but perfecting its various parts and replacing the "moving furnace" with a faucet (a system already invented by Savery)—Newcomen managed to create a functional machine, easily handled and useful enough.

The machine built and patented by **Watt** in 1769 also served to pump water, but was more refined than the others of its type and quickly revolutionized industry. In later machines, Watt replaced with a more simple connecting rod the double gear used here to move the large flywheel.

# Steam comes of age

the "firsts" of Cugnot's car is that of being the first "front-wheel drive" vehicle in history. The large boiler of the steam engine was mounted in front of the front wheel, while the two cylinders were almost perpendicular to that wheel, which also had a rudimentary kind of steering-wheel mechanism. With a bore of 304mm and a stroke of 356, a displacement of almost 50 liters was obtained.

But the example that has come down to us, built in 1770 and tested between the end of that year and the first half of 1771, was not the first model built by Cugnot. The inventor, who was a young artillery officer in the French army in the reign of Louis XV, proposed to the Minister of War, Marquis de Choiseul, a steam vehicle for transporting heavy artillery. The Minister was quite naturally enthusiastic about the idea and gave his consent, and Cugnot built a small-scale prototype that was tested a few times in Brussels and then presented to a large crowd in the French capital in 1769. The vehicle, with four people in it, seems to have done almost 10 km per hour. The test lasted a mere twelve minutes because of the small size of the boiler and the even smaller level of mechanical reliability of the machine itself. This experiment was a milestone in the history of the automobile, at any rate.

Nicolas Joseph Cugnot soon followed up his first prototype with another car, larger and more powerful than the original. In creating it, he made good use of the superior technological competence his fellow Frenchman General Gribeauval had gained in boring cannons. Cugnot thought that would help to make the new vehicle's cylinders perfectly circular. Another one of Cugnot's "firsts" was the first automobile accident in history. The young officer, driving the car now in the Paris Museum, was unable to avoid a wall during a

In 1825, Goldsworthy **Gurney** inaugurated a public passenger transportation service from London to Bath on a route 171 km long, making use of a steam carriage he invented himself. This "horseless diligence" could easily carry eighteen passengers, twelve outside and six inside.

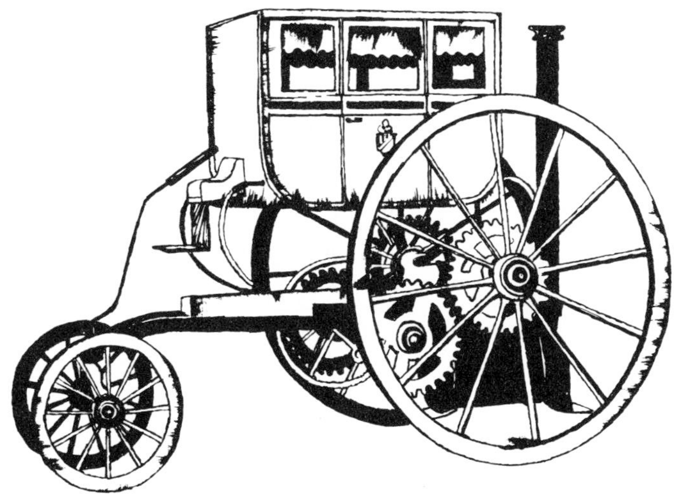

In 1802, English engineer Richard **Trevithick** built, with his cousin Vivian, a steam vehicle for passenger transportation. Contemporary accounts note that the vehicle carried eight people for a kilometer, "faster than a walking man." Trevithick was unable to find financial backing for his machine, which was abandoned; however, the motor was bought by a farmer who used it to power his mill.

The steam carriage built by **Hill** in 1839 is marked by the huge boiler in the rear. It was used in regular service on the Birmingham–London line.

trial run, either from distraction or because of the deficiencies in the steering mechanism. Cugnot was granted a pension of 600 francs for his ingenuity in 1772, but was soon forgotten in the agitated years that followed the French Revolution. He died in poverty in Brussels on October 10, 1804.

In those same years, on the other side of the Channel, a young Scotsman named James Watt (1736–1819) was carrying out studies and experiments on the practical use of steam. If Cugnot gave us the automobile, we must give Watt the credit for giving us its engine—a simple, efficient engine that also became the main factor in the English Industrial Revolution.

Of course, Watt's steam engine made use of the contributions of many other people. In particular, there are those of the Italian Evangelista Torricelli (1608–1647), the German Otto von Guericke (1602–1686), the Dutchman Christian Huygens (1629–1695), and the Frenchman Denis Papin (1647–1714). The first two concentrated mainly on research in the field of atmospheric pressure.

Atmospheric power had been spectacularly demonstrated by von Guericke in 1654 in an experiment carried out in Magdeburg, the city of which he was burgomaster. Von Guericke had two equal hemispheres made, each 3½ meters in diameter, and then joined them together with an air-tight lining. He then had the air removed from the globe with a pump. It took eight pairs of horses, four on each side, to separate one half of the globe from the other!

Huygens and Papin planned and realized, around 1670, the first internal combustion engine. (It should be remembered that the

**An English steam wagon (1828).** Note the original driving mechanism: the driver conducted the heavy vehicle by the use of a long bar linked to the two small front wheels.

Walter **Hancock** built nine steam vehicles, which he gave strange names (Infant, Automaton, Era, Enterprise, etc.); he used them to organize an efficient public transportation service that carried more than 4000 passengers in three months. Hancock was the first to make use of high-pressure steam—and caused one of that era's most serious accidents. The boiler of the Enterprise was put under too great a pressure and exploded, killing and wounding many. This accident led to the "Red Flag Act" of 1861, a law which slowed down the evolution of the steam vehicle with its tight restrictions.

steam engine is run by external combustion, since the steam is produced by the boiler outside the cylinders and put into them through ducts.) Their engine worked on gas produced by gunpowder explosion. In leaving a cylinder, the gas caused a space below the piston, which was then lowered by atmospheric pressure and exerted a certain force.

Later, Papin replaced the gas produced by the explosion of gunpowder with steam, the properties of which he had known for years. Papin, in fact, is the inventor of the pressure cooker, which he named "Digester," destined "to soften and extract nourishing substances from meats and bones." He had, in fact, discovered that when water was boiled in a very strong, hermetically sealed pan, so that the high pressure created by the steam had no outlet, the boiling-point temperature went well above 100 degrees centigrade, thus making the food cook rapidly.

Papin then took the step from the pressure cooker worked by steam to the engine run by steam; he planned a very slow and rather impractical machine for pumping water from wells. Papin's machine managed to pull up in a minute, from a well about 20 or 30 meters deep, a bucket containing thirty liters of water, with the aid of an operator—who might have done the job more quickly without mechanical aid.

Englishman Thomas Savery gets the credit for having separated the boiler from the cylinder, making it more simple for the engine to function. Since there was no longer any need for shifting the fire from beneath the cylinder to let it cool, it sufficed to turn a

This steam carriage, designed by General Virgilio **Bordino,** was built in the Turin military arsenal in 1854. Driving power was sent to the vehicle by steam released from a boiler set in the rear.

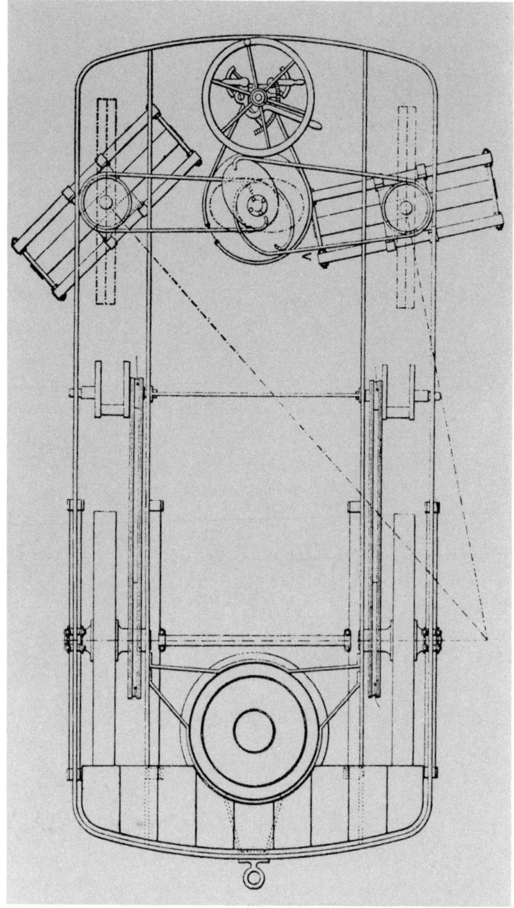

faucet that opened or closed the flow of steam to the boiler. Another great "perfector" of the steam engine before Watt was Englishman Thomas Newcomen, who thought of directing a stream of cold water inside the cylinder to condense the steam quickly; up until then the vacuum had been obtained by bathing the cylinder from outside. Newcomen added other practical touches to his heavy and very large machines, which were quickly adopted and exported all over the world, soon becoming indispensable in mining. But the greatest contribution to the construction of light steam engines—powerful, efficient, and fairly cheap—was made by James Watt. Thanks to Watt, it was possible to build engines small and powerful enough to do without a static position, so that they could be used on vehicles such as automobiles, trains, and ships.

Watt's first patent dates from 1769, when he was thirty-three years old. At the time he worked in the scientific laboratory of the University of Glasgow, where one of Newcomen's first machines had been installed. At first Watt merely tried to perfect the Englishman's engine; he eliminated a number of friction points that reduced the limited power of the engine. Soon, however, he realized that if the engine was to function really well it had to be completely redesigned. Above all, the serious loss of heat that marked all the engines of that period had to be eliminated; Watt therefore enclosed the boiler in a thick protective screen of wood and put numerous ducts in the interstices to make greater use of the hot gases produced by combustion. He also put insulating material around all the steam ducts. He then placed the condenser, to which the hot steam came after having moved the piston, to a separate place; here the steam became water again, thereby heating the water that was about to become steam and requiring, at the same time, less heat from without. But Watt was still not satisfied and obtained, in 1781, a patent for a truly revolutionary engine, so advanced that, from that time to our own, very few improvements have been made on it—and most of those that have were added by Watt himself, with later patents dealing with the double effect (on the basis of which the steam is admitted alternately to the two ends of the piston), the slide valve, and the centrifugal governor. But the Scottish inventor was not yet content with what he had done for the steam engine, and on April 27, 1784, he filed for a patent on an automobile—steam-driven, of course—which had a three-gear transmission system. This machine was never built, however.

With his partner, the manufacturer Matthew Boulton, Watt produced more than 500 steam engines; these contributed greatly to the Industrial Revolution in England, which took place at the end of the eighteenth century and during the first half of the nineteenth.

The early nineteenth century also marked England's triumphant entrance into the world of motorization. There was a great flowering of famous names and vehicles, such as the famous locomotive "Rocket" by Robert Stephenson, the world's first train, and vehicles by Richard and Vivian Trevithick, William Murdock, Walter Hancock, Henry James, Goldsworthy Gurney, and many others.

Among Great Britain's "firsts" in those years (including the first regular train service, the first connections with steam diligences, and the first motorized mail service) there was also the first nationally instituted regular toll

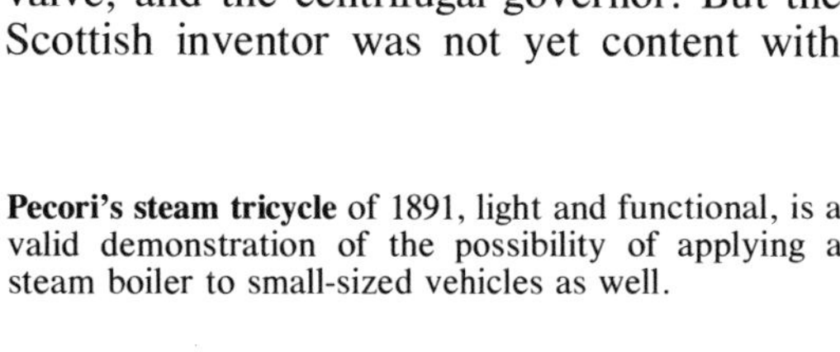

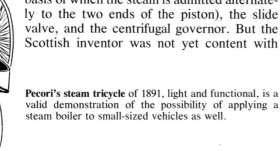

**Pecori's steam tricycle** of 1891, light and functional, is a valid demonstration of the possibility of applying a steam boiler to small-sized vehicles as well.

The work of Amédée **Bollée** can be considered fundamental in the development of the modern motor vehicle. Among the steam vehicles he built, the **Mancelle** and **Obéissante** were the most refined. The latter, a coach that could carry twelve people, was the first vehicle to get a driving "permit" in France. The **Obéissante** was also the world's first vehicle with independent wheels. We see in the plan (left) the corrected steering mechanism which acted on the two independent front wheels.

Below: The **Mancelle** was a six-seater break. Its front engine and transmission shaft predated some solutions adopted many years later.

Two views of **turnpikes**—road toll booths that sprang up like mushrooms in England in the early nineteenth century.

payment on roads. And, since more and more money was needed to build new roads and repair old ones, a solution was reached: instead of increasing the tolls, the number of tollgates (the so-called "turnpikes," of an octagonal shape so one custodian could look in all directions without obstacles) was increased beyond reason—so much so that on certain roads near London there was one every hundred meters!

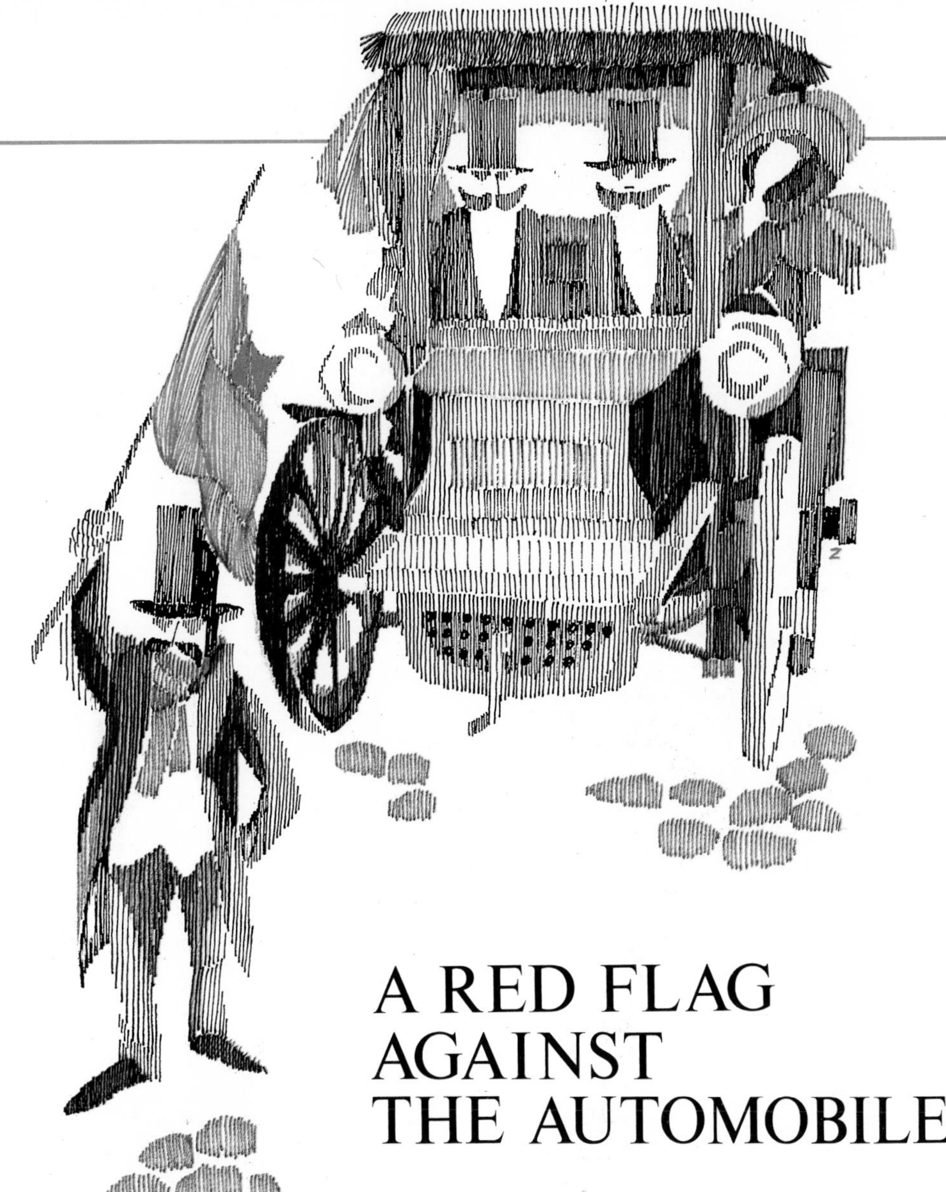

# A RED FLAG AGAINST THE AUTOMOBILE

Road motorization got off to a promising start in England in the first decades of the nineteenth century. It almost resembled the Industrial Revolution boom of those years. Even though they were heavily taxed, steam vehicles carried out regular and long service on the main English roads, competing with the railroads, also in full development at that time. But a law passed by Parliament in 1861—the "Locomotive Acts"—quickly blocked the growth of motorization. This law, made even more rigid in 1865, limited the speed of all motorized vehicles to 2 miles per hour (3.2 km/h) in the city and to 4 miles per hour (6.5 km/h) on country roads. It also obliged all drivers of motor vehicles to be preceded at a distance of about 50 meters by a man walking and waving a red flag to warn anyone else on the same road of impending danger. The motor vehicle was also obliged to stop for any cart driver who raised his hand. The law stated that the only party responsible for any eventual accident was purely and simply the driver of the motor vehicle. The pretext for the "Locomotive Acts" (also known as the "Red Flag Act") was a series of bad accidents due to steam vehicles in the years preceding the new law; but in reality there were a number of members of Parliament who had business connections with the railroads.

The Red Flag Act was repealed in 1896.

Giovanni Agnelli

Karl Benz

Amédée Bollée

Gottlieb Daimler

Albert De Dion

Rudolf Diesel

Charles Edgar Duryea

Henry Ford

Louis-René Panhard

Ettore Bugatti

# The automobile is born

John Boyd Dunlop

Louis Renault

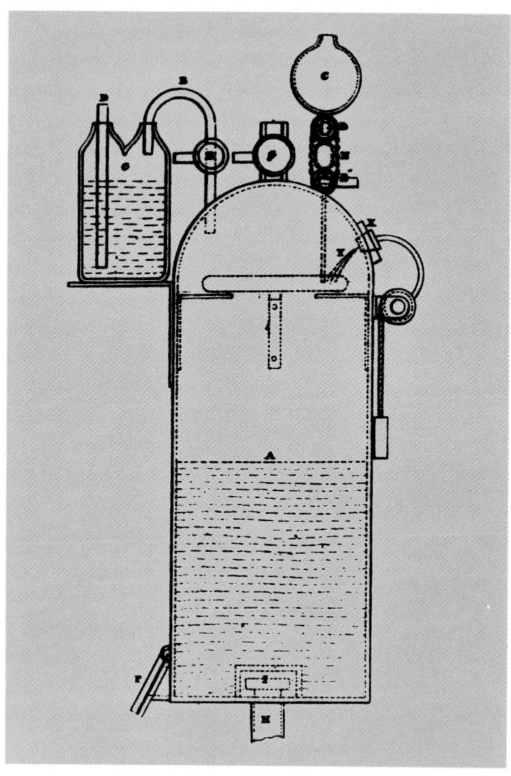

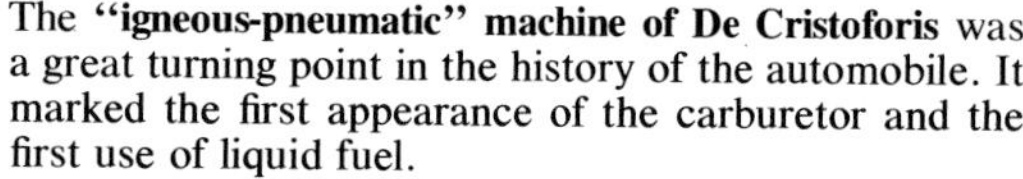

The **"igneous-pneumatic" machine of De Cristoforis** was a great turning point in the history of the automobile. It marked the first appearance of the carburetor and the first use of liquid fuel.

It is very hard to decide just who invented the internal combustion engine. Such an invention cannot be considered the creation of one person and this achievement cannot therefore be assigned to one particular nation. It is clear, though, that the studies of **Barsanti** and **Matteucci** (as well as those of Lenoir, Brown, and others) contributed to the development of the internal combustion engine. The two drawings show the motor with two counteropposed pistons patented by the two Italians in 1858.

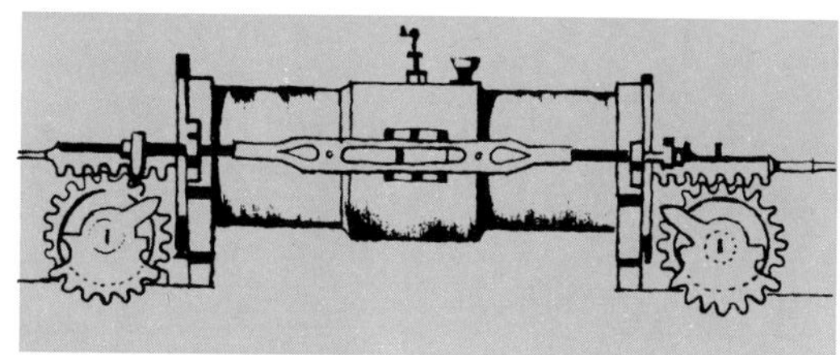

**Lenoir's** vehicle bore an external resemblance to the carriages of that era, but contained an important novelty: it had a gas explosion engine, patented in 1858 by Lenoir himself.

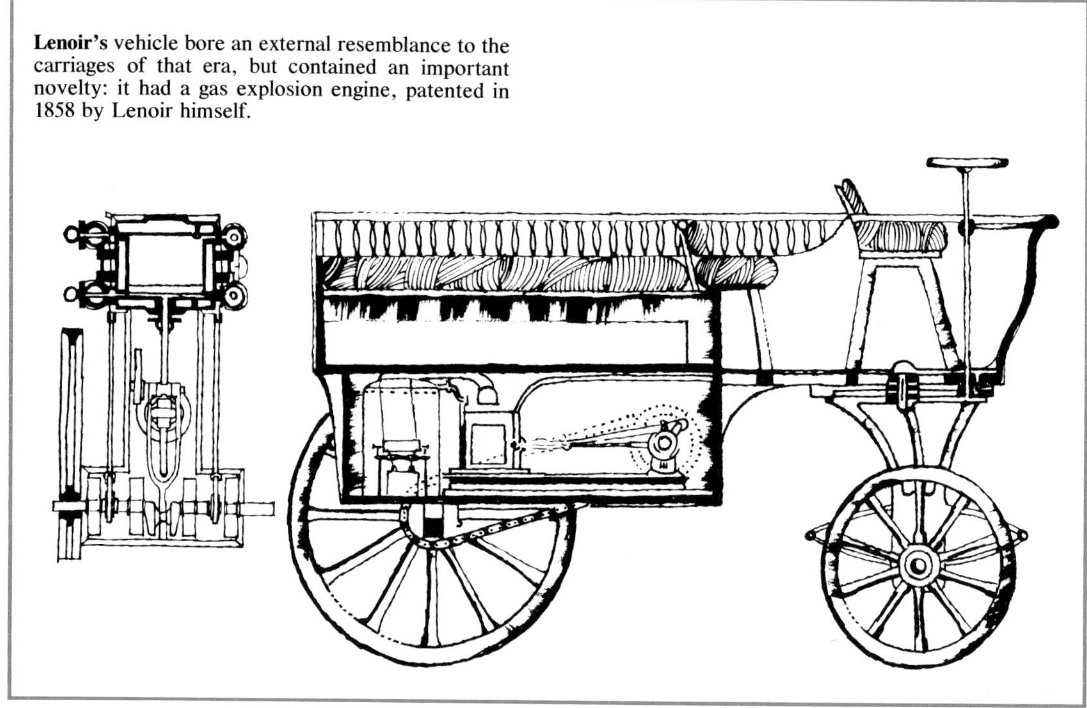

# The automobile is born

In the preceding chapter we traced a picture of the rapid development, especially in Great Britain, of steam vehicles for mass transportation.

We are therefore on the threshold of the birth of the actual automobile, by which we mean the first means of transportation for the individual. Man is an extremely individualistic animal, but for once—with the automobile, that is—he yielded his own interests to those of the majority.

The experience accumulated with mass transportation vehicles driven by steam was most useful in the birth of the private gasoline-driven car, and the contribution of steam did not vanish overnight. Steam vehicles were discussed for a long time after that, and some of them (for instance those built by Bollée *père* and Serpollet and the light vehicles of De Dion and Bouton) hold an important place in the history of the automobile. They stole the scene until after the First World War, when the last steam cars—the American White and Stanley makes—silently left the stage. Even electric cars—born at the end of the nineteenth century and defunct by the start of the First World War—vanished surprisingly fast. The last to die were the American makes Baker, Ohio Electric, and Detroit Electric—rather pathetic vehicles from the very beginning, with a very limited driving capacity and a speed that rarely managed to exceed 40 km per hour.

In the second half of the nineteenth century, the future was said to belong exclusively to one kind of driving force: the internal combustion engine. What a shame that it still remained to be invented for all practical purposes! But history loves to repeat itself—isn't the "fuel cell" automobile (it too yet to be invented) unanimously considered today the heir of the gasoline-run car?

As for the internal combustion engine, let us note first of all that we will not try to attribute patents and priority to anyone in particular—especially since almost every encyclopedia proposes a different name for its creator. Chauvinism, even in the field of who invented the car engine, has neither limits nor modesty. Too, it is almost impossible to establish a factual basis for who came first, since in those days the idea of patenting an invention hardly existed. If we really must give some kind of geographical position to the first inventors of the internal combustion engine, we could take Switzerland as a center on our map: all developments took place within a range of barely more than 500 kilometers from that center.

A share of the Barsanti and Matteucci "Società Anonima Nuovo Motore," issued in 1860.

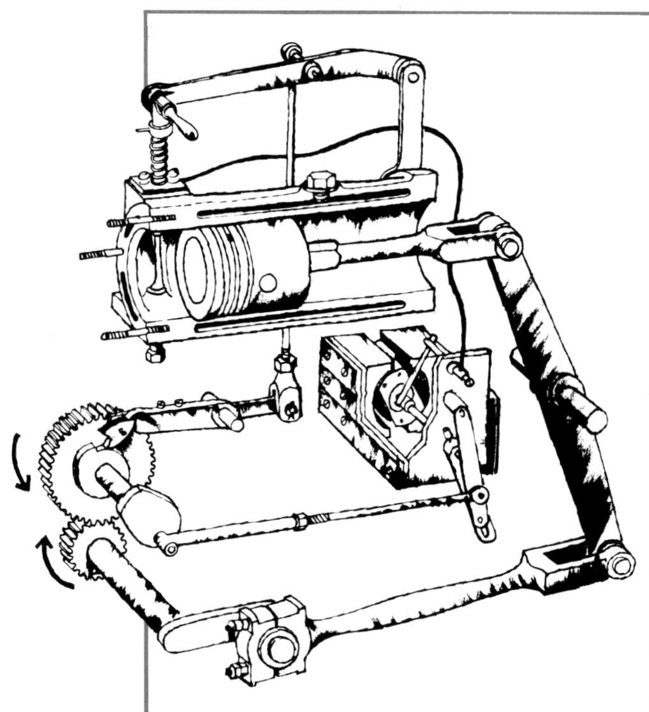

Even though the question is still highly controversial, Siegfried **Marcus** is probably the inventor of the first automobile to run on gasoline. The model he built in 1874 is preserved in the Technisches Museum in Vienna. It had a four-stroke, one-cylinder engine (above) with an ignition magneto, a wooden body, and iron-ringed wheels.

One thing can be stated with certainty: the internal combustion engine too had its Watt, that is, a man who built on the experiences of others—without hiding the fact—but planned everything in a wholly new way, creating a machine that was precise, efficient, and dependable. For the internal combustion engine, this man was the German Gottlieb Daimler. Daimler's contribution to the growth of motorization is shown by the adoption, in the nineties, of his two-cylinder V engine by all the important car makers of the time (Panhard & Levassor, Peugeot, et al).

Others were important in the development of the engine, too. For example, the first man to study the practical use of gas—apart from the experiments of some inventors in the preceding century, who used gunpowder—was Alessandro Volta (1745–1827); he thought of priming the gas he used in his experiments (natural gas collected in a swamp) with an electric spark. (We should also remember Volta's research and discoveries in the field of electricity.) But the Italian inventor was not thinking of an engine in this experiment; he was creating a gas pistol. It was this pistol he described in a letter to a friend in 1777: "It is a small firearm that is not loaded with powder but with gas . . . which is inflammable and goes off at the smallest elec-

tric spark." This type of pistol also occurred to Swiss inventor Isaac de Rivaz years later: after producing a steam-driven vehicle in 1787, he devoted himself to the internal combustion engine and in 1804 planned and made a car model moved by such an engine. De Rivas left testimony of this experiment in a patent filed in 1807.

Another vehicle propelled by an internal combustion engine was produced in May 1826 by the Englishman Samuel Brown, who, it is said, tested it near London. And Joseph Wilkinson, also English, gets the credit for having been the first to use liquid fuel instead of coal for feeding the steam boiler of a motor vehicle, a fact of no small importance; this record was contested by the Frenchman Joseph Ravel, however.

This rear-engine, 1.5 hp car was built by **Daimler** in 1889. It could do 18 km an hour.

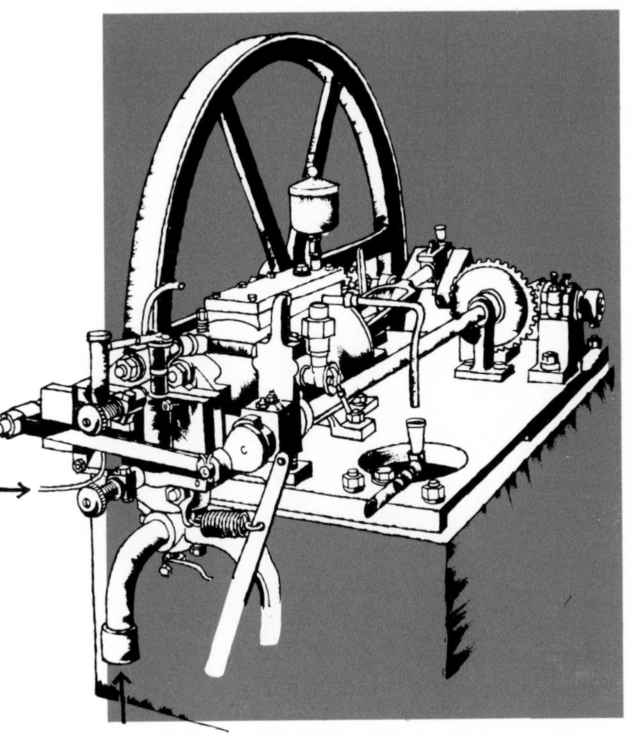

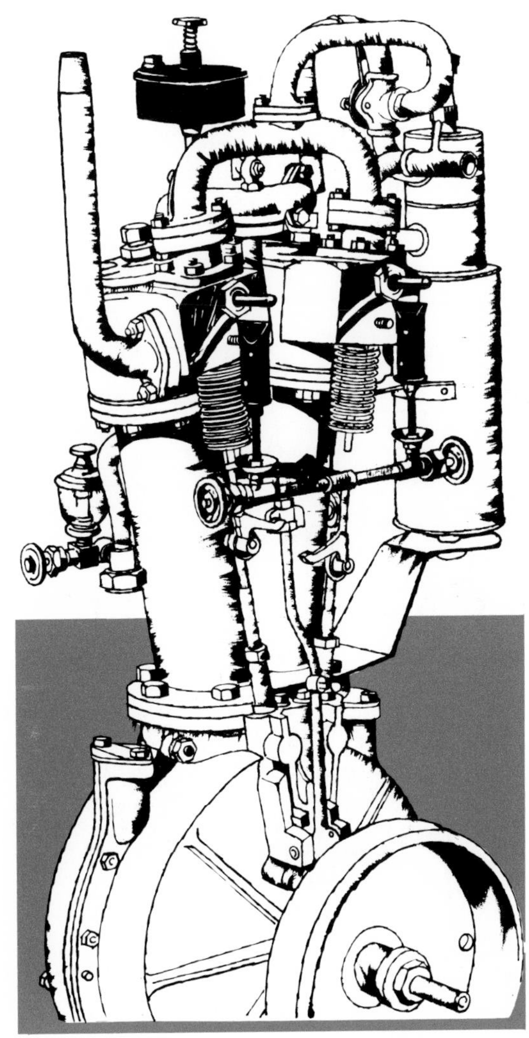

In 1876, the Gasmotoren-Fabrik Deutz, founded by Otto and Langen, with Daimler as technical director and Maybach as foreman, constructed a four-stroke, 8 hp engine (above) which can be considered the forerunner of our modern motors. It was never used in a vehicle because of its excessive weight. Daimler, who dreamed of a light, high-speed gasoline engine, left Otto and Langen and continued to work on his project with Maybach. Finally, in 1899, he patented a 15-degree V engine with two cylinders (right), with 1100 cc displacement and 3.35 hp. This engine had great success, and construction licenses for it were granted all over Europe; it was also used in the French cars of Peugeot and Panhard & Levassor.

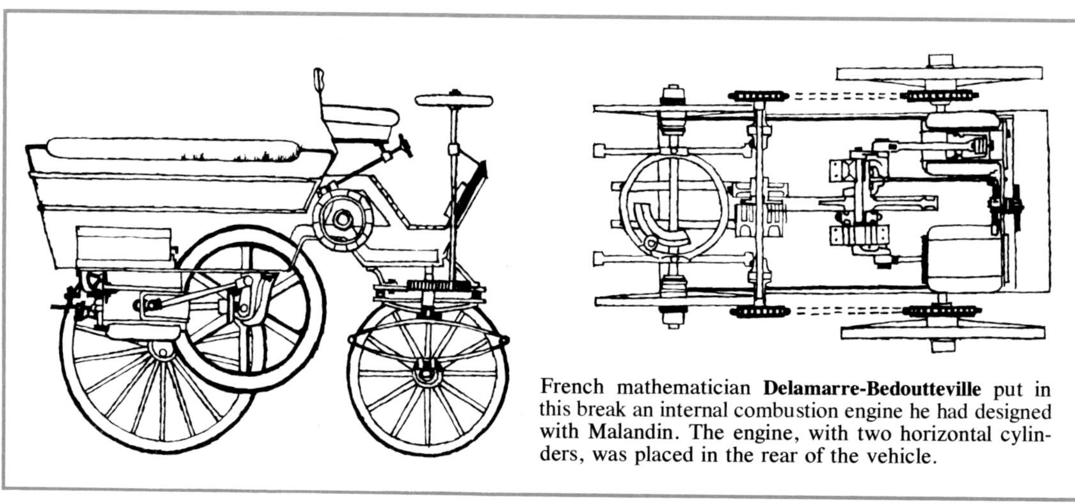

French mathematician **Delamarre-Bedoutteville** put in this break an internal combustion engine he had designed with Malandin. The engine, with two horizontal cylinders, was placed in the rear of the vehicle.

As for the internal combustion engine itself, however, after de Rivaz there were no further developments until 1860, when Frenchman Etienne Lenoir filed an interesting patent for a two-stroke internal combustion engine—one which Lenoir himself applied to a horseless carriage two or three years later. (The exact date is still controversial, but the fact of the experiment is certain.) This carriage covered the 18 kilometers between Paris and Joinville-le-Pont in three hours. It was probably the world's first automobile in the modern sense of the word, even though the velocity of the machine was even slower than that of a horse-drawn carriage.

Lenoir's vehicle, rudimentary as it was, was a milestone in the history of the automobile; among other firsts, it was the first vehicle to use electric ignition.

Even before Lenoir patented his two-stroke engine, the Italians Barsanti and Matteucci carried out extensive research on the internal combustion engine, and in 1854 they obtained an English patent for an atmospheric direct-action engine. In 1858, the two inventors also took out an Italian patent for a concurrent-piston engine, which they later produced on a small scale. It does not seem, though, that the experiments of Barsanti and Matteucci were ever devoted to making a vehicle move. Their studies were, however, most certainly made use of by the Germans Otto and Langen for their four-stroke-cycle engine, patented in 1867. Otto shares with Frenchman Beau de Rochas (who filed a

In 1885, Carl Benz built a tricycle called **"Velociped,"** on which he mounted a horizontal, one-cylinder gasoline engine. For the first time, ignition took place through a magneto and a sparkplug. The machine had block chain transmission and could develop 0.8 hp. As compared with Daimler's engine, that of Benz was slower and heavier, but the mechanical structure on which it was mounted was so balanced and compact that this tricycle was a completely new kind of vehicle and had immense success. It made its first public appearance on July 3, 1886, with a trial run at 15 km an hour. A year later, it was presented at the Paris Exposition, where Benz met Emile Roger, later to become the Benz Company's French representative. That was an important meeting, since it led to the great foreign diffusion of the Benz motor.

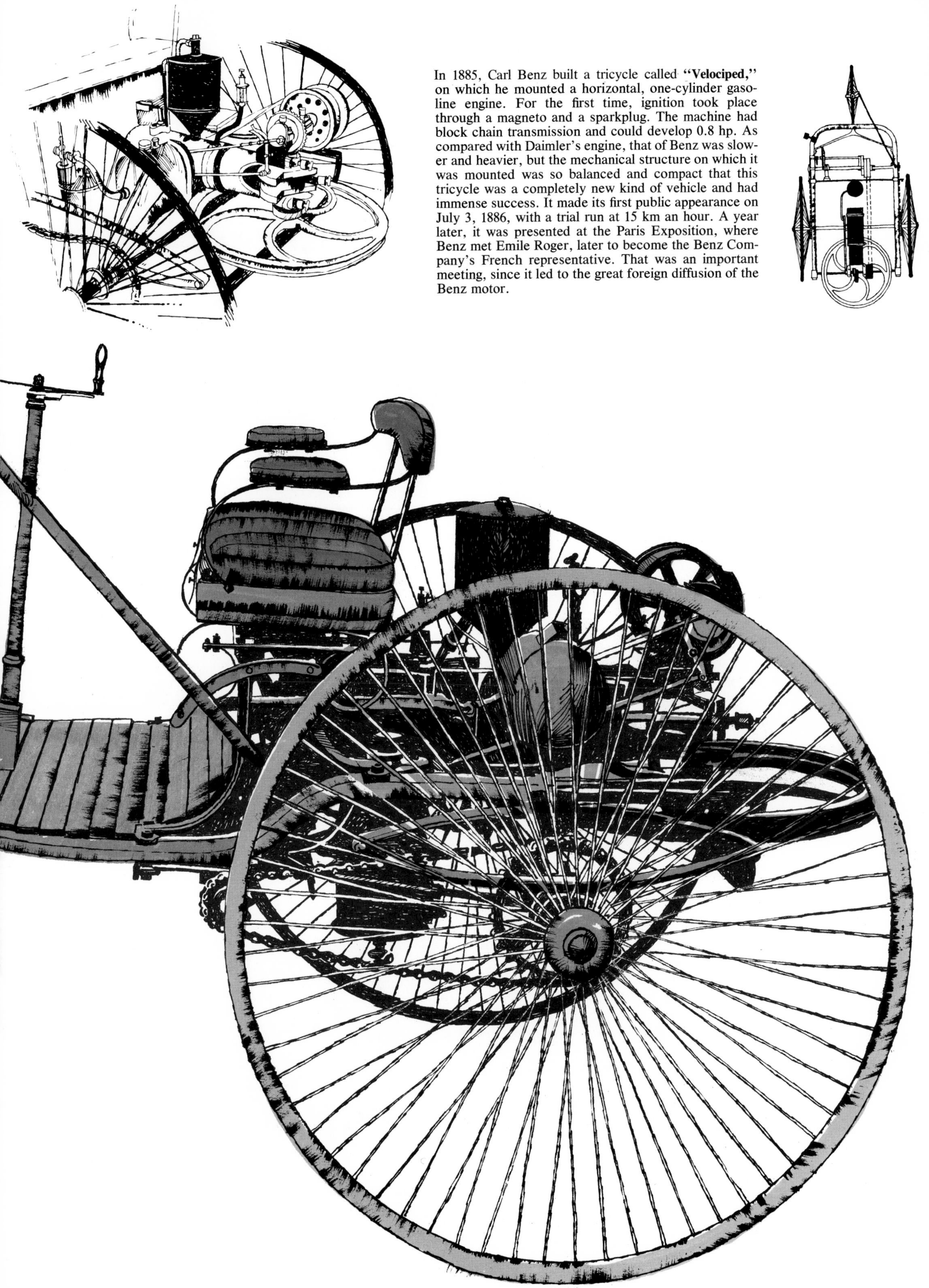

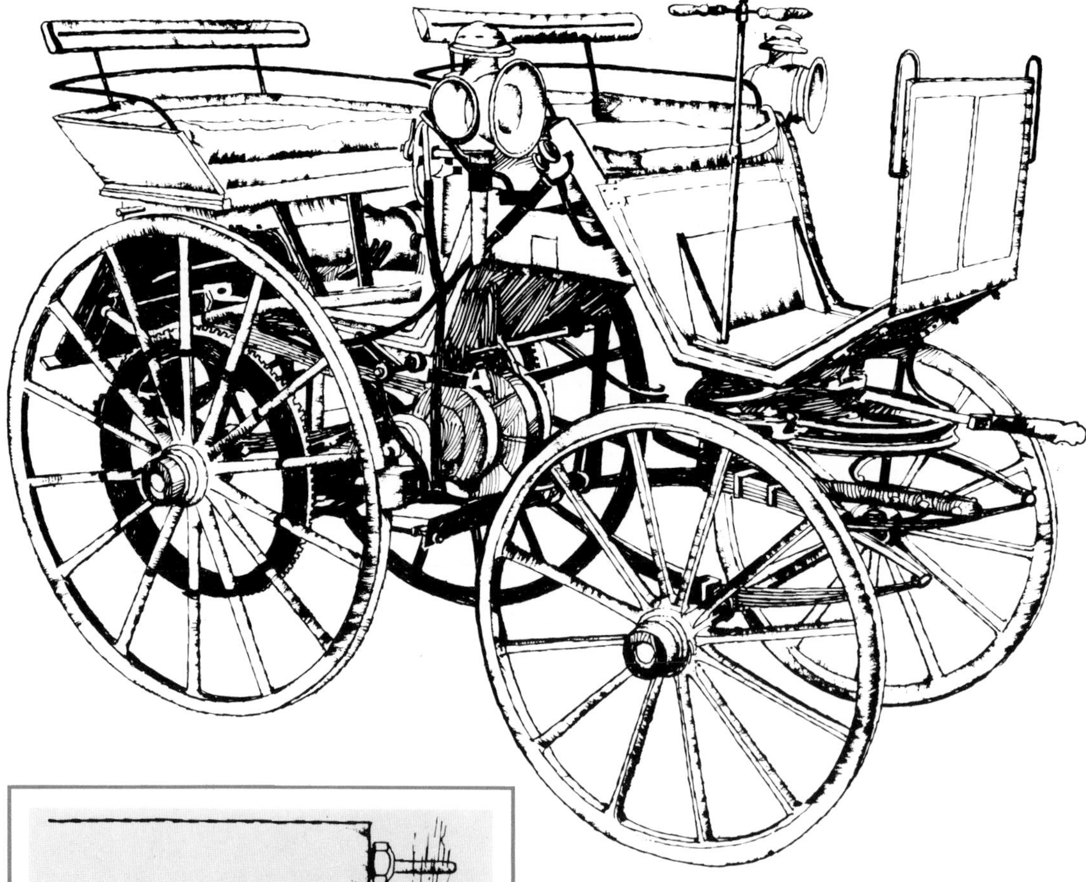

In 1885, Gottlieb Daimler commissioned from the body makers Wimpff and Son of Stuttgart a light and robust vehicle on which to mount the internal combustion engine he and Maybach had invented. This car (known as a **"Motorkutsche,"** or "motor coach") had a small gasoline engine which attained a speed of 15 km/h.

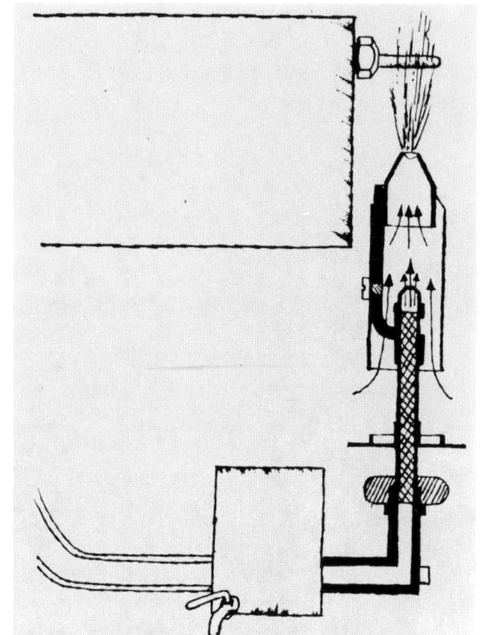

Daimler's **ignition system** consisted of a platinum tube made incandescent by a gasoline-fed Bunsen burner **(brûleur)** which crossed the cylinder head. During the compression phase, the mixture was pushed into the tube by the piston and exploded on contact with the incandescent platinum. This system was adopted by many builders but had more than one drawback, among them the danger of fire.

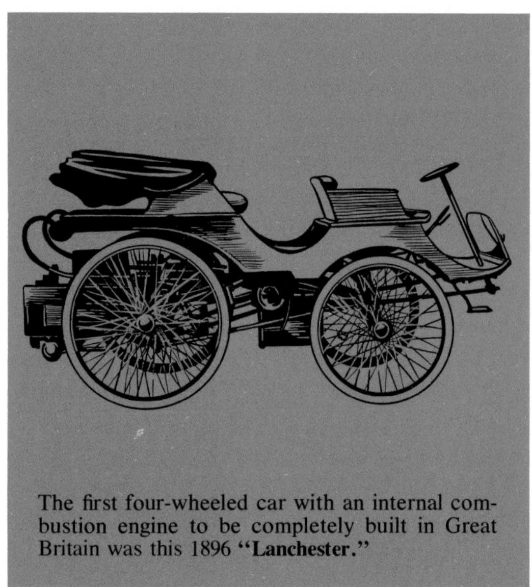

The first four-wheeled car with an internal combustion engine to be completely built in Great Britain was this 1896 **"Lanchester."**

With the **"Victoria,"** Benz & Company began, in 1893, the production of four-wheeled cars. This "horseless carriage" was an instant success, thanks to its clean and elegant lines and was built until 1898. It had a 3 hp, one-cylinder engine.

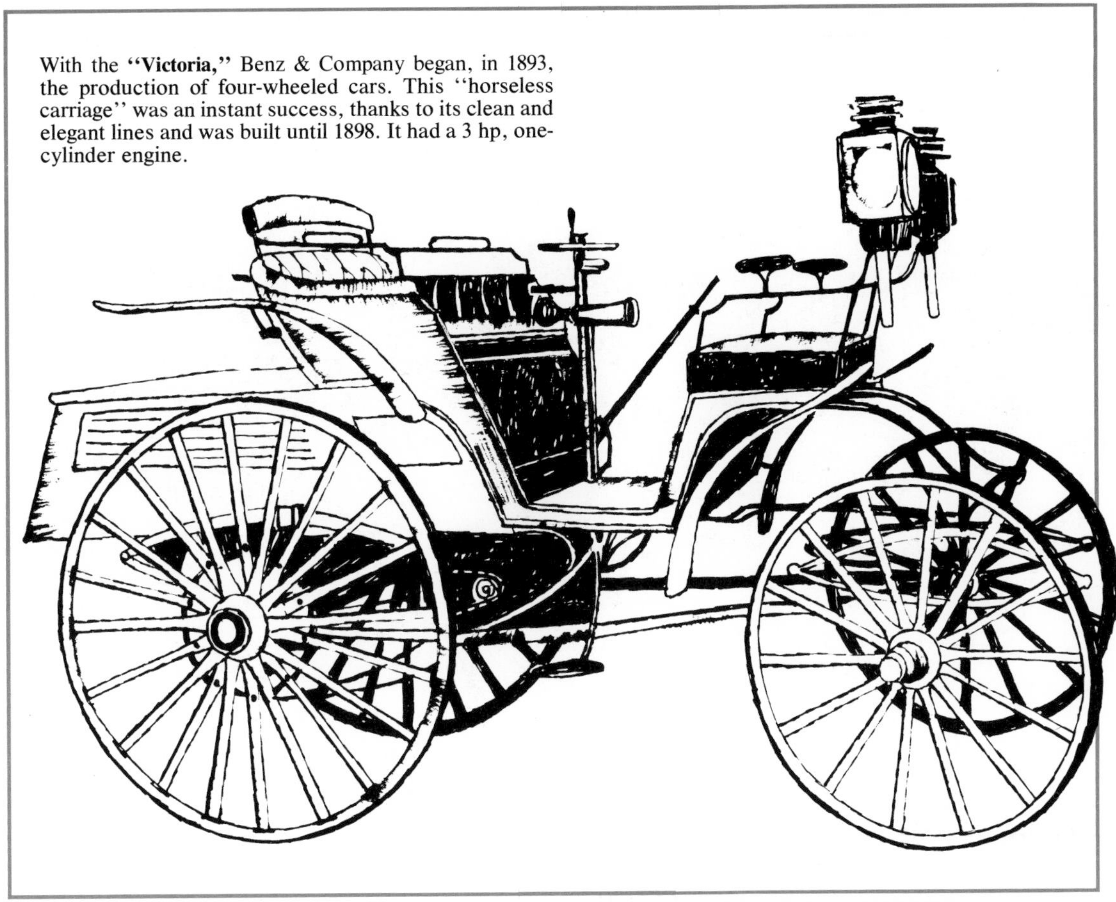

memoir expounding the theory of the four-stroke-cycle in 1861) the paternity of the modern four-stroke internal combustion engine which is called the Otto or Beau de Rochas cycle.

Although neither Beau de Rochas nor Nikolaus Klaus Otto ever built an automobile, the Austrian Siegfried Marcus used an Otto engine when he built one car in the year 1865 and another in 1874. The latter car is still preserved in the Technisches Museum in Vienna.

Among the originators of the automobile we have yet to mention the Italian Bernardi and the Frenchman Delamarre-Deboutteville. The former built, in 1874, a static gas engine and later another static engine (1878) with the Otto cycle, equipped for the first time with a carburetor; the latter inventor built in 1884 a

Nesselsdorf, a company that made horse carriages and railroad cars, produced this car in 1897. It was called **"Präsident"** and had a two-cylinder, 5 hp Benz motor. It won quite a few car races in 1899–1900, with Baron von Liebig as the driver. In 1918, Nesselsdorf adopted a new name, Tatra.

**Benz Ideal (1898)**

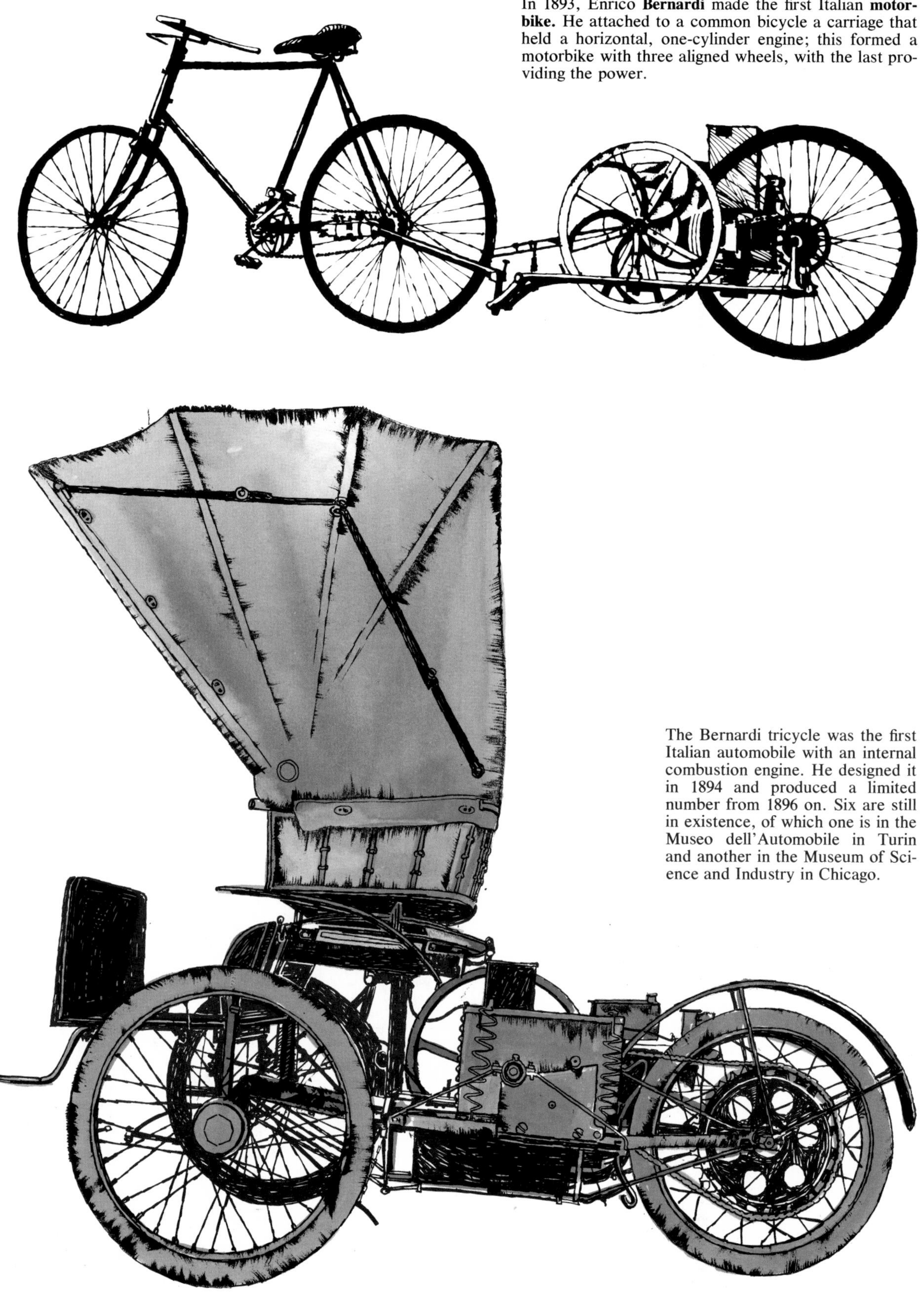

In 1893, Enrico **Bernardi** made the first Italian **motorbike.** He attached to a common bicycle a carriage that held a horizontal, one-cylinder engine; this formed a motorbike with three aligned wheels, with the last providing the power.

The Bernardi tricycle was the first Italian automobile with an internal combustion engine. He designed it in 1894 and produced a limited number from 1896 on. Six are still in existence, of which one is in the Museo dell'Automobile in Turin and another in the Museum of Science and Industry in Chicago.

Presented in 1894 and sold for 2000 marks, the **Benz Velo** was one of the first attempts to produce a popular-type car and is, at the same time, one of the earliest examples of a mass-produced vehicle. It was rare in that period to find two cars produced by the same factory exactly alike, but with the ''Velo'' Benz achieved the goal. As was usual with the Benz technique, the engine was a horizontal one-cylinder motor with 1140 cc and 3 hp at 400 rpm. This car too had electric ignition with sparkplug, coil, and battery. Unfortunately, the energy supplied by the battery did not last very long, and it had to be replaced frequently. The car reached a speed of 25 km/h and weighed less than 300 kg. The engine was water cooled.

car moved by the first high-compression engine.

But the internal combustion engine emerges from the technical shadows after the studies and practical realizations of Germans Karl Benz and Gottlieb Daimler. These two were, almost contemporaneously, the first to produce automobiles that were light, economical, and efficient, opening new paths to the new means of locomotion. It was the year 1886.

Automobiles with electric motors appeared in 1885 and were quite successful, due to their light weight and lack of noise. This is a **Woods** electric of 1899.

# DAIMLER

## I AM THE CAR

Gottlieb Daimler was born in Schoendorf, Württemberg, on March 17, 1834. His father, a mechanic, introduced him into the world of machines at an early age, when he sent him out to work as a factory apprentice. He entered the Stuttgart Polytechnical Institute at twenty-two and, after getting his degree, went to England to study the practical results of the English development of the steam vehicle.

When he returned to Germany, he became the director (1872) of the Gasmotoren-Fabrik Deutz, which specialized in the production of internal combustion engines. He left the company in 1882 and went, with his faithful friend Wilhelm Maybach, to Cannstatt, where he continued his longtime studies on the internal combustion engine. His first engine dates from 1883; it was a one-cylinder motor with *brûleurs* ignition and had a force of 1.1 hp. In 1885, Daimler mounted it on a motorcycle—the first in history. The same engine was later used on a horse carriage slightly modified for the occasion—the Motorkutsche—in 1886. Daimler soon began producing vehicles, and in 1888 the world's first taxi with an engine began regular service at the Stuttgart railway station.

But Daimler's name became famous throughout the world with his two-cylinder V engine with air cooling and *brûleurs* ignition, produced in 1888. It was presented at the Universal Exposition in Paris in 1889 and soon led to the French automobile "revolution" which started in 1891 with the cars of Panhard & Levassor, equipped with Daimler engines (like the Peugeots of the same period).

The **motorcycle** built by Daimler in 1885 had a vertical one-cylinder engine that was air cooled.

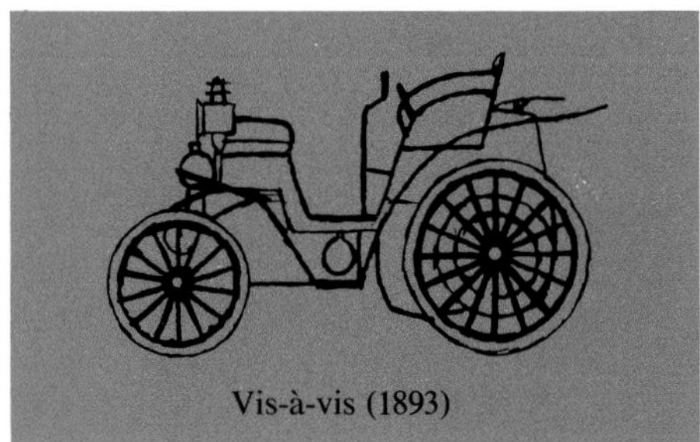

Vis-à-vis (1893)

Phaeton (1897)

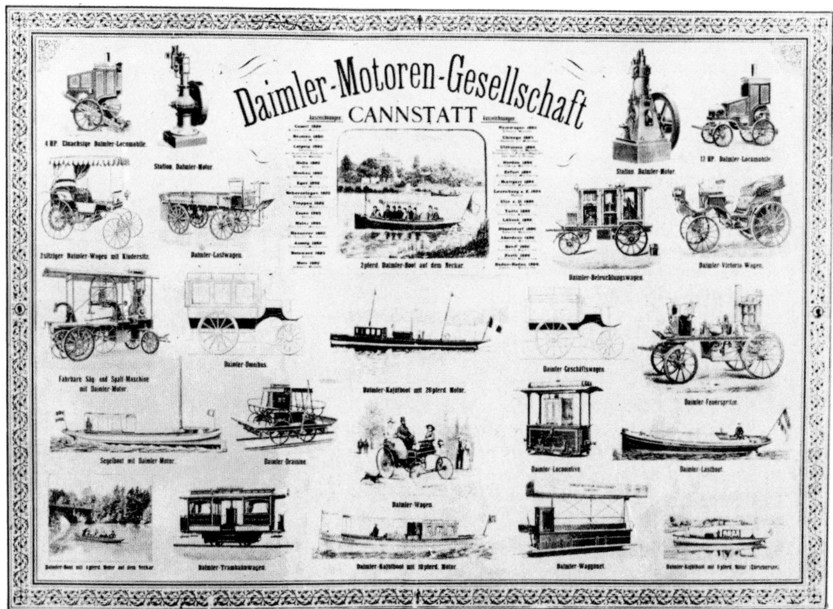


This publicity poster issued by Daimler in 1898 gives a good illustration of the German factory's choice of models.

# THE FUTURE LIES IN QUANTITY

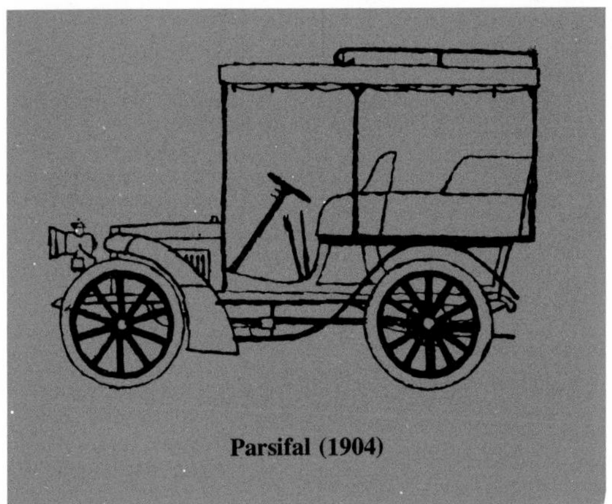

Parsifal (1904)

Karl Benz was born in Karlsruhe on November 25, 1844; his family had only modest economic means (the father was a railroad engineer who died when Karl was two), and his mother had to make great sacrifices to let the boy study. He entered the Karlsruhe Polytechnical Institute and received his degree when only twenty years old. He immediately found work in a steam boiler factory and remained there until 1871, when, at the age of twenty-seven, he moved to Mannheim and opened a small mechanical workshop. There he began his first research and experiments on a two-stroke internal combustion engine, which he finished in 1880. But the fragile economic status of his workshop soon obliged him to take two partners, with whom he founded the Benz und Cie Rheinische Gasmotoren-Fabrik in Mannheim.

At that point, Benz was finally able to dedicate himself wholly to his inventions. His first automobile, the "Velociped," was born in the autumn of 1885 (but only patented on January 29, 1896). It was more of a tricycle than an automobile, since Benz had strong doubts about current steering systems and preferred to use a single front wheel. He was not convinced by the studies of the German Ackermann or by those of the Frenchman Jeantaud of the value of the corrected steering system, dating from a few decades before. Not long thereafter Benz went on to invent and patent his own original steering mechanism, with a turning central spring.

From the start, Benz began the limited production of his own tricycles, which had considerable success both at home and abroad. From 1888 on, the French importer of Benz machines mounted the cars on the spot, thus founding the Roger-Benz company.

Benz began producing the "Velo"—the world's first small, mass-produced car—in 1894. In 1903, after a falling-out with his partners, he left his firm, which merged in 1926 with Daimler. Karl Benz died in 1929.

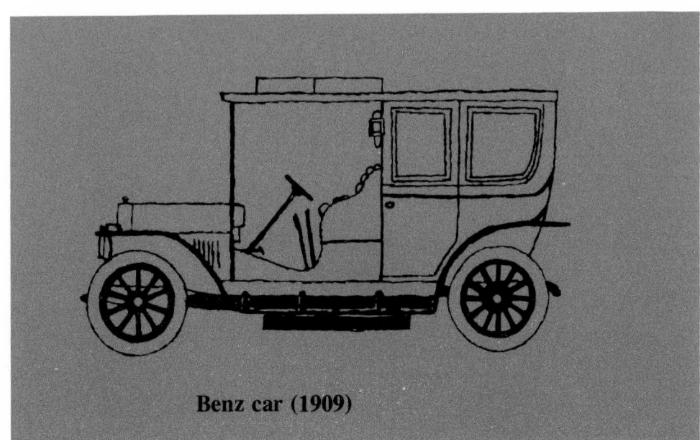

Benz car (1909)

Tonneau (1902)

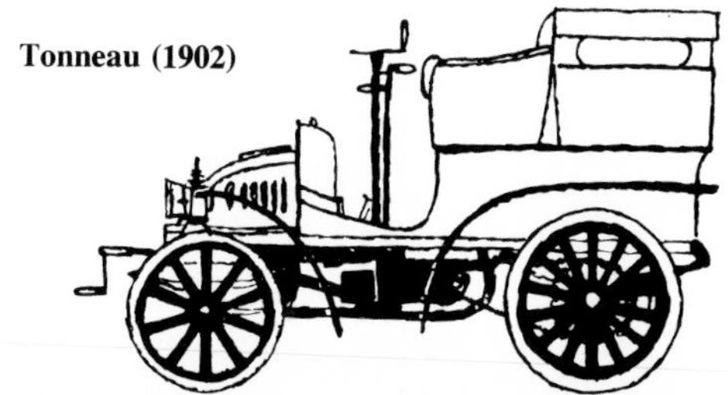

Touring car (1907)

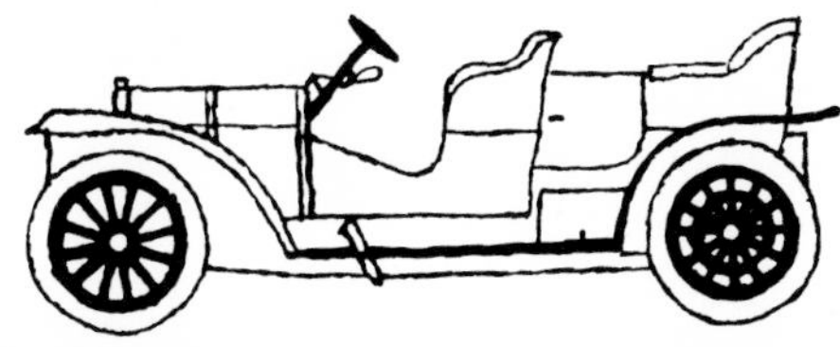

AUTOMOBILES
DELAHAYE
10. RUE DU BANQUIER
PARIS

# La belle époque

Fig. 1. Voiture à 4 places forme dog-cart

Fig. 2. Voiture à 4 places forme Wagonnette

Fig. 3. Voiture à 2 places avec parasol

Fig. 4. Voiture à 2 places avec petit siège à l'arrière

BATEAUX

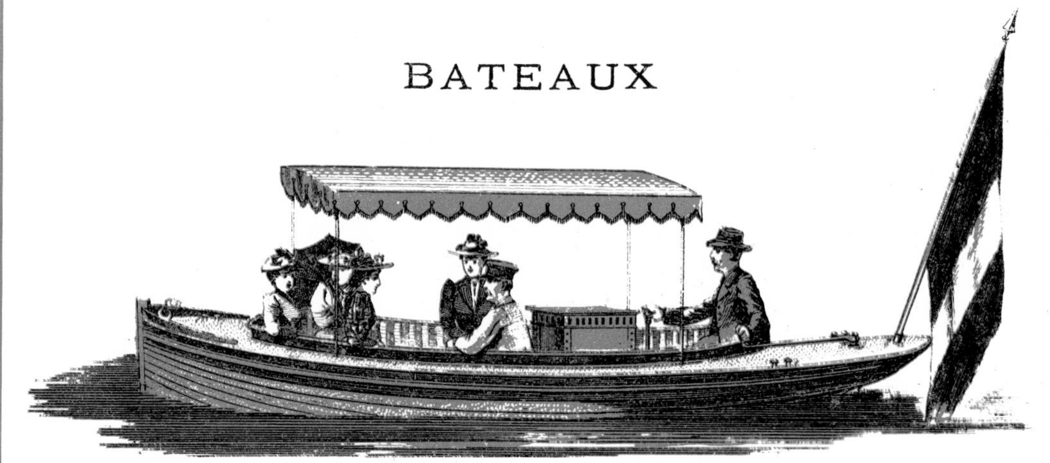

The first Panhard & Levassor catalogue, published in Paris, was also the first really modern automobile catalogue. A boat can be seen at the bottom; the firm produced marine engines as well as automobiles.

# La belle époque

Germany gave birth to the automobile, and France was its cradle. At the turn of the century, and especially in the last decade of the 1900s, Paris rose to the rank of automobile capital of Europe, and not only of Europe (those years, in fact, saw the first beginnings of motorization in the United States).

Daimler and Benz—particularly the first—started automobile driving in France. The agent for this process was Edouard Sarazin, a young French engineer entrusted by Gottlieb Daimler—who had discovered in him exceptional business acumen—with the task of finding a commercial outlet in France for his inventions. Sarazin had just recently entered the firm of Panhard & Levassor and proposed to that company the purchase of Daimler's patents. Negotiations were well under way when Sarazin died suddenly in 1889, but the agreement went through thanks to Sarazin's widow, who not only yielded the German inventor's patents but also married Emile Levassor in 1890.

The French house had been founded in 1845 by Périn, a very clever but very poor fellow who began from scratch and built wood-working machines. The business was already prospering when, in 1867, the young engineer René Panhard joined it and gave it his name. A third partner soon entered the field, Emile Levassor, and when Périn died in 1886 the firm took the name of Panhard & Levassor.

**Panhard Dog-Cart (1894).** The catalogue cover showed one of the first front-engine Panhards. It was a two-cylinder V, built on a Daimler license.

Right after the 1870 war between France and Prussia, the business was transferred to Paris, in Avenue d'Ivry, where it remained for almost a century until it closed.

Everything began on a cold morning in the early months of the year 1891, when an unsteady but rather impressive vis-à-vis four-

**Panhard covered body.** Panhard competes with Renault for being the first to offer this kind of body, which finally protected the driver from road dust and rain.

seater with a central engine placed under the floorboards managed to cover—without mechanical difficulties, a record for that period—the 10 kilometers that separated Avenue d'Ivry from Le Point du Jour. The venture was an immediate success. Even though the two partners had begun producing automobiles at a decent rhythm, there were so many orders that one sometimes had to wait two years for a Panhard & Levassor.

They were good machines: some of those in existence today are still in perfect working condition. But the main merit of the French firm was the conviction that mass production of the automobile was absolutely necessary. At first it was a rather primitive kind of mass production, because there were no two Panhards exactly alike. Too, there was a very limited choice of models, since all the cars had the same mechanical system; this is made clear in the catalogue, which was, by the way, the first modern automobile catalogue and thoroughly illustrated.

In 1894 Panhard & Levassor adopted an engine situated in the front of the car—Daimler's two-cylinder V with 4 hp, placed under the hood with a group containing the trans-

**Panhard dos-à-dos (1891).** Originally organized for woodworking, the Panhard firm soon began building motor vehicles. Its first car, with a Daimler engine set in the center, was tested in 1891. The front-engine was adopted later.

**Peugeot vis-à-vis (1891).** The bicycle-type spoked wheels show clearly the origins of the first cars made by this French firm. To be exact, this is the first four-seater vis-à-vis quadricycle built by Peugeot, and it had a Daimler engine group. This motor vehicle, which weighed 530 kg and reached a speed of 16 km/h, marked the shift made by the firm from an exclusively cycle-type production to a broader one with the possibilities for expansion that later made it one of the greatest French automobile manufacturers.

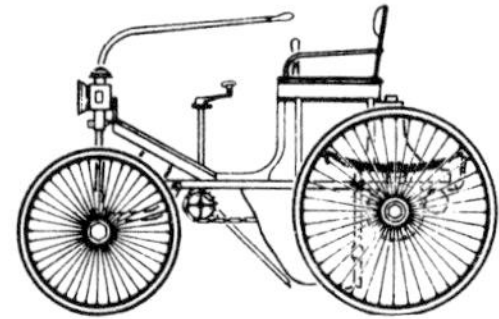

**Peugeot two-seater quadricycle (1891)**

**Peugeot two-seater quadricycle (1894)**

mission and the differential gear. The firm also began to simplify the construction of the car as much as possible, the first step toward the assembly line. The merits of Panhard & Levassor are indisputable, but we should not overlook the important role played by Peugeot at the end of the century. Panhard, considered at the time a medium-sized firm, employed about 100 workers, while in the same period Peugeot employed more than 2000.

The firm originated in the eighteenth century, when two brothers, Frédéric and Jean-Pierre Peugeot set up a foundry in the Montbéliard region, followed by a factory that made blades and one that produced bicycles. At the Paris Universal Exposition of 1889—that of the Eiffel Tower—the Peugeot firm offered a brand new steam tricycle propelled by a Serpollet engine; it was shown along with the bicycles, kitchen utensils, springs of all kinds, and various steel objects that had made the firm famous.

Everyone knew, in those years filled with novelties, that the Peugeot brothers had gotten rich due to a thoroughly nineteenth-century fashion: women's corsets. In fact, they alone possessed the secret of manufacturing the special steel needed for producing such corsets.

It was no small step from corset ribs to automobiles, but Peugeot took it by degrees, using the experience accumulated in the construction of the proverbially robust and efficient bicycles that had been the boast of the firm for decades and are still in its catalogue after more than a century. The firm was also aided by the high technological skill created by years of mechanical production (such as the springs, axles, and carriage joints which had been turned out for decades). It also made use of the experience gained from the Serpollet engine and the steam tricycle it powered; four examples of this tricycle were built and two of them still exist, one in the Conservatoire National des Arts et Métiers in Paris and the other in the Deutsches Museum in Munich.

The steam-driven car, clearly derived from a carriage, was large and heavy; the new gasoline-driven cars produced by Peugeot—and clearly derived from the bicycle, with spoked wheels and a chassis made of steel

**Peugeot 2½ hp (1894).** The production of Peugeot quadricycles continued practically unchanged until 1897. In the example shown here we find, as a result, the same characteristics seen in the 1891 model, such as the Daimler two-cylinder engine. This car was also built in Italy, by the Officine Costruzioni Meccaniche of Saronno.

**Peugeot vis-à-vis (1892).** One of the first Peugeot chassis to be fitted with a Daimler two-cylinder V engine. It reached a speed of 25 km/h.

**Panhard (1899)**

**PEUGEOT**

**Break (1894)**

**Omnibus (1895)**

Peugeot publicity when the firm still produced only bicycles. To the left can be seen the lion which is still the trademark of the French house.

**Phaeton (1899)**

tubing—were light and manageable. Just as its steam tricycle engine had used a thoroughly reliable engine produced by a specialist in the field, so the Peugeot gasoline-driven cars were produced with an engine created by someone in whom absolute trust could be placed: Daimler.

Almost up to the end of the century, all the cars produced by the French firm (slightly more than 200) were equipped with the famous Daimler closed-V, two-cylinder engine, with a displacement of between 565 and 1645 cc.

Since Panhard & Levassor had the French concession for Daimler engines, Peugeot, of course, had to turn to them to obtain the machines. Ironically, the first Peugeot equipped with a Daimler engine built with the Panhard & Levassor license was consigned to a client—the first Frenchman to buy a gasoline-driven car, a certain Eldin of Lyon—a few months before the first Panhard!

In 1891, the Peugeot Number One, a quadricycle, set a record when it went round-trip from Valentigny to Brest and back again (Valentigny was the site of the Peugeot factory) at an average of 13.5 km per hour, with no mechanical trouble at all. This was exceptional for the times, since the maximum speed of the quadricycle was only 18 km per hour, and to go a few kilometers without a breakdown was thought impossible. But the Peugeot firm has always had the tradition of turning out goods of the highest quality; for instance, the quadricycle in question—the so-called "Number One"—was really the sixth gasoline-driven vehicle built by the firm. The firm, however, was not happy with the results of its engines in the years 1889 and 1890 and never put the five prototypes built on the market, preferring to turn to others who had greater experience with gasoline engines. This is an example of modesty and conscience the like of which very few other automobile makers can point to in their past. And we should not

**"Voiture de livraison" (1900)**

**Peugeot Double Phaeton (1903).** This vehicle, refined and rational at the same time, had four comfortable seats and could do 80 km/h. The front mudguards were designed to deflect wind and dust from the passengers.

**Phaetonnet (1901)**

**Phaeton (1894)**

**Spider (1901)**

**Léon Bollée Tricycle (1896).** The first Bollée vehicle with an internal combustion engine was built by Léon, son of Amédée Bollée (considered the French pioneer of the steam-driven automobile). This tricycle, with two tandem seats, had a one-cylinder, 3 hp engine, water cooling, and three-speed gears. It began its career in the Paris–Marseilles race and in 1898 won the world record in the 100 km race at Etampes.

forget that in those days five vehicles could mean an entire year's production.

The tradition of the firm was that an automobile should be a light, economical, simple, and efficient machine, all the more efficient because simple. (Henry Ford was to adopt this principle in the years to come with the famous phrase: "What's not there can't break.") To simplify the transmission to the utmost, the nineteenth-century Peugeot had a posterior engine (that of Panhard & Levassor was in front).

The automobile became so popular in those years that many people were carried away by it. Among them was a remarkable French aristocrat, the Marquis Albert de Dion, with a mania for mechanical inventions. In 1876, at only twenty, he had managed to construct all by himself a complex hydraulic machine. Some of the world's most important mechanical patents bear his name, such as the De Dion "tube" still used today on many sports and luxury cars to improve road holding (it was invented in 1893!). After a casual meeting with George Bouton—an equally talented artisan—Albert de Dion founded with him and Bouton's brother-in-law, Jean Trépardoux, the firm that was to bear their names.

The De Dion-Bouton company got under way slowly, but ideas were not lacking—indeed, there were all too many. At the start, they concentrated on steam engines, light, powerful, and practical. Back in 1883 the three partners produced a small quadricycle with the first engine made in partnership; tests went very well, but there were no practical results from the model. A year later another steam vehicle was made, this time commissioned by a private client: a 1 hp engine and a

**Delahaye Break (1896).** This car participated in the famous Paris–Marseilles–Paris race. Note that the front seats are higher than the back ones and that the car has oil headlamps, solid rubber wheels with wooden spokes, and a luggage hamper in the back.

**Delahaye (1909)**

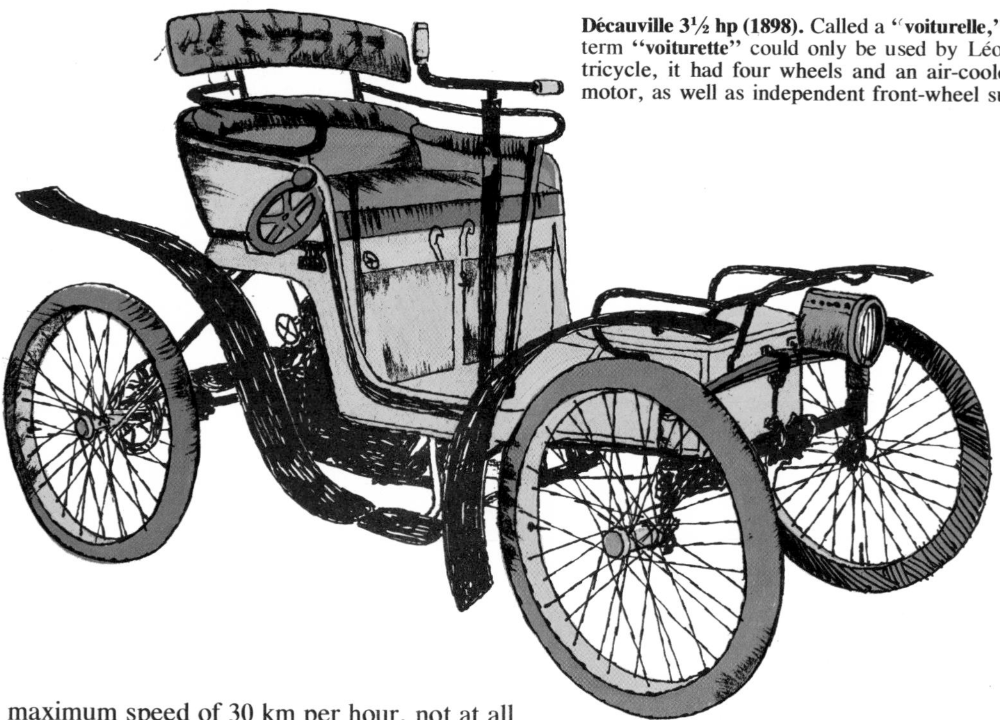

**Décauville 3½ hp (1898).** Called a "**voiturelle**," since the term "**voiturette**" could only be used by Léon Bollée's tricycle, it had four wheels and an air-cooled, 3.5 hp motor, as well as independent front-wheel suspension.

maximum speed of 30 km per hour, not at all bad for that era.

A tricycle like the above vehicle took part in the first "motor race" in history. It was organized by the editor of the magazine *La Vélocipede* and held on April 28, 1887; there was only one competitor in the race, the tricycle built by De Dion, Bouton, and Trépardoux, which managed to finish and win at the same time—automatically. An eye-witness timed its speed for a short distance: 60 km an hour! It is hard to believe the original documents.

The same tricycle engine was mounted on a boat and served as the locomotive force. The boat went up the Seine so fast that the police were forced to halt experiments in the water by the three partners after many complaints by local boatmen. The firm went on for a few more years, what with engines never produced and a commission from the French Navy for more engines that were never produced. At last the three partners decided to split up. One of them believed exclusively in the future of the steam engine (Trépardoux); another had great hopes for the gasoline engine (De Dion). De Dion managed to convince Bouton he was right. Time has wiped out all memories of Trépardoux.

In 1893, the De Dion-Bouton company took part—for the last time with a steam-driven vehicle—in the Paris–Rouen race. They came in first but did not win because the rules forbade carrying anyone in the car but the driver—and a steam engine needed a fireman. That same year saw the two partners busy at last with "their own" gasoline motor; De Dion and Bouton would never have made use of other people's engines. In 1894 the first of a long series was ready: a small, one-cylinder air-cooled engine with a driving force of ½ hp, which De Dion managed to raise to 1500 revolutions per minute (a fine rate for that time, and one which paved the way for fast engines). It was a great success, but instead of mounting it in a car of their own the partners decided to build it for other firms. Thousands of these engines were sold in Europe and in America as well. In the last years of the nine-

Publicity for the French car "**Hurtu.**" This firm had bought from Léon Bollée the production license for his **voiturette.**

**De Dion Bouton Tricycle (1896).** The tricycle on which De Dion and Bouton mounted their first engine, destined to spread throughout Europe.

The first engine built by the two partners. It was an air-cooled, one-cylinder motor which had ½ hp (left).

teenth century the De Dion engines—others, all of low displacement, followed the small, air-cooled one-cylinder motor—initiated entire nations into the use of the car, which was of course then homemade.

In the United States, Pierce Arrow, Packard, Peerless, Skriner, and other important firms in the automobile world used De Dion-Bouton engines for years. In Italy, the engines of the French firm were used by Ceirano, Marchand, Bianchi, and Ricordi. In Germany, by Adler, Opel and Kleyer. In Great Britain, by Ariel, Argyll, Humber, Empress and Lawson. And there is, of course, a long list of French manufacturers, among them one name that would soon be famous—Renault—but also others, such as Delage, Darraq, Phébus, Chenard, Rochet, and Latil. All in all, no fewer than fifty automobile manufacturers all over the world used the De Dion-Bouton engine.

Since the engine existed and was excellent, De Dion decided to apply it to a tricycle in 1896; it didn't sell too well at the start, but that wasn't important since the engines themselves sold very well indeed. The tricycle weighed about 250 kg, was driven by a 3 hp engine, and was very fast for its age, winning prizes in all the races in which it was entered. Production went on without interruption for a decade. In 1899, the De Dion company presented its first car—or, rather, its first small car—the 3.5 hp "vis-à-vis," a car that was really popular, light, and economical and that was produced in large numbers, making the

**De Dion Coupé Docteur (1900).** This model took the name "Coupé Docteur" from its success with the medical profession; a one-cylinder engine that reached 30 km/h was mounted on a closed body with only two seats.

**The engine of the De Dion vis-à-vis of 1898.**

**De Dion Bouton Populaire (1903).** A utility passenger car with a one-cylinder engine and a bold design that had great success from its first appearance. Various models were produced until 1907, when the firm devoted its production to large luxury cars.

firm famous as the first factory to turn out a cheap, useful family car.

As long as the two partners concentrated on such cars, business prospered; early in this century, the De Dion-Bouton became one of the world's largest and most important automobile industries (3000 persons were employed by it in the year 1906).

A year later, along with the presentation of the 3.5-hp engine, a model was born that was to become the best-seller of the Parisian firm at the opening of the century: the famous "Populaire." This car was produced until 1907 in various models—27, to be exact—with one-, two-, or four-cylinder engines.

In 1908, the De Dion-Bouton extended its

**Renault 3½ hp (1899).** At the end of the last century, many young men concentrated on building cars, fascinated by the new means of locomotion. One of them, Louis Renault, started off by mounting a De Dion engine on a tricycle he designed. This illustration shows the model preserved in the Museo dell'Automobile in Turin; it has a De Dion engine, three-speed gears with reverse, third in direct and cardanic transmission.

gamut of models and produced a brand-new engine, a V-8 (another first of the firm); clients could thus choose between 2-, 4-, and 8-cylinder cars with between 6 and 35 hp. Thus was born the modern idea of a complete series.

But times were evidently not ripe for such a wide variety of models. Anyone who wanted a luxury car had a wide range of brands to choose from, and De Dion, which had become famous for its low-cost family cars, could not hope to draw to itself overnight a clientele already oriented toward more illustrious names in the luxury field.

The decline of the De Dion name began with the First World War, during which it manufactured arms and aviation engines; after the war the firm never recovered completely, even if its death agony lasted for many years. In 1933 it finally closed down, unable to compete with such great luxury names as Hispano-Suiza, Delage, and Voisin.

Albert De Dion was a mechanical genius but not a great salesman.

The same cannot be said for Louis Renault, who already had many orders for his first prototype—a small car little more than two meters long and just a few hundred kilograms in weight—before it was finished. And what seemed to be a big toy (and almost certainly was born as a game, the result of the hobby of Louis and his brother) was to become the foundation of one of Europe's most prolific automobile factories.

Louis Renault had a passion for machines, but was also an extremely practical man. Still very young—when his first car was born, in November 1898, he was about twenty years old—he had accumulated a great deal of experience handling, dismantling, and reassembling engines since childhood. And it was a happy childhood, no doubt of that; he always had everything he wanted. His father bought him a Panhard & Levassor engine even before he turned fourteen; and he practiced with it in the small repair shop set up in the garden of the country house at Billancourt, on the Seine just outside Paris. That garden was soon to become a smoky workshop. The Renault factory is still in that same garden, which, as the years passed, swallowed up all the nearby gardens and the small island (Seguin) in the river. A repair shop that becomes a factory is a rare thing; inside the Billancourt factory, the repair shop is preserved in its original state.

Louis had been fascinated by the De Dion engines and by the idea of the automobile held by its builder: that of a simple, practical, and economical machine. Renault

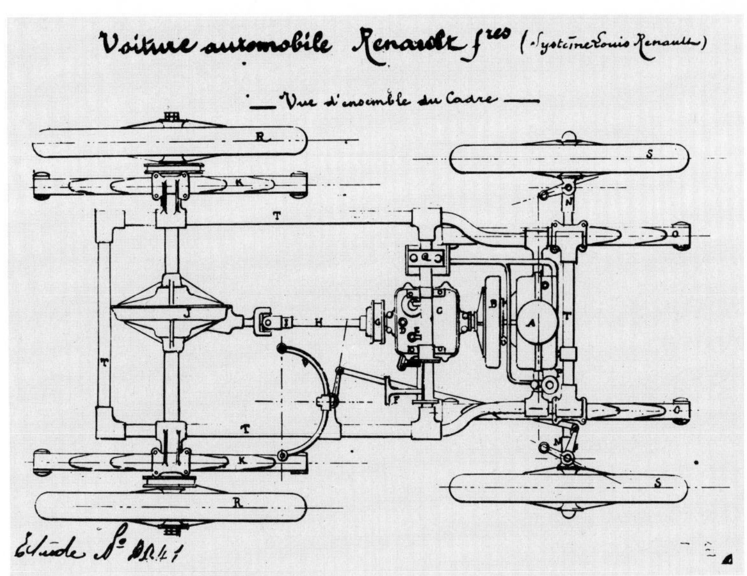


The plan of the first car designed in 1899 by Louis Renault for filing his patent. We owe to him, among other things, the invention of the direct-transmission gear box.

Another of Louis Renault's firsts worth recalling: **inside driving,** attained through the use of the chassis of his first car.

adopted this philosophy and remained true to it for years, even if he produced cars with a 9-liter displacement (the "40 hp"). But the economical car remained the basic one for Renault.

Economical did not necessarily mean banal, though—on the contrary. The important thing was a highly refined and "clean" mechanical foundation based on the well-tested De Dion 3½ hp engine, a solid steel chassis, cardanic transmission, and a direct contact gear box (that is, one in which the upper gear made use of two equal gears which made its use more regular and silent). This last discovery was patented on February 9, 1899, and guaranteed Louis Renault indisputable priority. Another French factory, the Décauville, also claimed this priority, however, for its 3½ hp of 1898, a small car which also had a De Dion engine; but no one at the Décauville plant had thought of patenting the invention.

On March 30, 1899, the Renault Frères company was founded, with an initial capital of 60,000 francs.

**Darracq type N (1901).** Alexandre Darracq preferred the one-cylinder engine, of which the "Type N" made use. It had a one-cylinder front engine with 9 hp and a speed of about 50 km/h. The wheels were of wood, of the artillery type—a common feature at that time.

In the meantime, as the century ended and even before Renault Frères opened for business, the activity of Léon Bollée continued at full rhythm in his father's plant in Le Mans, in the heart of France. For years Léon

**Darracq 9½ hp (1902).** This rear-entrance tonneau is characteristic of the many cars built by Alexandre Darracq; it had a one-cylinder engine and a tubular chassis and did 40 km/h.

Bollée claimed to be the head of the oldest automobile factory in France and in the world. That is correct, if we take into account as well the activity of his father, Amédée, in the field since 1865. The elder Bollée was undoubtedly the pioneer maker of automobiles in France, linking his name to steam-engine vehicles, while Léon's activity was oriented toward internal combustion engines.

The first vehicle planned and produced by Léon Bollée was really a tricycle, so simple, efficient, and robust that it became very popular at the end of the nineteenth century. It had a one-cylinder motor, designed by Bollée himself, placed horizontally and supplied with a *"bruleurs"* ignition; it had a force of 3 hp—four times greater than that of the other popular tricycle of the period, the De Dion-Bouton. While the latter was a one-seater with pedals, because of its low power, the Bollée tricycle was a comfortable two-seater equipped with a simple, three-gear-belt transmission. It was presented to the public in 1896 and called "Voiturette" (a name patented by Bollée himself); it began at once to take part in all the main meets of the day, and always ended up in the top classifications. In 1898, a Bollée "Voiturette" managed to break through the 100-kilometers-per-hour "barrier."

In 1896, Léon Bollée licensed the manufacturing rights of his tricycle to the Englishman David Salomons for the enormous sum of £500,000. He later yielded the same rights for France to the Hurtu Company and then to the Société des Voiturettes Système Léon Bollée (in which he became a minority shareholder). Like Ferdinand Porsche later, Bollée was very busy developing projects for third parties, licensing patents left and right, above all to American manufacturers who were fascinated by the Bollée name.

Let us note particularly the license of a patent for an automobile, which Léon made at the end of the century, to the manufacturer Alexandre Darracq. Darracq then began to produce in his own factory (Usines Perfecta), the first real automobile designed by Léon Bollée.

The Darracq company's success began with that car, and the plant became one of the most important in the field early in the twentieth century. With its exceptional multinational characteristics—it had great amounts of capital behind it—it contributed in one way or another to the birth of quite a few European car plants of great prestige, such as Opel in Germany, Alfa Romeo in Italy, and Talbot in Great Britain.

The automobile had at last grown up.

**Bollée Limousine (1901).** Highly appreciated for its roominess, it had two outside front seats and six inner ones, as well as a luggage rack on the roof and a wicker basket behind. Note the two characteristic round radiators set on each side of the hood.

**Ettore Bugatti's first car (1901)**

# DE DION BOUTON

## TWO MEN AND A CYLINDER

**De Dion-Bouton & Trépardoux Steam Wagon (1889).** This primitive vehicle is preserved in the Museo Storico della Motorizzazione Militare in Rome.

**Vis-à-vis (1898).** This vis-à-vis with a one-cylinder, 3.5 hp engine was the first four-wheel car model built by Albert De Dion and George Bouton. De Dion's fame is also linked to an original suspension system patented in 1893 and known as the "De Dion bridge."

If, one day during Carnival season in the year 1883, Marquis Albert De Dion had not gone to a toy shop on the Boulevard des Italiens in Paris to buy some prizes for a ball, one of the most important names in the history of the automobile might be missing.

It is true that history is not made of "if's"—but no meeting was more unlikely than that between De Dion and Bouton. Rich and noble Albert De Dion, whose great passion was machinery, discovered in that toy shop a small model of a steam engine that worked perfectly. He got the name of the craftsman and went to see him at once, never showing up at the ball, of course—a sacrifice that changed both their lives. As soon as he met George Bouton, De Dion proposed that they become partners. And that very year, 1883, saw the start of the De Dion, Bouton & Trépardoux Company. (Trépardoux was Bouton's brother-in-law, his partner in the small workshop in which the toy machines were made.) Things went slowly at first, despite ideas and patents. All their efforts were concentrated on steam engines—which Bouton and Trépardoux favored—while the great new idea of those years was the internal combustion engine, which was light and compact and thus better adapted for the first wobbly automobiles.

Since Albert De Dion was the only one of the three partners to believe in the gasoline engine, a split in the company was inevitable. De Dion was joined by Bouton, and Trépardoux left the firm. From then on, it was a long series of triumphs. The small but solid and inexpensive De Dion-Bouton engines literally invaded the world—even before the French company prepared some kind of vehicle on which to mount them. A popular tricycle was produced in 1896, and in 1899 there appeared an equally popular car which made the firm's fortune. Then, in the first decade of the new century, the abandonment of the "popular" formula slowly brought about the decline of the name of De Dion-Bouton.

# A HOPELESS PATENT

Even though he was born to be an inventor, his family wanted him to become a lawyer. But as soon as George B. Selden—born in 1846—got his degree, he left the United States for Europe. He wanted to observe, study, and "get inspiration" from what Europe's greatest inventors were then—it was the 1860s—about to perfect: the internal combustion engine. Selden sensed the idea's great future, went home, and decided to make use of his exceptional legal knowledge, in regard to the future means of locomotion.

It cannot be denied that Selden was more a great lawyer than a great inventor. In fact, in 1879, he applied for a patent on a vehicle with "nonanimal traction"; in this patent he managed to "foresee" everything, even if in an extremely vague and imprecise way.

No one before then had ever patented an entire motor vehicle—just parts, such as the engine, the steering mechanism, or the brakes. Selden filed a patent for the whole thing.

With legal ups-and-downs, he was able to prolong his patent rights proceedings until 1885. George B. Selden thus claimed the title of "inventor of the automobile," although he had managed only to build a prototype vehicle many years after he had filed for a patent. The invention had finally been invented.

From that moment on, Selden simply had to sit back and claim the royalties which had legally matured on his patent: so much for each car built in the United States, and every car had to have "his" metal plate on it. Some car makers rebelled, went to court—and lost their cases. Finally Henry Ford decided to wage bitter war on Selden; this war lasted from 1903 to 1911 and ended with the defeat of George B. Selden.

Opel

AUTOMOBILI e VELOCIPEDI
F.lli MARCHAND
PIACENZA

AUTOMOBILES MARTINI St-BLAISE
NEUCHÂTEL (SUISSE)
MARTINI
PREMIÈRE ET PLUS ANCIENNE MARQUE NATIONALE

5

# A new century

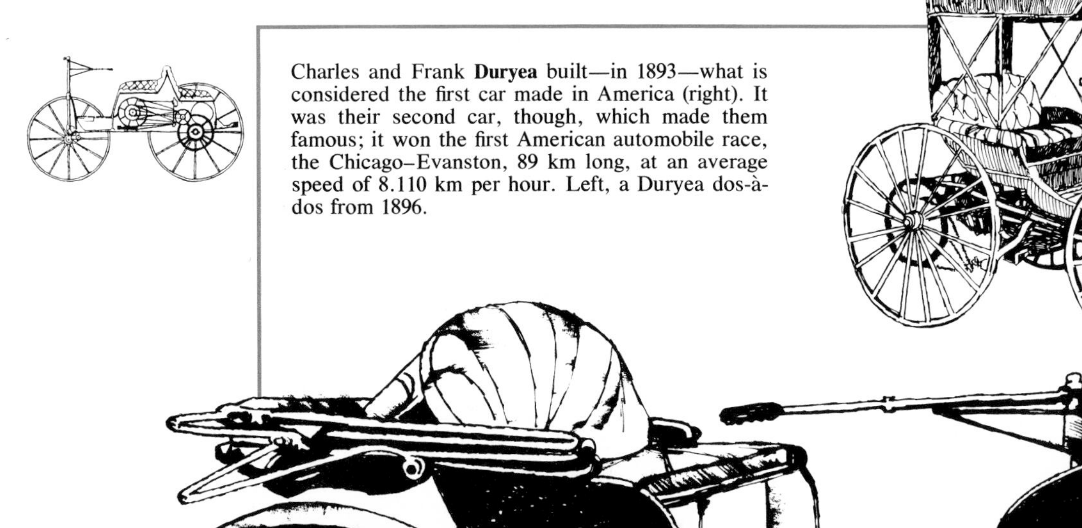

Charles and Frank **Durvea** built—in 1893—what is considered the first car made in America (right). It was their second car, though, which made them famous; it won the first American automobile race, the Chicago–Evanston, 89 km long, at an average speed of 8.110 km per hour. Left, a Duryea dos-à-dos from 1896.

**Columbia (1901).** Columbia had a complex history. The firm originally produced electric cars that were distributed in England under the name of City and Suburban and in France under that of Electromotion. In 1899, it turned to building gasoline cars, with the name of Pope-Columbia. The model shown here had a vertical one-cylinder, 5 hp engine and could reach a speed of 45 km/h.

# A new century

While France had the automobile fairly early, the other European nations and the United States suffered delays. There were various reasons for these delays, and they almost always differed from one country to another. In England, for instance, the slow development in motorization was due to the presence of the severe "Red Flag Act," which obliged anyone who used a motorcar to advance preceded by a man on foot, carrying a red flag by day and a lantern by night. Germany, on the other hand, was full of projects and ideas, to the point of letting them overflow into nearby France; what was lacking was the courage of factory owners to gamble all they owned on the new invention. As for Italy, there too there were many inventors, but there was no capital and no basic industry on a level with the French.

In the United States, things were different: a few inventors were forced to work without any real contact with their European colleagues (in those days, the oceans did divide the continents literally). All these factors were aggravated by the lack of roads in the United States.

Though these seem to be very different problems, combined they were serious enough to retard the development of the automobile outside France for some time. All these countries, some to a greater and some to a lesser degree, had to wait patiently for the arrival of the new century to see a modern automobile industry arise in their own territory. Now let's look at the situation nation by nation at the turn of the century, beginning with the United States.

Even though lawyer George B. Selden claimed that he had filed a patent as far back

**Oldsmobile (1897).** The first motor vehicle built by Ransom Eli Olds, founder of the first automobile factory in the United States.

# OLDSMOBILE

## CURVED DASH: THE AUTOMOBILE IS MASS PRODUCED

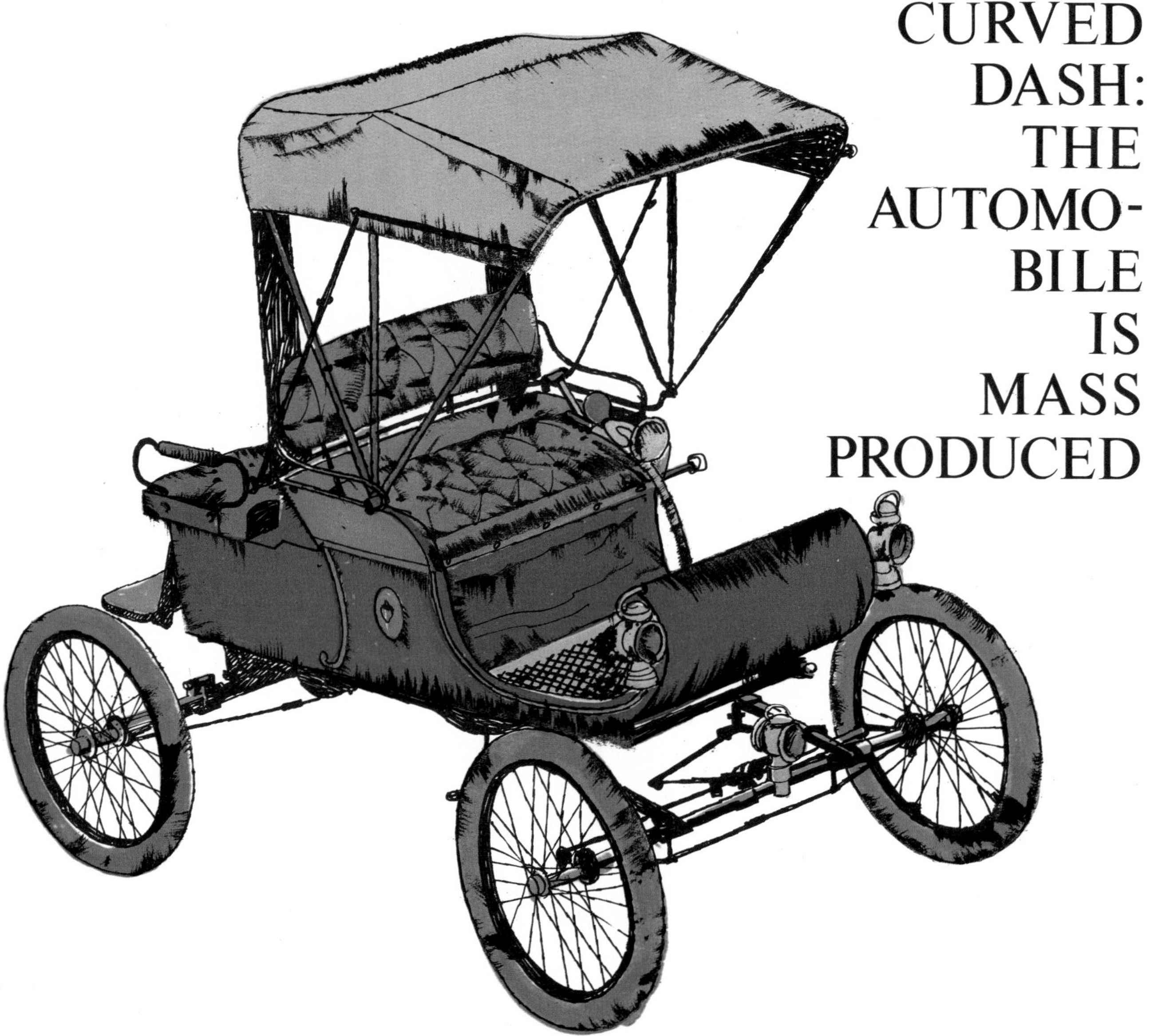

Apart from any technical or aesthetic virtues, the Oldsmobile "Curved Dash" must be remembered for having been the first four-wheeled car produced on a large scale in identical examples and, to top it off, available in only one model. These criteria of mass production were to be applied on an even larger scale a few years later, and are thus responsible for the birth of the assembly line.

The Curved Dash had all the traits of a truly popular car: it had a simple mechanical setup and was easy to maintain, trustworthy and cheap. When it was presented in 1901, it cost about $650. It was powered by a one-cylinder, 5 hp engine and could do a bit more than 30 km/h; it had a gear box with two forward gears and one reverse. The car could carry up to four people, due to the addition of a rear seat facing backward.

It had great success on the market and was built from 1901 to 1907; in 1903, 3750 were built—a third of the 11,235 vehicles made in the United States that year. The prototype of this car was saved by a miracle from a 1901 fire that completely destroyed the factory Ransom Eli Olds had built in Detroit. Since all the costly and not very salable models in production were destroyed, Olds was literally forced to concentrate all his hopes on the little Curved Dash.

as 1877 (but which in reality was filed in 1879 and granted on November 5, 1895) and therefore attributed to himself the title of "the inventor of the automobile," there really were very few "firsts" in America in this field. Selden's patent was just a very clever trick to get money from the real inventors; the lawyer had in fact patented "everything," even extending his patent to any vehicle moved by a motor.

As if the lack of roads were not enough, because of Selden the few American inventors kept their projects under wraps for too long. The fact is that at the start of 1895 there were hardly 4 machines in operation in the whole United States; the number rose to 16 the next year, as compared with nearly 1000 that wobbled over the roads of France. Too, those few cars were almost all imported, since the first "real" American car dates from 1893; the month was November, and the name of the inventor that of the Duryea brothers, Charles and Frank. The two brothers were soon followed, in July 1894, by their compatriot Elwood Haynes. Haynes later contributed to the birth of the first authentic automobile industry in America when he became the advisor to Albert A. Pope, then owner of the largest American bicycle factory. However, due to the lack of roads and to the immense distances involved, even the bicycle had trouble getting started in the United States.

This is why Pope first turned to a very talented inventor, Hiram P. Maxim (better remembered for a machine-gun bearing his name), who in 1895 had designed an automobile with an internal combustion engine. The Pope Company then concentrated on electric propulsion, and at the start of the 1890s began producing a small car called the "Columbia" which was soon successful.

The first manufacturers of American automobiles were, in any case, the Duryea brothers, as we have mentioned, but their

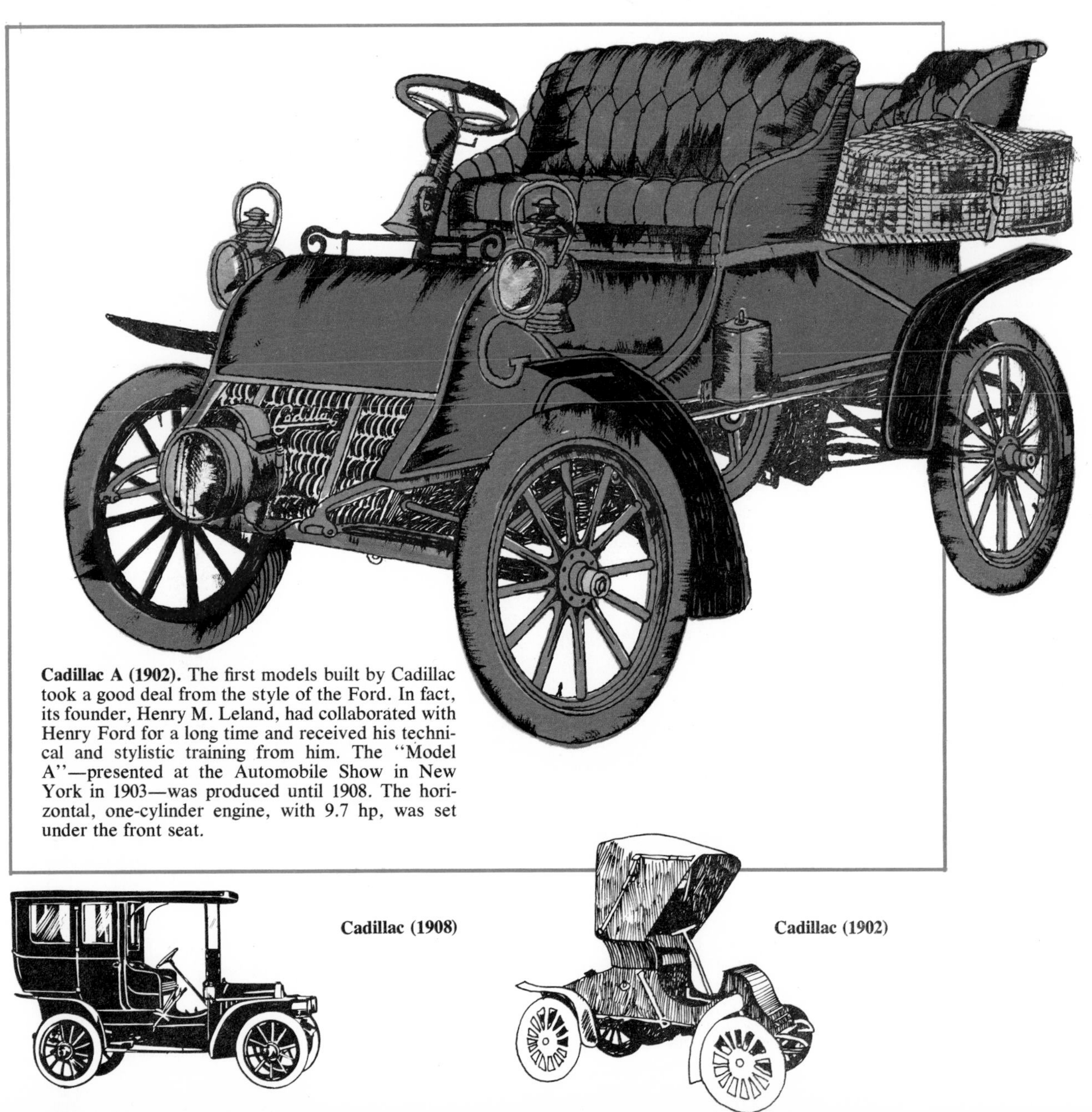

**Cadillac A (1902).** The first models built by Cadillac took a good deal from the style of the Ford. In fact, its founder, Henry M. Leland, had collaborated with Henry Ford for a long time and received his technical and stylistic training from him. The "Model A"—presented at the Automobile Show in New York in 1903—was produced until 1908. The horizontal, one-cylinder engine, with 9.7 hp, was set under the front seat.

**Cadillac (1908)**

**Cadillac (1902)**

**Oakland (1908).** The first Oakland, designed by A. D. Brush, had a vertical two-cylinder engine (2.5 liters) with an epicyclic gear box and water cooling. In 1909 the firm was absorbed by General Motors.

production was very limited (only a few dozen cars up to the beginning of the twentieth century), although they had a moment of great popularity after the highly controversial victory won in the first American automobile race, the Chicago-Evanston, which took place on November 28, 1895. The Duryeas were followed by other pioneers who in turn set up factories; among them was Haynes, who, with the Apperson brothers, founded the Haynes-Apperson Company. Another pioneer was Winton, who founded the Winton Company. Thus, even though the automobile arrived late in America, the country made up for lost time. In 1897 there were already nine makes of automobiles, all present at that year's Boston Fair; and by 1900 the overall production in the country reached exceptional heights; 4000 vehicles, which became 7000 a year later. Also in 1897, American manufacturers managed to get a law passed fixing a 45 percent customs tax on imported cars, even though many of them went on using European engines in their own models.

From the start, then, the American automobile industry showed clearly what its path would be, and a very simple path it was: large-scale production. Before the arrival on the scene of Ford and his industrial revolution, another talented young man began "mass production" in Detroit. In 1901 Ransom Eli Olds managed to produce more than 400 "Curved Dash" Oldsmobile cars in a few months; they were all exactly alike and the client was unable to choose different types of chassis (an unusual happening for those years). It was a simple, strong, and economical little car, and it could be sold for only $650, thanks to mass production. It was driven by a one-cylinder motor and barely weighed 360 kg. A year later more than 2500 of these cars were made, guaranteeing Olds and his partners immense profit; it was becoming very good business to produce automobiles.

Now let's have another look at the Old World—at Great Britain, to be more exact. The land that had given birth to automobile driving—or to the steam engine, anyway—had suddenly plunged into a medieval apathy

The 1907 **Pope** was one of the last electric cars made by that firm. This kind of car was given up in 1910 because of its limited power range.

**Buick (1903)**

**Cadillac,** later famous for its highly luxurious models, was, in its early years, oriented toward a middle-income market. The car shown here was aimed for such a market.

because of the notorious "Locomotive Acts" passed in 1861 and strengthened in 1865. These laws limited the speed of all motorized vehicles to 2 miles an hour in the city and 4 miles an hour on country roads—and obliged each car driver to see to it that he was preceded at a distance of about 50 meters by a man waving a red flag. Naturally, English interest in the automobile was sinking rapidly, to be transferred to the bicycle, especially after an invention patented by a Scottish veterinarian, John Boyd Dunlop, in 1888; the pneumatic tire, a feature that would pass from the bicycle to the automobile and make a great contribution to the automobile's diffusion throughout the world. Dunlop's original tire was then perfected by the Michelin brothers. In 1896 the Michelins, to overcome a natural public suspicion regarding their product, bought 200 Bollée cars and 100 De Dion tricycles, which they then sold at auction at the respective

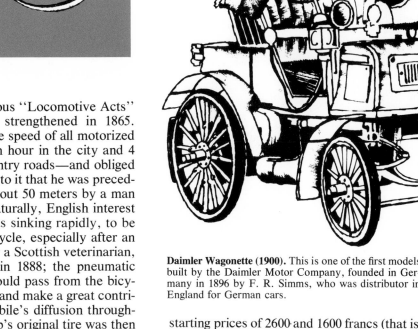

**Daimler Wagonette (1900).** This is one of the first models built by the Daimler Motor Company, founded in Germany in 1896 by F. R. Simms, who was distributor in England for German cars.

starting prices of 2600 and 1600 francs (that is, a lower price than was charged by the two firms) with great success. Bollée and De Dion were later the most fervent supporters of the pneumatic tire as against the solid rubber one.

It was not until 1896 that a courageous

**Wolseley 6 HP (1904).** The Wolseley factory was founded in 1895 by Herbert Austin. Production began with a series of tricycles based on Léon Bollée's *voiturette*. The cars produced after that, supplied with a horizontal engine, were highly admired for their simplicity and efficiency, even if they were highly criticized for their noisiness. This model, preserved in the Montagu Motor Museum, is interesting for its radiator made up of many rows of finned tubes winding around the hood.

**Daimler Open Tourer (1907)**

**Buick Model D (1907)**

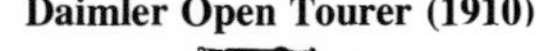

**Daimler Open Tourer (1910)**

**Rover 8 HP (1904).** This is the first four-wheeled vehicle produced by Rover. It was designed by E. W. Lewis and had a one-cylinder 8 hp engine, mechanical brakes, and the gear lever on the wheel.

British politician, Sir David Salomons, managed to get Parliament to repeal the oppressive laws against driving motor vehicles. That victory was celebrated, on November 15, 1896, with a sightseeing competition—the London-Brighton race, still repeated every year with old cars—in which quite a few foreign contestants took part, including one who had come over from America. Earlier, Salomons himself had founded with four partners (Lawson, Duncan, McRobie, and Turrell) the British Motor Syndicate for the development of motorization in Great Britain, in the expectation that the restrictive laws would soon be repealed. Although the British Motor Syndicate had gotten exclusive rights for the British market on many French and German patents, the company soon failed; as a result, the first car factory founded on British soil was the Daimler Motor Syndicate Ltd. (still in existence under the name Daimler Company Ltd.) for the exploitation of Gottlieb Daimler's motor patents. Before the end of the century, other English factories were established and in full production, such as Lanchester, Wolseley, Armstrong-Siddeley, Rover, Standard, Singer, Sunbeam, Lea-Francis, Morgan, Hillman, Humber, Albion, Austin, Crossley, Jensen, Jowett, and Napier.

From Great Britain to Germany: for almost twenty years (that is, until the start of the twentieth century) after the studies of Otto and Langen and before those of Rudolf Diesel, the German car was linked to just two names—three, if we want to add to Daimler

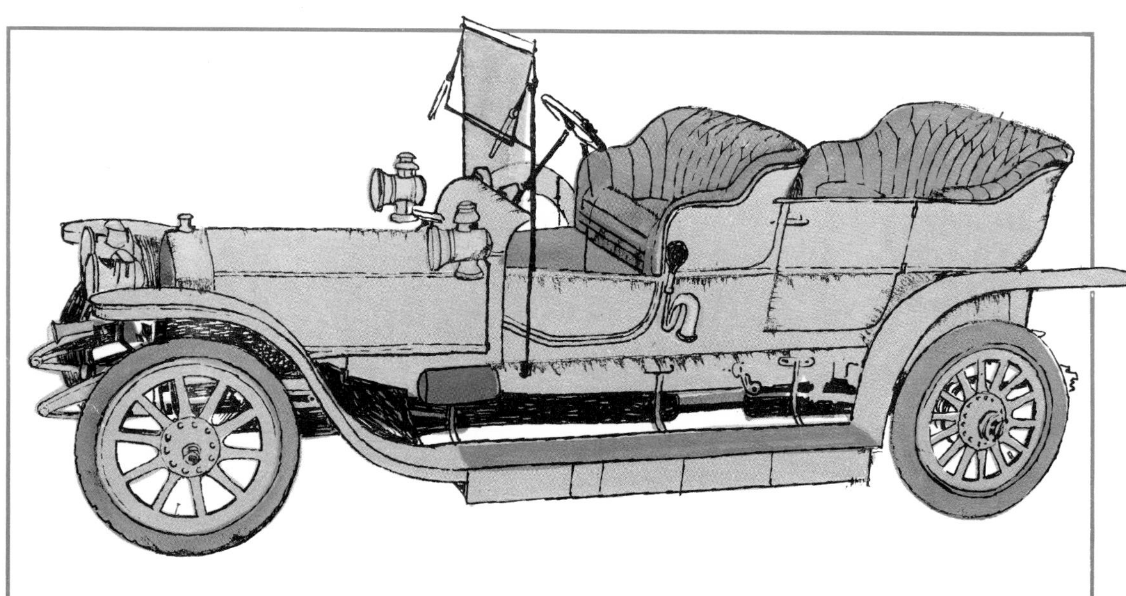

**Rolls-Royce Silver Ghost (1907).** The Rolls-Royce story began in 1903, when F. H. Royce became dissatisfied with his Décauville and decided to build a car for himself. C. S. Rolls, who imported luxury cars from the continent, was struck by the accurate finishing of the car and quickly set up an agreement with Royce. It was 1906. The "Silver Ghost" model is so famous that it hardly needs description; this is the car that, over a period of nineteen years (1907–1926), made the firm of Rolls-Royce a byword for perfection. The engine had six aligned cylinders and could reach a speed of 100 km/h. Officially entitled the "40/50," this car was nicknamed the Silver Ghost because the first one—extremely quiet—was painted Silver for publicity reasons.

**Auburn (1903)**

**Auburn (1907)**

**Benz Coupé Milord (1897).** A strange car with heavy lines, and large solid-rubber spoked wheels. The engine was new and interesting: it had counteropposed cylinders and was called "kontra-motor," a kind of forerunner of the "boxer."

and Benz's names that of Maybach, Gottlieb Daimler's right-hand man. Unlike the situation in France, the automobile had trouble asserting itself in Germany, because of suspicion felt by German industrialists. As a result, the two great German inventors had to turn into manufacturers themselves and even into traveling salesmen to advertise and sell their own patents throughout the world. We have already mentioned the patents licensed by Daimler earlier in this book; let us now mention two industries set up on Benz's patents: the Roger-Benz company in France and the Lutzmann company in Germany.

For these two German inventors, the Universal Exposition in Paris in 1889—organized for the centenary of the French Revolution—was an excellent launching ground for spreading the fame of their patents. Another French show, the Salon of 1900 in Paris (held from December 19 to 25), marked a basic step forward for the automobile industry, and particularly for the German industry. There the world's first really modern car, the Mercedes Simplex, had its international premiere. Gottlieb Daimler never saw it, though; he had died a few months earlier at the age of 66.

**Ajax Landaulet (1908).** This extremely well-finished and strong car had a four-cylinder engine and could reach 60 km/h; it was the first built by the "Ajax SA" Company, founded in 1907 by a Swiss financial group that had taken over the "Dr. G. Aigner Fabrique d'Automobiles, Zurich" after bankruptcy.

**Studebaker electric car (1902)**

**Studebaker Garford (1904)**

Lutzmann 4 HP (1895). Production of the Lutzmann car began in 1895 with this typical "horseless carriage" partly based on the first Benz models both in line and technical setup. This model did not sell well, and in April 1899 Lutzmann became part of the Adam Opel bicycle factory.

**Opel 4 HP (1898).** This is the first car produced by the new Lutzmann-Opel factory. Built in the Rüsselsheim plant, it was also sold in a 6 hp version. It was exceptionally advanced in comparison with other models of that era and even had pneumatic tires.

**Opel "Darracq" (1908)**

Even though it was produced by the Daimler firm, the Simplex already bore the name Mercedes (which has always remained with it) for commercial reasons, since the word Daimler was thought to be too "German" for foreign buyers. And Emil Jellinek, the French importer of the famous German cars, suggested giving it his own daughter's name—Mercedes.

The Simplex had been designed by both Daimler and Wilhelm Maybach, though only the latter remained to produce it and reap the profits. It was truly a revolutionary car. It had, for the first time, a chassis of stamped plate (instead of wood or rolled plate) to which all the mechanical parts were firmly attached, and it also had a slanted—not a vertical—steering-wheel shaft. The timing system worked through mechanically controlled valves (in those days the inlet valve opened by depression). A gear box with differentiated control was used for the first time, so that the gears no longer had to be patiently

**Paul Daimler car (1900)**

sought out with the lever; ball-bearings were mounted on all moving parts; and cooling took place through a very modern and highly efficient beehive radiator that, from the Simplex on, replaced the serpentine type. Last, the Simplex used for the first time an ignition system with a high-tension magneto, the only valid one until 1925 and the arrival of coil ignition by battery.

Motorization in Italy, as in Germany, got under way rather slowly. In 1899 there were only about 111 motor vehicles in circulation, while a few thousand moved over French roads. But if the means for starting actual production were lacking, inventors were plentiful. Among them were such illustrious

**OM Züst 10 HP (1908)**

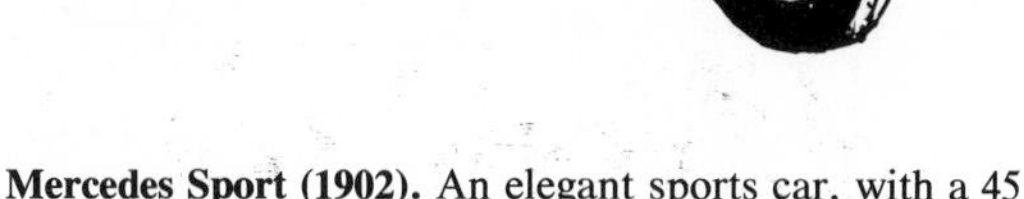

**Mercedes Sport (1902).** An elegant sports car, with a 45 hp engine and a speed of 70 km/h.

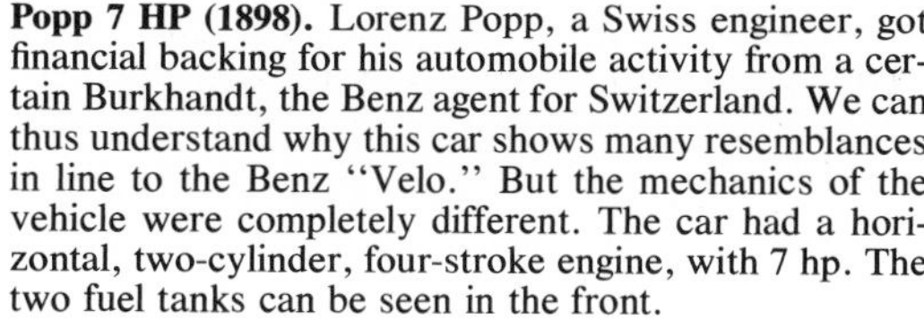

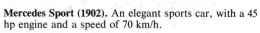

**Popp 7 HP (1898).** Lorenz Popp, a Swiss engineer, got financial backing for his automobile activity from a certain Burkhandt, the Benz agent for Switzerland. We can thus understand why this car shows many resemblances in line to the Benz "Velo." But the mechanics of the vehicle were completely different. The car had a horizontal, two-cylinder, four-stroke engine, with 7 hp. The two fuel tanks can be seen in the front.

**Benz touring car (1906).** It had a 28 hp engine with a speed of 70 km/h.

**Mercedes Autobus (1903).** The German firm not only produced automobiles, but also turned out industrial vehicles as well.

**Pierce-Arrow Motorette (1901)**

**Pierce-Arrow Great Arrow (1907)**

**Mercedes Simplex (1902).** This vehicle, created by Maybach and distributed in France by Emile Jellinek, who also contributed to the financing of its construction, was a sensation because of its completely new lines. Its steel chassis and beehive radiator marked the end of the "motor carriage" and opened the era of the automobile.

Jellinek was an Austrian merchant who moved to France and began selling cars; he bought a number of Daimlers and business flourished. To increase the public's interest in the new vehicles, he changed the name from Daimler to that of his daughter, Mercedes. The Daimler firm liked the name, and from that time on all the cars built in the Cannstatt factory were called "Mercedes."

**Welleyes 3 HP (1899).** This car can be considered the forerunner of all the Fiat models. It was made by a company founded by Giovanni Ceirano, and designed by engineer Aristide Faccioli. The vehicle pleased a group of Turinese manufacturers (including Agnelli) who had just founded the Fabbrica Italiana Automobili Torino (Fiat); they realized that this sector was due for development and first bought the patent, later absorbing the entire factory.

**Isotta Fraschini 40 HP Landaulet (1906)**

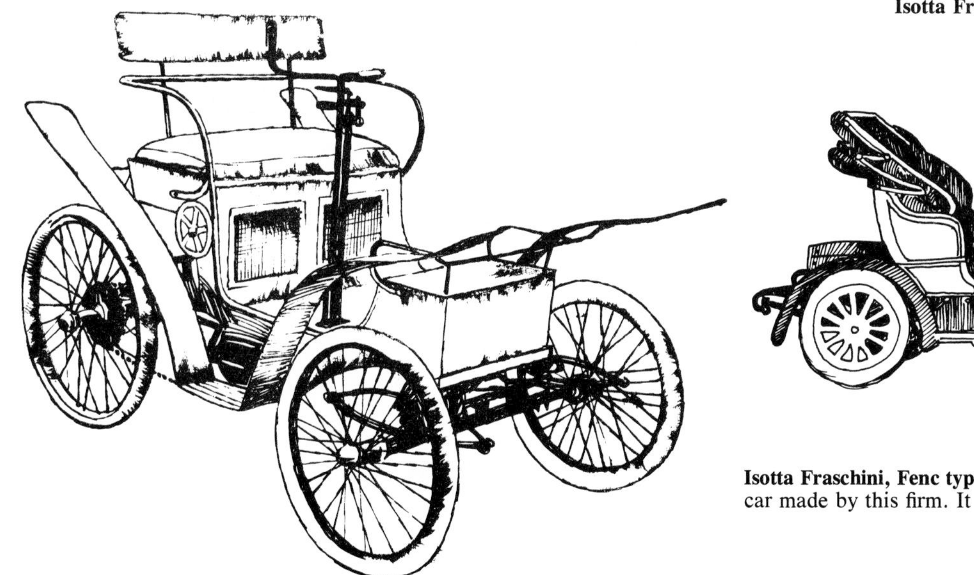

**Isotta Fraschini, Fenc type 10 HP (1906).** The first utility car made by this firm. It had a four-cylinder engine.

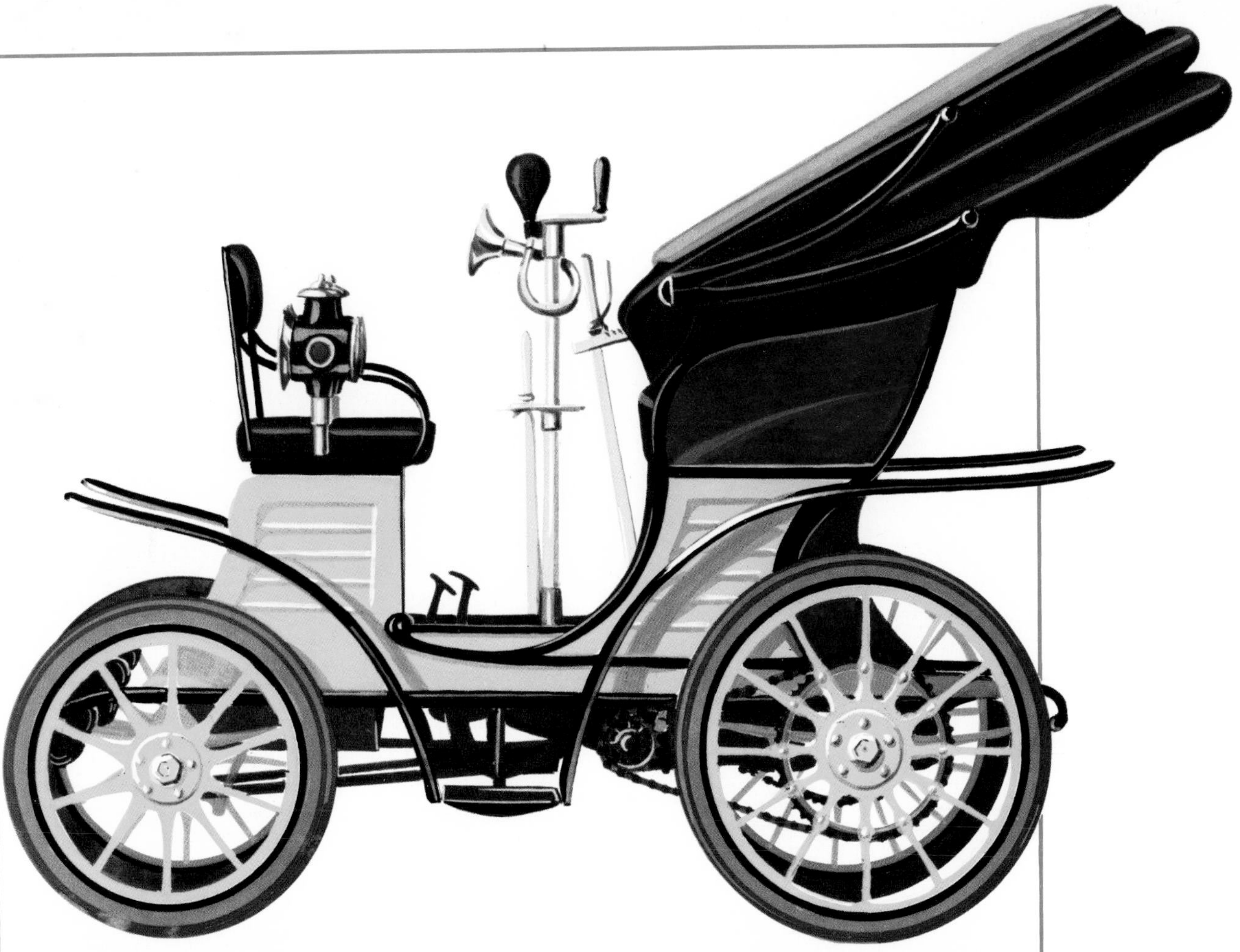

**Fiat 3½ HP (1899).** "We must give the client a car that never stops!" It was with this aim that Giovanni Agnelli, after the experience with the Welleyes, proceeded with production of the new Fiat cars. The first model, which came out of the old Ceirano plant in Turin, was this small "duc" with two to three seats. It was created by Marcello Alessio, who designed the body and by engineer Faccioli, who set up the mechanical system. It had a 600 cc, horizontal two-cylinder engine. Eight cars in all were built and three are still in existence: one in the Museo dell'Automobile in Turin, one in the Centro Storico Fiat, and one in the Ford Museum in the United States.

names as De Cristoforis, Barsanti, and Matteucci, and, above all, that of Professor Enrico Bernardi from Padua (1841–1919). Among Bernardi's firsts are considered to be the detachable head cyclinder with mechanical overhead valve control (1889); the uniform-level carburetor with vaporization, adopted by Daimler five years later; air and gasoline filters; and the automatic lubrication of all moving parts. These are important firsts and, because Bernardi filed patents on them, there can be no doubt as to their existence or patent. Then too, Bernardi had already made, in 1874, a small static engine that worked on gas, followed by another static engine in 1878 that worked on the Otto system. Bernardi later produced, in 1893, an original bicycle propel-

**Fiat 16/24 HP (1903).** In 1902, the engineer Enrico became technical director of Fiat. From that time on, technical innovations were made in production—for instance, this 16/24 with important novelties such as the four-cylinder engine and friction clutch plate.

**Fiat 24/32 HP (1903).** This was the first Fiat with a Landaulet body. It had a pedal accelerator, a multiple-plate clutch, and four-speed gear box.

led by a small motor placed on an attached carriage.

The automobile only got under way in Italy with the founding of the Fiat company on July 11, 1899. It was a very small beginning; the slight industrial capacity of the nation at that time and the even slighter consumer demand did not allow Fiat and the rest of the Italian automobile industry to reach the then-current French levels. In fact, Fiat produced only 8 cars in 1899, 24 in 1900, and 73 in 1901, in a national production of 300 machines in 1901. This, when as early as 1897 the French automobile industry—unquestionably the most important in the world at that time—succeeded in turning out more than 3000 cars a year, for a total sales value of 15 million francs, equal to about $20 million today! Of the 15 million francs taken in, 624,000 came from exported models.

To get back to the Fiat, we should note that the most important Italian automobile factory was born practically from osmosis, by absorbing another Turinese brand, the Welleyes, founded in 1898 by Giovanni Battista Ceirano—whose family later made a great contribution to the Italian automobile industry—and who up until then had concentrated on producing bicycles.

The Fiat absorbed the Welleyes with all its executives, its skilled workers (among them Vincenzo Lancia, the future racing driver of the Fiat and founder of the company of the same name), and also the design for a 3½ hp car planned by engineer Aristide Faccioli. Fiat soon produced its first car, a light and

**Ceirano 5 HP (1901).** Ceirano is famous not so much for its models, which were not particularly successful with the public, as for the fact that the Ceirano brothers founded many companies—among them Rapid, Itala, Spa, and Scat. The 5 hp model, which had an Aster motor, had a light and pleasing form. It was built a year before the Ceirano Brothers firm went out of business.

**Duesenberg "Mason" (1906)**

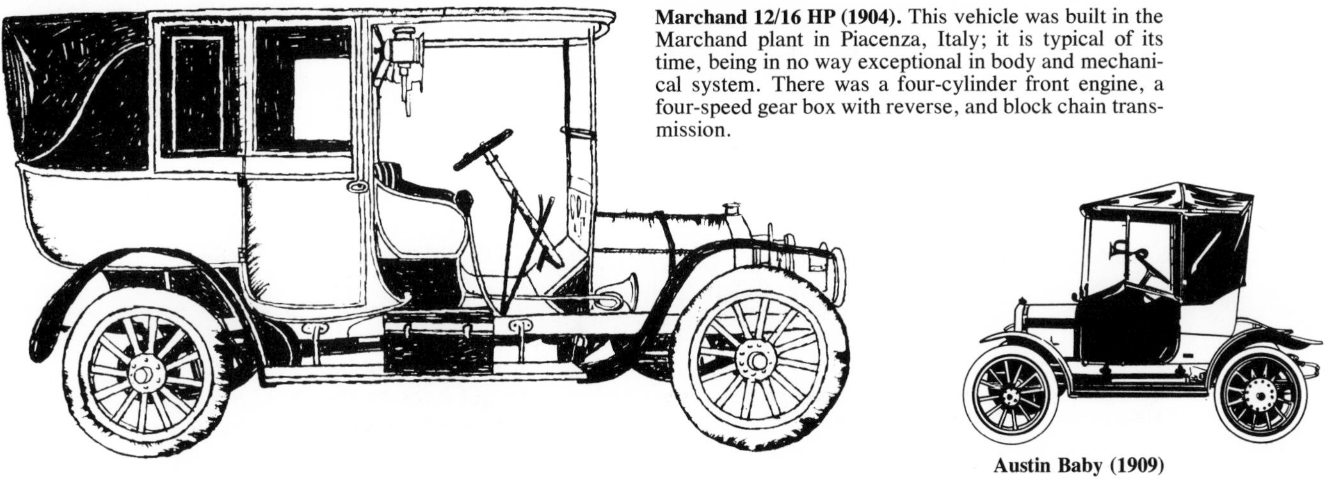

**Marchand 12/16 HP (1904).** This vehicle was built in the Marchand plant in Piacenza, Italy; it is typical of its time, being in no way exceptional in body and mechanical system. There was a four-cylinder front engine, a four-speed gear box with reverse, and block chain transmission.

**Austin Baby (1909)**

economical vis-à-vis equipped with a horizontal, two-cylinder, 679 cc, 4.7 hp engine. The gear box was quite refined, with a crown gear and three forward and no reverse gears, while the maximum speed was about 35 km/h with the very contained gas consumption for those days of about 8 liters per 100 km.

With the birth of Fiat, Turin was definitely confirmed as the capital of the automobile industry in Italy. The first four-wheeled vehicle designed in Italy was born in Turin in 1895: it was the "Wagonette," created by Michele Lanza and built in the workshop of the Martine brothers.

**Maxwell 14 HP (1908)**

**Itala 35/45 HP (1909).** This vehicle belonged to Queen Margherita of Savoia who named it "Palombella" (small dove)—it was a tradition in the Savoia family to name their cars after animals. The body, which was refined and well finished, was done by Cesare Sala.

**Packard 12 HP (1902)**

Vauxhall

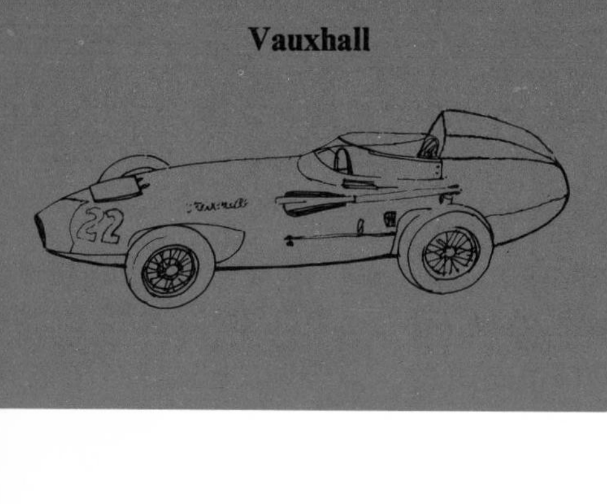

BRM

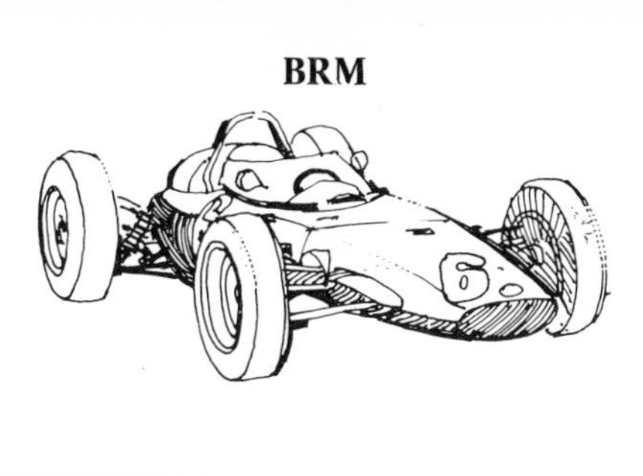

Jaguar

Monroe

Delage

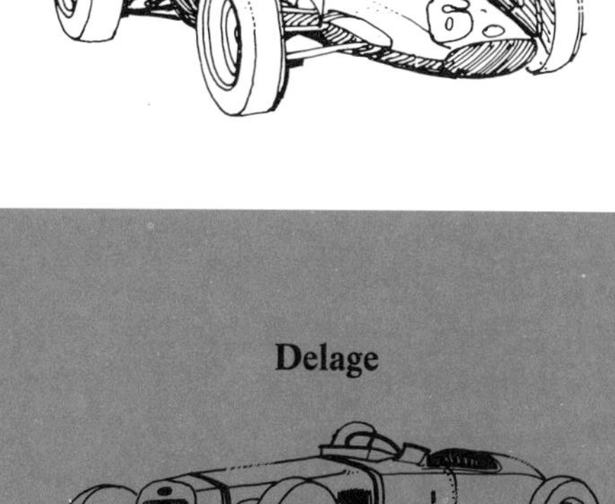

Auto Union

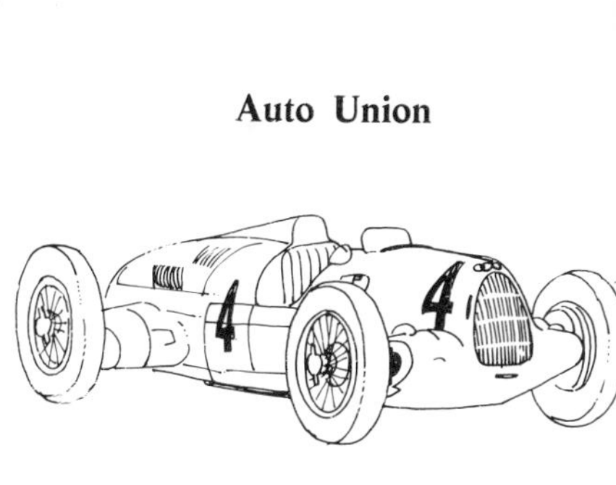

Fiat

Lagonda

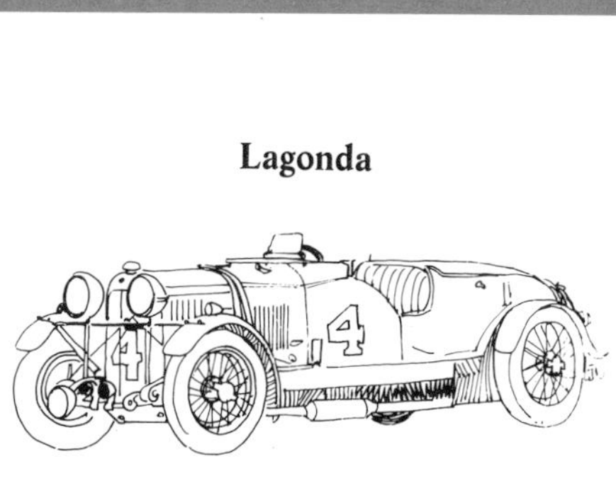

Bentley

Bentley

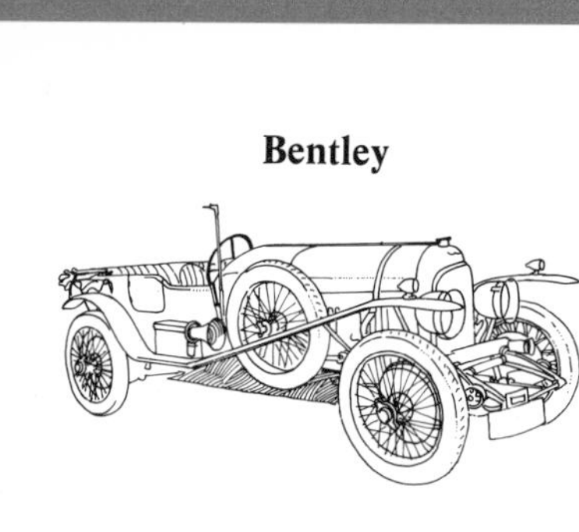

Aston Martin

Delahaye

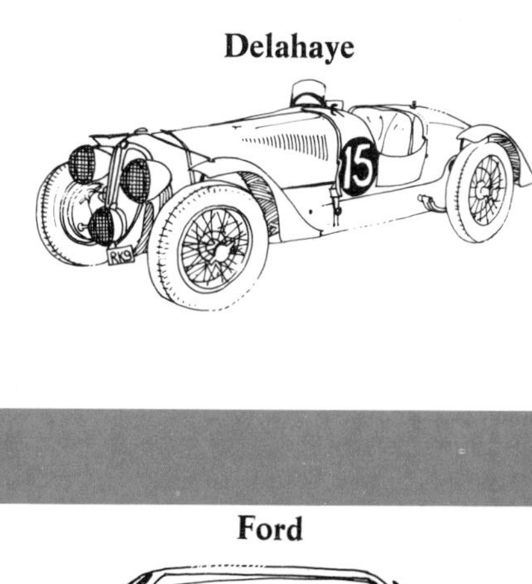

La Lorraine

Bugatti

Ford

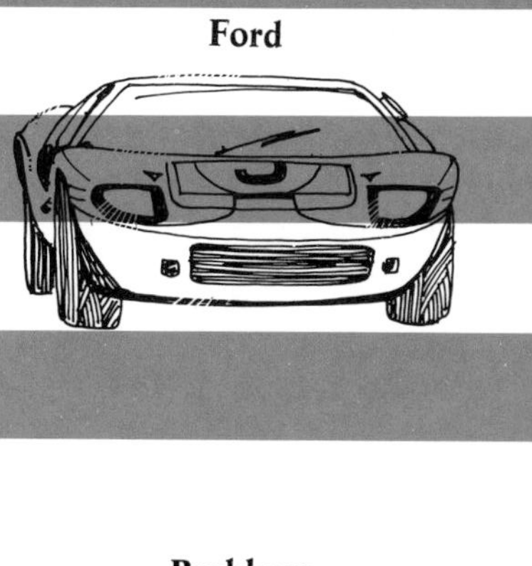

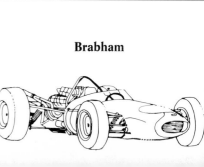

Eagle

Talbot-Darracq

Brabham

Maserati

Matra

Porsche

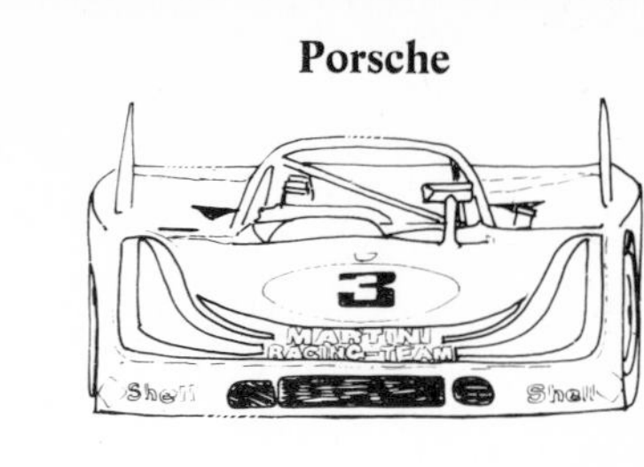

Cooper

Lotus

McLaren

Mercedes

Alfa Romeo

Chaparral

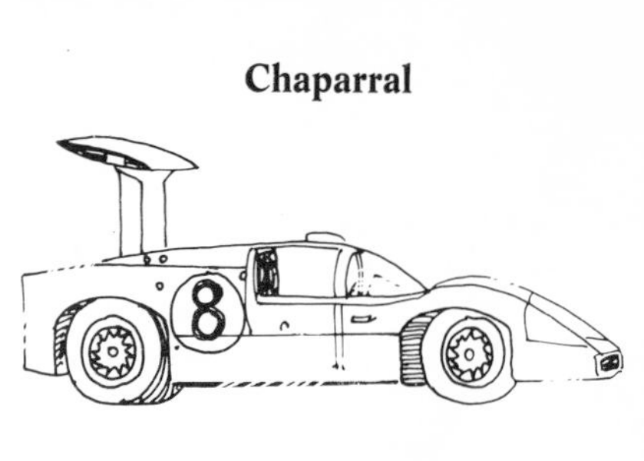

# Dust and glory

Talbot

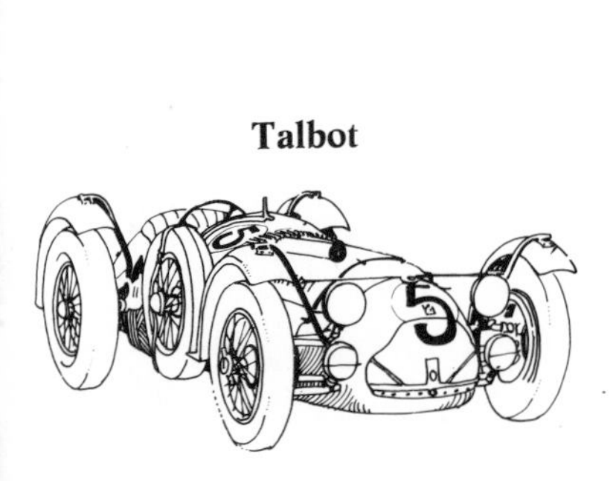

Ferrari

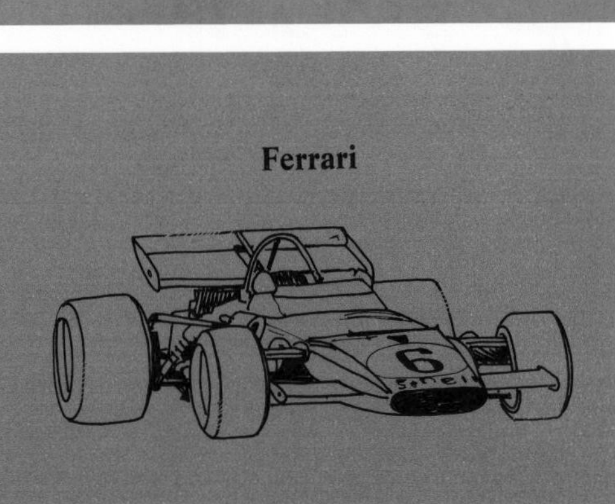

Tyrrell

Chaparral

Honda

Mirage

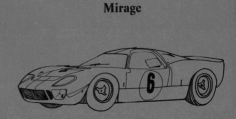

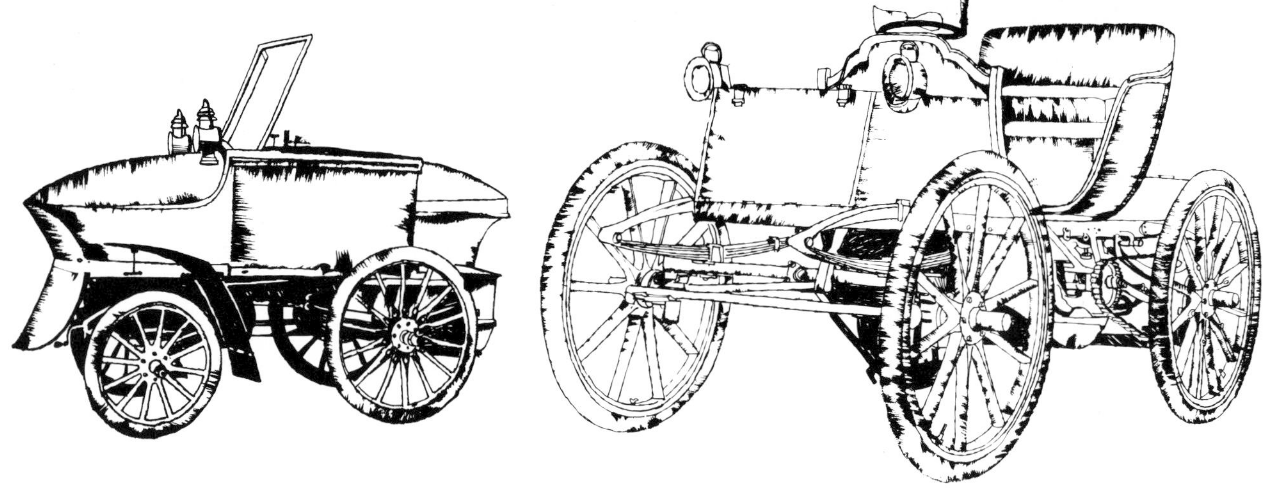

**Amédée Bollée (1898).** Four of these cars were built to take part in the Paris–Amsterdam–Paris road race. They had a two-cylinder, 3042 cc engine.

**Jeantaud (1899).** The first car to surpass the limit of 100 km per hour. It had electric traction, weighed 1400 kg and had 36 hp, and was driven by Count Gaston de Chasseloup-Laubat.

The French **Mors** car had its name linked to the sport of automobile racing from 1900 to 1904. The vehicle shown here won two great races: the Paris–Bordeaux and the Paris–Berlin. It had a 10,087 cc, 60 hp, four-cylinder engine.

**Serpollet (1903).** This was definitely an original car, powered by a four-cylinder, 40 hp steam engine.

**Wolseley (1904).** Like all the machines of this name, born between 1895 and 1905, it was designed by Herbert Austin. The car had a four-cylinder engine, 11,896 cc and 96 hp.

# Dust and glory

Automobile driving as a sport is closely connected with the historical evolution of the automobile itself. With the birth of the motor vehicle, competition between one man and another expanded to include competition between machines, retaining all the basic characteristics of the athletic contest.

The automobile as a vehicle for the masses has benefited from motorized competition. This is clear from the mechanical evolution brought about by the car, with the adoption of ever more sophisticated solutions, the use of avant-garde material and building techniques, the exploitation of resources that also exist in sectors that only touch on automobile driving (aeronautical building techniques, for example, can testify to this tradeoff of knowledge).

The bond between the racing car and the ordinary passenger car was closer and more evident in the first years of the existence of the four-wheeled vehicle. However, as time passed and production techniques improved, always bound to the steady rhythm of production lines, the need for containing expenses won out over the adoption of certain useful and valid, but rather costly, solutions. In other words, manufacturers did not always find it convenient to transfer technical improvements that had emerged from the grinding use of the vehicle in competition to the mass-production side of the budget. To do so, they would have had to use more valuable materials and expensive machinery; that in turn would have made the cost of their product rise too high and made it less competitive on the commercial market.

The very famous Itala, the car that crossed Asia in 1907, was a stock production car adapted for the long trip. The **Itala 35/45 HP** had a four-cylinder, 7433 cc engine.

The automobile as a sport, today almost wholly entrusted to small firms specializing in the creation of racing cars, was really born in the workshops of the first builders of passen-

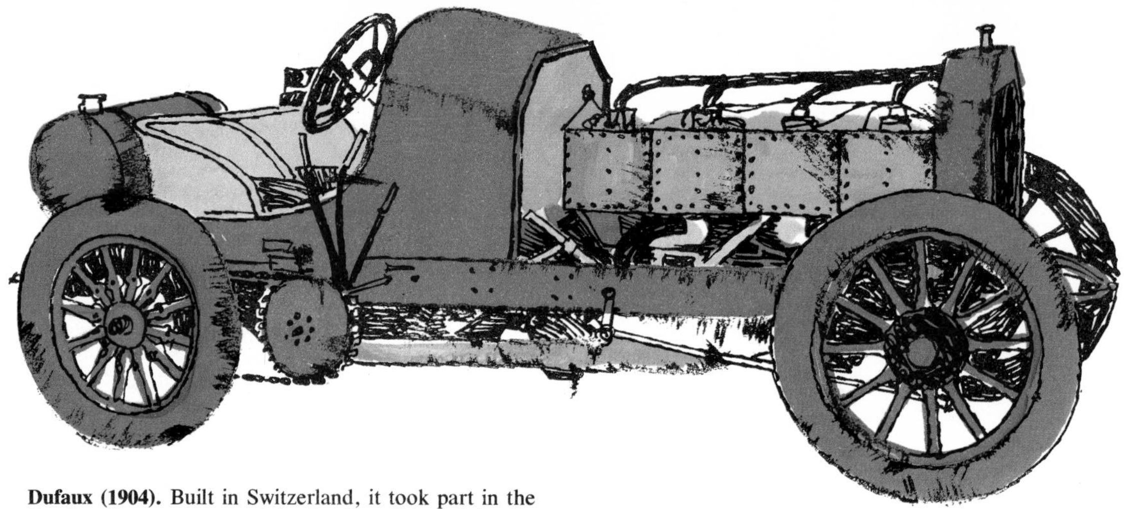

**Dufaux (1904).** Built in Switzerland, it took part in the Gordon Bennet race and in the first Grand Prix. Its special characteristic was an engine with eight aligned cylinders.

**Thomas Flyer, Type 35 (1907).** This car won the New York–Paris endurance, speed, and resistance race over a distance of more than 20,000 km, including the United States–Japan sea crossing. The "Thomas Flyer" had a 9369 cc, 70 hp, four-cylinder engine.

ger cars. But it developed with the consolidation of the great producers, such as Fiat, Ford, Renault, Mercedes, Peugeot, and Opel.

The first automobile race took place on July 22, 1894, and covered the Paris–Rouen route. Twenty-one automobiles took part in this race, organized by the *Petit Journal* and promoted by journalist Pierre Giffard. There were 14 cars with gasoline and 7 with steam engines; 5 Panhard & Levassors (2 built by the firm itself, another 3 entrusted to Mayadex, Dubois and Vacheron), 7 Peugeots (driven by Lemaitre, Doriot, Kraeutler, Machaux, Rigoulot, Le Brun, and de Bourmont), a Benz by Roger, and a Gautier by Gautier itself. The

**Peugeot (1912).** This car drew attention for its use of an engine with a double overhead camshaft, 7600 cc, which let it triumph in races over cars with far greater displacement but with piston rods and compensators.

**Fiat Grand Prix (1907)**

steam-driven cars were the two Le Blant-Serpollets of the brothers Maurice and Etienne Le Blant, the De Prandières-Serpollet of De Prandières, the Serpollet of Archdeacon, the Scotte of Scotte, the Brasier of de Montais, and the De Dion-Bouton tractor of Albert de Dion.

As the rules of the race show, that far-off Paris–Rouen meet was not an actual speed race. In fact, an elimination heat was planned to prove that all the machines taking part in the race were able to do 50 km in no more than three hours. In order to be admitted to this elimination heat, the cars had to have certain qualifications, as the rules announced: "They must not be dangerous, must be manageable and comfortable for the passengers and must not be too costly."

This first meet turned into a speed race, however, because of the high rate (an average of 20 km/h!) imposed by the steam car of Marquis de Dion. The jury assigned a first prize of 5000 francs, to be divided equally between Panhard & Levassor and Peugeot, since "using the gasoline motor invented by Daim-

**Fiat S76 (1911).** Well known, along with the names of "Brooklands 300 HP" and "Mefistofele," this car set the world record for the mile twice, in Brooklands, England, with 195 km per hour, and in Long Island, U.S.A., in 1912, with 290 km per hour. It was a 4-cylinder engine of 28,338 cc displacement.

ler, their cars fully responded to the needs of the competition, even if they are still not fully attuned to the dreams of the passengers."

Historians say that the first real meet took place a year later over the 1178 km that separate Paris from Bordeaux; the race was won by a Panhard, with an average speed of 24 km per hour. Automobile racing continued steadily from that time on. The first international race, the Paris–Amsterdam–Paris, was held in 1898. In 1901 the cars taking part in the

**FIAT RACING MODELS**

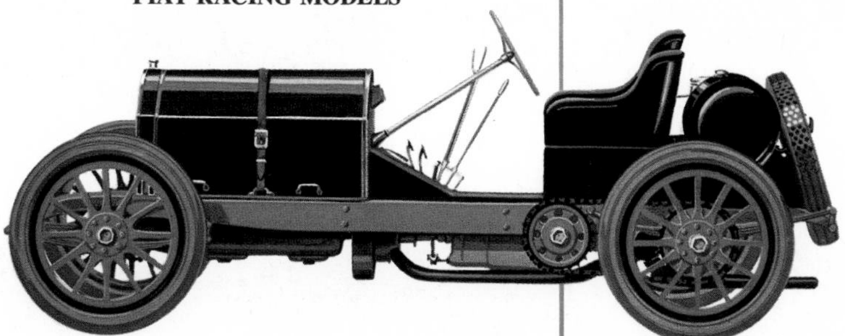

**75 HP racing model (1904)**

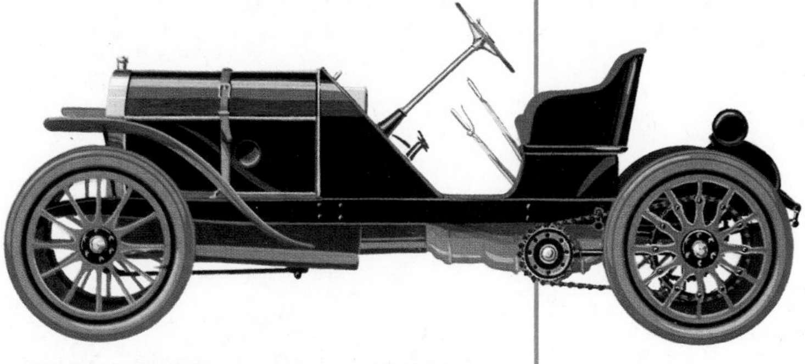

**100 HP Gordon Bennet racing model (1905)**

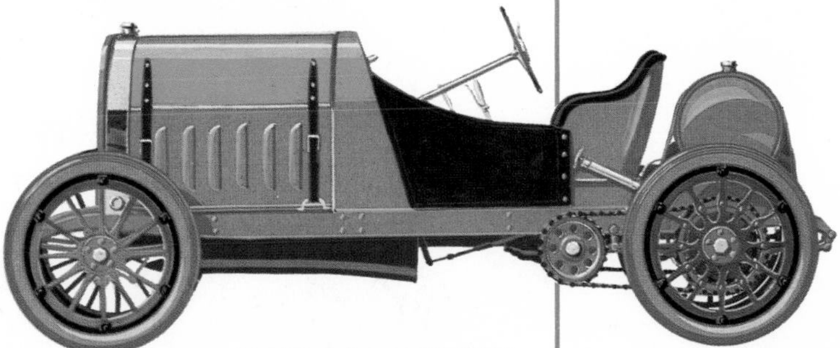

**S 74 racing model (1911)**

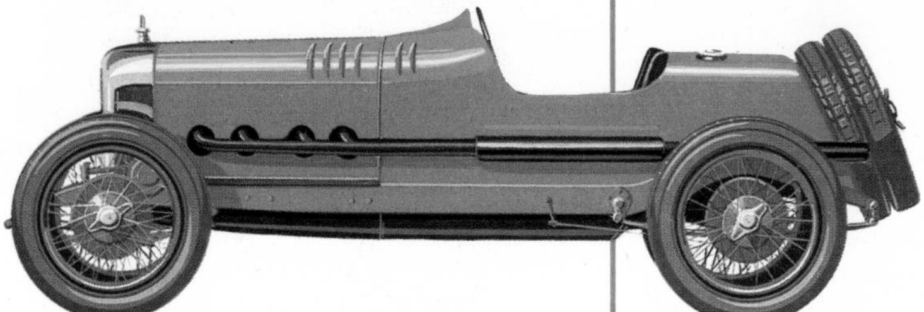

**S 57/14 B racing model (1914)**

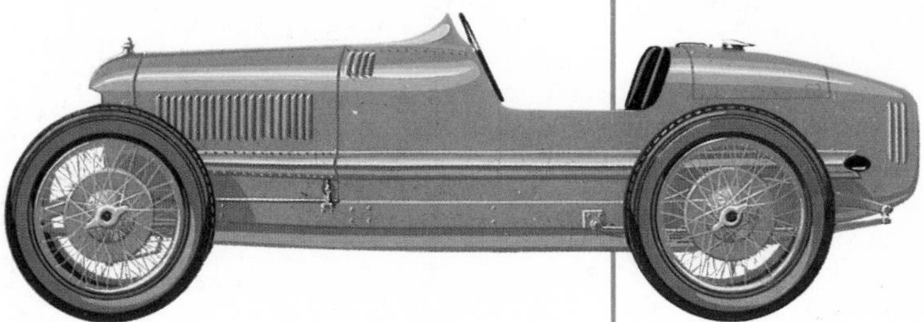

**Grand Prix 804 model (1922)**

**Mercedes Flying Dutchman**

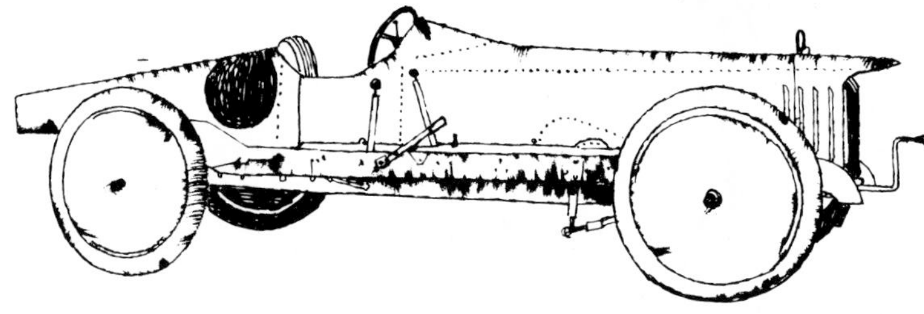

**Vauxhall (1910).** One of the first 3-liters to be timed at a speed above 100 miles an hour (160.9 km/h).

After having built small cars powered by one-cylinder engines for a few years, the French **Sizaire-Naudin** firm produced, in 1912, three cars with four-cylinder, 2962 cc engines with four horizontal valves per cylinder. These vehicles took part in some races—with very poor results.

Paris–Berlin race were divided into three categories: large cars weighing more than 650 kg, lighter cars weighing from 400 to 650 kg, and little cars, the weight of which could not exceed 400 kg. This was the first attempt to regulate the various categories of automobiles. In 1902 the first race on a closed road circuit took place; it was held on the Ardennes Circuit and the contestants had to do six laps. This race may be considered the forerunner of our present-day competitions.

A year later, in 1903, the races between one city and another were suspended because of the dramatic accidents that had taken place during the Paris–Madrid race. That race had been interrupted at Bordeaux. The high speed now used by the cars competing (when the race was suspended, the Mors of Fernand Gabriel had averaged a speed of 105 km per hour!), and the crowds using the roads (along which both normal traffic and the cars in the race passed at the same time), created the preconditions for a series of terrible accidents which cost the lives of both drivers and spectators. The authorities decided to stop the meet at Bordeaux and to end all meets between city and city.

In the meantime, a new racing formula had been invented in 1900, one reserved for teams of cars from one country. It was named after James Gordon Bennett, a rich American newspaper publisher who donated the trophy and whose papers highlighted the races that marked the first years of life of the automobile. Teams of three cars per nation took part in the competition for the Gordon Bennett Cup, and the rules demanded that these machines had to be built in the nation using them, though not necessarily designed in that nation. Thus, there were examples of Darracqs built in France, Germany, and England and of Daimlers produced in Germany and Austria.

The strict limits to the number of participants aroused annoyance in France, where many builders and drivers wanted to be part of the team of three cars admitted for the Gordon Bennett Cup. In 1904 the Automobile Club of France laid the foundation for a new type of meet, open not to national teams but to single builders. The Gordon Bennett was held until 1905 (the last race took place on the Clermont–Ferrand circuit), while the Auto-

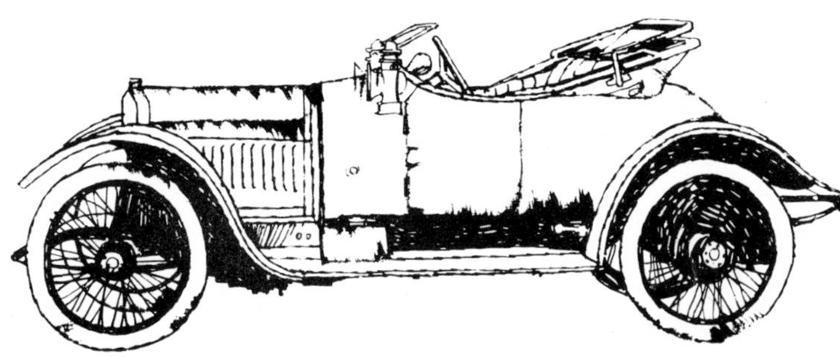

**Hispano-Suiza (1913).** Powered by a four-cylinder, 3620 cc, 64 hp engine.

**Delage (1913).** This firm, known for its small cars, only began taking part in Grand Prix races in 1913, when it entered a team of two cars with four-cylinder, 7032 cc engines with four horizontal valves per cylinder and a five-speed gear box.

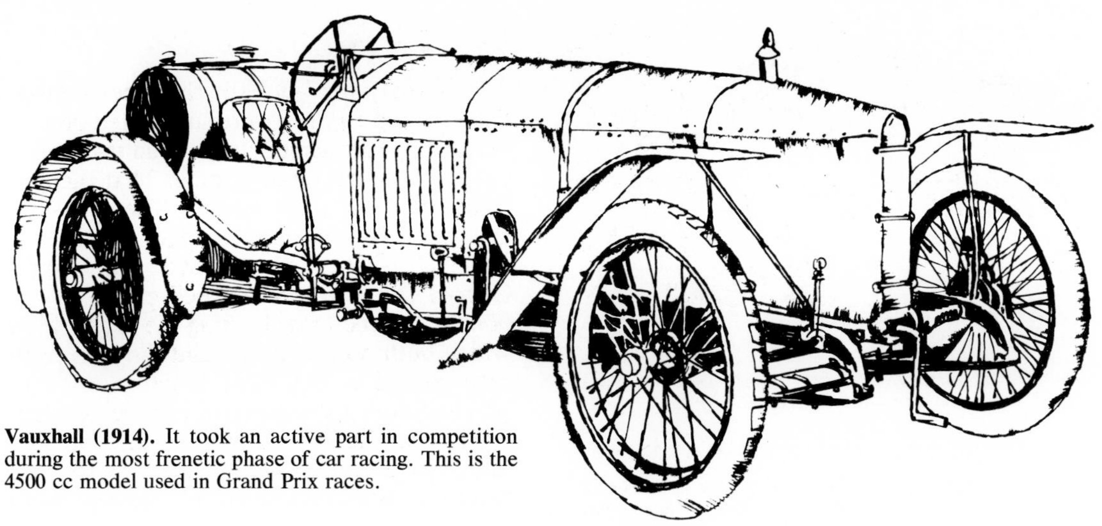

**Vauxhall (1914).** It took an active part in competition during the most frenetic phase of car racing. This is the 4500 cc model used in Grand Prix races.

mobile Club of France defined the details of what was to remain the most fascinating of all automobile races: the Grand Prix.

The first Grand Prix of France took place in the year 1906 on a road circuit near Le Mans. The contestants (32 cars from three different builders) did six laps on the circuit for a total of 103.180 km, and the trials lasted two days. The winner of the first Grand Prix was proclaimed on June 26, 1906: Szisz, in a Renault, won over ten other drivers who crossed the finish line, with an average speed of 101.200 km/h. The meet was reserved for cars that did not weigh more than 1007 kg.

The sport of automobile racing was thus taking shape, with its well-defined dimensions, its precise rules, its ever more popular manifestations, and the participation of organizations that grouped together and represented sports fans of each separate nation: the Automobile Clubs.

The Grand Prix opened a new chapter in the history of the automobile, because it became clear that, if all the contestants were to be put on the same level, common limiting denominators had to be found to make the race interesting for the public and significant for the results of technical research. Thus, the weight limitation was replaced by a limit on fuel consumption (30 liters per 100 km) so as to avoid the presence of "monsters"; for instance, the Renault that won the first Grand Prix had a displacement of 13,000 cc and a power of 105 hp. Then limits were put on displacement volume and on the size of the car. As the years passed, the elements that remained to determine the various formulas were weight and displacement, two precise and clear measures essential to the performance of motor vehicles.

**Aston Martin (1922).** This English car took part in many races. It had a four-cylinder, 1486 cc engine with lateral valves.

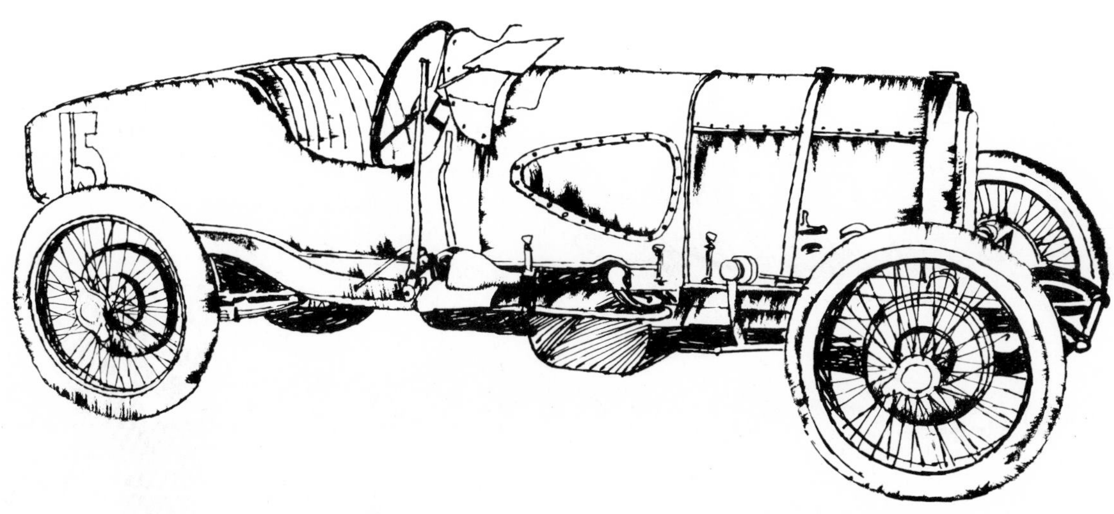

**Fiat Grand Prix (1924).** Fiat has had a glorious racing history and won races all over the world. The Grand Prix model had an eight-cylinder, 2000 cc engine with supercharger and 130 hp.

**Maserati 1500 (1926).** One of the first of a long series of sports cars built by the firm in Modena. It was a Grand Prix called "Type 26" and won, on its first appearance, the victory in its category in the Targa Florio race of 1927.

The year 1906 was an important one for car racing. While the Grand Prix was being created in France, in Sicily the first Targa Florio was taking place—on May 9, to be precise—thus preceding the Grand Prix and becoming the oldest car race run regularly through the years up to our own time. The Targa Florio came into being in a special atmosphere, one in which the moods of Sicily mingled with the free and adventurous spirit of Vincenzo Florio, the youngest member of a rich family from Palermo.

"There is an undeniable relationship between the race set up by Vincenzo Florio

**BUGATTI**

The French Bugatti car was one of the protagonists on the sports scene in the 1920s and 1930s. These cars won on the Spanel circuit in 1929, 1931, and 1934.

**Bugatti, Type 35 (1927).** The "Type 35" was unquestionably the most famous of the Bugattis and won many races between 1924 and 1930. The original version had a 1990 cc engine with 105 hp and eight aligned cylinders. Smaller motors (of 1500 and 1100 cc) were also used to fill the needs of the Grand Prix formulas of 1925 and 1926.

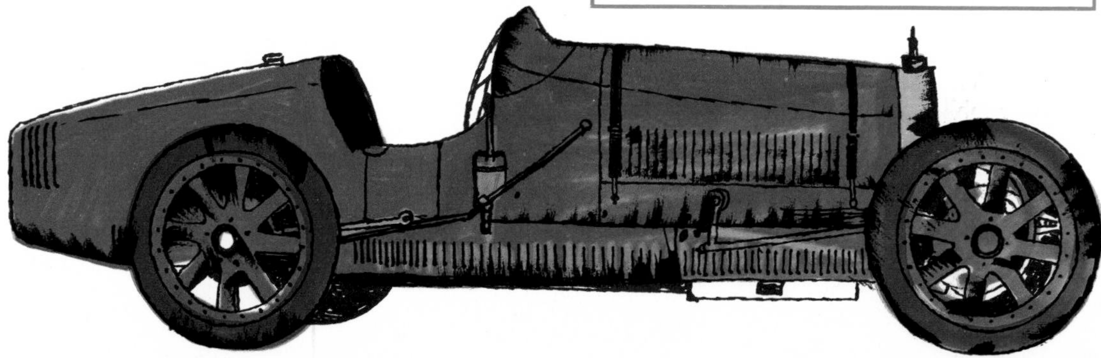

**Mercedes W 25 (1934).** From 1934 on, Mercedes took an active part in racing for many years. Model W 25, the first in a long series, had an over-fed, 3360 cc engine with eight aligned cylinders, double overhead camshaft, and four valves per cylinder.

**MERCEDES**

The **Mercedes** won many victories on the German Nürburgring track. These cars won in 1927, 1928, and 1931.

Those were the years of the tycoons who sought thrills for their own personal pleasure, often counting on that new, wonderful, and fascinating mechanism called the automobile for their excitement. That same era saw another race set up by a rich American: the Vanderbilt Cup, the first internationally famous race to take place in America, thanks to the immensely wealthy William K. Vanderbilt, who had gained his experience in Europe and then proposed to the Americans a racing formula very much like the Gordon Bennett one. This race has always taken place in the United States and was won for the first time by an American only in 1908, in its fourth trial (the first dates to 1904 but the 1907 race was omitted). A driver named George Robertson, the first American winner, raced in a Locomobile.

**Citroën Petite Rosalie (1933).** This car ran 133 laps in Montlhéry without stopping, and won the world record of 300,000 km, with an average of more than 93 km per hour.

and that organized by American tycoon Gordon Bennett with the important trophy that bears his name,'' writes Giovanni Canestrini in the preface to his book *The Fabulous Targa Florio.* ''Gordon Bennett and Florio sensed that the future of the automobile lay in competition. . . . Gordon Bennett had opened the way to the so-called racing formulas, while Vincenzo Florio wanted to improve the automobile's performance.''

**Alfa Romeo** won many victories in the ''24 Hours'' of Le Mans, one of the classic endurance races. Below: The machines that won in 1931, 1932, and 1934.

# ALFA ROMEO

## A FOUR-LEAF CLOVER TO WIN

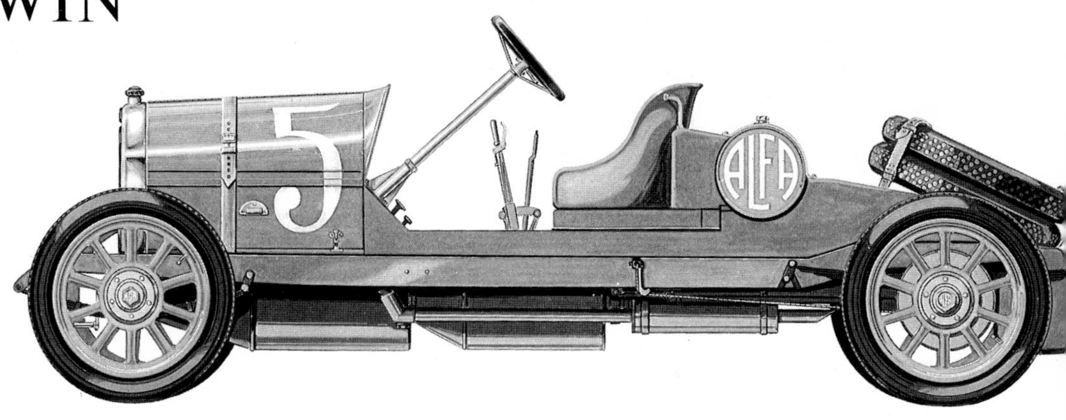


**24 HP racing car (1911).** The first sports model built by Alfa. It was designed by geometer Merosi, who began planning it in 1909. The touring version was found to be both brilliant in performance and comfortable.

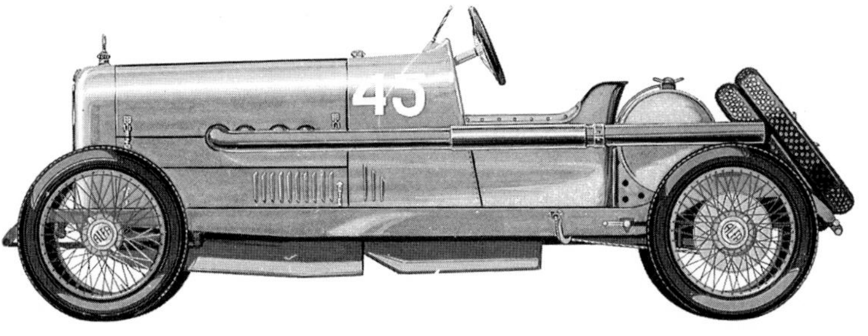


**40/60 HP (1921).** This car had a long evolution, both aesthetic and technical, since it was "born" in 1913 and used until 1922.

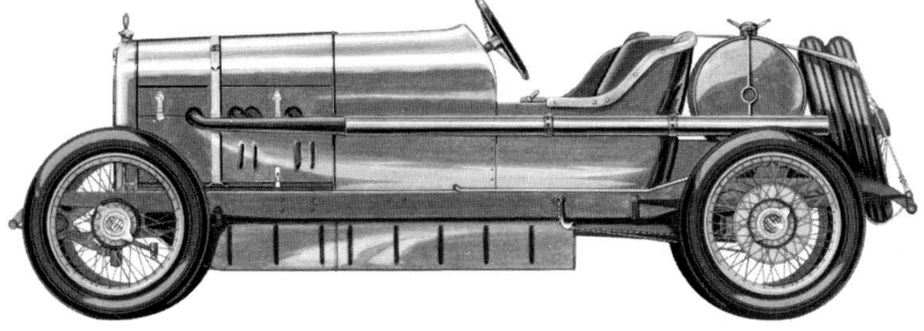

**20/30 ES (1921).** This was just a further stage in the prewar model, even if it first appeared in 1921.

**RL Super Sport (1925).** The RL was created in 1921 and went into production in 1922, in both stock and sports models. In 1925, the type was improved and took the name "Super Sport."

# ALFA ROMEO

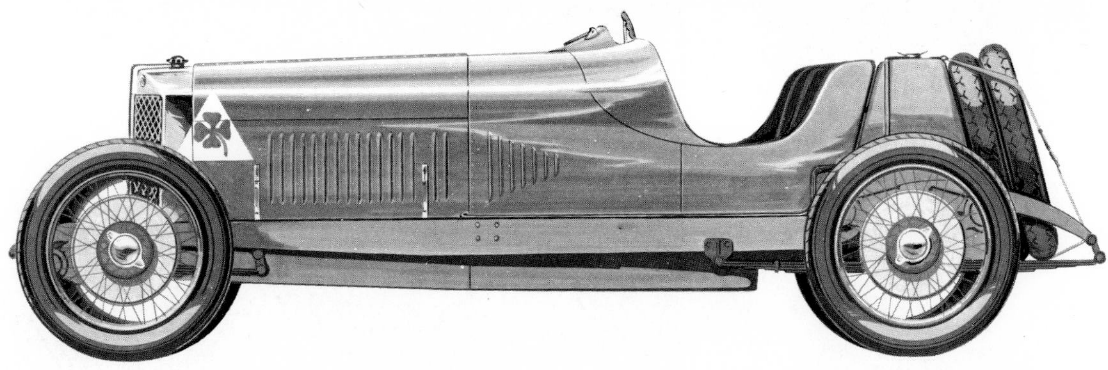

**RL Targa Florio (1924).** From the same technical derivation, there came a new Targa Florio version of the Alfa "RL" series. This one had a shortened chassis with room for two seats only. The engine displacement was increased to 3,154 cc, and 95 HP.

Among the great names that make up the "Gotha," or blue book, of automobile sports competition, that of Alfa Romeo deserves a place by itself. The Italian firm made a choice from the start to link its name to racing—not to give publicity to its car, but as the only possible way to perfect the quality of its product and adapt it to the expanding needs of its highly sophisticated clientele.

Founded in 1910, ALFA (Anonima Lombarda Fabbrica Automobili) took over the Darracq plant (8000 square meters in the Portello district near Milan); one hundred workmen and about twenty office clerks sufficed for the first phase of production, and Alfa was already taking part in races in 1911 with the first models designed by geometer Giuseppe Merosi.

The First World War interrupted the growth of the business, which had to produce war matériel and not automobiles. It was at that time that engineer Nicola Romeo joined the company. The end of the war saw the new partner determined to start the company (which had become "Alfa Romeo") in the racing field once more. An official team was set up with first-rate drivers like Antonio Ascari, Giuseppe Campari, and Enzo Ferrari. They won some epoch-making victories in Italian meets. To make the firm's name better known abroad, Romeo decided to have Alfa participate in all the more important international races. Machines designed by Merosi and Jano were prepared, and success soon followed—thanks to the skill of Ascari, Ferrari, Campari, Sivocci, Masetti, Brilli Peri, De Paolo, and Wagner. In 1925, Alfa Romeo won the world title and attained international glory. Success in competition opened up new market outlets for the company from Milan, including that of aviation equipment.

The Alfa Romeo name became even more famous internationally with the start of the finest of all road races: the "Thousand Mile" race. The firm won eleven victories, eight of them consecutive, in this meet in the years between 1927 and 1947.

In fact, every great racing driver has driven and won with an Alfa Romeo: among others, there were Nuvolari, Varzi, Caracciola, Chiron, Fagioli, Brivio, Farina, Trossi, and Pintacuda. In this long period of racing competition, Alfa Romeo cars took part in meets both in official teams and as part of the Ferrari squad, created by the man who was later to build racing cars.

**6C 1500 Super Sport (1928).** This car, a Jano project, was considered an avant-garde vehicle as it preceded the trend of European production. The design of the "6C" was based on the successful Alfa straight-eight supercharged "P2."

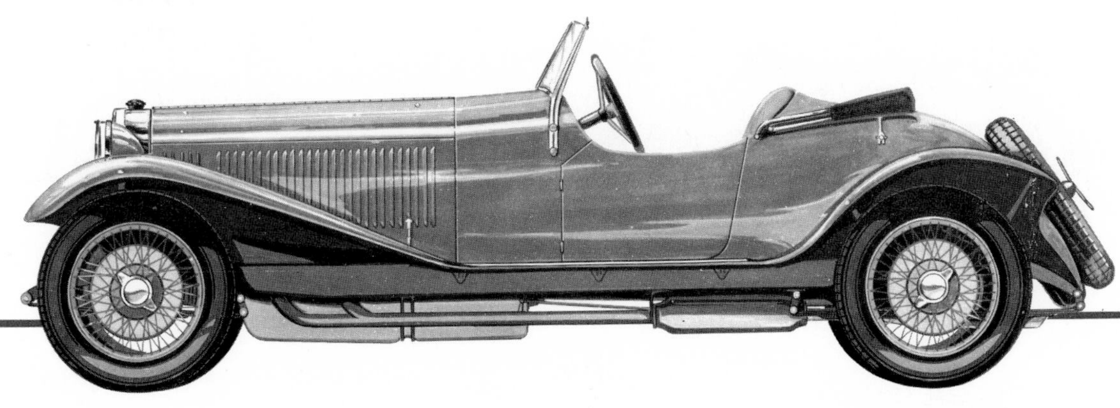

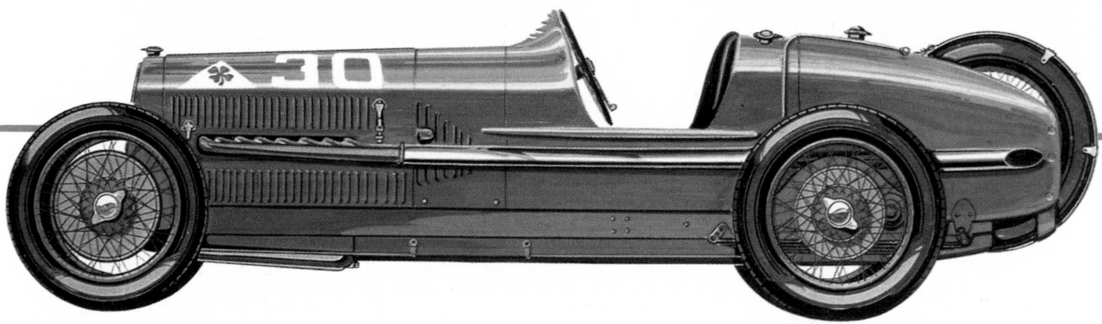

**Grand Prix P2 (1930).** One of the most important cars in the Alfa sports line. The P2, designed by Jano, had a 2-liter, 175 hp engine.

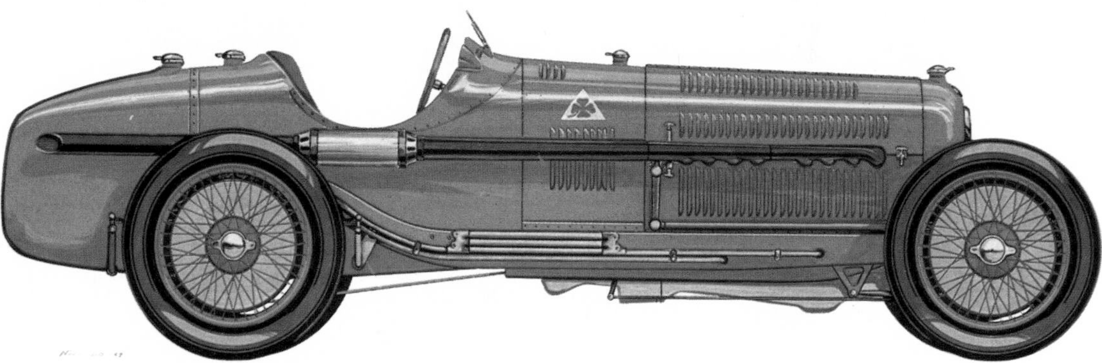

**Grand Prix type B P3 (1932).** Also planned by Jano, it was the worthy successor of the famous P2. Even though it was christened "Type B," it ended up being called the "P3".

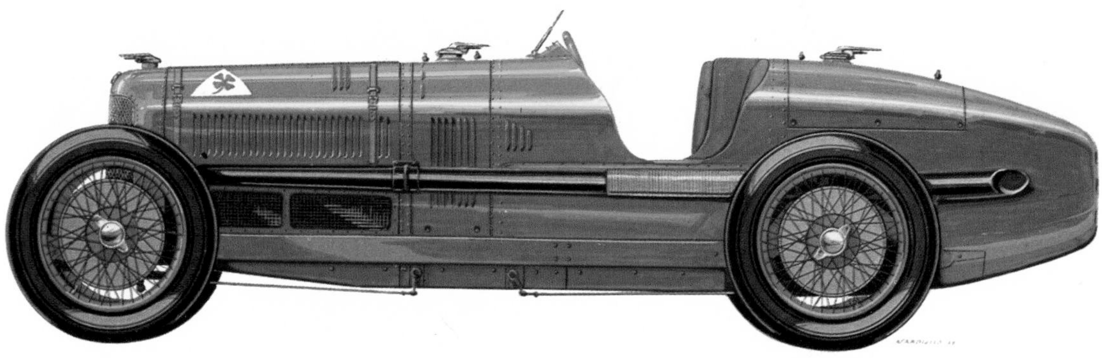

**Grand Prix P2 (1924).** The first overfed-engine Alfa Romeo. It resulted from the Milanese firm's decision to produce a car that could compete with the foreign racing cars with overfed engines. The designer of this machine was Jano, who began working for Alfa in 1924.

After a very dark period from 1935 to 1937 (when Mercedes and Auto Union imposed their strength), the Alfa racing sector brought the company back to the top in 1938. The famous single-seater "Type 158" was created, and entrusted to champions like Nuvolari, Farina, Biondetti, and Sommer, and victories soon followed.

The Second World War blocked Alfa Romeo's ambitious plans, and the Type 158 was only taken out of the closet again in 1946. The one-seater designed by Colombo and Massimino won many victories with Varzi, Wimille, Trossi, Farina, and Sanesi. In the meantime, the engineer Satta had designed the "159". The World Driving Championships, founded in 1950, saw the triumph of Farina; the machine took part in 11 Grand Prix and won them all with Farina, Fangio, and Fagioli. A year later, Fangio—again with the Alfa "159"—won the world title. After this second success, the heads of the Milanese firm decided to give up racing and concentrate on stock models.

In 1965, after a gap of fourteen years, Alfa returned to top-level international competition in the sport category with the "33". And this car too, imitating the years of glory, brought success to the Italian colors due to drivers such as Adamich, Andretti, Merzario, Pescarolo, Peterson, and Vaccarella.

# ALFA ROMEO

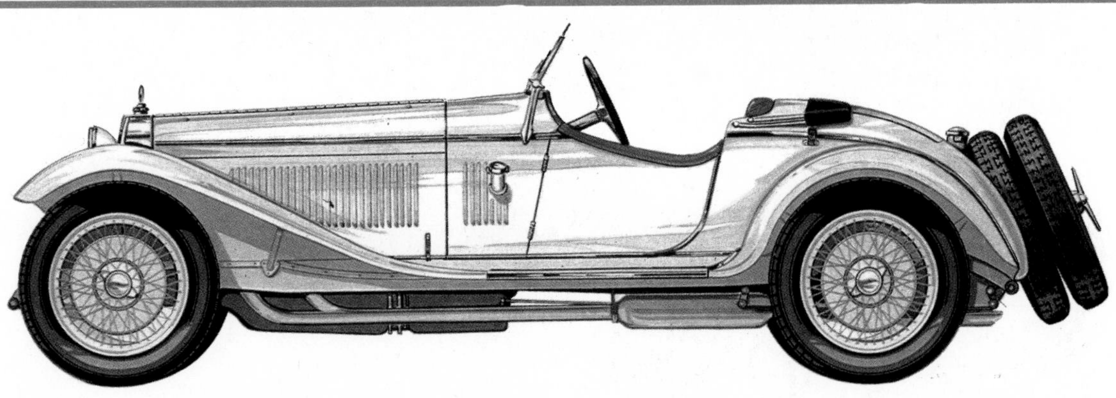

In the tradition of cars created especially for sports competition, Alfa Romeo produced many cars, like this **6C 1750 Gran Sport (1930)** (above), adapted for fast roads as a touring car. The same can be said for the **Spider 8 C 2300 (1931)** (right), it too the result of racing experience.

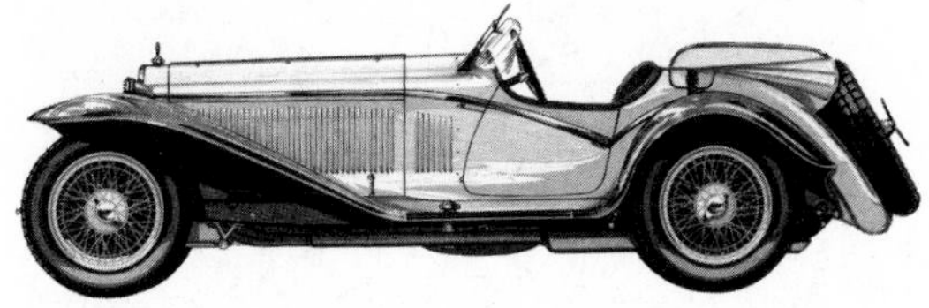

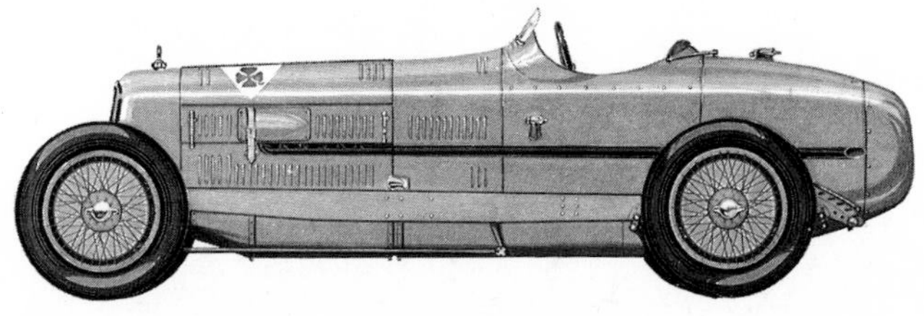

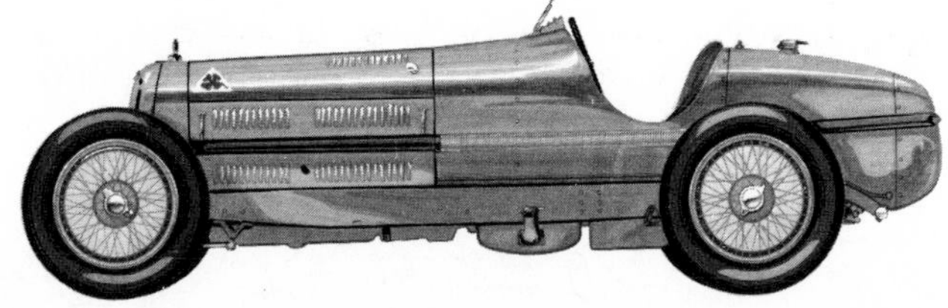

**Gran Premio Type A (1931).** The single-seater series of Alfa began with this car designed by Jano; it had two independent and parallel 6C 17,500 engines.

**Gran Premio 8C 2300 Monza (1931).** In 1931, a very limited series of cars, with a rear fuel tank for racing long endurance meets, was produced.

**Gran Premio Type 158 (1938).** Also known as "Alfetta," it was another milestone in the sports history of Alfa Romeo. This single-seater had great success both before and after the Second World War. Study on the "158" began at Alfa in 1937; it was planned by Colombo and Massimino and the car—with a 1500 cc engine—made its debut in 1938.

ALFA-ROMEO MILANO

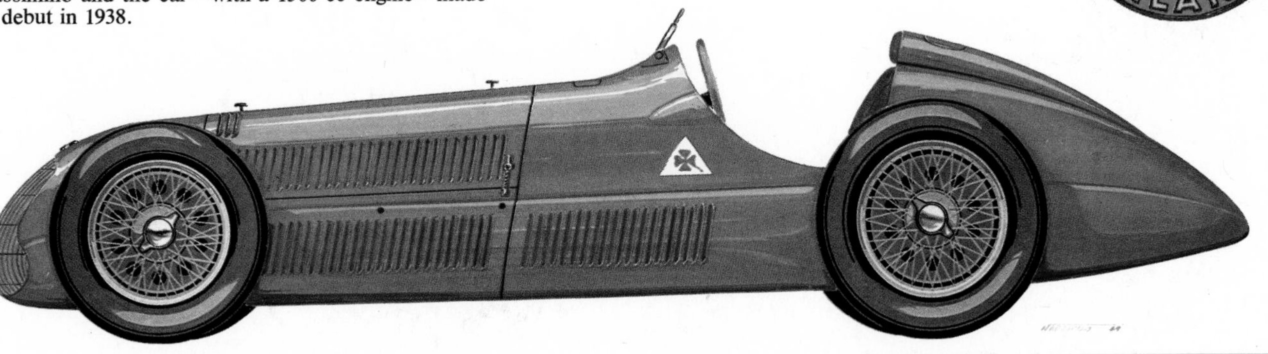

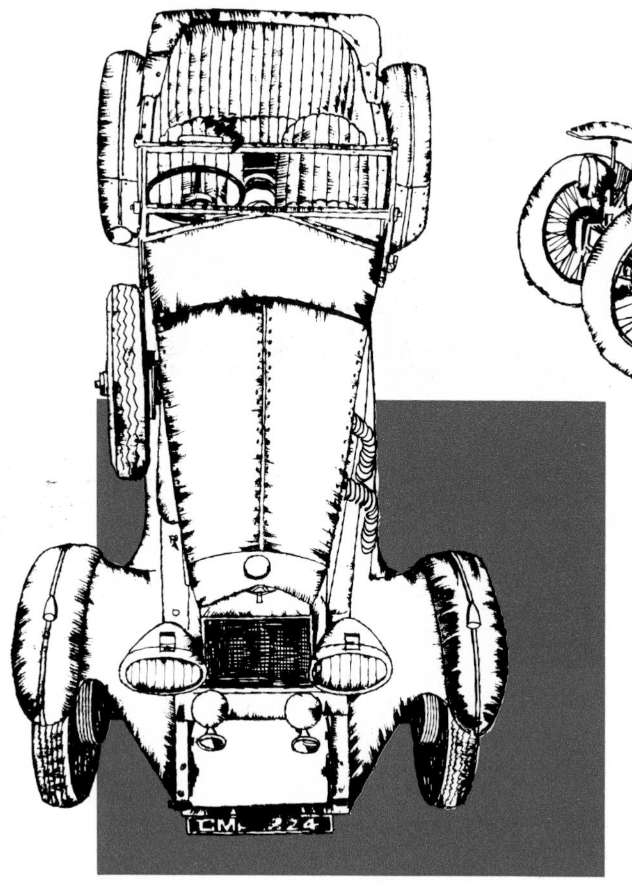

**Tracta Gephi.** Engineer–designer–driver Jean-Albert Grégoire built this car, which he then drove in the 1927 Le Mans "24 Hours."

**Invicta (1930).** An excellent British sports car. In 1931, Donald Healey won the Monte Carlo Rally with one of these machines. It had a six-cylinder, 4467 cc, 120 hp engine.

Another great moment in the sport of automobile racing was the construction in 1909 of the Indianapolis Motor Racing Speedway, which from 1911 on played host to the world-famous "500." At first the races were competitions between amateurs who only wanted to show off the power of their new models; but soon a new idea took hold: auto races in specially built stadiums might offer a paying public a highly entertaining spectacle. Then too, the speed attained by the cars suggested removing all races from roads open to normal traffic.

If we want to respect chronology, we must note that the first automobile racing track was that of Brooklands in England, built in 1906 and inaugurated in 1907. This racecourse was designed by Colonel Holden of the Royal Engineers, and was directed by railroad engineer Donaldson. The first race on the Brooklands Motor Course took place on July 6, 1907. The new policy, based on laps, pleased both fans and promoters. Many projects were laid aside temporarily, though, either because the moment did not seem right for large investments or because the threat of war overshadowed sporting events. After World War I, life began its normal course again, and science, pushed forward as usual by the needs of warfare, turned once more to the automobile.

Three cars that won first prize at Le Mans: the **Chenard Walcker** in 1923, the **Bentley** in 1924, and the **La Lorraine** in 1925.

**Delahaye Competition (1936).** In 1939, it won a Brooklands race as "the fastest touring car." It had a 3500 cc engine, like that used on the trucks of the same name.

**Delage Competition Model.** It won the famous Tourist Trophy in 1938, with a six-cylinder, 3-liter engine.

The early twenties saw the birth of a race which, along with the Targa Florio and the Indianapolis 500, is a classic of its kind: the 24 Hours of Le Mans. In the same period, a long-distance race destined to become another classic began: the Rally of Monte Carlo.

The 24 Hours of Le Mans was really born to speed up the evolution of stock cars, but it was transformed as the years passed. Today it is reserved almost exclusively for real "monsters." In the beginning it was meant to stimulate solutions for both large and small technical problems. For instance, the rules declared that convertible cars had to appear with the tops open and that the driver had to close the top before the car could leave the starting line. Needless to say, the means of closing the tops were refined just to make the task easier for driving champions. It once took about 10 minutes of hard labor to close a canvas top, and if the same maneuver can be done today in a few seconds and with one hand alone, it is because of the constantly evolving improvements made in the 1920s by the organizers of the 24 Hours of Le Mans.

As for the Monte Carlo race, the formula of heading for a single point after departures from various cities was applied for the first time by the organizers of the Monte Carlo Rally in 1911. After the second trial, in 1912, however, the race was suspended and only resumed after 1924. In this case too, the competition has given birth to interesting technical solutions. Since this race takes place in January every year, the main problem to be resolved has always been that of road holding. Nail-studded tires proved themselves in the

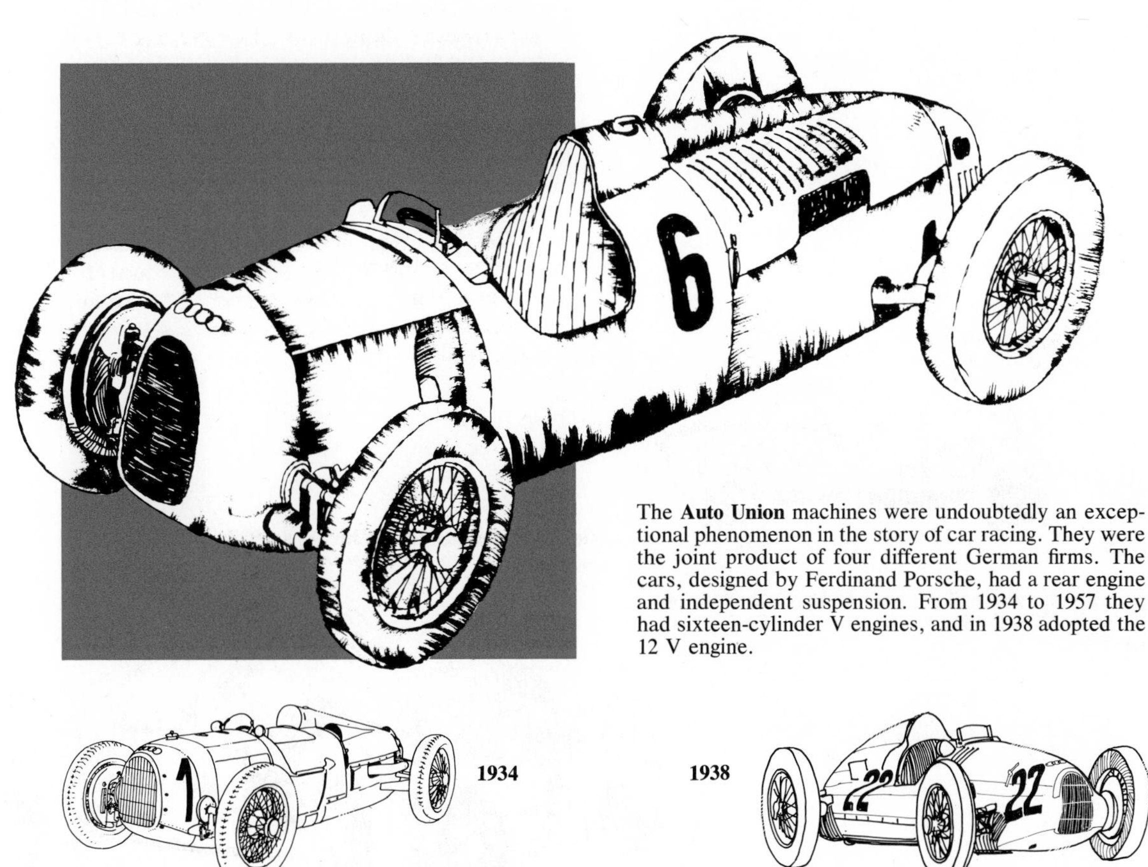


The **Auto Union** machines were undoubtedly an exceptional phenomenon in the story of car racing. They were the joint product of four different German firms. The cars, designed by Ferdinand Porsche, had a rear engine and independent suspension. From 1934 to 1957 they had sixteen-cylinder V engines, and in 1938 adopted the 12 V engine.

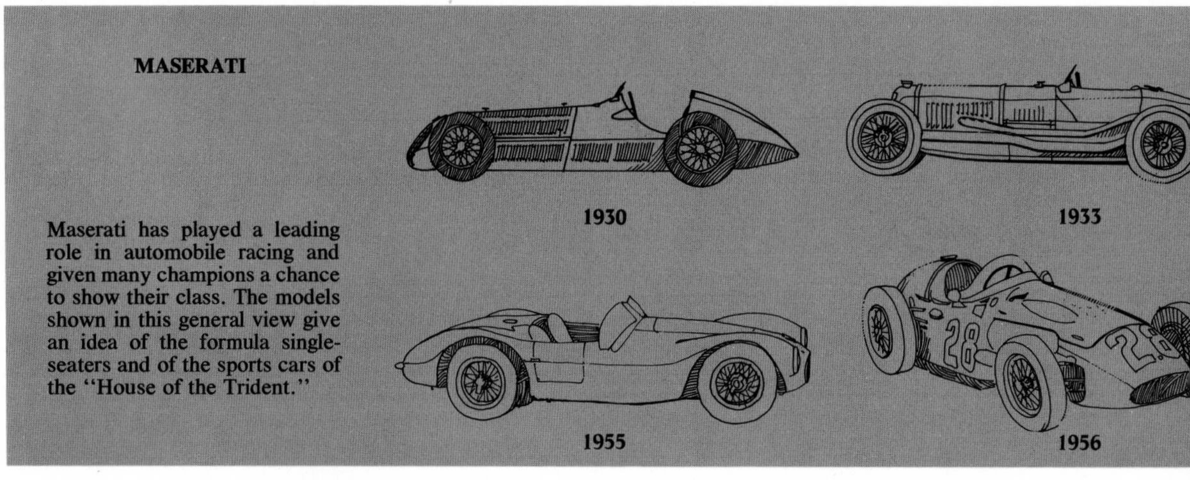


**MASERATI**

Maserati has played a leading role in automobile racing and given many champions a chance to show their class. The models shown in this general view give an idea of the formula single-seaters and of the sports cars of the "House of the Trident."

**Cooper Mark IV (1950).** British sports history owes much to the Cooper. This small Formula 3 car with a 500 cc engine brought out the talent of quite a few drivers, including Stirling Moss, Peter Collins, and Stuart Lewis-Evans.

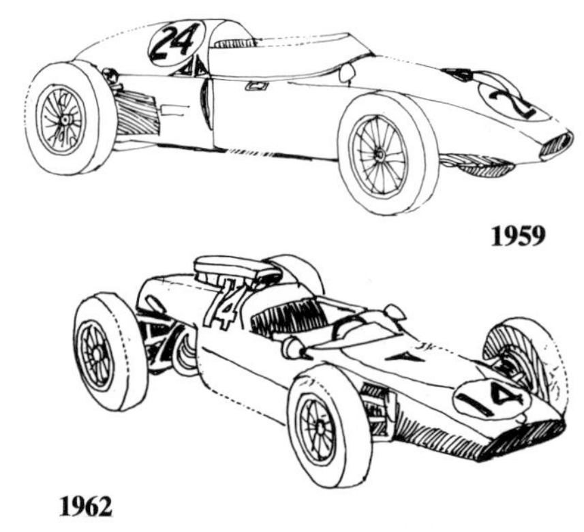


**Cooper** also built single-seaters for Formula 1 meets; here are three that won many victories and conquered the world title with Jack Brabham as driver. From above: single-seaters from 1959, 1962, and 1967.

struggle for the victory in the Monte Carlo Rally and, thanks to that race, are now widespread.

At that time, the great automobile industries thought they could make use of racing for publicity. The need to put the public in suitable arenas for the fascinating spectacle of cars racing at top speeds led the organizers to demand racecourses worthy of the show. This led to the construction of great motor-racing tracks and famous circuits, some of which are still popular today: the Avus track in Germany, built in 1920; the Monza in Italy, 1922; Montlhéry, the French track near Paris, 1924, and the permanent track laid out in Spa-Francorchamps dates from the same year; Reims, 1925; Nürburgring, 1927; and Modena, 1927. The principality of Monaco proposed a toboggan-type course through the narrow streets of Monte Carlo (which gave birth in 1929 to the most typical of the Formula 1 Grand Prix).

The twenties also saw the start of another exciting race, which ran for thirty years because of the exploits of world-famous champions: the Italian "Mille Miglia" (Thousand Miles) race, created by Aymo Maggi, Franco Mazzotti, Giovanni Canestrini, and Renzo Castagneto. The race began and ended in Brescia, and the contestants had to cover about 1600 km on ordinary roads. This very difficult race was for years a unique testing ground, and all the great champions have triumphed in it, showing that the Mille Miglia was a race that only really great drivers could win.

These competitions also saw a battle among the great automobile builders, anxious to publicize their products in all possible ways, often with memorable results. The exceptional Fiat team, with Bordino, Felice Nazzaro, and Salamano, had great success

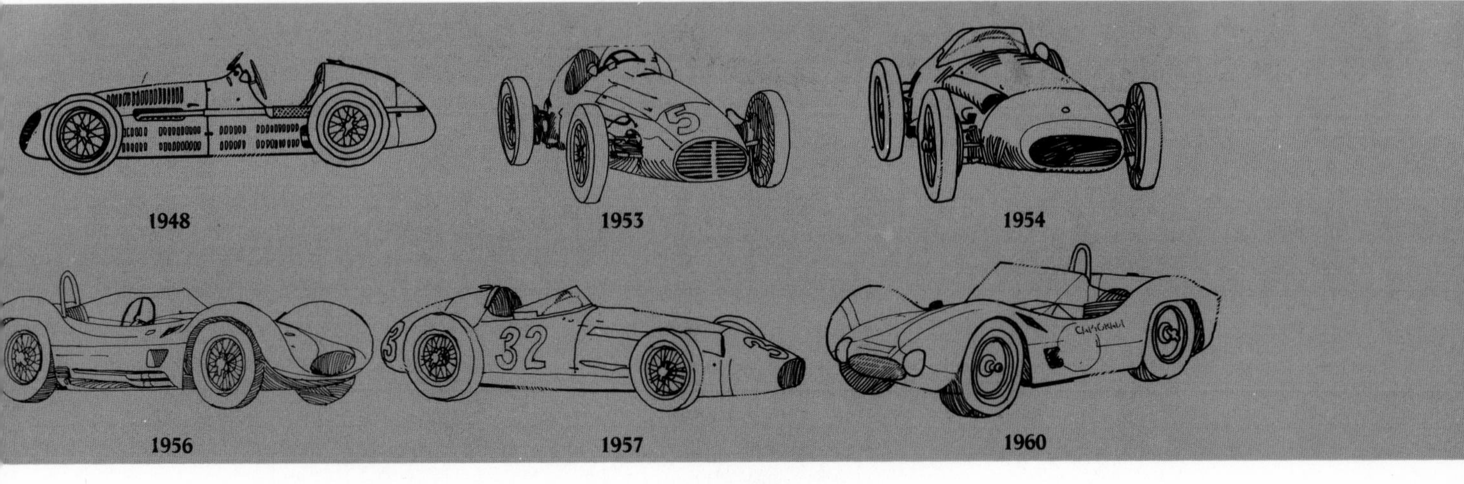

**Jaguar XK-120 Type C (1951).** Even though it never took part in a Grand Prix, the Jaguar played an important part in the sporting life of the roaring years of racing. At Le Mans, for example, the British car won well-deserved laurels with the model illustrated here.

and only left the scene in 1927 after another victory by Bordino in the Milan Grand Prix. Alfa Romeo too came to the fore with Antonio Ascari, Sivocci, Campari, Enzo Ferrari (later to become the "wizard" of Maranello), Varzi, Brilli-Peri, and the inimitable Tazio Nuvolari, a driver who won all there was to win, with every conceivable type of motorcycle and automobile. Too, there was the great Maserati team, with Borzacchini, Varzi, and Nuvolari; the Bugatti squad, with Wimille, Benoist, Chiron; the Mercedes team, with

Among the cars "made in England," the BRM merits special mention for the stubbornness with which it took part in competitions, finally managing to win a Grand Prix. The 1962, 1965, and 1972 models all won prizes in title races.

**Cooper-Climax.** In 1959 and 1960, it brought Jack Brabham the World Driving Title. The success of this English machine marked the start of the era of single-seaters with rear engines.

**Ferrari 246 (1960).** This six-cylinder car won just one success in the world driving meets of 1960: the Grand Prix of Italy, with Phil Hill as driver.

**Lotus 25.** This car is particularly important in the story of this English firm, because Colin Chapman built it to fit the body of champion Jim Clark—and the Scotsman won his first world title with this car.

**1961**

Colin Chapman, who might be considered the British Ferrari, created the **Lotus,** a racing car that attained international fame in a very short time, winning both world titles and dozens of Grand Prix, thanks to champions like Moss, Clark, Hill, Rindt, Fittipaldi, and Peterson.

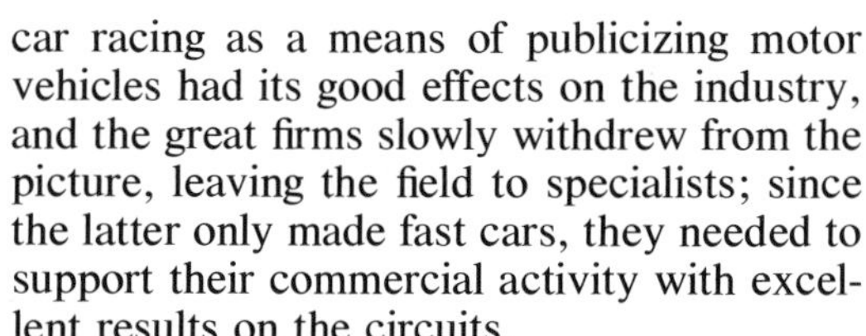

**1968**

Caracciola, Masetti, Neubauer, Fagioli; and the Auto Union (the first racing car with a rear-end engine) with Rosemeyer, Stuck, Nuvolari (the Italian ace drove almost every car of his day).

As the years went by, the exploitation of car racing as a means of publicizing motor vehicles had its good effects on the industry, and the great firms slowly withdrew from the picture, leaving the field to specialists; since the latter only made fast cars, they needed to support their commercial activity with excellent results on the circuits.

Just before the Second World War, automobile racing took on a political tone because of Hitler, who chose the automobile as a power symbol. The Mercedes, and especially the Auto Union, were "ordered" to win. Luckily that period was an exception, for, aside from the Nazi reign, the sport of car racing has always managed to stay outside complicated political struggles.

While new racecourses sprang up everywhere, bringing fame and fortune to racing cars and drivers (it was a particularly fruitful season for the Italians), the roar of cannons and the rumble of tanks distracted the world's attention from the events of sport. War was at hand. The more technically advanced nations were all involved in the conflict and automo-

**Ford GT 40.** It marked the entrance of the great American firm into the modern world of automobile racing competition. After a long series of disappointing tests, the machine finally won the "24 Hours" of Le Mans, beating Ferrari. That same year, Ford won the world title, repeating the feat in 1968.

**Lotus 49 (1970)**

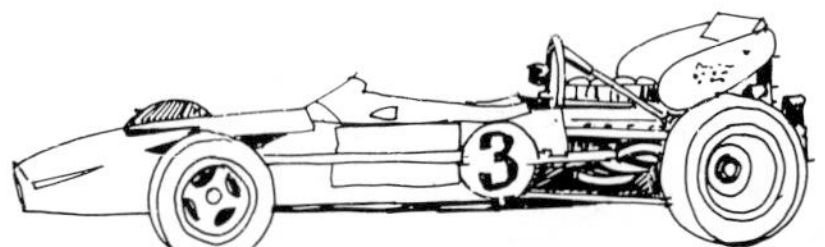

**Lotus 72 (1973)**

**Brabham F1.** Jack Brabham, world champion in 1959 and 1960, decided to build his own one-seater in which to take part in the World Driving Championships. He was the first driver–builder to win the title (his third success) in 1966. The Brabham Formula 1 had a Repco engine built in Australia.

biles were painted grayish-green. Designs for racing cars were never realized, since all the technical staffs involved were called upon to use their experience in war industries. Those were hard times for the sport of auto racing, and some champions even paid personally for their part in the conflict—for example, Robert Benoist, arrested in Paris by the Gestapo for taking part in the French Resistance and killed at Buchenwald on September 12, 1944.

The first postwar European race was held in the Bois de Boulogne in Paris in September 1945. The contestants were racing fans driving prewar cars that had been kept in mothballs all during the conflict.

A strange category of small 500 cc machines with motorcycle engines appeared in Great Britain in 1946. It was the Formula 3 of the day, and it brought to light a number of Anglo-Saxon champions, one of whom was Stirling Moss.

As the years passed, the situation became completely normal once more, and international relations became easier, at least on the sports level, among the nations of Western Europe. This relaxed climate saw the birth of the first Formula 1 World Championship, in 1950. The technical regulations had been launched in 1947 and were based on 1500 cc motors with supercharger or on 4500 cc motors without supercharger; there were no other limitations. The first Formula 1 single-seaters were born right after the war and created the highest expression of automobile racing as a sport. Time and the technical perfection of mass-production vehicles have naturally changed the meaning of this aspect of racing, since the technical research and experimentation that had marked racing in its first glorious years slowly gave way to other motivations, which took shape in the 1960s. There was in fact a research phase from 1950 to 1959, with first Alfa Romeo and then Mercedes directly involved in the races; the field was then slowly handed over to the small firms that built highly specialized vehicles (like Ferrari, Maserati, and Porsche) and later to brands born exclusively for racing, like the Lotus (which then started making touring cars), Cooper, and BRM; and finally to those which were named after driving champions who had gone into business for themselves making single-seaters (McLaren, Brabham, Surtees). The Anglo-Saxon names of the teams and the British sports training of the

**PORSCHE**

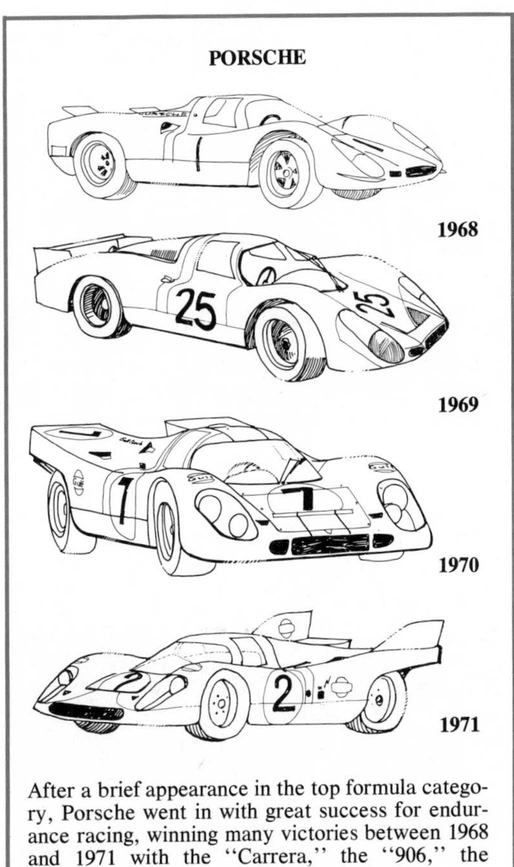


After a brief appearance in the top formula category, Porsche went in with great success for endurance racing, winning many victories between 1968 and 1971 with the "Carrera," the "906," the "908," and, last, with the "917."

**Brabham (1969)**

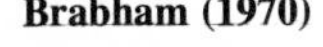

**Brabham (1970)**

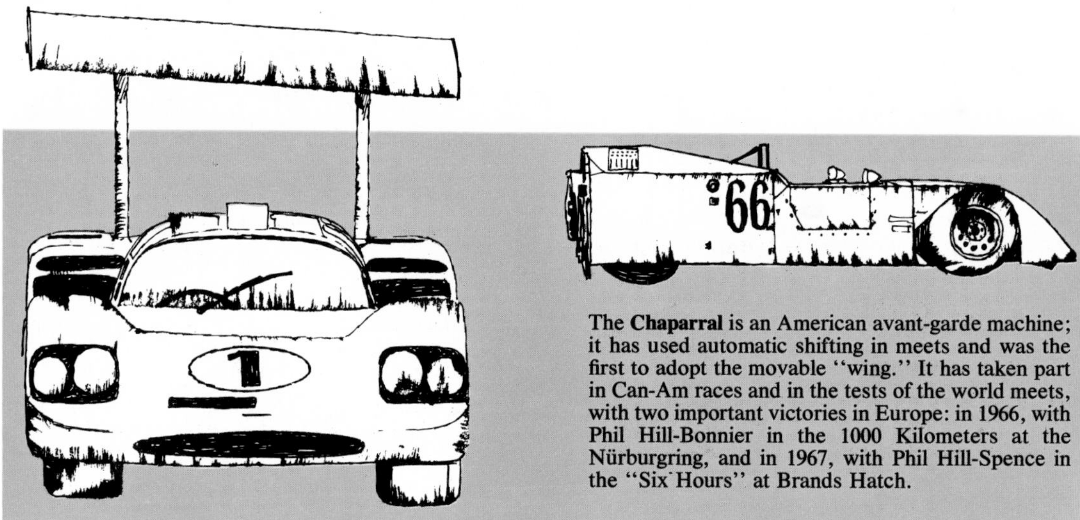


The **Chaparral** is an American avant-garde machine; it has used automatic shifting in meets and was the first to adopt the movable "wing." It has taken part in Can-Am races and in the tests of the world meets, with two important victories in Europe: in 1966, with Phil Hill-Bonnier in the 1000 Kilometers at the Nürburgring, and in 1967, with Phil Hill-Spence in the "Six Hours" at Brands Hatch.

drivers are no accident; they show that at the end of the fifties car racing received new blood from Great Britain, with a new flowering of drivers, cars, and tracks (Brands Hatch dates from 1949, Aintree from 1954, Goodwood from 1948, Mallory Park from 1956, Oulton Park from 1953, Silverstone from 1948, Snetterton from 1951, and Thruxton from 1950). The English began winning the formula races, due to an "assemblers'" technique (with this word, Enzo Ferrari distinguishes real racing-car builders from those who use parts made by different firms), which foreshadows the designing of a chassis entrusted to a specialized firm, and on which the engine and other components supplied by specialized builders—Cosworth for the engines, Hewland or ZF for the gearboxes—are then mounted.

The evolution of the position of the motor, in the more sophisticated racing cars, is important on the technical level. In Europe, between the last years of the 1950s and the middle of the 1960s, use of the rear engine became fairly widespread, and the Cooper-Climax with which Jack Brabham won the Formula 1 World Championships in 1959 and 1960 had its engine placed behind the driver (the Auto Union had already set a prewar precedent). This new trend spread rapidly among British builders, and from there to Italy and the United States, where Ford ordered a 3,000 cc engine for the new Formula 1 that was set up in 1966. It is said that Ford—which used the publicity slogan "Sport Improves the Race" for promoting the sales of its vehicles—spent £100,000 for the "3-liters"

**MATRA**

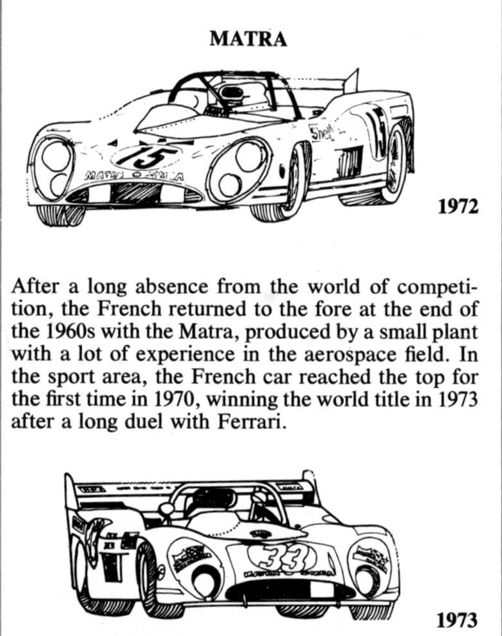


After a long absence from the world of competition, the French returned to the fore at the end of the 1960s with the Matra, produced by a small plant with a lot of experience in the aerospace field. In the sport area, the French car reached the top for the first time in 1970, winning the world title in 1973 after a long duel with Ferrari.

**Porsche 917.** The first version, which had a flat, twelve-cylinder, air-cooled engine, did not have much success because it was hard to control. The later, aerodynamically improved version of the "917"—entrusted to the JW Automotive team—proved excellent and won the world title in 1970 and 1971.

**Gulf Mirage (1973)**

designed by Keith Duckworth. The money was well spent, in any case, since from 1966 on that engine has won the Grand Prix almost without interruption. In fact, from 1968 to 1974 it conquered the title without a break, with the Lotus (three times), with the Tyrrell (twice), with the Matra and McLaren, once each.

Before Henry Ford II set up his sports program, he tried to buy out Ferrari. "That little Italian brand gets more free publicity every time it wins a race than we do by paying for it!" said the American tycoon. When negotiations bogged down, Ford decided to go into racing anyway, aiming first at a victory at Le Mans and then at an indirect and less costly solution like that mentioned above—building an engine adapted for Formula 1 to hand over to other single-seater builders. This had very interesting results, and on a publicity level it amply repaid the initial expense. Ford has also supplied motors for Formula 2 and Formula 3, to the point of practically controlling the market; for a long period of time only those motors were used in racing cars.

Thanks mainly to the support of Ford, English technique came to the fore; and British business sense suggested finding new forms of financing. At first (in the days of Stirling Moss) the banks could be depended on to use the single-seater as a means of propaganda; then more radical solutions were found, such as cars that even changed names to "honor" the donor's financial commitment. Recently the giant cigarette manufacturers have linked their products to racing, and this union of sport and youth in publicity seems to have paid off quite well. Today the sport of car racing—in its more sensational forms, such as Formula 1, sports car competitions, Formula 2, and even the great international meets—is closely bound to the publicity for an incredible variety of products. The fabric is so tightly woven that one cannot even predict the chances for survival of these kinds of sport should the support of its sponsors one day be withdrawn.

Even though it is no longer the basic testing ground for stock-car production (with perhaps the rally sector as an exception), automobile racing has discovered a new form of expression that attracts great crowds of spectators and has aroused a completely new interest, thus demonstrating its intact vitality as a sport.

For a long time, the **McLaren** was the absolute protagonist of the Can-Am championships; it was a "two-seater racer" made especially for the tests on the tracks of Canada and the United States. Bruce McLaren (in 1967 and 1969), Denny Hulme (in 1968 and 1970) and Peter Revson (in 1971) became Can-Am champions in these cars.

**Tyrrell (1971)**

Ken Tyrrell, a lumber dealer and discoverer of sport talent, became a builder of single-seaters at the insistence of Jackie Stewart. He has had the satisfaction of seeing his cars win many Grand Prix and take the world title in 1971 and 1973, thanks to the Scottish champion. The Tyrrell used Ford Cosworth 8V engines.

**Alfa Romeo 33/3 (1971)**

**Ferrari 312 (1972)**

# THE INDIANAPOLIS RACING CARS

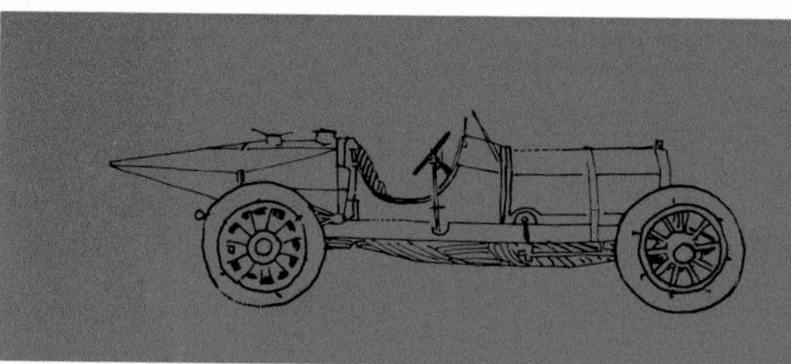

**1911 Marmon « Wasp »**

**1915 Mercedes**

When, in far-off 1908, four men from Indianapolis (Carl Fisher, Arthur Newby, Frank Wheeler, and Jim Allison) decided to build a track both for motor races and to give car builders a place to test their machines, no one imagined that in time that track would become famous all over the world for a race: the Indy 500.

In Europe there are only two examples of places that have become as famous in the history of the sport of automobile racing as Indianapolis: Le Mans, known for the extremely difficult and highly interesting "24 Hours," and Sicily.

Indianapolis owes its fame to the "500," a race in which the love of competition is mixed with the fascination of strong emotions—and with economic interests. The Indy track is an oval with two straight stretches, 1005 meters long, and two shorter ones, only 201 meters long, linked together by four curves of different shape, all 402 meters long, and is commonly called the "oval" or "brickyard." The automobile races that take place on this track are organized by USAC (United States Auto Club) and Indianapolis Motor Speedway. From the very first meet, held on August 19, 1909, Indy was paid its tribute of blood; a driver, two mechanics, and two spectators were killed on the hot, sunny day of its inauguration.

From then on, the "500" has been a steady sacrifice of human life on the dual altars of speed and the dollar. A victory at the brickyard means more than a world title; for Americans the idols of Indy are living gods. Among many others, the faces of famous drivers such as De Palma, Resta, Chevrolet, Shaw, Rose, Foyt, Clark, Graham Hill, Bobby and Al Unser, and Andretti decorate the large silver cup that is the sought-after trophy. The "500" has not been generous with European drivers and car builders. The Indy is a classic American motor race, and for many years American design technique has triumphed there. Even Ferrari, which has won almost all the most important races, could not break the spell.

The design philosophy of the Indy single-seater has yielded only once: when the great Jim Clark appeared at the starting line in Indianapolis with a rear-engine Lotus-Ford. Up until then, Indianapolis cars had always had the motor set in the front. After the Scotsman won the race, a rapid shift took place, and now only machines with rear engines compete at Indy. Still, after the short European reign (Clark and Graham Hill), American drivers have once again become the masters of the 2½ miles of the Indianapolis motor speedway.

**1921 Frontenac**

**1925 Duesenberg Special**

**1929 Simplex Piston Ring Special**

**1933 Tydol Special**

# INDIANAPOLIS

1912 National

1913 Peugeot

1914 Delage

1916 Peugeot

1919 Peugeot

1920 Monroe

1922 Murphy Special

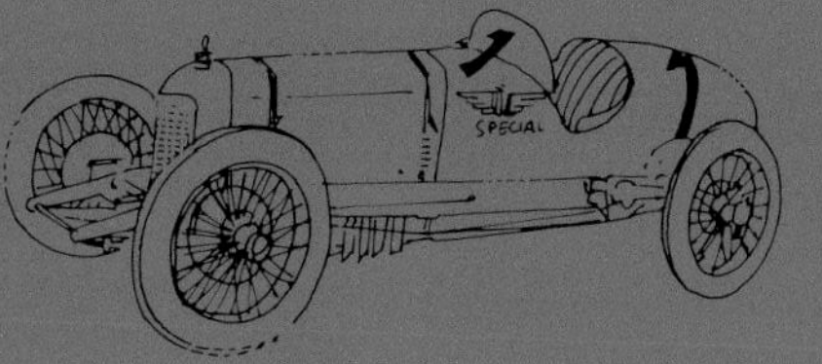

1923 H.C.S. Special

1924 Duesenberg Special

1926 Miller Special

1927 Duesenberg

1928 Miller Special

1930 Miller-Hartz Special

1931 Bowes Seal Fast Special

1932 Miller-Hartz Special

1934 Boyle Products Special

1935 Gilmore Speedway Special

1936 Ring Free Special

# INDIANAPOLIS

1937 Shaw-Gilmore Special

1938 Burd Piston Ring Special

1939 Boyle Special (Maserati)

1947 Blue Crown Spark Plug Special

1948 Blue Crown Spark Plug Special

1949 Blue Crown Spark Plug Special

1953 Fuel Injection Special

1954 Fuel Injection Special

1955 John Zink Special

1959 Leader Card 500 Roadster

1960 Ken Paul Special

1961 Bowes Seal Fast Special

1965 Lotus-Ford

1966 American Red Ball Special

1967 Sheraton-Thompson Special

1971 Johnny Lightning 500 Special

1972 Sunoco-McLaren

1973 Eagle-STP

# INDIANAPOLIS

1940 Boyle Special (Maserati)

1941 Noc Out H.C.

1946 Thorne Engine Special

1950 Wynn's Friction Proofing Special

1951 Belanger Special

1952 Agajanian Special

1956 John Zink Special

1957 Belond Exhaust Special

1958 Belond AP Special 1

1962 Leader Card 500 Roadster

1963 Agajanian Willard Special

1964 Sheraton-Thompson Special

1968 Rislone Special

1969 STP Oil Treatment Special

1970 Johnny Lightning 500 Special

# THE LEGEND OF SPEED

The absolute record for land speed is a title of great prestige, one which frightens even drivers used to racing at 300 km an hour in automobile competition. This kind of racing calls for real specialists, and the most famous were probably Malcolm and Donald Campbell. Absolute record means the average speed in two courses on the mile or kilometer at top speed, made in two different directions so as to compensate for eventual wind advantages. Until 1964, the FIA declared that the record had to be obtained with a four-wheeled vehicle, which had to have at least two driving and two directing wheels. No power limit was set on the engine.

After 1964, as a result of the use of jet engines in these record trials, the FIA modified the rule and said

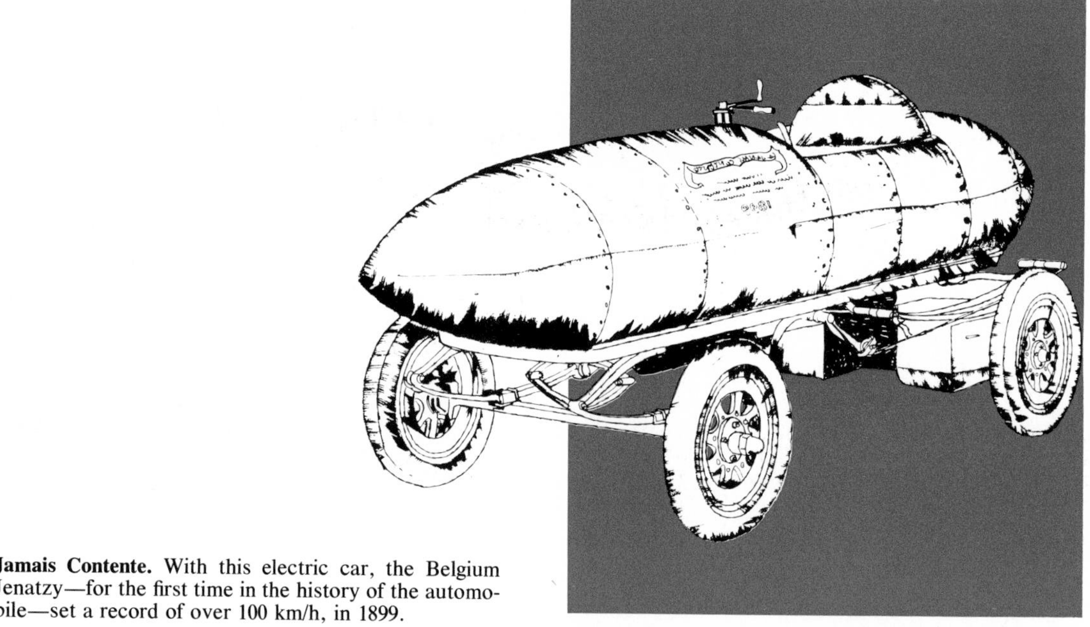

**Jamais Contente.** With this electric car, the Belgium Jenatzy—for the first time in the history of the automobile—set a record of over 100 km/h, in 1899.

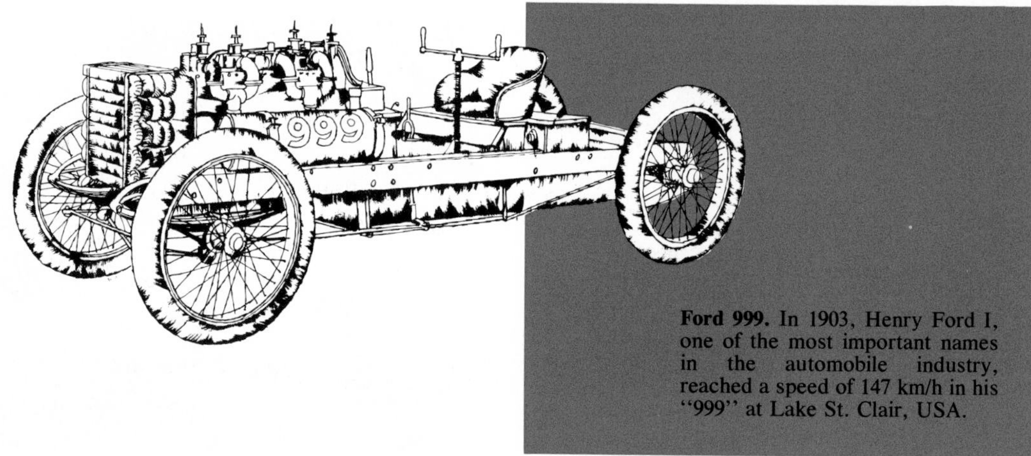


**Ford 999.** In 1903, Henry Ford I, one of the most important names in the automobile industry, reached a speed of 147 km/h in his "999" at Lake St. Clair, USA.

# RECORD

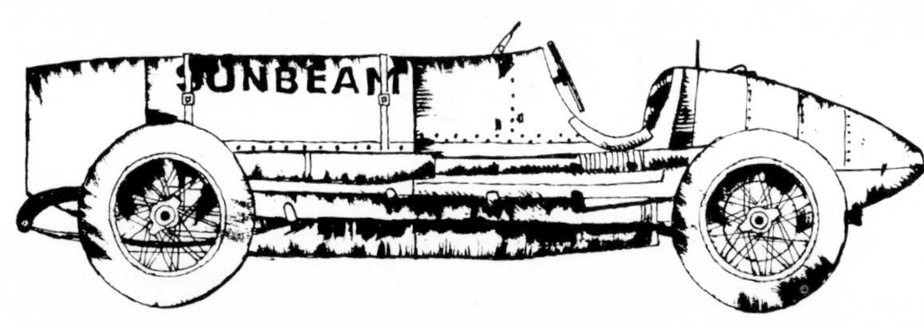


**Sunbeam 350 HP.** K. Lee Guinness drove it at a speed of more than 215 km/h on the famous Brooklands track in England in May 1922.

that any vehicle depending on the ground for support (that is, which had its wheels resting on the earth) and that contained a driver could compete for the absolute speed record. At the same time, it established a new record category reserved for vehicles with conventional internal combustion engines and wheel traction, and called the World Record for Automobiles.

Naturally, the absolute speed record draws the greatest attention; and the idea that a man driving a wheeled vehicle has gone more than 1000 km an hour (Gary Gabelich with the "Blue Flame" in 1970) will lead other proponents of speed-for-its-own-sake to try to surpass that record.

It all began in 1898, when an electric Jeantoud machine, driven by Chasseloup-Laubat, reached a maximum speed of 63.153 km/h, a speed that in that period could easily be compared with the 1000 km/h of today. Until 1899, the top speed contest was reserved for electric cars; and it was one of these—the "Jamais Contente" of Jenatzy—that exceeded the fatal 100 km/h mark at Achères, France.

From that moment on, there were duels between specialists trying to better the speed attained by their adversaries, in trial after trial. Let us recall, in this respect, the names of Vanderbilt, Hourgières, Duray, Malcolm Campbell, Segrave, and Parry Thomas; and in more recent times, those of John Cobb and Eyston and Donald Campbell, until we reach the duel between Arfons with the "Green Monster" and Breedlove with the "Spirit of America," interrupted in 1970 by the appearance of the "Blue Flame." This vehicle (a rocket-car) was driven by Gary Gabelich at more than 1000 km/h over the Salt Flats at Bonneville, a place where the bold apostles of pure speed have celebrated their rites since the 1930s.

At any rate, the speed of 1000 km/h is just a step in the fascinating history of speed.

**Fiat** too is among the names which have held the absolute speed record, thanks to Ernest Eldridge, who was timed at Arpajon in France, in July 1924, at a speed of almost 235 km/h.

Another **Sunbeam** that reached the maximum speed record was that driven by Henry Segrave at Southport in Great Britain, where he surpassed a speed of 245 km/h.

**Higham Special "Babs."** Parry-Thomas set a record twice in 1926 in the space of a few months (272 and 275 km/h). The "Babs" had a twelve-cylinder engine of almost 27,000 cc and was an old machine that the British champion had bought from Count Zborowski.

**White Triplex.** This car won at Daytona Beach in 1928, driven by Ray Keech at more than 334 km/h; it had a 26-liter, twelve-cylinder V engine.

## THE FASTEST IN THE WORLD

| | | |
|---|---|---|
| 1898 | Chasseloup-Laubat with a Jeantaud (Achères, France) | 63,153 |
| 1899 | Jenatzy with a Jenatzy (Achères, France) | 66,645 |
| 1899 | Chasseloup-Laubat with a Jeantaud (Achères, France) | 70,297 |
| 1899 | Jenatzy with a Jenatzy (Achères, France) | 80,321 |
| 1899 | Chasseloup-Laubat with a Jeantaud (Achères, France) | 93,724 |
| 1899 | Jenatzy with a Jenatzy (Achères, France) | 105,904 |
| 1902 | Serpollet with a Serpollet (Nizza, France) | 120,771 |
| 1902 | Fournier with a Mors (Dourdan, France) | 123,249 |
| 1902 | Angères with a Mors (Dourdan, France) | 124,102 |
| 1903 | Duray with a Gobron-Brillié (Ostenda, Belgium) | 136,330 |
| 1903 | Henry Ford with a Ford "999" (Lake St. Clair, USA) | 147,014 |
| 1904 | W. K. Vanderbilt with a Mercedes (Daytona Beach, USA) | 148,510 |
| 1904 | Rigolly with a Gobron-Brillié (Nizza, France) | 152,501 |
| 1904 | De Caters with a Mercedes (Ostenda, Belgium) | 156,941 |
| 1904 | Rigolly with a Gobron-Brillié (Ostenda, Belgium) | 166,628 |
| 1904 | Baras with a Darracq (Mongeron, France) | 168,188 |
| 1905 | Arthur Mac Donald with a Napier (Daytona Beach, USA) | 168,381 |
| 1905 | Hémery with a Darracq (Aries-Salon, France) | 175,422 |
| 1909 | Hémery with a Benz (Brooklands, England) | 202,655 |
| 1910 | Barney Oldfield with a Benz (Daytona Beach, USA) | 211,500 |
| 1922 | K. L. Guinness with a Sunbeam (Brooklands, England) | 215,250 |
| 1924 | René Thomas with a Delage (Arpajon, France) | 230,634 |
| 1924 | E. A. D. Eldridge with a Fiat (Arpajon, France) | 234,986 |
| 1924 | Campbell with a Sunbeam (Pendine Sands, England) | 235,217 |

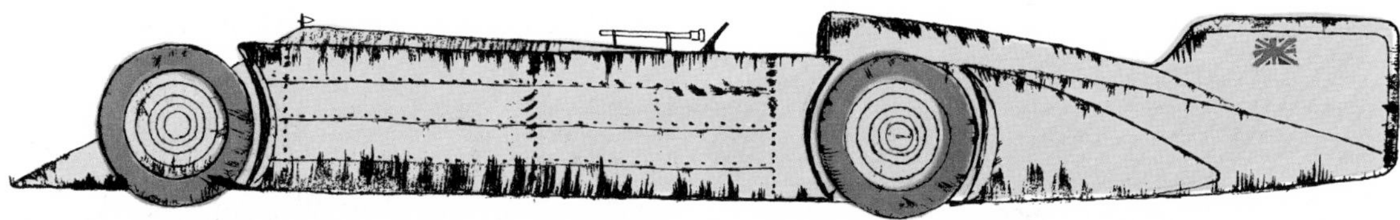

**Irving Napier Golden Arrow.** Henry Segrave's Golden Arrow did more than 372 km/h on the Daytona track in March 1929; it had a 26,900 cc, 925 hp engine.

**Bluebird.** This car, linked to Campbell's legendary successes, let Malcolm cross the mark of first 445 and then 484 km/h in March and September 1935. The two records were made on the Salt Flats at Bonneville.

# RECORD

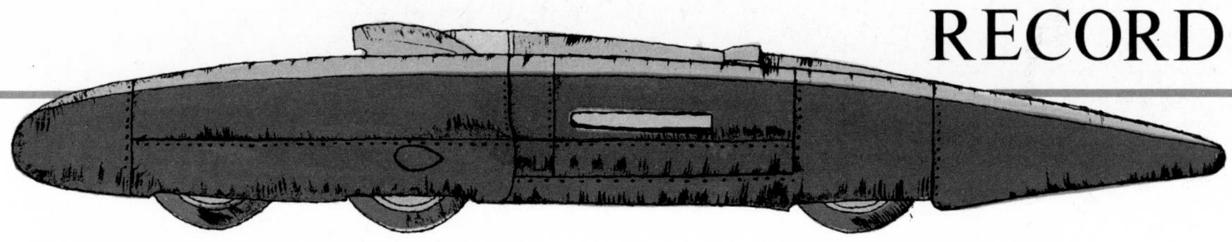

**Thunderbolt.** In September 1938, Eyston drove this car, powered by a twenty-four cylinder, 36,500 cc, 2350 hp Rolls-Royce engine, to the new speed record of 575 km/h.

| | | |
|---|---|---|
| 1925 | Campbell with a Sunbeam (Pendine Sands, England) | 242,800 |
| 1926 | Segrave with a Sunbeam (Southport, England) | 245,149 |
| 1926 | J. G. Parry-Thomas with a Thomas Special (Pendine Sands, England) | 272,458 |
| 1926 | J. G. Parry-Thomas with a Thomas Special (Pendine Sands, England) | 275,229 |
| 1927 | M. Campbell with a Napier Campbell (Pendine Sands, England) | 281,447 |
| 1927 | H. O. D. Segrave with a Sunbeam (Daytona Beach, USA) | 327,981 |
| 1928 | M. Campbell with a Napier Campbell (Daytona Beach, USA) | 333,062 |
| 1928 | Ray Keech with a White-Triplex (Daytona Beach, USA) | 334,022 |
| 1929 | H. O. D. Segrave with an Irving-Napier (Daytona Beach, USA) | 372,340 |
| 1931 | M. Campbell with a Napier Campbell (Daytona Beach, USA) | 395,469 |
| 1932 | M. Campbell with a Napier Campbell (Bonneville Salt Flats, USA) | 408,621 |
| 1933 | M. Campbell with a Rolls Royce-Campbell (Daytona Beach, USA) | 438,123 |
| 1935 | M. Campbell with a Bluebird Special (Bonneville Salt Flats, USA) | 445,703 |
| 1935 | M. Campbell with a Bluebird Special (Bonneville Salt Flats, USA) | 484,818 |
| 1937 | G. E. T. Eyston with a Thunderbolt (Bonneville Salt Flats, USA) | 501,374 |
| 1938 | John Cobb with a Railton (Bonneville Salt Flats, USA) | 536,471 |
| 1938 | G. E. T. Eyston with a Thunderbolt (Bonneville Salt Flats, USA) | 555,909 |
| 1938 | G. E. T. Eyston with a Thunderbolt (Bonneville Salt Flats, USA) | 575,217 |
| 1939 | John Cobb with a Railton (Bonneville Salt Flats, USA) | 593,560 |
| 1947 | John Cobb with a Railton (Bonneville Salt Flats, USA) | 634,267 |
| 1964 | Donald Campbell with a Bluebird II (Lago di Eyre, Australia) | 648,728 |
| 1964 | Craig Breedlove with a Spirit of America (Bonneville Salt Flats, USA) | 655,151 |
| 1964 | Art Arfons with a Green Monster (Bonneville Salt Flats, USA) | 698,756 |
| 1964 | Craig Breedlove with a Spirit of America (Bonneville Salt Flats, USA) | 843,590 |
| 1964 | Art Arfons with a Green Monster (Bonneville Salt Flats, USA) | 863,570 |
| 1965 | Craig Breedlove with a Spirit of America (Bonneville Salt Flats, USA) | 893,390 |
| 1965 | Art Arfons with a Green Monster (Bonneville Salt Flats, USA) | 927,846 |
| 1965 | Craig Breedlove with a Spirit of America (Bonneville Salt Flats, USA) | 966,571 |
| 1970 | Gary Gabelich with a Blue Flame (Bonneville Salt Flats, USA) | 1001,667 |

**"Green Monster."** This car belongs to the modern history of speed records. Driven by Art Arfons, it dueled for the title with Craig Breedlove's three-wheeled "Spirit of America."

**"Blue Flame."** With this three-wheeled, rocket-car, Gary Gabelich crossed the 1000 km/h limit for the first time in history.

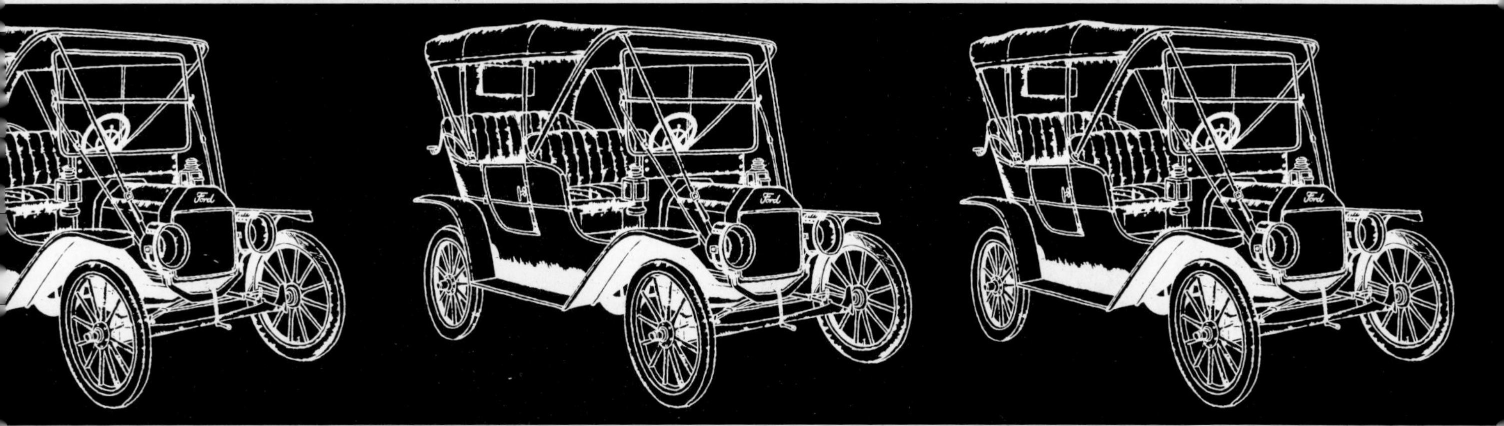

# Ford's revolution

**Ford S (1908).** The last model in the series that preceded the famous "T." Like the latter, the "S" was made to be built and sold cheaply and had some points in common with its successor, such as front suspension with transverse leaf springs. Only the "Model K"—of the cars that preceded the "T"—was an expensive car, and very few were sold at a price of $2500.

**Ford A (1903).** The "A" was the first car produced by the Ford Motor Company, which was founded on June 16, 1903. The first "Model A" left the small factory just one month after the company had been set up. It was an inexpensive car, with a two-cylinder engine, and cost the fairly low price of $800. Almost two thousand of them were turned out in little less than a year and a half.

# Ford's revolution

When on October 1, 1908, Henry Ford started to produce his "Model T," he probably never dreamed that the car would transform the face of America. Profound social changes were to accompany the physical changes of the nation's cities; mass production, higher salaries for workers, and a heightened consumption of goods were born; and all this because of—for better or worse—the Model T. "Someone should write a learned essay on the moral, physical and aesthetic effect of the Ford Model T on the American people," John Steinbeck wrote in *Cannery Row:*

> Two generations knew more about Ford's gadgets than about the clitoris, more about shifting gears than about the solar system. Part of the conception of private property disappeared with the Model T. Monkey wrenches stopped being private property and pumps belonged to the last person who handled them. Most of the babies of that period were conceived in Model T Fords and quite a few were born in them. The Anglo-Saxon ideal of the home suffered so much that it's never been the same since. . . .

But it wasn't just the ideal of the home that disappeared with the success of the Model T; handicraft work methods and low pay for workers also vanished. Henry Ford did what he could to set up a balance between production and labor after the introduction of the assembly line, since higher production did in fact lead to a reduction in working hours and to much higher pay. The announcement of the new labor contract on January 5, 1914, caused much more of a sensation than that of a year earlier informing the world of the birth of the assembly line. It even aroused more emotion in America than did the start of the war in Europe a few months later.

The **quadricycle** that Henry Ford completed in 1896 was his first vehicle. He devoted all of his spare time to it for years, even working nights to get it finished.

It was indeed big news: overnight, the 15,000 employees of the Ford factory went from a daily pay of $2.34 for a nine-hour working day to a pay of $5 a day for eight hours! On the morning of January 6, 1914,

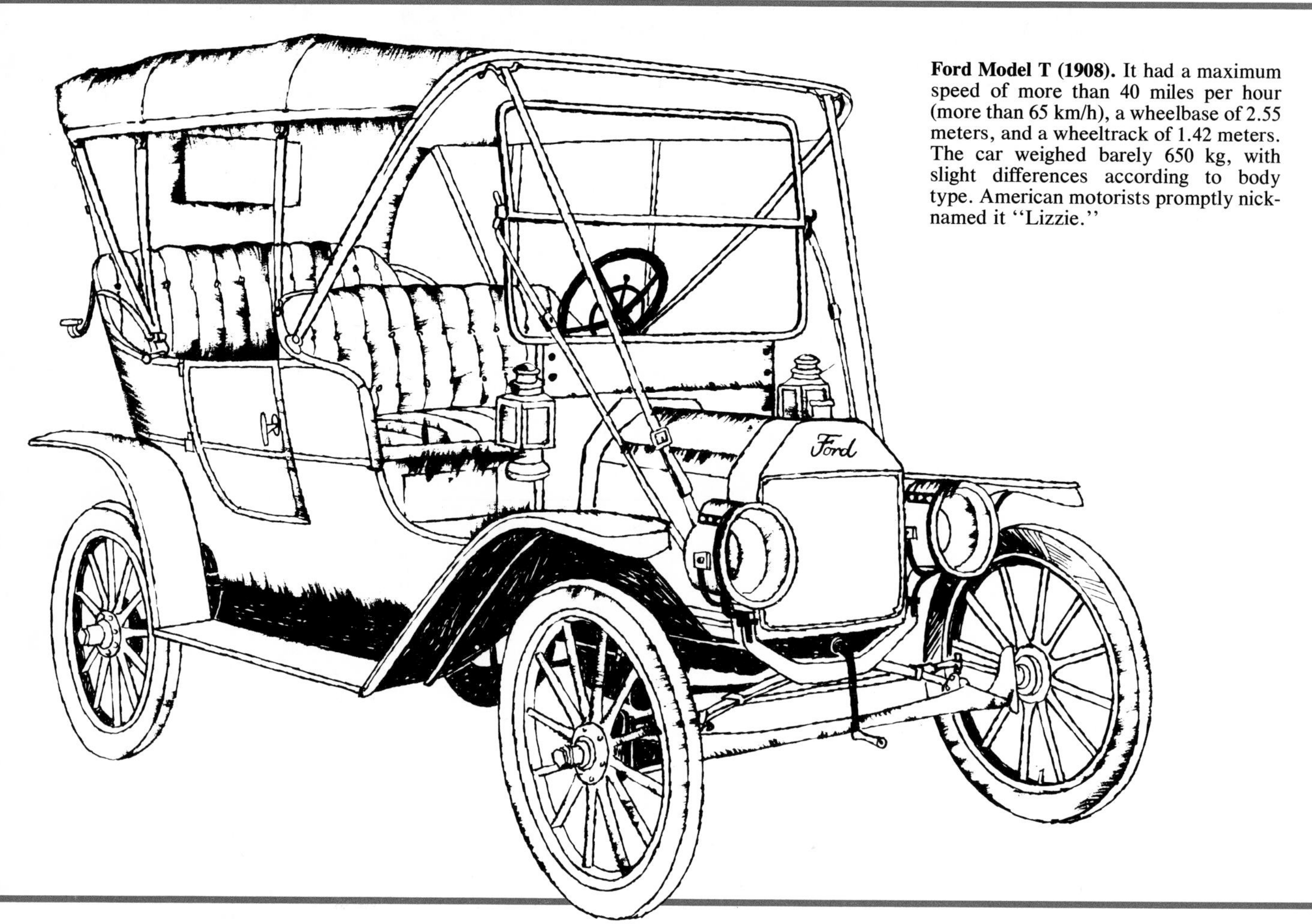


**Ford Model T (1908).** It had a maximum speed of more than 40 miles per hour (more than 65 km/h), a wheelbase of 2.55 meters, and a wheeltrack of 1.42 meters. The car weighed barely 650 kg, with slight differences according to body type. American motorists promptly nicknamed it "Lizzie."

more than 10,000 men from all over the area (some had come hundreds of miles) crowded around the gates of the Ford factory in Detroit hoping to find work; but no jobs were available. This pilgrimage went on for weeks, and hundreds of thousands of Americans saw the Ford plant in Detroit for the first time.

Years later, *The New York Times* recalled that an agitated America expected at least four tragic results from that reckless move by Ford: Detroit would be changed from a great industrial city into a country town, since no other manufacturers would keep their plants open; the few manufacturers who remained in Detroit would quickly go bankrupt; Ford itself would soon go bankrupt; and, last, Ford workers would quickly be ruined by this sudden and unexpected prosperity.

Of course, none of this happened. Detroit consolidated its fame and power as the world capital of the automobile; no one went into bankruptcy in Detroit, or, at least, no one did so because of Ford's decision (those on the verge of bankruptcy went into bankruptcy, but not because of Ford); and the workers quickly went out and bought Model T's, thus doing exactly what Henry Ford had counted on their doing.

The "divine mechanic"—the American phrase for Henry Ford—was born in a modest farmhouse in Springwells, not far from Detroit, on July 30, 1863. He was the oldest of six children; his mother died in childbirth when he was thirteen, and he and his father, William, an Irish immigrant, had to care for the other five children. He and his father soon fought over one point: Henry had no intention of becoming a farmer. Little Henry's sole passion was machinery—the small amount of machinery available to an Irish farmer: a watch, a farm machine, a cart. Henry disman-

# THE MODEL T

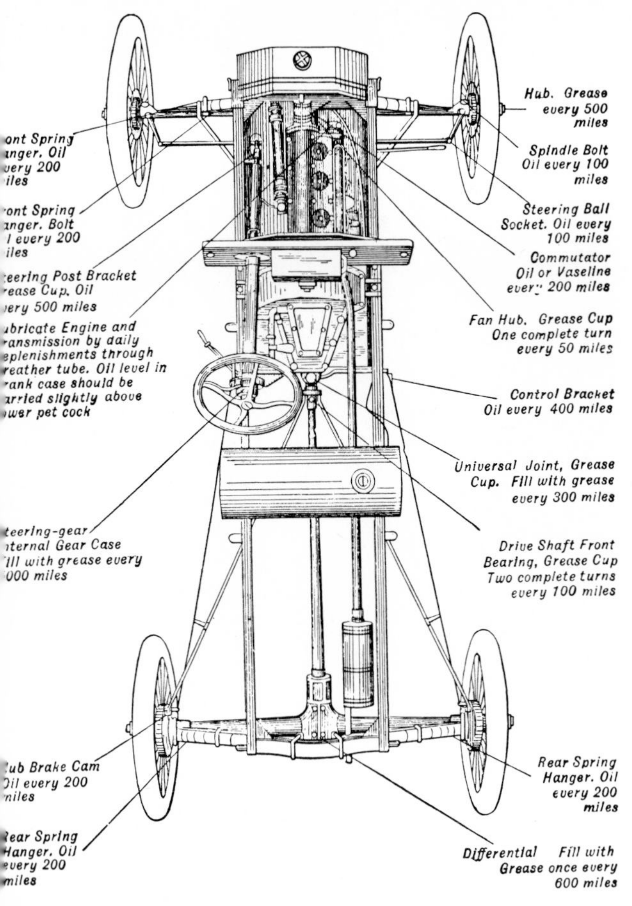


The car that really set off widespread motoring in the United States had a fairly large engine: four aligned cylinders, 2892 cc (bore of 95 mm and stroke of 102). Because of "throttled" feeding, which took place through a rudimentary carburetor, it only had 21 hp and barely 1500 rpm. Henry Ford wanted "Lizzie" to have limited power and few revolutions so that she would have a long life, be very dependable, and show high torque capacity. The Model T was so flexible that it allowed the use of a gear box—with epicyclic gears—with only two forward speeds (plus reverse, of course). But everything about Lizzie was both practical and simple: gravity led the gasoline from the tank (set beneath the front seat) to the carburetor; there was radiator-type water cooling, pumpless—and even lubrication (of the "splash" type, through the movement of the flywheel and the driving shaft) was pumpless. The flywheel itself also contained the coils of the generator; over the years, the electric system was completed with electric—rather than acetylene—lights, with a battery and with an electric starter.

Driving was quite easy as compared with other cars of that time: the spark lead and accelerator were controlled by two small levers beside the steering wheel; and there were three pedals, one on the left for first, one in the center for reverse, and one on the right for the brakes. Once the motor was started, it sufficed to push down the left pedal and unblock the handbrake lever. When some speed was gained, releasing the left pedal put the car into second. The left pedal had to be pushed down steadily if a long slope was to be climbed.

tled, reassembled, repaired, greased, modified, and transformed all he could get his hands on. When still very young, he managed to get a job in one of the very first electric power stations in Detroit, and said good-bye to his father and brothers and, above all, to the good, fertile earth.

The story of Henry Ford is that of the American self-made man: from the plow to the million-dollar bank account. It would be a mistake, though, to confuse Henry Ford with the great figures in the American financial world, such as John D. Rockefeller, Henry Clay Frick, William B. Astor, Cornelius Vanderbilt, George Pullman, Jay Gould, Jim Fisk, and others. There is a great difference between Ford and the American tycoons of his time—the difference between an inventor of genius who knew how to make the most profit out of his ideas, and the looters who were no more than dynamic speculators and clever manipulators of capital. It was to slow down the activities of the various Rockefellers, Vanderbilts, et al., that the federal government had to create the Interstate Commerce Act and then, when that turned out to be inadequate, the Sherman Antitrust Act. In the meantime, twenty-five-year-old Henry Ford, without a dime, was designing his gasoline motor at night.

To offer some philosophical excuse for their bold methods, the American tycoons of the turn of the century even turned to Darwin's theory of evolution, which (according to them) was perfectly adapted to American society. John D. Rockefeller declared: "The growth of a great industry is only a question of the survival of the fittest. It has nothing to do with an evil tendency of business. It is simply the correct functioning of nature and divine law." That inevitable and fitting mention of divine law—keeping in mind the puritanism of

American society at that time—sums up much. The activity and future achievement of Henry Ford fit into such a picture. Economist John Kenneth Galbraith, formerly advisor to President Kennedy, expressed shock, in his book *The Liberal Hour,* at certain of Ford's methods; but to be shocked would be to judge Ford outside of the natural historical reality of an era and a system. Galbraith himself has to admit that "Ford's activity may have been negative, but is still above all blame" and he concludes, "the fact remains that Henry Ford built the most famous automobile of all time, apart from definitely creating the largest mechanical undertaking of his time."

"The largest mechanical undertaking of his time"—this is perhaps the most interesting element in the picture, considering the fact that Ford had started with next to nothing. In 1898 he founded a small company with five partners who had pooled their savings. In 1899 the Detroit Automobile Company was born, but in the following year the company collapsed for lack of capital. Ford did not give up; a year later, he prepared an interesting prototype vehicle with which he beat quite a few records. Then, with some of his former partners in the Detroit Automobile Company, he founded the Ford Motor Company on June 16, 1903. The first car produced was an economical two-cylinder model that cost $800: the Model A. From then on, Ford went from one success to another. On October 22, 1906, Henry Ford replaced J. S. Gray as president of the company—of which he had hitherto been technical director and vice-president—and at the same time took over shares worth 58.5% of the total capital.

The naked chassis of one of the first Model T's. Note the gasoline tank under the front seat; it fed the carburetor through gravity.

Between 1903 and 1908, the Ford Motor Company ran through almost the entire alphabet, presenting cars from "A" to "S," one after another (even if some remained in the prototype stage). The idea was to produce automobiles that were light, very strong, and quite economical. The price should always be just a bit less than that of competition; this was Ford's intention, and the validity of his plan was demonstrated first by the success of the "A" and then of the "N"—which generally foreshadowed the "T" and was a four-cylinder utilitarian passenger car sold for only $500. The Model K, on the other hand, was not a success; it was a prestige car of 7000 cc, made at his partners' insistence, and sold for $2500. At a time when the automobile was considered a luxury, Henry Ford was the only one to see the possibility of its becoming a necessity for the common man. The failure of the Model K and the exit from the company of the partner who was mainly responsible for insisting on that model—events which led to Ford's rapid rise—were certainly important moments in the history of the Detroit firm. In any case, disagreement among the shareholders was for Ford just a small setback compared to the "Selden racket." We have already spoken of Selden and his activities; suffice it to note here that this clever lawyer was able to demonstrate the fact that he had really "invented" the automobile in every part, thanks to an extremely vague patent filed years before involving any vehicle that moved through "nonanimal traction."

Ford vigorously opposed the claims of Selden and after very long and complex legal proceedings finally won his case in 1911. This

One of the first **town cars** (1909), the more luxurious version of the Model T. The "Runabout" was the cheapest available of that type.

A **TT truck,** which made use of the reinforced chassis of the Model T.

was not just a Henry Ford triumph, but a victory for the entire young American automobile industry, and it may well explain why production almost doubled from 1911 to 1912, going from 210,000 to 378,000 cars.

But Henry Ford certainly did not sit around waiting for the complications of the Selden case to be resolved before giving new impetus to his factory. The context in which Ford was functioning was undoubtedly just right for accepting an automobile boom; let us examine the reasons why. As the century opened, the United States was a mainly rural nation (only 33 percent of the population was concentrated in the cities, as against 77 percent in England) with great space (about thirty times that of England), a less than primitive road network, a transport system based on horse-driven carts, and an inadequate railroad network. On the other hand, the country had a real desire to do things and to progress. Thus, industries were born, but they could not develop because of the inadequate transport system; agriculture could not reach the levels to which it seemed destined because railway rates were very high and because of the need for mechanized farming. Now more than ever before, the railroads showed that, although indispensable, they were inadequate for the needs of such a large country.

Ford entered this picture with his low-priced car, a machine at one and the same time simple, strong, trustworthy, roomy, and able to cross a field of grain or ford a stream. America asked for nothing better. No one can deny that Ford understood the market long before the existence of a market was even suspected; we might even say that he created marketing.

But, apart from marketing, we also owe to Ford one of the most loathed and at the same time most useful inventions of our age: the assembly line, as it was applied to automobile manufacture—and employed in grand style. Even before Henry Ford, other American manufacturers had used the assembly line, though to a limited degree: for instance, Whitney and Colt for rifles and revolvers, respectively, even before Ford was born, and Eli Terry for watches. Ford gets the credit, though, for having studied the most rational use of it, for having set the standards for the production of the assembly line—in other words, for having made of it an efficient monster.

Thanks to the use of the assembly line—and thanks as well to the theories of the utilization of labor of F. W. Taylor, who studied how to increase production on the basis of an

**"T" Station Wagon (1921).** Ford was the first to offer a station wagon, with wooden superstructure, in his catalogue—as far back as 1915.

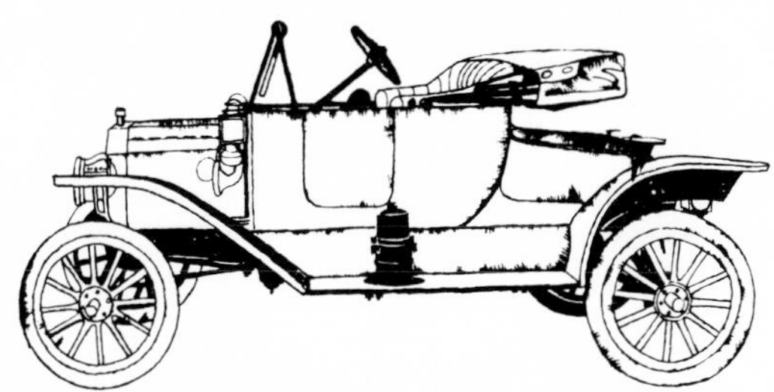

The **Runabout** version **(1913).** On the footboard, the acetylene generator of the gas for the two headlights; the two parking lights on each side of the windshield, and the rear light, ran on kerosene.

**Four-door sedan (1924).** By 1915, acetylene lights were replaced by electric ones.

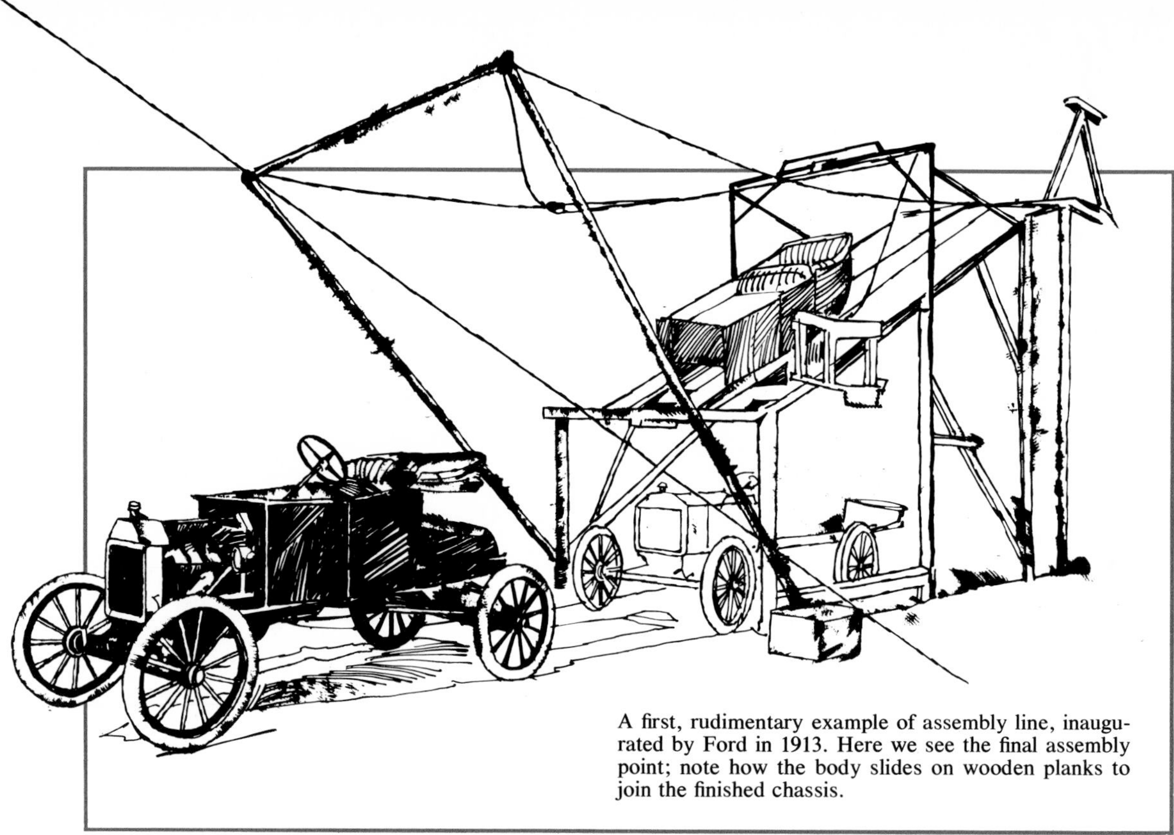

A first, rudimentary example of assembly line, inaugurated by Ford in 1913. Here we see the final assembly point; note how the body slides on wooden planks to join the finished chassis.

analysis of the workers' movements and the division of their labor—Ford was slowly able to lower the price of his Model T, in the torpedo touring version, from the original $850 of 1908 to a minimum of $380 in 1926 (despite the fact that in the meantime the car had been improved and even equipped with an electric starter and circuit).

Ford managed to get these excellent results because of the exceptional concentration of his production resources, as well as for other reasons. For instance, the Model T's were equipped with tires made in his own factories, and the raw material came from his own plantations in South America or in Indonesia; the steel was made in the Ford steel mills with coal taken from Ford mines and carried to Detroit on Ford ships; and so on. This was all the more extraordinary at a time when factories, and not only the small ones, usually suspended production for a few months every year, either to get production of a new model under way, or to clear out old stock, or to clean out the workshops, or even merely to take inventory. When these factories opened again, they often had to face immense problems to find labor; not all the workers were prepared to remain unemployed for a few months because of a lack of industrial organization.

Taylorism (the basic slogan of which was that there was only one way to make something, the "one best way") and Fordism (which we might define as a practical variant of the first) were soon welcomed throughout the world, including the communist world. Back in 1918, Lenin stated that "Taylorism must be put at the service of communism." And at the beginning of the thirties Ford himself was asked for advice in setting up the newly born Soviet automobile industry. Thus

| YEAR | FORD Production | UNITED STATES Production |
|---|---|---|
| 1903 | 1.708 | 11.235 |
| 1904 | 1.695 | 22.830 |
| 1905 | 1.599 | 25.000 |
| 1906 | 8.729 | 34.000 |
| 1907 | 14.887 | 44.000 |
| 1908 | 10.202 | 65.000 |
| 1909 | 17.771 | 127.287 |
| 1910 | 32.053 | 187.000 |
| 1911 | 69.762 | 210.000 |
| 1912 | 170.211 | 378.000 |
| 1913 | 202.667 | 485.000 |
| 1914 | 308.162 | 573.039 |
| 1915 | 501.462 | 696.930 |
| 1916 | 735.020 | 1.617.708 |
| 1917 | 664.076 | 1.873.949 |
| 1918 | 498.342 | 1.170.686 |
| 1919 | 941.042 | 1.876.356 |
| 1920 | 463.451 | 2.227.349 |
| 1921 | 971.610 | 1.616.119 |
| 1922 | 1.301.067 | 2.544.176 |
| 1923 | 2.011.125 | 4.034.012 |
| 1924 | 1.922.048 | 3.602.540 |
| 1925 | 1.911.706 | 4.265.830 |
| 1926 | 1.554.465 | 4.300.934 |
| 1927 | 417.288 | 3.401.326 |
| 1928 | 743.936 | 4.358.759 |
| 1929 | 1.862.585 | 5.337.087 |

the Gorki factory came into being, and it was no accident that the first car made there, the Gaz A, was a faithful imitation of the 1928 Ford A.

Naturally, the assembly line had its faults, but at that time it was the only way Ford knew to increase production from a few thousand cars a year to more than two million, the latter a figure that was to remain unequaled for many years. With his assembly line, Ford managed to produce in one day—October 31, 1925—9109 Model T's, another record that was to last for a long time. Ford went from the 10,202 cars turned out in 1908 (about a sixth of total American production), to the 69,762 of 1911 (about a third of American production), to the 202,667 of 1913 (little less than half of the overall American output), to the 501,462 of 1915 (more than half), to the 971,610 of 1921 (about 60 percent).

But if it is true that Ford produced most of the American cars of that period, it is also true that the total value of the Model T came to barely more than 30 to 35 percent of the total cash sales in America; it remained always by far the cheapest car on the world market. After sales peaks, a slow decline began for Ford in 1924; the public had more experience and began to get tired of the same model, which was a bit too "utilitarian" for the new tastes of the American buyer. In 1927, Ford produced only 380,741 cars, barely one eighth of that year's American production. The Model T's last year of life was 1927; on May 31, with number 15,007,033, the world's most famous car ended its long (nineteen years) and prosperous career.

"The Model T is vanishing from the American scene," wrote Lee Strout White in 1936, "but this is a limiting judgement, because for millions of Americans who grew up with it, the old Ford *was* the American scene."

The king is dead—long live the king! For the first time in his life, Ford shut down the assembly line for a few months to set up production of a new model, which was to start the alphabet all over again. And at the end of 1927, the Model A was presented with great publicity. There was such high expectation for this new Ford that half a million Americans put out money for the new Model A without even having seen it and without knowing its final price—another unbroken record! The new Ford was shown in Madison Square Garden in New York, the only covered hall that could hold the crowd foreseen. The crowd went wild, as newspapers of the day report.

One of the last Model T's produced: the 1927 **touring car,** the cheapest version available. More than 15 million Model T's were produced by Ford.

The Model A was shown in New York while the Motor Salon was going on right across the street, but Ford didn't want to present his car in that show. Once again, he was right; he managed, in fact, to draw more people in to see his car in one day than the Motor Show attracted during its entire run!

**Ford A (1928).** This car was presented to the public at the end of 1927, after the Ford assembly lines had remained inactive for several months to get the new model under way.

PIERCE - ARROW
Dual-Valve Six

for Economical Transportation
CHEVROLET
The aristocrat of small enclosed cars—smart, dependable and, above all, easy to drive.
CHEVROLET MOTOR COMPANY, DETROIT, MICHIGAN
Touring - $510
Roadster - 510
Coupe - - 645
Coach - - 645
Sedan - - 735
Landau - - 765
f.o.b. Flint, Mich.
QUALITY AT LOW COST

RENAULT

la sagesse
vous conseille
de choisir
une
DeDion
Bouton

# The war is on

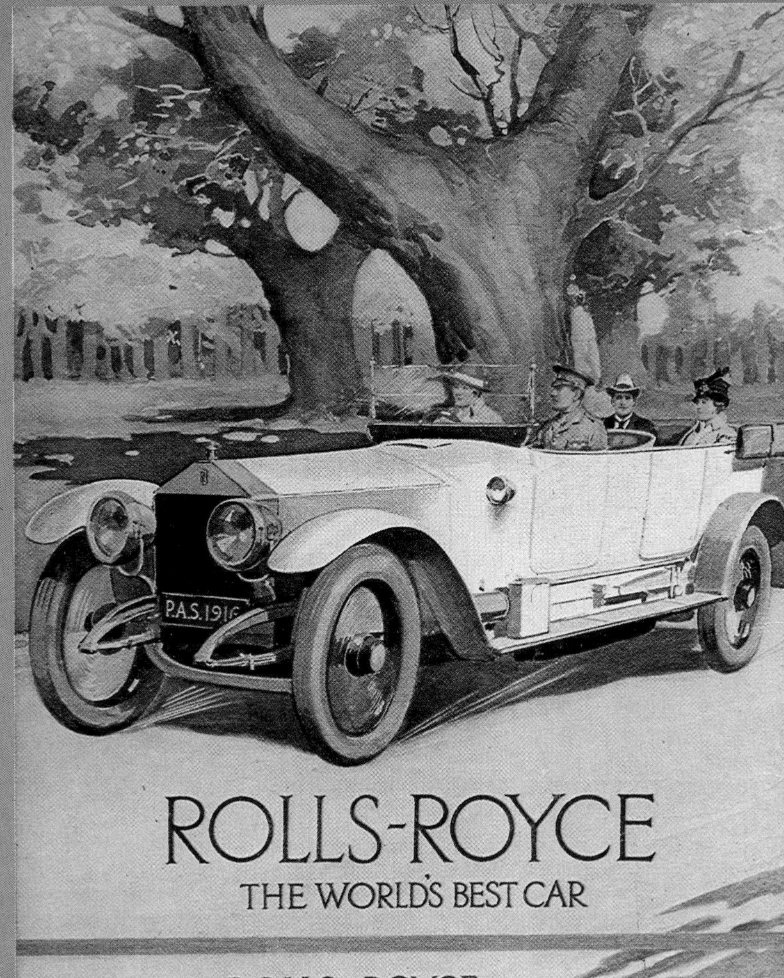
P.A.S. 1916
ROLLS-ROYCE
THE WORLD'S BEST CAR
Telegrams
ROLHEAD. LONDON
ROLLS - ROYCE LIMITED.
14 & 15 CONDUIT ST. LONDON. W.
Telephone
GERRARD 1654 (3 LINES)

DIATTO

FIAT
509

LA 10 H.P.
CITROËN
Conduite intérieure
3 Places
ÉLÉGANTE, RAPIDE, LA CONDUITE INTÉRIEURE CITROËN EST
LA VOITURE INDISPENSABLE POUR VOS COURSES ET

**White Steamer, Type 0 (1909).** Born as a factory for making sewing machines, the White Company turned out its first steam vehicle in 1900; but in 1911 it began producing gasoline-driven cars.

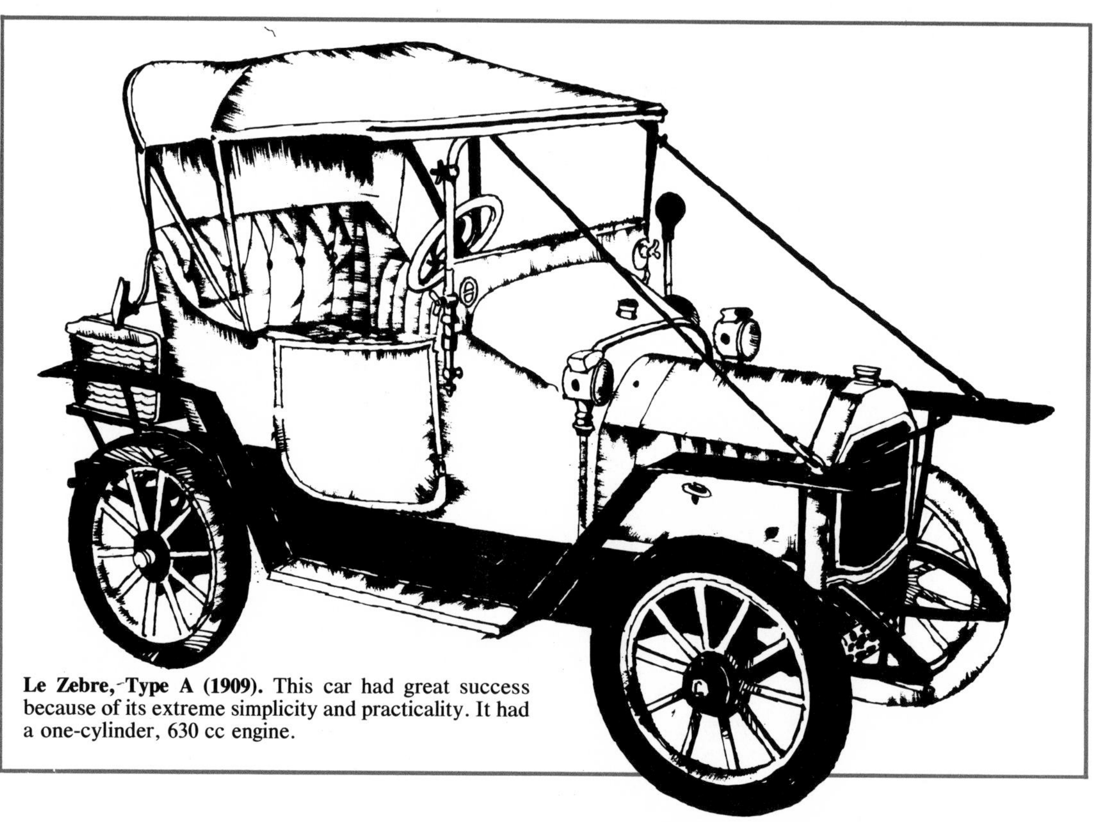

**Le Zebre, Type A (1909).** This car had great success because of its extreme simplicity and practicality. It had a one-cylinder, 630 cc engine.

# The war is on

The first years of the twentieth century, those which preceded the First World War, were filled with significance for the automobile. In that decade the motor-driven vehicle left the mists of prehistory and lost almost all of its pioneering aspects to become part of daily life; in other words, it became goods for consumption. Most of the credit for that goes to Henry Ford and his industrial revolution (the assembly line, "a car for every purse," etc.); but it would not be fair to leave unmentioned the contribution of many other firms, large and small, which in one way or another helped to make the automobile widespread and popular.

This popularity can be summed up in a few figures. As for the United States, for instance, car traffic rose from 8000 vehicles in 1900 to 2,300,000 in 1915; France leaped from a couple of thousand cars to more than 100,000 in the same period of time; Italy had a small-scale boom from 300 cars to 25,000. It is clear, however, that the figures for Europe are nothing as compared with those for America, and the latter would probably have remained

**Brixia Züst 10 HP (1909).** An elegant and comfortable car that was built in Brescia until the Brixia Züst company was absorbed by OM. It had a four-stroke, three-aligned-cylinder engine, one of the few made in the entire history of the automobile.

on European levels if it had not been for the Ford Model T, which spurred on the entire American automobile industry and, later, that of Europe.

The Model T introduced, along with the concept of the assembly line, also that of the big factory; no longer a series of small workshops in which the cars were built by purely handicraft methods, but a few large plants so well equipped as to be able to turn out thousands of cars a year—naturally at much lower prices.

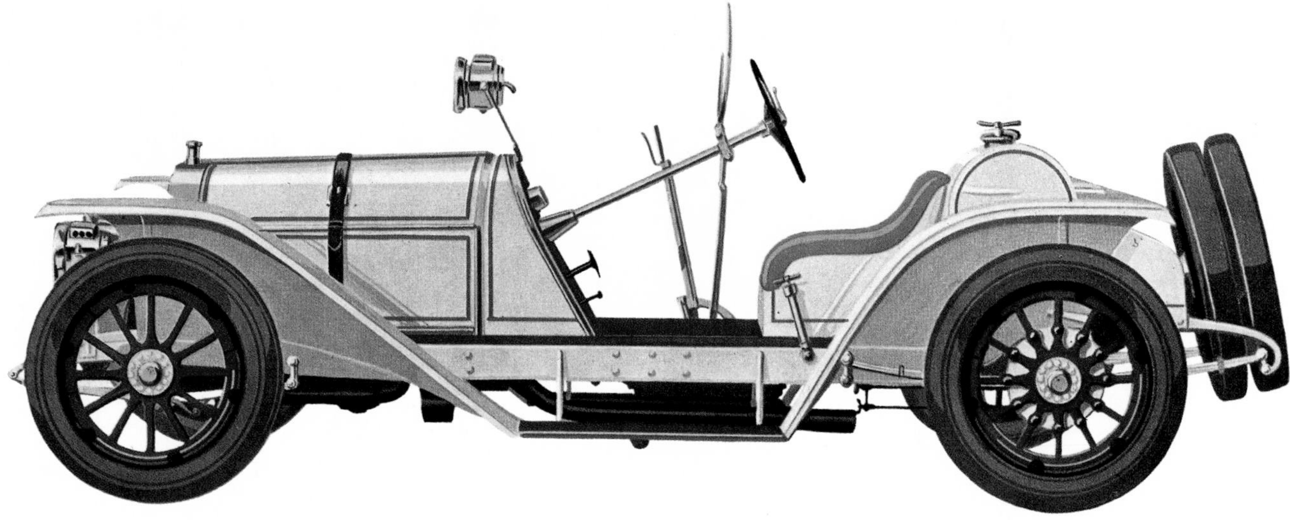

**Mercer 35 T (1912).** Better known as a "raceabout," this car had success thanks to its easy handling and its good road holding. The body was simplified to the maximum and characterized by a round windshield fastened to the shaft of the steering wheel. In the center of the front there was a large mobile headlight. The maximum speed was about 120 km/h.

In the United States at least, this trend led to fast processes of transformation in industry and to the more or less rapid bankruptcy of the less powerful companies. Only those companies whose production was extremely specialized or which were devoted to luxury goods managed to survive for a certain number of years—but those of the latter type succumbed to the 1929 depression. The future belonged to "big business."

As far back as 1913, Ford alone succeeded in producing 202,000 cars out of a national total of 461,500, quite a record when one remembers that the number two builder of the time—Overland, founded by John N. Willys—only made 37,000 machines and the number three—Buick, which was already part of General Motors—barely reached 28,000. But at that time there were almost 200 automobile factories in the United States, and more than 500 all over the world, including America.

The year 1914 saw the top ten automobile makers of America control almost four-fifths of the national market, with a production of 412,000 cars—more than 300,000 of which were built by Ford—out of a national total of 548,139. The great firms were lining up with Ford to make life hard for small producers.

We cannot use the phrase "great firms" without thinking at once of General Motors, which created more than one company in this

**Austin 18/24 (1911).** The first 18/24 Austin model appeared in 1907. The 1911 version, a solid touring car, had its bore increased in regard to the earlier series; with 45 hp it reached a speed of 80 km/h.

**Berliet (1910).** Known today as a truck factory, Berliet began making automobiles in 1895. In 1910, the firm put seven models on sale, with two-, four-, and six-cylinder engines. The type illustrated here, which had a four-cylinder engine, was used by the President of the Republic of France.

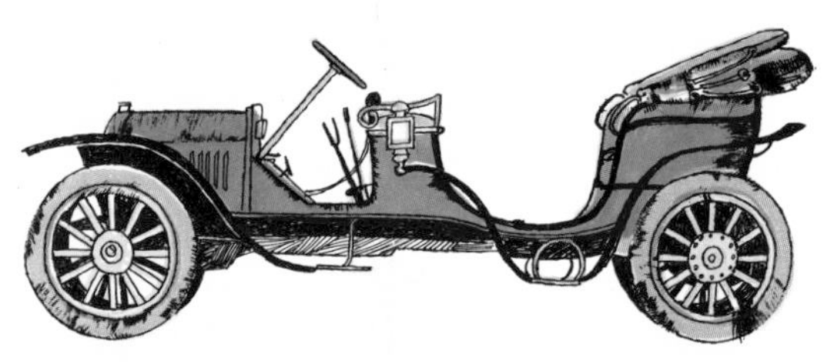

**Studebaker 20 (1911)**

**Chevrolet Baby Grand (1912)**

**White (1912).** This was one of the first Whites equipped with an internal combustion engine, after the American firm decided, in 1911, to stop making steam engines from then on. This car belonged to President Theodore Roosevelt, a devoted client of the firm for years.

field, in both America and Europe. General Motors sprang up practically out of nothing, due to the practical genius of William C. Durant (1860–1947). Durant began his career when still very young, building light horse-drawn carriages with a partner, about 1885. It was then just a short step from the carriage to the car. In 1904, Durant took over Buick for very little money, since it was on the verge of bankruptcy; he reorganized it from top to bottom, with a brand new gamut of models. From the day he entered the automobile manufacturing field, William C. Durant followed his conviction that a great automobile firm must offer the widest possible choice of models so as to follow the client in his evolution—that is, as he climbed up the social ladder. These are the first signs of that theory of consumption of goods that Henry Ford codified a few years later.

Durant carried Buick to the top in just a few years. Famous as a great industrialist, he then tried to create a large automobile trust, in 1908, which was to include Buick, Ford, Reo, and Maxwell-Briscoe. This plan was never completed. On September 16, 1908, Durant founded the General Motors Company and in a couple of years merged with or bought out

**Buick Roadster (1910).** This was one of the many models offered by this firm after W. C. Durant's reorganization of the company. It had an engine with four aligned cylinders.

**Oldsmobile (1912)**

**"Packard Six" (1912)**

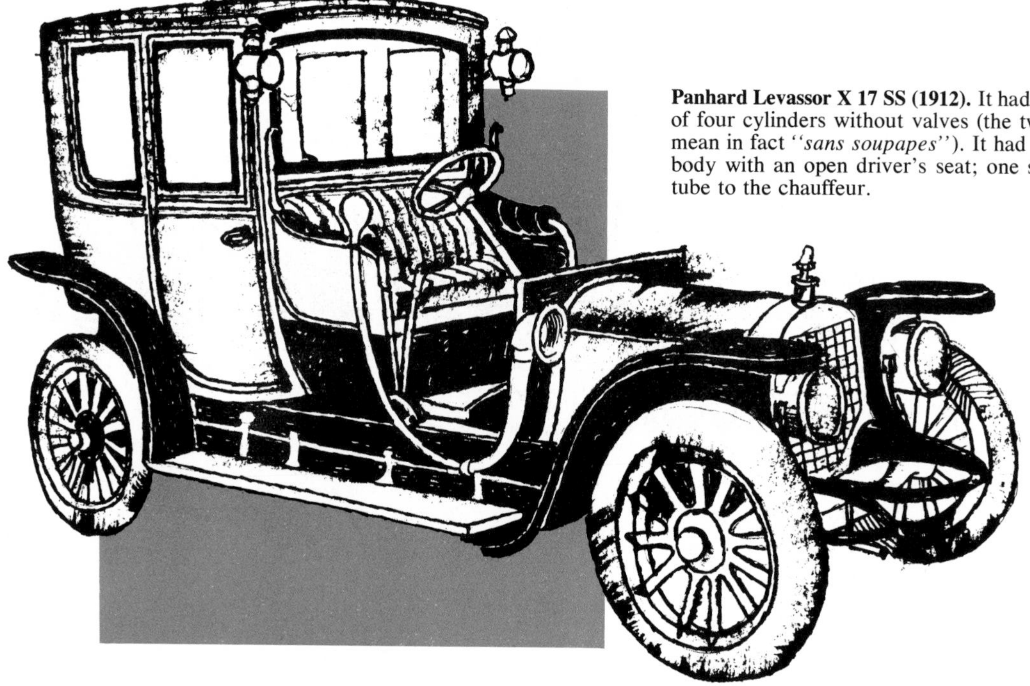

**Panhard Levassor X 17 SS (1912).** It had a Knight engine of four cylinders without valves (the two letters "SS" mean in fact *"sans soupapes"*). It had a coupé de ville body with an open driver's seat; one spoke through a tube to the chauffeur.

for a small sum of money Cadillac, Carter, Elmore, Ewing, Oakland, Oldsmobile, Welch, and other less important brands. As a result of economic difficulties in 1910, Durant was forced to give up the presidency of General Motors to Charles W. Nash, another pioneer of the American automobile industry and founder of the firm that was later to bear his name. However, Durant did not retire from the field and a year later founded Chevrolet, which from the thirties on was to become the most popular American car. The immediate success of Chevrolet led to Durant's return, in 1915, to the presidency of General Motors; GM, we need hardly add, bought Chevrolet in 1918. A sudden tumble in the value of General Motors stock, from $400 down to $12, forced Durant to retire from the company once and for all. He later founded the Durant Motors Company, transformed in

**Vauxhall Prince Henry (1913).** A four-cylinder engine that developed 75 hp let this machine reach a maximum speed of 120 km/h and maintain it even in long-distance travel. This quality and its excellent road holding ability made it one of the era's most popular touring cars.

**Opel (1914)**

1927 into Consolidated Motors, with the obvious intention of making war on General Motors. Consolidated did turn out many and at times excellent cars (apart from the Durant, it produced the Dort, Stars, and Flint, and it owned the Mason truck factory); but Consolidated couldn't survive the 1929 crash. Durant died in 1947 in New York, the almost-forgotten owner of a chain of restaurants.

The control of General Motors went to Alfred P. Sloan, Jr., after Durant withdrew. Sloan, unlike Ford—and in this he was a better prophet than the "divine mechanic"—was firmly convinced that in every business, even the most active and efficient, there was a need for steady development and constant reorganization. Sloan believed above all in good administration understood as market research, imposition of a certain "need" for consumption, and a continual contribution of new ideas by new men in the executive sector of the business. Ford, on the contrary, was stubbornly convinced that a line of production—no matter of what kind—should be followed through at all costs once it was established; he was a firm believer in his own actions and inventions and supported them to the end. Ford was a real precursor, but unable to accept any valuable contribution from others. In other words, he was an extremely proud man.

He was the last American car maker to adopt hydraulic brakes in a nation that had

**Lancia Theta (1914).** The first cars made by Lancia in 1908 were called "Alfa." From that date and until 1931, the year in which the "Artena" and "Astura" models were launched, all the firm's models were called by letters of the Greek alphabet. The "Theta" had a four-cylinder, 70 hp engine; it was the first European car to use a mass-produced electrical system.

**Hispano-Suiza Alfonso XIII 2.5 liters (1913).** Built in Barcelona by Swiss engineer Marc Birkigt, this was one of the first sports cars to be mass produced, apart from being one of the fastest of its time. Many versions of this model were made; the best-known and at the same time the most powerful was the 3.6-liter.

**Peugeot Bébé (1913).** The French firm gave this name to a small 652 cc car it launched in 1902. But the most successful model was that designed by Ettore Bugatti and produced from 1913 to 1916. This version had a four-cylinder, 855 cc, 6 hp engine.

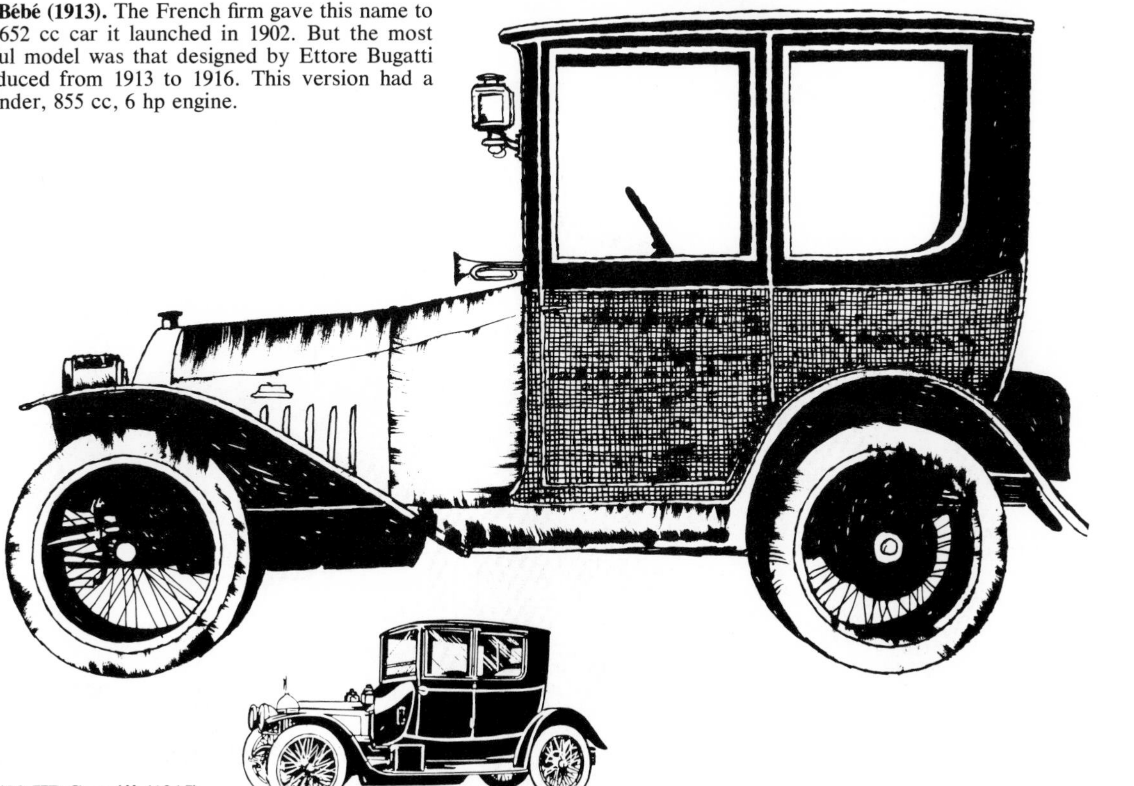

**Daimler "20 HP Coupé" (1915)**

# RENAULT

## A TAXI FOR THE MARNE

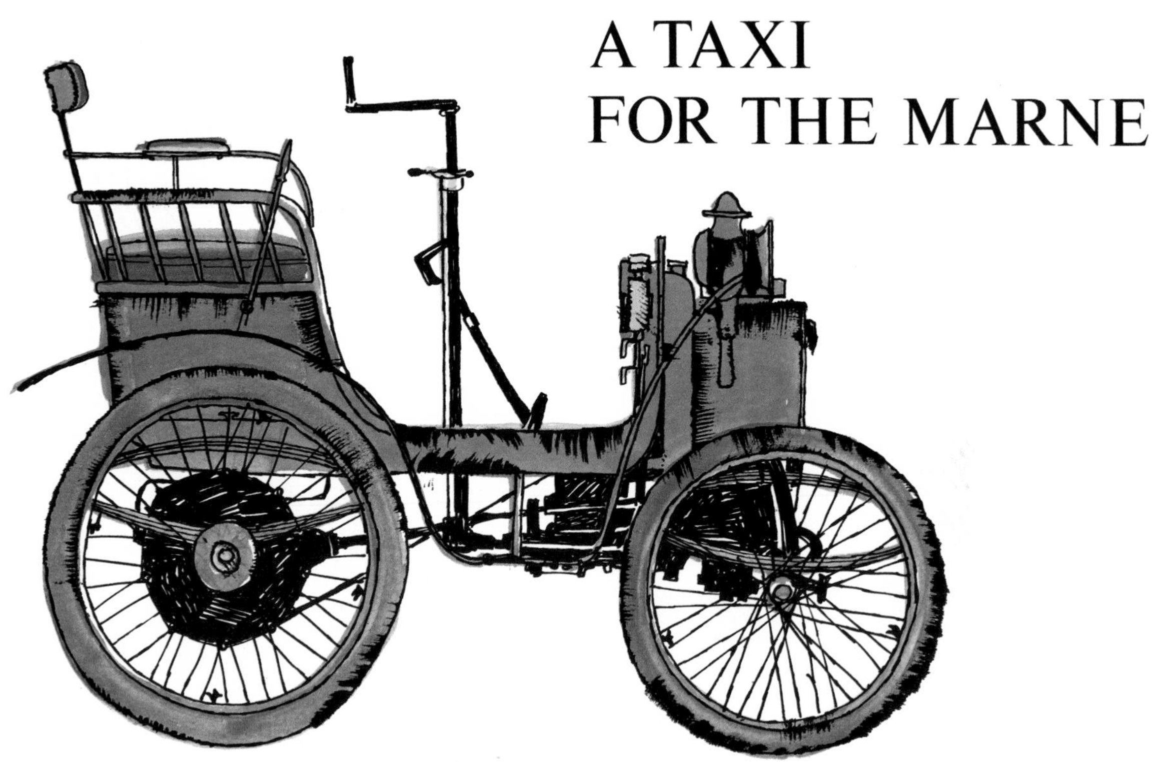

**Voiturette, Type A (1899).** The first Renault car. It had a De Dion air-cooled front engine with 1¾ hp; the gear box had direct transmission in the top gear, and the maximum speed was 36 km/h.

**Voiturette, Type C (1900).** This car had a one-cylinder, 3½ hp motor.

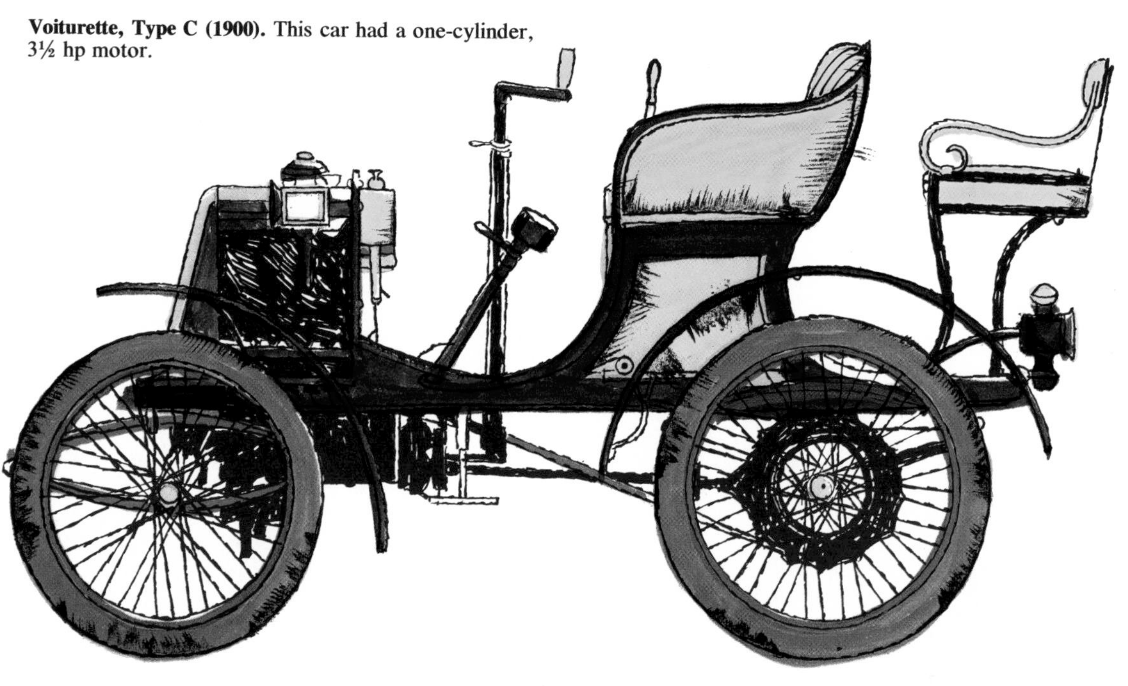

# RENAULT

**Marne Taxi (1906).** This robust "fiacre," the AG model, was the most popular taxi in Paris in the years that preceded the First World War. It had a two-cylinder, 1.2-liter engine. Thousands of these taxis were effective in stopping the German advance on Paris by permitting French troops to reach the front quickly.

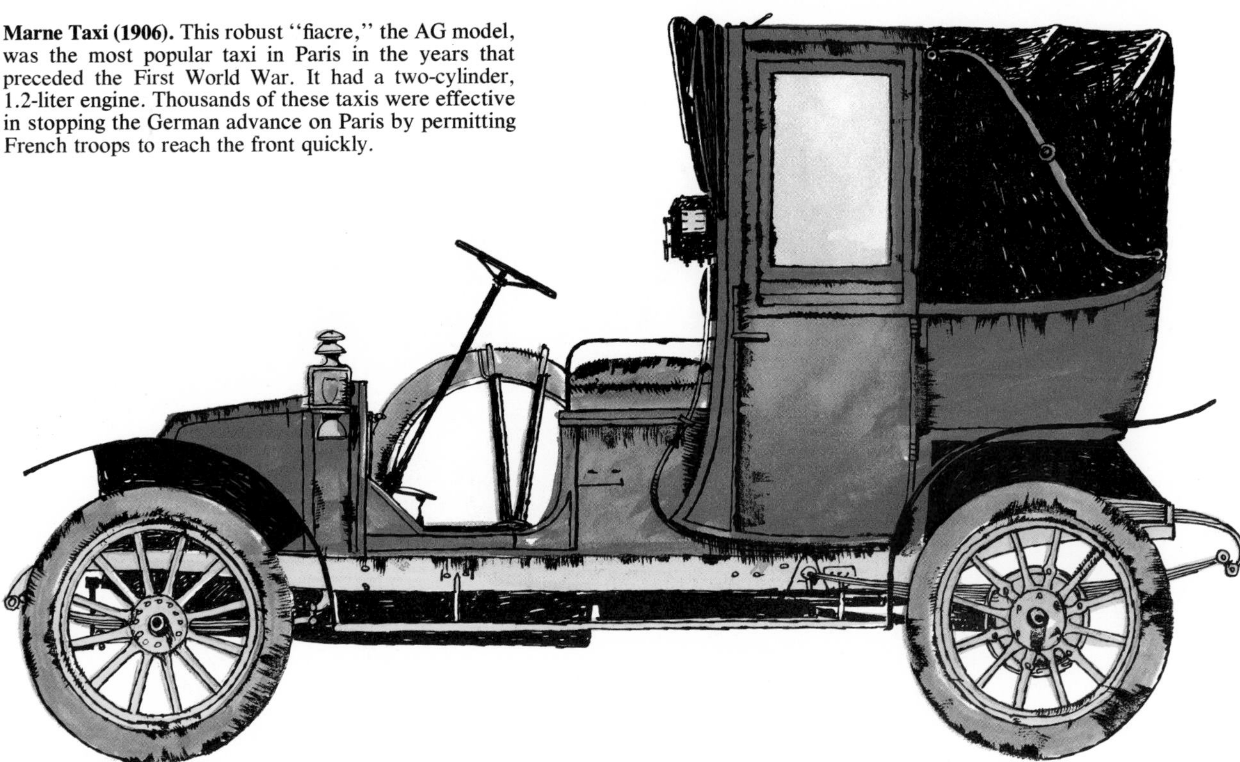

There are at least three events in the history of Louis Renault that would suffice to change the destiny of any man: his patent on the direct-transmission gear box; the part his taxis played in saving France during the First World War; and his having opened his factory—perhaps in the hope of saving it—to the Germans in the Second World War. The last was certainly the most tragic event in the life of Louis Renault for it led to his being imprisoned in 1944 and to the confiscation of his plant by the government. Louis Renault did not survive the blow and died that same year. The other two events made the Paris firm into France's most important automobile industry.

Even though the first car designed by Louis Renault used the famous De Dion two-cylinder, 3½ hp engine, everything else was highly original. It had a new 3-speed-and-reverse gear box incorporating a direct top gear which was quickly patented by Renault. This patent turned out to be an unexpected gold mine for the French inventor. It not only established his right to an invention already claimed by others (in fact, the Décauville of 1898, which came out a year before Renault's car, had direct-transmission gears, but no one had thought of patenting the idea), but it also brought him substantial royalties from all the firms that had used that kind of gear box during the early years of the new

**Torpedo (1912).** With a six-cylinder, 35 hp engine.

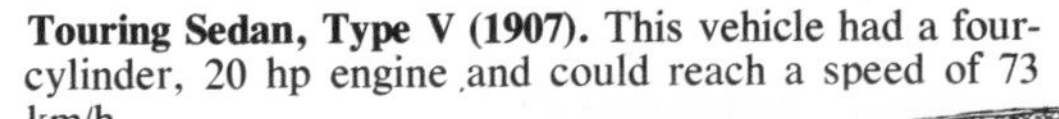

**Touring Sedan, Type V (1907).** This vehicle had a four-cylinder, 20 hp engine and could reach a speed of 73 km/h.

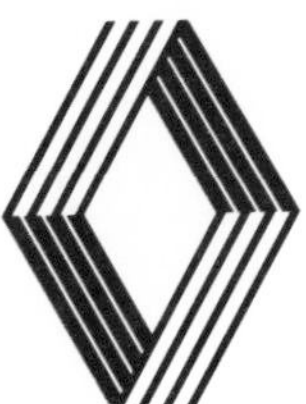

# RENAULT

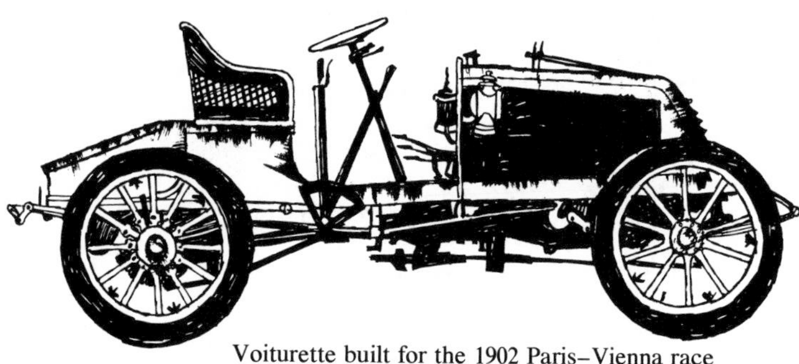
Voiturette built for the 1902 Paris–Vienna race

century—and there were many of them, in view of the utility of the invention.

Renault's claims for royalties were strengthened by the fact that the Copperau factory had objected, and lost its case when Renault went to the courts. The enormous royalties collected by the young industrialist were used to enlarge his plant. The result was that his firm was the leader on the French market until the First World War. For instance, almost every taxi in Paris in those years was a Renault. And the best tanks were by Renault, too; they were agile and easy to maneuver, with a revolving cannon turret, and were used by the Allied belligerents at the start of the First World War. But despite the Renault tanks, in 1914 the Germans came within cannon range of Paris and the range of the shots of "Big Bertha," the largest cannon ever made, which moved on rail tracks. The French counteroffensive, headed by General Gallieni, succeeded in blocking the Germans at the Marne, due to the action of General Maunouri and to the rapid

Voiturette built for the Grand Prix of the A.C.F. of 1906.

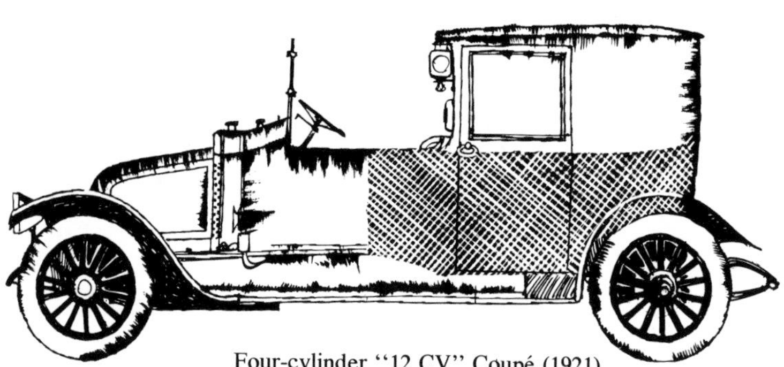
Four-cylinder "12 CV" Coupé (1921)

Coupé de Ville "18 CV" (1923)

Tous-temps by Million-Guiet

Five-seater Torpedo

Three-seater Cabriolet

Convertible Sedan by Binder

# RENAULT

requisition of a thousand Renault taxis (of the Fiacre AG 1910 type) which circulated throughout Paris. This was the only way in which a huge number of French soldiers could reach the front and stop the German advance. As a monument to the Renault taxi's contribution to the victory, one of these cars is carefully preserved in the Invalides Museum in Paris.

The postwar period saw Louis Renault still at war, but this time metaphorically; the battle was with the new manufacturer André Citroën. The latter, using American production techniques and a huge publicity campaign, tried at all costs to dethrone the Renault firm from its position as the top French car industry—and partly succeeded, due to the incredible acceptance of the small and popular Citroën "5 CV." But in the 1930s Renault took over the market once more. His rival's financial misfortunes—which came despite the superior mechanical quality of Citroën cars—worked to his advantage.

Reinastella (1929). It had an eight-cylinder engine.

Manoquatre Sedan (1933)

Three-seater Torpedo

Sedan by Weymann

Two- or three-seater Cabriolet

Cabriolet by Letourneur and Marchand

Monastella Convertible Cabriolet (1929)

Nervasport (1932). This car had an eight-cylinder engine.

Nerva Grand Sport (1937)

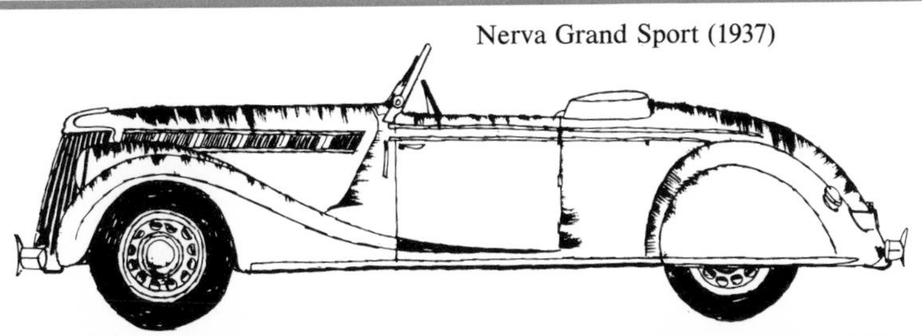

**Panhard Levassor Sport Skiff (1913).** Built by the body maker Labourdette, this car was called "skiff" because of its nautical appearance. It was covered with a three-ply layer of wood and did not have doors. The long hood and small windshield gave it a streamlined appearance.

become the standard bearer of that way of braking—thanks to the research of Californian Malcolm Loughead, who, from 1920 on (after founding Lockheed), began licensing his patent to the major automobile industries.

He was also a steady and stubborn supporter of rigid-axle suspension with transversal leaf springs, even in the forecarriage. Not until 1948, after his death, did the Ford company adopt independent front suspension.

Even though Ford himself was a prophet of the "marketing" perspective, he was always opposed to any kind of market research, the use of which he was unable to imagine, and to the artificial creation of early obsolescence in products when they could go on functioning for many years.

Ford was also against any kind of group leadership of his company and rejected a more sophisticated type of bookkeeping in favor of that which made use of recycled envelopes—envelopes, once opened, were turned over and used again to save paper. Ford used this system for many years, and only the immense success of the Model T convinced him to spend a few more dollars for paper and office supplies.

Alfred P. Sloan, Jr., perhaps the first real "manager"—in the more modern meaning of the term—in the automobile industry, was

**Oldsmobile "Touring 45 A" (1918)**

**Packard Twin Six (1916).** Packard began producing its cars with a modified Winton model. It later offered a vast range of high-class cars, among them the Model C, famous for having done the San Francisco–New York route in sixty-one days, the Model L, which inaugurated the classic Packard radiator, and, last, the Model Twin Six, the world's first twelve-cylinder car to be mass produced (until 1923).

**Itala "22/35 HP" (1912)**

**Opel (1917)**

**Super-Fiat dorsay torpedo (1921).** The Super-Fiat was a luxury car produced in very few examples and with two different kinds of body. It had a twelve-cylinder, 6805 cc, 80 hp V engine.

**Fiat 501 (1919).** This was the first small-displacement (1460) Fiat to be built after the First War. It was a great success, and more than 45,000 machines were produced between 1919 and 1926.

made of far different stuff. If a car did not have the success hoped for—because, perhaps, it did not function to perfection—he was ready to suspend production of that model after only a few months; that was the case with the 1923 Chevrolet with an air-cooled engine. Unlike Ford, Sloan thought it necessary, as we have noted, to offer the market a large range of models (which nevertheless made use of as many common parts as possible); he also believed in a more subtle type of marketing and was always ready to listen to suggestions from his collaborators; and, finally, he always adopted the most modern and up-to-date methods of administration. Sloan did have at least one trait in common with Henry Ford, though: he was a superb organizer of his own and other people's work.

While Ford, Durant, and Sloan made great contributions to the use of the automobile throughout the world, much is also owed to those who made of the machine the highest technical expression of their time. There were, for example, the efforts of Bugatti, Royce, Lancia, Citroën—and Marc Birkigt of Hispano-Suiza.

When the Hispano-Suiza firm was founded in Barcelona in 1904, with Spanish capital

**Rolls-Royce Continental (1913).** Driven by Radley, it won the famous "Alpine Trials" in 1913. Note the unique radiator cover and the electric headlights adopted especially for this meet.

**Crane Simplex, Model 5 (1918).** Designed by Henry M. Crane, this was one of the most important American cars. It was built with infinite care and attention—so much so that the first buyer got an unconditional lifetime guarantee! It had a six-cylinder engine with 9-liter displacement.

**Studebaker (1913)**

**Studebaker "Light 6" (1921)**

**Isotta Fraschini, Type 8 (1920).** These cars, elegant and very expensive, were mainly produced for the American market. They were very sought-after as prestige models by kings, tycoons, and famous actors. The model shown here, with a body by Cesare Sala, had an eight-cylinder, 80 hp engine, and also had brakes on all four wheels.

but Swiss technical supervision, Marc Birkigt was only twenty-six years old; but he was already famous in the Swiss railroad world as a designer of rail vehicles. Birkigt viewed the activity of Hispano as a way of avoiding the dull life in Geneva. In 1904, the brilliant Swiss designer—who many years later was to be awarded the degree of engineer *honoris causa* by the Zurich Polytechnical Institute—prepared a "double phaeton" model that was quite large and extremely well designed. Just two years later he commanded the attention of the automobile world with his "20/24," a four-cylinder, 3758 cc machine with some noteworthy technical features. And, in fact, note was taken by Alfonso XIII, king of Spain and a well-known automobile fancier. After turning out some fine sports cars, Hispano launched (in 1911) the legendary "15 T," a four-cylinder, 3604 cc model that was named "Alfonso" in honor of the Spanish ruler. The "15 T" was a low-slung car, powerful and endowed with excellent performance, as well as with fine gearing (first with three, then with four gears) and a precise steering mechanism. It easily won, not only numerous sports laurels, but also the reputation for first-rate mechanical quality to be found in every Hispano-Suiza which is legendary even today.

A great contribution to the firm's reputation was supplied by the designing and practical realization by Birkigt of a still-famous V-8 airplane engine with air cooling and a timing system with valve control by an overhead

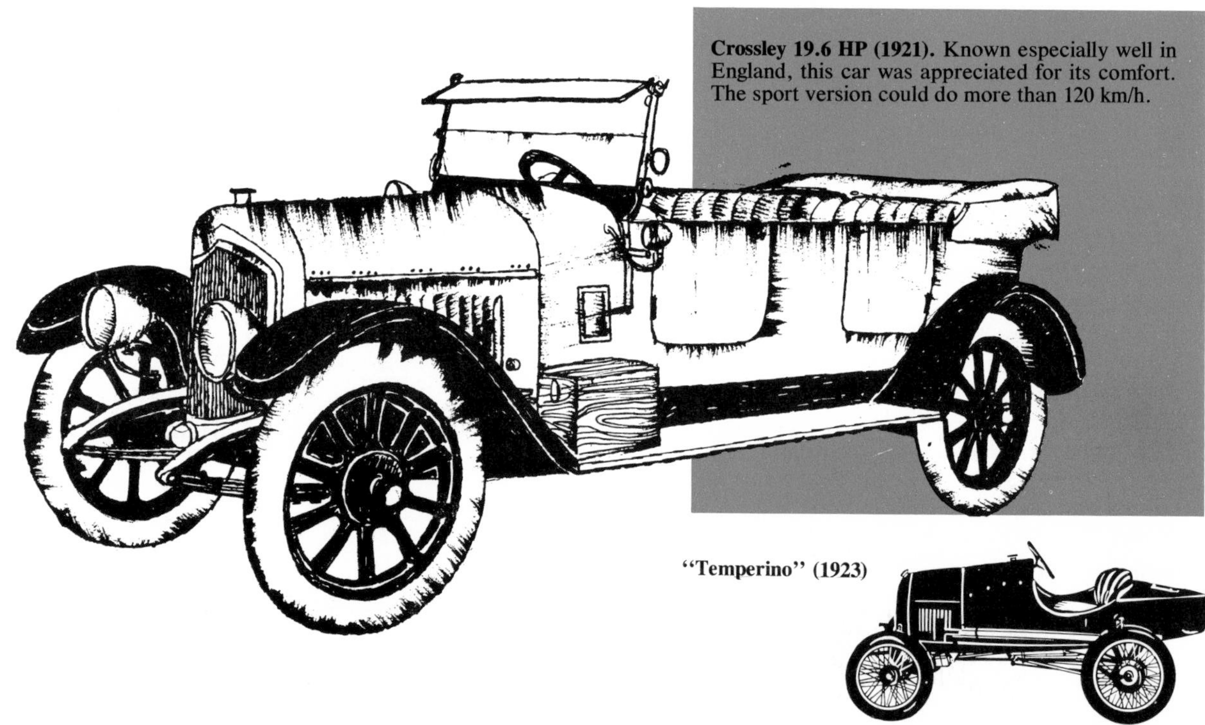

**Crossley 19.6 HP (1921).** Known especially well in England, this car was appreciated for its comfort. The sport version could do more than 120 km/h.

**"Temperino" (1923)**

**Fiat 520 coupé (1927).** The 520 was presented at the Paris Motor Salon in 1927 as the Turin firm's luxury model. It had a six-cylinder engine and was the first Fiat car with coil ignition and left-hand drive.

camshaft for each bank of cylinders. This motor had immediate success and was produced during the First World War in France—where Hispano had opened a factory in 1911—and on license in Great Britain and the United States. When the war ended, the Birkigt V-8 served as a model for a number of American car engines in the 1920s. (In some cases, like the 1921 Wills-Sainte Claire, it was outright plagiarism.)

The war helped turn a number of small plants into big industries. This was the case with Hispano-Suiza, but also with the Italian Isotta Fraschini and Fiat firms; the latter got important military orders for a water-cooled machine-gun and a very strong truck, the "18 BL." War enlarged the automobile industry to dimensions hitherto undreamed of: in 1917, Italy reached a record production of 25,280 cars, a record only surpassed in 1924.

André Citroën, a talented engineer short of cash but full of ideas, created for the French army—out of nothing—a great weapons factory right in Paris on the banks of the Seine. Once the factory had been transformed into an automobile plant right after the war, it produced the first Citroën cars. At the start, the Citroën was far from being the avant-garde machine it later became. The French manufacturer merely limited himself to applying in Europe the techniques he had learned during his frequent trips across the Atlantic from Ford and other great builders in the field: that is, mass production through assembly lines which produced highly standardized models that were fully equipped. (Citroën did not offer chassis for body fitting, and its cars were already furnished with electrical circuits, spare wheels, etc.—all unusual for that time.) Later, Citroën added all-steel bodies for the first time in Europe. But Citroën caused the great revolution in 1934 when it introduced its famous "Traction," the first "all-in-front" vehicle to be mass produced.

Long before André Citroën, however, another new manufacturer had upset the automobile world: Vincenzo Lancia. Born in 1881, he began his activity when very young with Giovanni Battista Ceirano and went over to Fiat in 1899, after it bought out Ceirano and

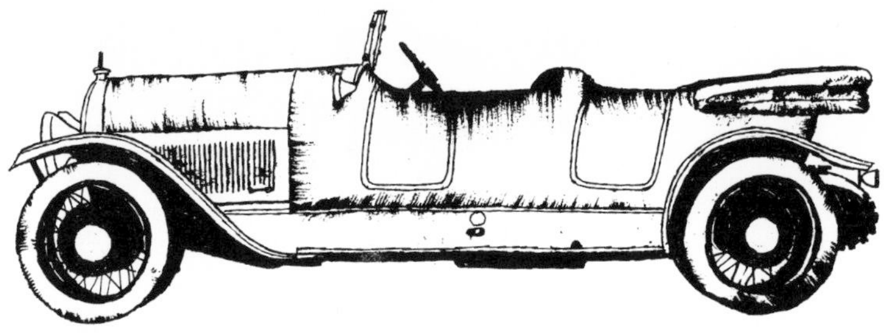

**Darracq V8 (1921).** Not a very manageable car; it was only mass produced for about a year, and it had 3.2-liter displacement.

**Opel (1925)**

**Bianchi S4 (1925)**

**Chrysler "Six" (1924)**

# AUSTIN

# THE MAGNIFICENT SEVEN

Four-seater sedan with leatherette body.

Two-seater Wembley sedan by Gordon England

Two-seater coupé by Mulliner

Four-seater sedan with body designed by Mulliner

# AUSTIN

On a much smaller scale, the Austin Seven was for the English what the Ford was for the Americans—the first step to mass motorization. Herbert Austin, builder and creator of the Seven, put his car on the market in 1922 with the slogan "The Motor for the Millions." The Seven, of which 300,000 were made, was a success only in England but not abroad where it was built by a special permit (Rosengart in France, Dixi and B.M.W. in Germany, Datsun in Japan, and in the United States by the American Austin Company).

Austin, after starting production of the Seven and fixing the price at 225 pounds, but before launching it in the market, took a trip to the United States to visit the Ford plant to study the success of the "Model T." He then hurried back to England where he made a change in the production of his car by using more steel in the body. This decreased hand labor considerably and permitted Austin to reduce his price by 60 pounds by the time the car was launched. With such a low price, the Seven was an immediate commercial success; in fact, its cost was just a little higher than the price of a motorcycle with a sidecar or a cyclecar (small vehicles with motorcycle engines, three to four wheels and a maximum of three seats).

The Seven, named for its fiscal power according to British standards, was a little less than 2.70 meters long (35 cm. less than a modern "Mini" or a Fiat 126) and less than 1.20 meters wide. It was equipped with a water-cooled, 4 cylinder in-line engine, displacing 696 cc (bore and stroke of 54 and 76.2 mm) which later evolved to a displacement of 747.5 cc by an increase of the bore to 56 mm. Originally, the Seven weighed only 360 kg., had a torpedo body, two doors and two seats, with two additional small seats in the back for children. It had a three-gear shift and a maximum speed of 60 km per hour, which changed to 80 km in later models with a four-gear shift in 1933. Like the Ford Model T, the Seven was constantly improved and the price lowered during its long life of seventeen years. The most economic version, the Torpedo (nicknamed "Chummy" by English motorists) reached the low price of 118 pounds in 1932, equivalent to about $1,000 in today's market. As the years passed, other versions were added to the original "Chummy," among them a small sporty "spider," which was guaranteed a top speed of 80 miles per hour, and a sedan with the rear of the chassis reinforced, since at first "Chummies" had frequent breaks and cracks in the body due to the excessive weight put on the back seats (for instance, two adults instead of two children). Unfortunately, the brakes were the weak spots of the Seven; even in the last models of 1938, when brakes had also been applied to the front wheels, the braking power was insufficient and the pedal was very stiff.

Two-seater fake cabriolet with body by Austin

The last series of Chummy-Torpedo

Four-seater regular sedan

Four-seater sedan by Swallow Sidecars

MG (1923). The first MG. It was built by Cecil Kimber, director of the "Morris Garage" and won many racing competitions, which led W. R. Morris to start mass producing it in 1924.

took over not only the equipment but also the employees of the latter. Vincenzo Lancia was soon put to work in the racing department of Fiat; and he represented the great Turin plant in many races in both Europe and the United States, winning a great number. He founded Lancia with a partner in 1906, but because of a fire which almost completely destroyed the machinery he was unable to present his first model, the "Alpha," until 1908.

From the start, the Lancia was noted for the great care with which it was built and the novelty of its technical apparatus. But the masterpiece of the young Italian designer and manufacturer was the "Lambda," officially presented to the world in 1923, the first mass-produced car furnished with independent

**Hispano-Suiza Boulogne (1924).** Famous for having been driven by André Dubonnet, this was the era's most modern car, due to its mechanical setup. Note the characteristic body with its wooden fillets.

**Morris Bullnose (1924).** This car was extremely easy to drive; it had a very smooth gear box and clutch—to a point where use of the clutch was no longer necessary.

front suspension. Another, and no less important, "Lambda" first was the use of a load-bearing body, replacing the chassis which had to support both the mechanical parts and the body. In the "Lambda" the body framework bore the weight of the parts, the panels, and the other elements of the body itself.

Vincenzo Lancia produced other important models after the "Lambda," among them the "Augusta," the "Artena," and the "Astura," all with load-bearing bodies, independent front suspension, and V engines. In 1936, he presented the "Aprilia," a splendid and very modern car.

Let us now go back in time—to England. Certainly the greatest English designer and

**Alvis 12/50 (1925).** This should be considered a sports car rather than a racing car. In fact, its size and excessive weight kept it from competing successfully with other cars of the same displacement, such as Bugatti and Aston Martin. It was available in both two- and four-seater versions and had a 1500 cc engine (a 1700 cc engine was available upon request).

**Chrysler "Six" (1925)**

manufacturer of automobiles in the early years of this century was Henry Royce, who in 1903 was already turning out extremely well-finished machines in a limited quantity. One of these cars came into the possession of C. S. Rolls, a man whose passion for cars was only exceeded by his wealth. Ecstatic over the precision and efficiency of the Royce, Rolls convinced its maker to set up a partnership for producing and selling high-class cars. Naturally, Rolls would contribute the money and Royce the talent.

The company was founded in December 1904 and legalized a year later, when production was already under way, using the famous Greek temple style radiator. In 1906, little more than a year from its birth, the Rolls-Royce company presented the legendary "Silver Ghost" (a name that came from its exceptionally silent performance); this car was produced for nineteen consecutive years, until 1925. It maintained the same high performance level and had a well-merited success. Quite a few "Silver Ghosts" are still functioning, and some of them have traveled more than a million kilometers—not unusual for a Rolls-Royce.

Royce and Ettore Bugatti had much in common: both were perfectionists. The talented Italian sought after perfection from the age of twenty, when he worked for the Prinetti & Stucchi tricycle factory in Milan. But perhaps Bugatti's most fertile period of creativity came around 1910, when he worked as an independent designer. In that period, he designed some wonderful engines for the De Dietrich, and the unforgettable Peugeot "Bebé" of 1913, the real forerunner of all later utilitarian passenger cars.

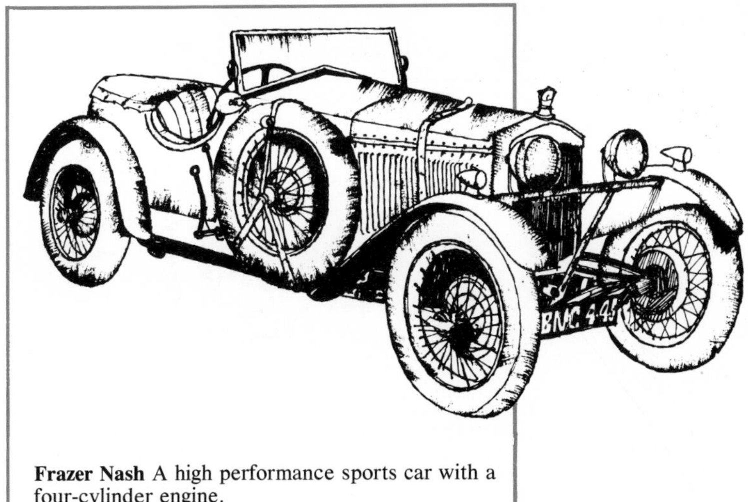


**Frazer Nash** A high performance sports car with a four-cylinder engine.

**Bugatti, Type 30 (1926).** Endowed with a 2000 cc engine, it could do 130 km/h. This car, directly derived from the prototype—it won second and third place in the 1922 Grand Prix of France—started off Bugatti's production of eight-aligned-cylinder engines.

**Bugatti, Type 43 (1927).** A fast sports car which had the engine of the type 35 B racing car, and could do a maximum speed of 160 km/h.

**Isotta Fraschini, type 8A (1926)**

**Pierce-Arrow, Type 80 (1926)**

A daring American flier dropped out of the night on Le Bourget—and won the adulation of the world.
An inspired American golfer conquered famed St. Andrews—and received the applause of kings.
A new American motor car swept into the spotlight scarcely four months ago—and encountered a public reception once undreamed-of. . . . A brilliant new car: vivid, poised, distinguished, staunch—the Oakland All-American Six. A car with all those qualities Americans admire . . . a car on which America has already bestowed success!
OAKLAND
ALL-AMERICAN SIX

LINCOLN
Sport Phaeton (by Locke)

8-88 ROADSTER $1995
80 Miles Per Hour
130-Inch Wheelbase
Five Passenger Capacity
Door for Rear Seat
AUBURN AUTOMOBILE COMPANY, AUBURN, INDIANA
AUBURN

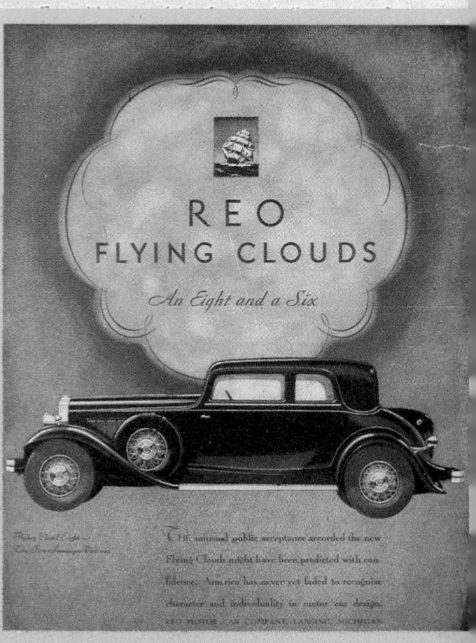
REO
FLYING CLOUDS
An Eight and a Six
THE unusual public acceptance accorded the new Flying Clouds might have been predicted with confidence. America has never yet failed to recognize character and individuality in motor car design.
REO MOTOR CAR COMPANY, LANSING, MICHIGAN

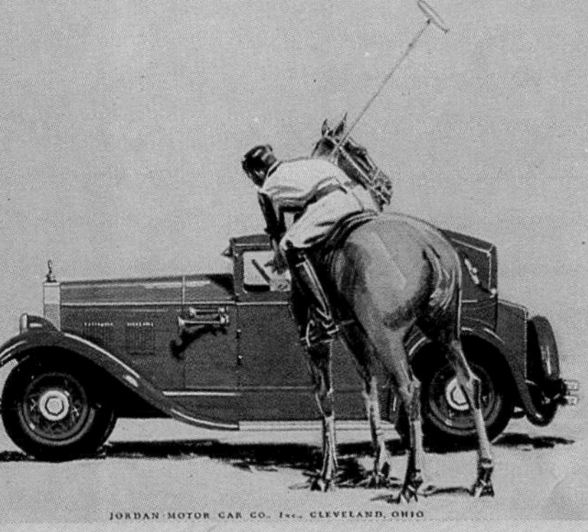

# The golden age

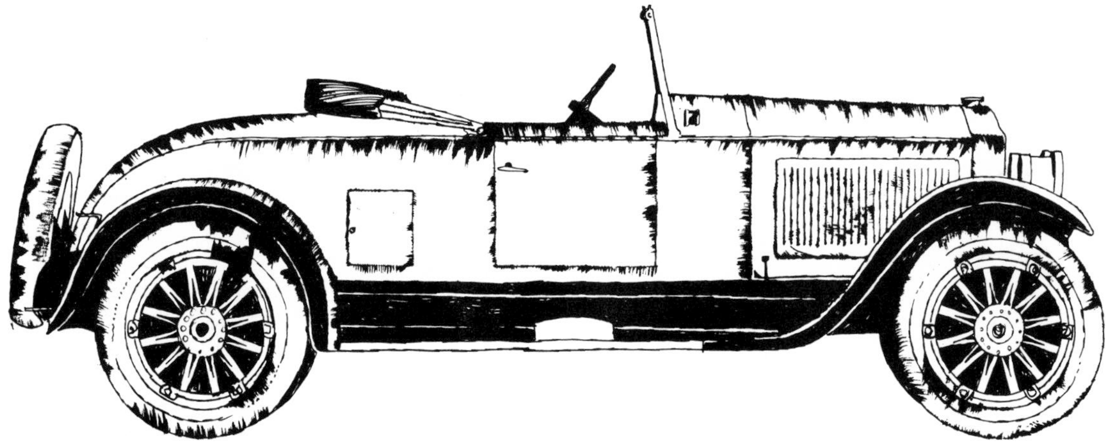

**Buick (1927).** One of the most important cars made by this firm, which was founded in 1903 by David Buick, taken over in 1904 by William C. Durant, and absorbed by the General Motors group in 1908.

**Rolls-Royce Phantom I (1928).** After the First World War, the English car manufacturers began mass producing automobiles again, with renewed enthusiasm; and Rolls-Royce, which had stopped turning out the "Silver Ghost" in 1926 after nineteen years of production, presented this new "Phantom" with an extremely streamlined look. (Shown here is the version by the London body maker Barker.)

**Cord L-29 (1930).** The first machine produced by Errett Lobban Cord, former owner of Auburn and Duesenberg, was also the first American car with front-wheel drive to be mass produced. It had an eight-aligned-cylinder Lycoming engine and a maximum speed of 125 km/h.

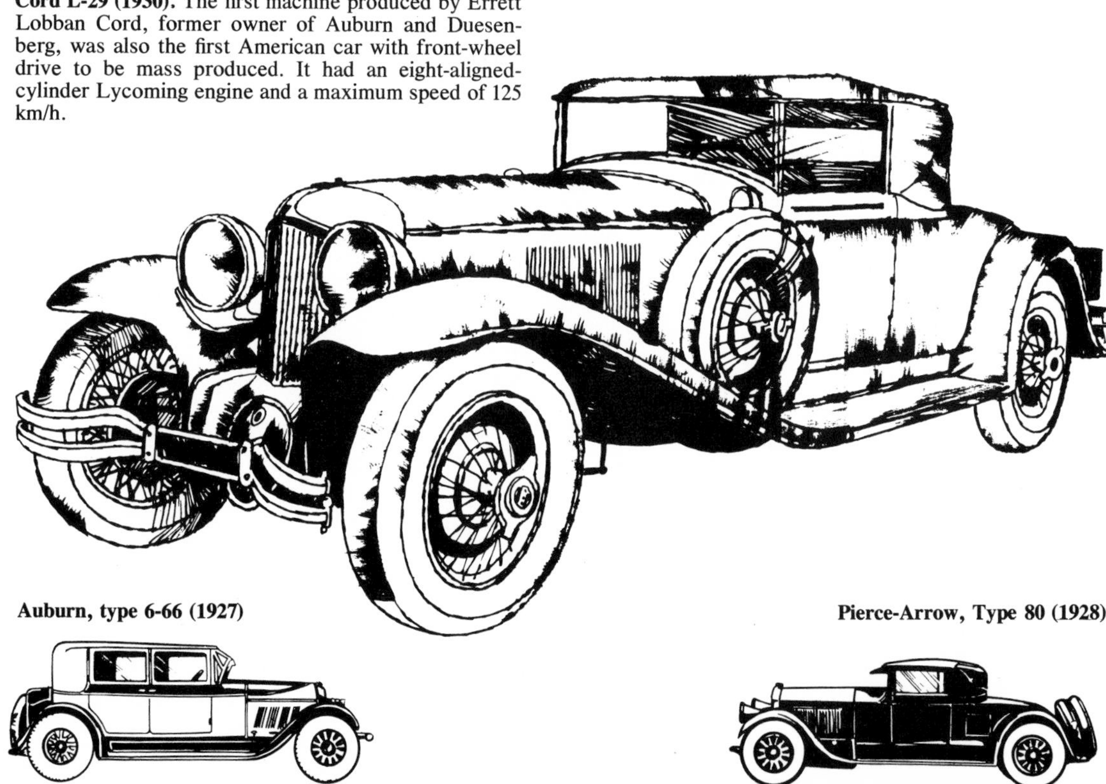

**Auburn, type 6-66 (1927)**

**Pierce-Arrow, Type 80 (1928)**

# The golden age

The "Roaring Twenties" marked a period of great development in the history of the automobile. For instance, in 1929 we discover that 6,274,400 cars were produced in the world, of which 5,337,100 were made in the United States and 262,000 in Canada (which manufactured them on American concession). In other words, America turned out almost 90 percent of the entire world production.

Henry Ford's theories on the consumption of goods ("You don't have to be rich to have a car, but you have to have a car to be rich") had easily seduced the American masses and were catching on in Europe too. At the end of the twenties, more than 26 million automobiles circulated in the United States—that is, one for every five inhabitants; there were more than a million and a half in Great Britain and about as many in France (almost one for every 25–30 inhabitants); Germany lagged behind a bit with 600,000 cars; then came Italy with not quite 250,000. Almost 35 million cars were in circulation all over the world.

But this incredible expansion was dealt a violent blow when on October 24, 1929—"Black Thursday"—the New York stock market collapsed after a short agony. It is hard to describe the effects that the end of American prosperity had on the world economy. America was to export a long period of crisis after her prosperity declined.

Yet it was all predictable, even if no one wanted or knew how to foresee it. The economies of all other nations were solidly bound to that of America, on which they depended for everything: from raw material to semifinished goods, down to the credit granted for importing it all. In fact, America had an absolute need of greater exports to support her strong production efforts, so that the powerful American banks of the time granted long-term, low-interest loans to all the European countries—loans that were obviously meant to finance the purchase of American raw

**Reo Flying Cloud (1929).** In 1904, Ransom Eli Olds, the founder of Oldsmobile, started a new company that took its name from his initials: R.E.O. The model illustrated here had a 6-cylinder engine and could do more than 100 km/h. In 1936, Reo stopped making cars and concentrated exclusively on industrial vehicles.

**Minerva (1927).** Minerva produced cars of very high quality, like the one shown here, and was among the most well-known and successful of the Belgian automobile manufacturers.

materials and manufactured goods. When Wall Street collapsed and the banks quickly tightened their pursestrings, both the Americans and the foreign customers of America were quick to feel the pinch.

So, in 1930, world automobile production sank to 4,130,000, of which 3,515,000 cars were made in America and Canada (about 85 percent of the total). But the bottom was reached in 1932, when world production was 1,873,000 cars, 1,332,000 made in the United States, and barely 60,800 in Canada (for a total of about 74 percent of world production). Only one nation escaped the violent crisis that shook the automobile industry: Great Britain, which between 1929 and 1932 kept her rhythm of production practically unchanged (from 238,800 to 232,700 cars), as well as her rhythm of exportation (from 42,200 to 40,300). In the same period, though, Germany lowered her production from 127,800 to 51,800 cars; Italy from 55,100 to 29,600; France from 224,000 to 163,000; and Canada from 242,100 to 60,800. In 1932, the United States only exported 70,100 cars as against the 546,200 of 1929 (that is, it went from 80 percent to about 40 percent of total world exports of automobiles). Italy too—by then famous for building luxurious cars—was hit hard in her exports: she went from 23,700 cars in 1928 to 6,400 in 1932.

The crisis was a terrible one and served to make the strong manufacturers stronger, wiping out the weak. Some of the most famous names in the blue book of the automobile of the time disappeared. In the end, however, this helped to rationalize production, which was dispersed throughout countless trade names and models, as compared with the consolidation of the field today.

**Lincoln (1928).** Founded by Henry Leland in 1921, this firm was taken over by Henry Ford barely a year later; he wanted these luxury cars to compete with Cadillac.

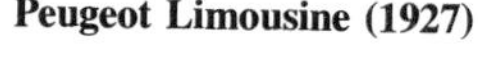

**Peugeot Limousine (1927)**

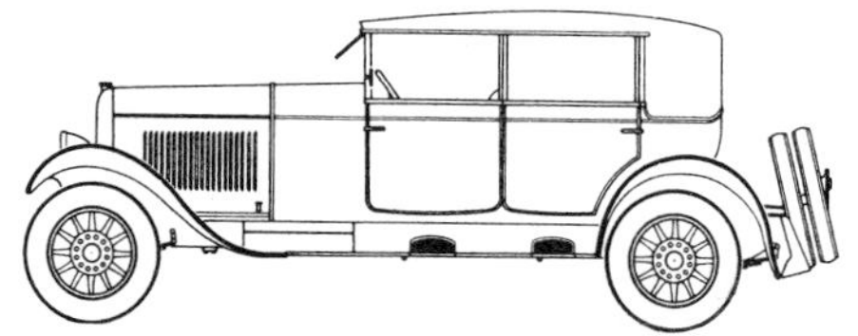

**Peugeot Sedan (1927)**

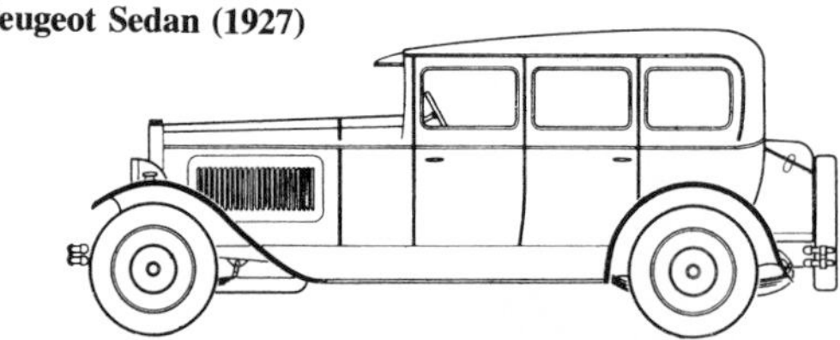

**Stutz 8 Club Coupé (1928).** After producing sports cars, Stutz turned to the luxury car market in 1926. The firm was famous for its eight-cylinder, 96 hp engines and also for the high quality of its finishings.

**Bucciali Double-Huit (1932).** This car, shown fairly often at the Paris Automobile Salon, never got beyond the prototype stage.

**Delage D 8 (1932).** The Delage D 8 line was impressive with its mixture of elegance and sports quality; it had an eight-cylinder, 4050 cc engine.

**Chrysler Imperial Coupé** by Le Baron **(1932).** The first eight-cylinder Chrysler, presented in 1930, was immediately successful, owing to its superb performance and its competitive price. This 1932 ''Imperial'' also had an eight-aligned-cylinder, 6.3-liter engine with 135 hp.

**Peugeot Cabriolet (1927)**

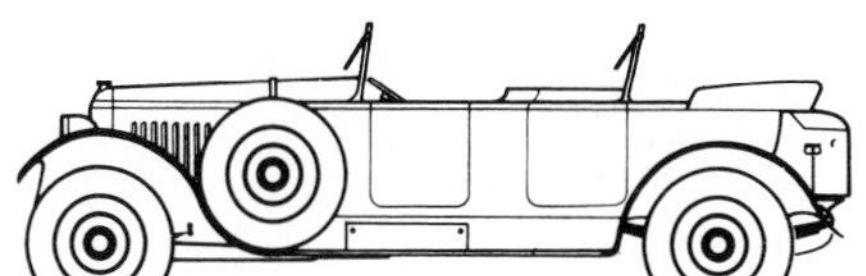

**Peugeot Coupé de Ville (1927)**

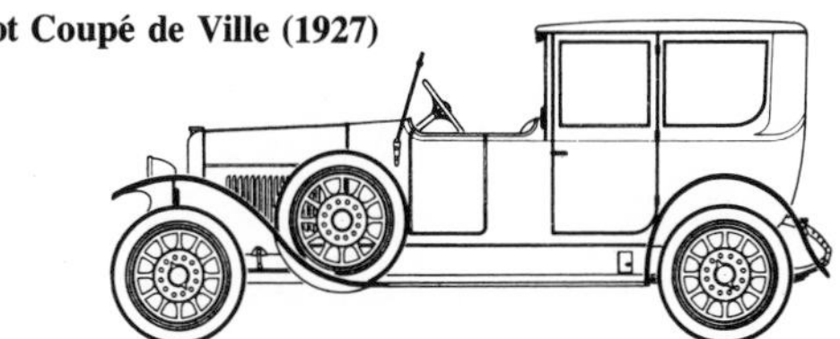

**Marmon 8/69 (1931).** The well-known American firm's cheapest model in the 1930s. It had an eight-aligned-cylinder engine with a lateral valve timing system.

**Bianchi S 5, Viareggio type (1932).** The "S 5" was one of the most economical of the medium-sized Italian cars: it used less than 10 liters of fuel in 100 km. It had a four-cylinder, 1.3-liter, 30 hp engine, with an overhead valve timing system.

**OM Alcyone (1934).** This was the last car made by the Brescia firm, which stopped building passenger cars (but not commercial vehicles) in 1934, after it was taken over by Fiat. It had a six-cylinder, 2198 cc, 60 hp engine.

**Auburn Speedster (1935).** The body was both pleasing and impressive; the Lycoming engine was an eight-cylinder, with 4575 cc and 115 hp. This was one of the cars preferred by sports drivers of the time.

It was during those years that the old industrial tycoons vanished and left their positions to our modern "managers." One-man decisions were replaced by directorate control; single proprietors became countless (and often small) shareholders; life-time jobs turned into constant turnovers in top posts. Many people felt the results of a decision in the automobile factories of that time. The name of the plant came to the fore, and the name of the owner passed into the background; man was surpassed by machines.

Strange as it seems, the most handsome and impressive cars of the golden years—golden years for the automobile, naturally—were almost all born after and not before the tragic collapse of the stock market on Wall Street. And they were almost always the last glories of firms that were shortly to vanish, famous names that did not survive the Great Depression. These names stood for a long, slow, and magnificent swan-song; their products were the unique masterpieces of the greatest artisans of the day.

As we noted, one of the nations hardest hit, apart from the United States, was Italy, which saw her car exports shrink drastically—almost all her production was for the luxury market—after the boom of the 1920s. After the stock market collapse, her car exports represented only 16.9 percent of her production (that is, 7070 cars out of the 41,700 built), in the year 1933.

It was the end of an era. No one wanted to buy splendid cars like the Isotta Fraschini, the Itala, and the Ansaldo. The domestic market was, of course, unable to guarantee an outlet for these great names, and the most important Italian firms were forced to close down. The end of the Isotta Fraschini, undoubtedly the most illustrious name that has ever existed in the Italian automobile world, should be noted in this respect. Led by Giustino Cattaneo, this great firm reached the

**Chevrolet Capitol (1927)**

height of perfection in 1931 when it presented the "8B," the production of which was short-lived. In 1932, when Isotta was at the end of its rope because of the decline in exportation—the cars made by the Milanese firm were almost all destined for foreign purchase—an agreement was made with Ford in America for broad collaboration, especially in the commercial sector. Ford was to guarantee Isotta an exceptional outlet in the American

**Austro-Daimler, ADR 6 type (1933).** With a body by Burgmeister, this car had a six-cylinder, 3614 cc engine that made it one of the company's fastest; in fact, it could do 145 km/h.

**Pierce-Arrow Silver Arrow V 12 (1933).** This vehicle, presented at the Chicago World's Fair, had a 7-liter, 175 hp engine. Ten cars in all were made. It was one of the first aerodynamic cars produced in the United States and had the high price of $10,000.

A six-cylinder **Chrysler Roadster** with a mass-produced body and typically American line, from the end of the 1920s.

**NSU Cabriolet 7/34 PS**

**Auburn Club Coupé (1927)**

# ISOTTA FRASCHINI

## THE DIVINE

The Isotta's moment of glory came around 1930, with the "8 A" and the "8 B," two well-known and impressive cars with eight-aligned-cylinder engines of 7.4-liter displacement. The high society of the day enjoyed the prestige of riding in them.

The immortal "8" was designed by engineer Giustino Cattaneo, also responsible for a series of superb plane engines. In reality, Isotta Fraschini lost in cars all it had earned with plane engines during two world wars. The fact remains that the Milanese plant turned out the best automobiles Italy has ever produced.

Founded in January 1900 with 500,000 lire capital and the aim of selling Renault cars in Italy, Isotta began assembling the French machines very soon, and from 1902 on produced its own chassis on which it mounted the French Aster engines. The firm would probably have been short-lived—as often happened in those days with small car makers, wiped out by frequent crises or taken over by larger manufacturers—if Giustino Cattaneo, a highly talented man full of new ideas, had not come along in 1905. With his technical knowledge and leadership, Isotta was the first to adopt (in 1909) front-wheel brakes. In fact, the firm had patented a mechanism that eliminated the difficulties involved in linking braking mechanically to the directional wheels. Cattaneo also designed a whole series of sports models

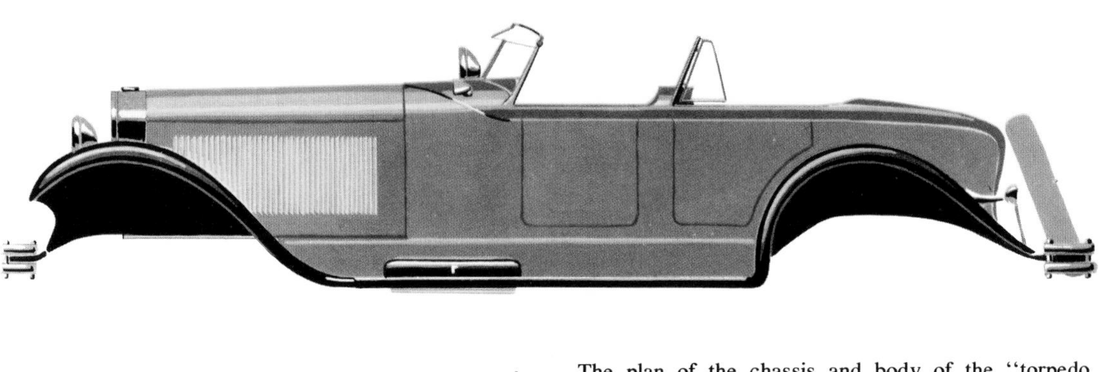

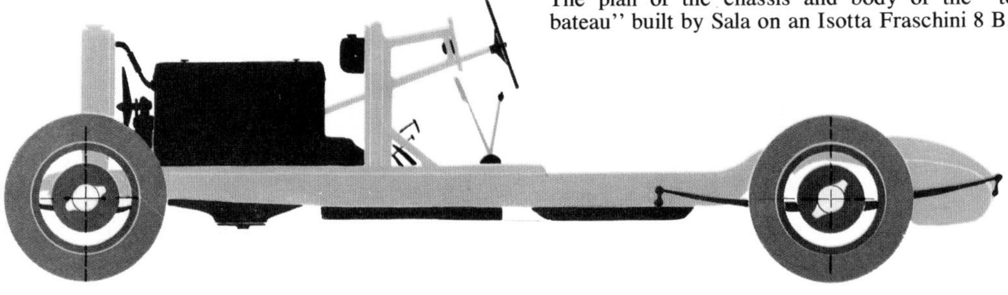

The plan of the chassis and body of the "torpedo bateau" built by Sala on an Isotta Fraschini 8 B.

# ISOTTA FRASCHINI

**8 A Torpedo Sport Bateau (1929).** The "8 A" was the most famous Isotta Fraschini. Like most of the firm's models, the body was by Ercole Castagna.

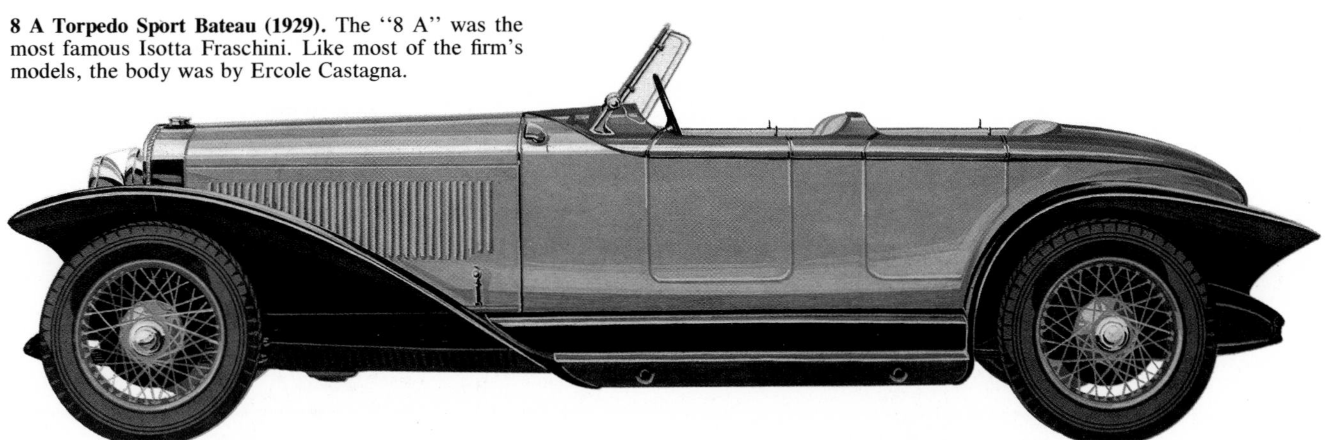

which won recognition and prizes all over the world and began, as far back as 1911, the successful manufacture of engines for airplanes and dirigibles.

During the war, Isotta filled a government order for 4000 airplane engines, and afterward decided to restrict its production and stake everything on a single luxury model, designed by Cattaneo and recognized as his masterpiece. The "8" was presented in August 1919. Its mechanical refinement and accurate construction were recognized at once. Most of the engine and the pistons were made of aluminum; there was an overhead-valve timing system; feeding took place through two Zenith carburetors; the brakes—to be found on all four wheels, of course—used a mechanical brake booster; the gear box had three speeds, and the clutch was of the multidisk type. The engine had a 5902 cc displacement (with a bore and stroke of 85 and 130 mm) and could develop about 80 hp at 2200 rpm.

In 1924, the firm presented the "8 A," with displacement raised to 7370 cc through a bore increase of 10 mm; engine power thus rose to 110–120 hp at 2400 rpm. The brakes too were modified; the diameter was increased, a push-down brake booster employed, and the steering wheel was improved by the addition of a shock absorber. In 1931 the "8 B" came out, even if very few cars of that type were to be built. Among its new features in respect to previous models were the

increased power (135–160 hp at 3000 rpm) due to various improvements in the engine; an improved gear box, now synchronized; and suspension that used hydraulic shock absorbers.

Even though from 1928 on, it was possible to buy an Isotta with a body supplied by the company itself, many clients preferred to buy the chassis alone, and then turn to the best body makers for a luxurious facade for their car.

**Type 8 C Monterosa (1947).** This car, presented at the Paris Salon in 1947, was called "Monterosa" from the name of the street on which the plant stood. It was designed by Fabio Luigi Rapi, one of the creators of Isotta's fame; the car was never produced regularly.

# HISPANO - SUIZA

## THE QUEEN

The 6 A Victoria model (1928)

A coupé built by the body maker Guiet

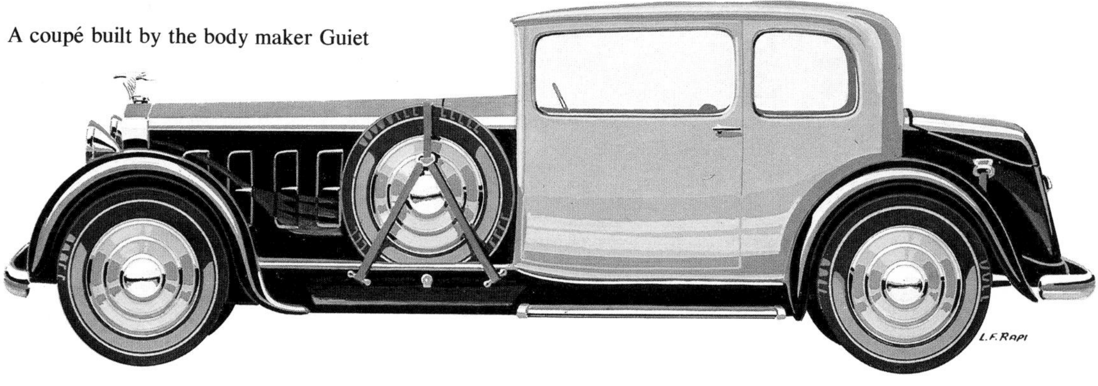

"In the blue book of the automobile, the Hispano-Suiza is the Queen." This phrase, taken from an old catalogue put out by that great firm, gives an idea of the image the Hispano had created for itself—an image that was far from inaccurate.

The Hispano story began in Barcelona, Spain, in 1906. The firm appeared on the market that year with a car that had a modern design and excellent technical performance. It was a 3.7 liter model that soon inspired a 7.5 liter one that already had the feature of a unified engine and gear box. The car, apart from its speed and performance on the road, also had efficient brakes, exceptional road-holding ability, and a superb gear system. These characteristics distinguished the Hispano for years from other top-category cars. One of that era's fastest cars was the famous Hispano "Alfonso."

After the First World War, activity began again in the Barcelona plant, under the stimulus of Marc Birkigt, one of the great names in automobile history and in that of mechanics in general. He designed an excellent eight-cylinder V engine for airplanes, produced during the First World War by twenty-one different manufacturers all over the world. His, too, were all the Hispano models produced until the end of the 1930s.

At the start of the 1920s, the firm moved to Paris, where its most famous models were created. Among these, we should mention the fabulous twelve-cylinder V Hispano produced from 1929 on in two versions: the 9424 cc "68" and the 11,310 cc "68B." The first was capable of 220 hp, the second 250; and the latter, in the coupé version, could reach a speed of 175 km/h.

# A WINGED AUTOMOBILE

A twelve-cylinder sedan (1930).

A twelve-cylinder sedan from the early 1930s.

"Mechanics is not a trade, it's a passion!" So said Gabriel Voisin when someone asked him about his profession, a profession to which the brilliant French builder always gave his all.

Gabriel Voisin came to the automobile after a highly successful career as a plane builder; in fact, the first airplanes built in France were constructed by Voisin Frères and were made almost at the same time as the "flying machines" of the Wright brothers. And the French Air Force fought the First World War with Voisin—as well as Farman and Blériot—planes.

After the war, Voisin gave up planes and threw himself into car making with all his energy—and the young aeronautical engineer had so many new ideas that his cars seemed to have everything but wings. Voisin himself designed all his cars, from the front bumper to the rear. His automobiles were highly original, futuristic—and they were powerful and luxurious as well, with large engines of four, six, eight, and even twelve cylinders.

But Voisin's masterpiece will always be the "C 23," built in the middle 1930s, a powerful car with twelve aligned cylinders created by lining up two six-cylinder, 3-liter engines, one behind the other, so that the motor ended up inside the driving area, "to assure better weight distribution and bring the engine as close as possible to the geometric center of the car," as Voisin declared. With 180 hp and 4000 rpm, the "C 23" could almost reach a speed of 180 km/h—exceptional for those days.

During the twenty-year period in which they were built, the Voisins were the cars of kings, princes, and tycoons, but almost never of the nouveau riche, who preferred more obviously luxurious machines. The last Voisin was made in 1939. After the Second World War, Gabriel Voisin designed just one car, a highly original 200 cc model, the "Biscuter," which helped Spain get mass motorization under way.

A twelve-cylinder sports car with a body (Weymann patent) made lighter, and covered with leather.

# BUGATTI

**Royale Coupé (1928).** A four-seater version of the well-known vehicle with a body by Weymann.

## AN ITALIAN AT THE COURT OF FRANCE

Perhaps more than any other car builder, Ettore Bugatti knew how to create a fantastic legend around himself and his work. Bugatti's story has to be heard to be believed and should really start with "Once upon a time. . . ."

Well, then—once upon a time, there was Ettore Arco Isidoro Bugatti. He was born in Milan, into a lower-middle-class family, on September 15, 1881. His father was an artisan whose specialty was working silver objects and who instilled in his son a love for things carefully and accurately made, with a precision that was almost fussy. Even apart from his father's influence, however it is likely that Ettore was born with a love for fine things and an innate artistic sense.

He would undoubtedly have ended up in his father's profession if, unlike his father, he had not been urged on by a wish to excell: "If I ever manage to build what I want, it will be a car above all criticism," he wrote to a friend in his mature years. Ettore Bugatti must have repeated the phrase to himself many times, ever since the days when, still very young, he entered the Prinetti & Stucchi firm with a rather vague job that soon led to his becoming the company factotum. He even mounted four one-cylinder engines on one of the light chassis the Milanese house produced for its tricycles.

When not quite twenty, he got his firm's permission to design cars for other companies, and in 1901 a beautiful mechanical creation came into being: the Bugatti-Gulinelli, accomplished with the financial support of Count Gulinelli of Ferrara. From then on Bugatti was always busy, particularly as a free-lance

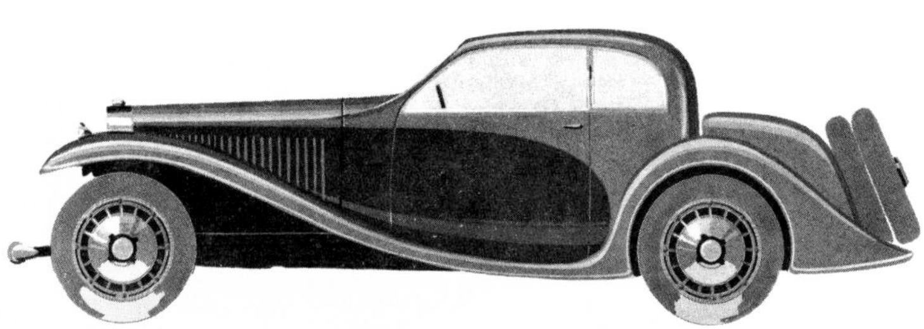

**Coupé, Type 44.** This touring car, with a Chapron body, was produced from 1927 to 1930.

# BUGATTI

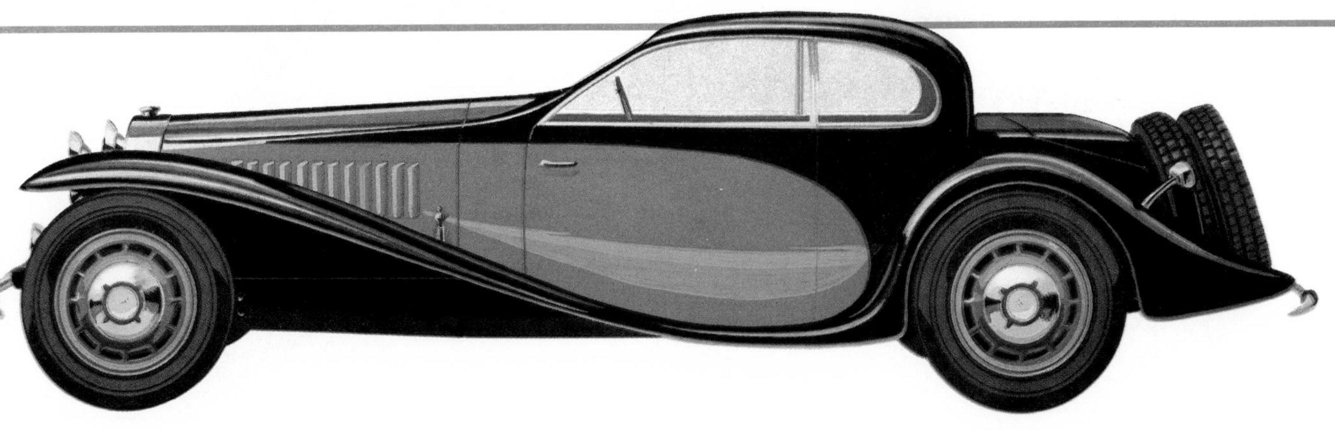

**Coupé, type 50 (1933).** Another body by Gangloff.

designer for the great automobile manufacturers of the day.

The design for his first car was bought by the Alsatian manufacturer De Dietrich, who soon asked him to transfer to Niederbronn and offered him the incredible sum of 50,000 gold lire, plus a 10 percent royalty on every car made. Bugatti moved to Alsace and shortly thereafter went to work for Mathis; then he designed a car for the Deutz Gasmotor Werke and later for Peugeot as well (the famous utility car, the 856 cc "Bébé," which had an incredible success).

In 1909, Bugatti decided to go on his own. He got a loan from the Darmstadt Bank and opened a plant at Molsheim in Alsace. The most important cars of the 1920s and 1930s—after Alsace became French following the First World War—came out of that factory and had a great influence on the period's style and technical development.

Bugatti thus became French, and he was so attached to his adopted country that he even used the language at home with his family.

In this period, and with the aid of his son Jean, Bugatti furthered the legend that had grown up around his cars. After the fabulous Grand Prix "Type 35," which won all of that era's important races, he decided to design what was to be his masterpiece, the "Royale," six of which were made and are still in existence. This impressive car had eight aligned cylinders with 12,760 cc, a very long hood (2 meters) and, naturally, exceptional performance. The three-speed gear box had second in direct transmission and a multiplied third; it was even possible to start in direct.

But all of Bugatti's cars had one weak point: the brakes. The great designer refused to use a brake booster, or even hydraulic circuits. When people complained about this problem, Ettore Bugatti would reply dryly: "I build automobiles for moving, not for stopping."

**Berlinetta Sport, Type 57.** This car was made from 1934 to 1940. The body was designed by Jean Bugatti and made by Gangloff.

# DUESENBERG

## LEGEND BECOMES ART

**Model J Beverly (1931).** A luxury body on the chassis of the era's most powerful car. The "J" had an eight-cylinder, 6882 cc engine and could do more than 175 km/h.

If there were any real need of an object that could in itself sum up and synthesize the idea of the Roaring Twenties in America, that object would certainly be the Duesenberg. The automobile industry—no matter of what nation—has never produced another image of power, luxury, and perfection like the Duesenberg—and mass produced, even if in small numbers, to top it off! The exceptional qualities of the Duesenberg were never equaled by either Hispano-Suiza, Voisin, Isotta Fraschini, Rolls-Royce, or Daimler. Perhaps only Bugatti—with his "Royale," of which only six were made—might have equaled the reputation created by Duesenberg cars, but even he never succeeded.

The Duesenberg: the most powerful, the fastest, the most expensive, the most desired, the most luxurious car to be had. An absolutely matchless machine, which led many firms that tried to imitate it into bankruptcy. And of course, such a car had its bards: even F. Scott Fitzgerald sung its praises.

It was the only American car to win a French Grand Prix, in 1921. It was the only car desired to an equal degree by kings, tycoons, actors, and gangsters; you had to be someone to own it, either Alfonso XIII, the King of Spain, or Gary Cooper, or John D. Dodge (the automobile tycoon), or William Randolph Hearst, or Jerome Medrano (the founder of the circus of the same name). The names of gangsters were not added to the impressive list of clients displayed in every Duesenberg showroom; the firm preferred to ignore its success with that segment of the population—a success partly due to the fact that they were the fastest cars to be bought (the "J" could do 185 km/h and the "SJ" 210 km/h). Both models were unrivaled in performance: the "J" had suction feeding and four valves for each of its eight cylinders; and the "SJ" had a supercharger, and was instantly recognizable by the chrome exhaust pipes that stuck out of the sides of the hood. The first had a 265 hp engine (exceptional even today) with 4250 rpm and 6882 cc; the second had a 320 hp engine with 4750 rpm and equal displacement. With its three-speed gear box, the "J" could reach 145 km/h in second and 185 in third, while the "SJ" could reach 170 and 210 km/h respectively. The dials and controls on the dashboard (including an altimeter) were almost totally duplicated on a panel for the backseat passengers! The controls also included some lights on a complex mechanism

**Model A Roadster (1925).** It had a 90 hp, 4260 cc engine and was the first American car—along with the Chrysler—to mount mass-produced hydraulic brakes.

# DUESENBERG

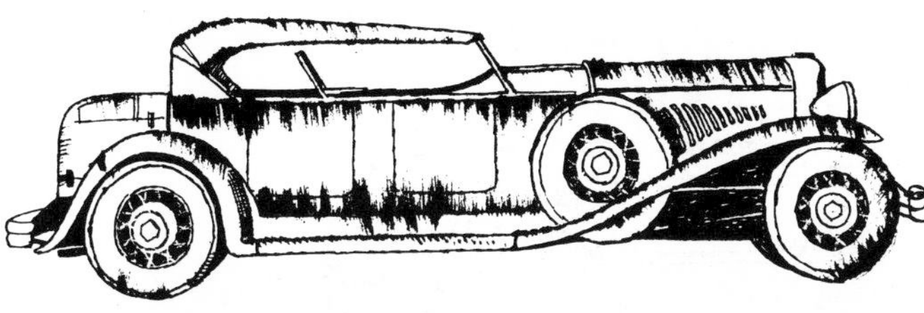

Tourster with body by Derham

Town Car with body by Murphy

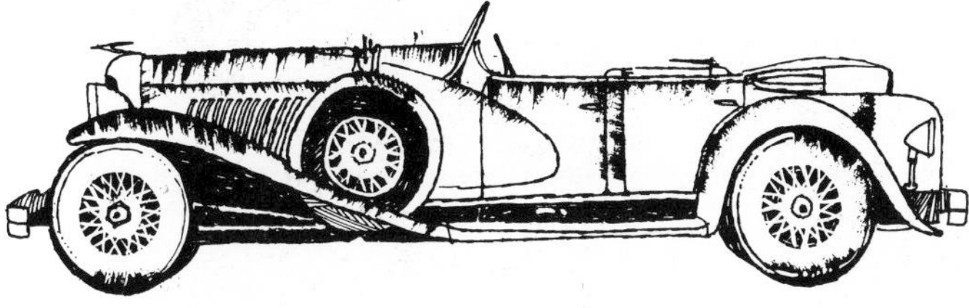

Phaeton with body by La Grande

Town Sedan with body by Willoughby

Convertible Sedan with body by Le Baron

Prince of Wales Sedan by Rollston

Phaeton Convertible with body by Derham

Coupé with body by La Grande

Victoria Convertible with body by Rollston

Arlington Model by Derham

Roadster Convertible with body by Murphy

All-Weather Town Landau by Rollston

# DUESENBERG

**Model J Roadster Convertible (1931).** Model "J", of which about 470 were made, was the first new vehicle produced by the Duesenberg factory after the firm was taken over by Errett L. Cord.

*He drives a Duesenberg*

The refined publicity—of a stylishness that was inimitably unique—printed by Duesenberg in some magazines from the 1930s. The phrase that accompanied each sketch was, "He Drives a Duesenberg."

linked to the speedometer; they lit up when it was time to lubricate the chassis, change the oil, etc. This marvel of mechanical technique of that era (and probably of today as well) was born from the ingenuity of two brothers of German origin, Frederick and August Duesenberg, who, after working for other American automobile makers, decided in 1913 to set up their own plant. From the beginning, the two brothers showed a preference for high-class products, with great mechanical precision and fine performance, even though

**Model J Convertible (1931).** Here too we see the impeccable and majestic line that marked the Duesenberg cars.

# DUESENBERG

**Model SJ Roadster (1933).** One of the rare Duesenbergs with a body by Weymann. The "bateau" end section, visible on the right, is typical of this model.

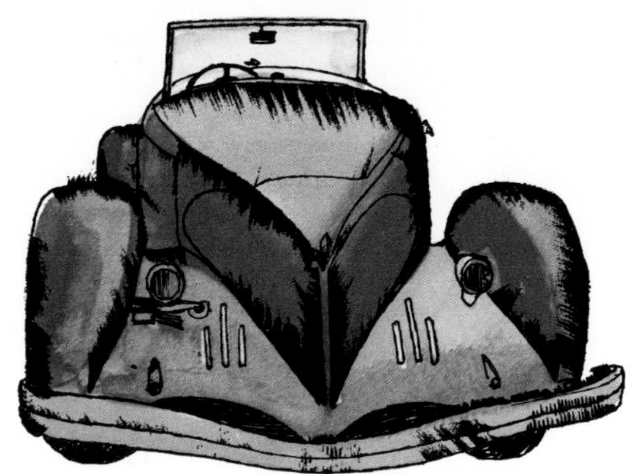

they did produce some less powerful cars under another name. But the real specialty of the Duesenberg brothers (they built airplane engines as well) was the fast car, which quickly brought them fame and fortune. In 1920, after the end of the First World War, they entered the prestige market with an interesting eight-cylinder, 90 hp model of superior performance, finally made commercial in 1922 as the "Model A." This car was the forerunner of the "J," then followed by the "SJ" with supercharger. These last two models were launched after the firm had been acquired by the brilliant banker Errett Lobban Cord, who decided to make the Duesenberg the pearl of his industrial empire.

The "J" made a triumphant debut at the end of 1928; its exceptional characteristics, combined with an intelligent publicity campaign (unique in style, as mentioned earlier), soon made it the world's most sought-after and exclusive car. The result of a very limited production—not more than 490 Duesenbergs were built in all, of which thirty-six were "SJ's"—many of these cars are still lovingly preserved by their owners.

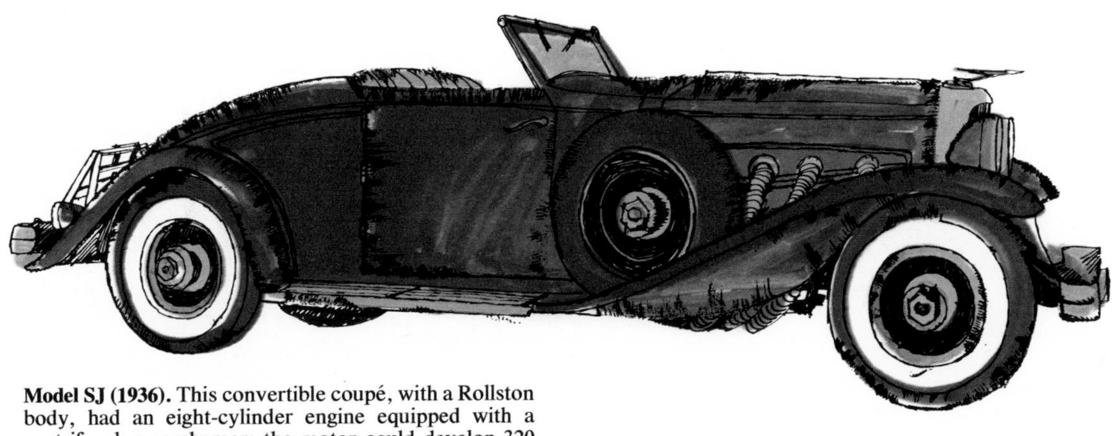

**Model SJ (1936).** This convertible coupé, with a Rollston body, had an eight-cylinder engine equipped with a centrifugal supercharger; the motor could develop 320 hp.

# CITROËN

## FULL SPEED AHEAD

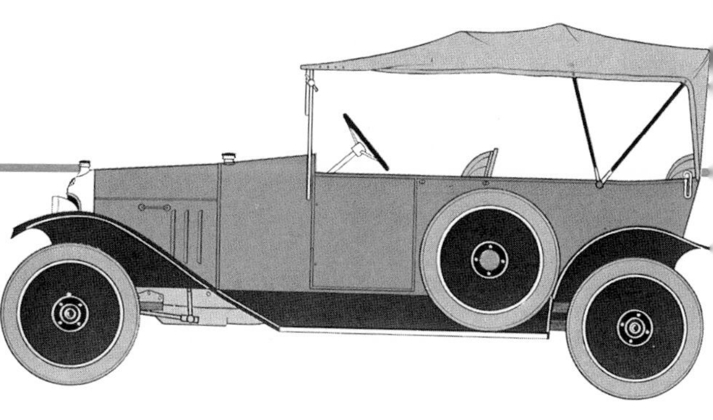

**Torpedo 10 HP, Type A (1919).** The first car made by this firm.

When, on June 4, 1919, André Citroën (an arms manufacturer who had been the major supplier of ammunition to the French Army during the First World War) presented his first car—the Model A—to public and press in his handsome showroom on the Avenue des Champs Elysées, few people thought the new activity of that arrogant and despotic man would be successful. Hadn't weapons brought him in enough cash? What was he trying to prove with that far from original car (a bit of Ford, a bit of Chevrolet, and a bit of Fiat), which had only one kind of body (torpedo) and no chance of being "personalized"?

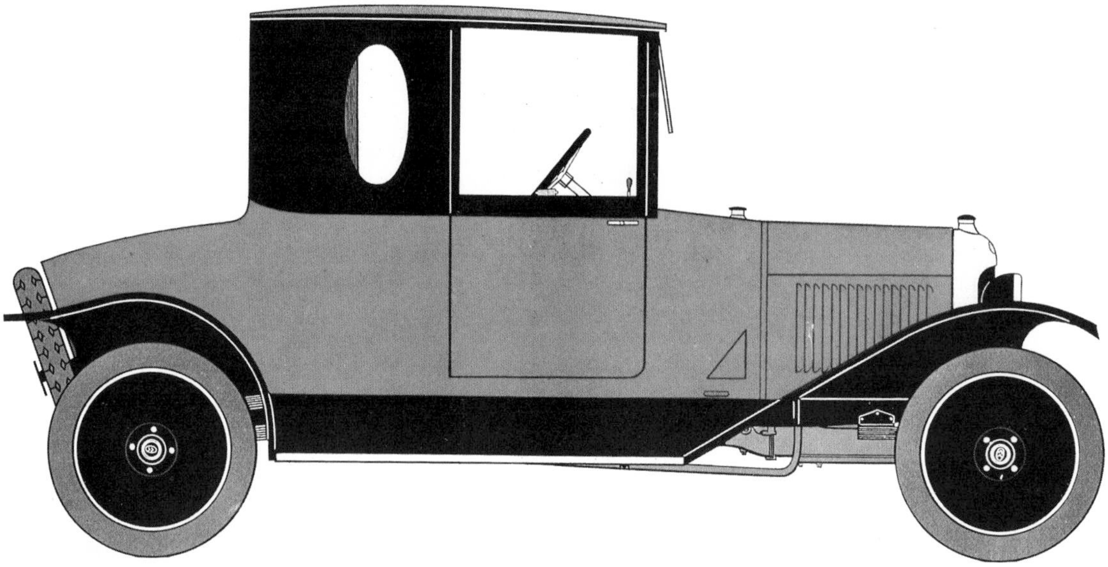

**B 2 Coupé Docteur (1922)**

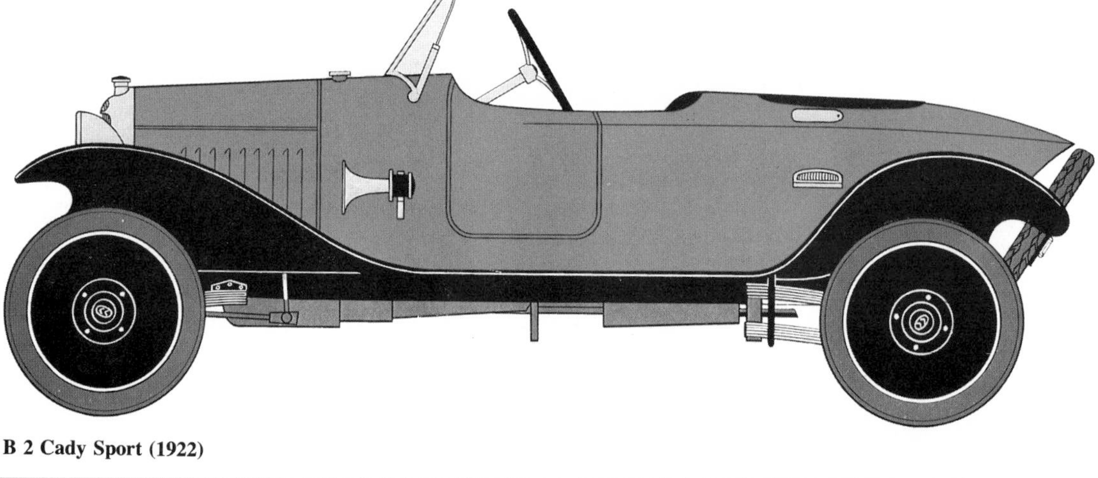

**B 2 Cady Sport (1922)**

**Sedan B 12 (1926)**

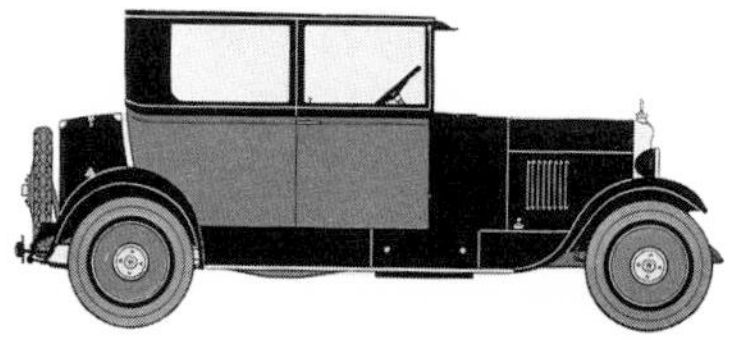

**Coupé B 14 (1927)**

# CITROËN

At that time the customer was always right. The manufacturer simply offered him a bare chassis, advised him where to find a body maker to "clothe" it, and was always ready to fulfill all requests for modification. Even Ford—from whom André Citroën had learned the lesson of the assembly line—offered its buyers a choice of four bodies and thus some kind of personal expression.

Yet the new car was a success. Production soon went from 100 cars a day—an output already exceptional for the Europe of that time—to 300 cars a day. Due exclusively to André Citroën, standardized mass production had finally arrived in the Old World.

Citroën went from one success to another: in 1920, the four-cylinder "B2" was created, with a 1452 cc engine as against the 1327 cc of the "A." In 1922, Citroën decided that the time was ripe for a small utility car of 856 cc, with just two seats. Only one color was available, lemon yellow, and the car was given the nickname *citron* (lemon). The result was a sales triumph that became even greater when a rear seat was added to the original two—hence another nickname, *trefle* (clover). This car reached a production level of 100,000 a year. It was Citroën who, along with the assembly line and the all-steel body (which guaranteed greater strength and a simplified production technique), introduced Europe to "consumerism." The French manufacturer was, in fact, the first in Europe to make use of spectacular publicity stunts; he even went so far as to place one of his cars on the Eiffel Tower—which was then lit up at night by thousands of lights spelling out his name—and he also organized races in Africa and the Far East (the Croisière Jaune, Noire, etc.) to propagandize the resistance and endurance of his machines.

All this brought Citroën to the top, and by the end of the 1920s it was Europe's largest automobile-producing firm, with 25,000 employees, second only to American companies.

The *trefle* was followed by the "B12," the "B14," and then by the new "C4" and "C6," strictly American in style and assembled in Italy by the Milanese branch of the company. The "Rosalie" was born in 1932; and a prototype with a rounded line and wholly mass-produced mechanical system, but with a lighter and simpler body, set an exceptional endurance record on the Montlhéry autodrome track: 300,000 km at an average speed of 93 km/h. But André Citroën's swan song (he died in 1935 at only fifty-seven) was the fabulous "7 CV" 1303 cc in 1934. It was soon followed by the "11 CV," the "15" (with six cylinders), and the "22" (the last, an eight-cylinder, V engine car, was never mass produced). They were all renamed "Traction" by the French because of their front-wheel drive which became a Citroën trait from that time on. The "Tractions," low and streamlined, and almost always black, soon became an integral part of the French landscape. Supplied with a solid load-bearing body on which the mechanical parts were bolted, these cars were so avant-garde in conception that they were produced until 1957, a record for longevity.

Sport Torpedo 10 HP (1923)

B 2 Coupé de Ville (1923)

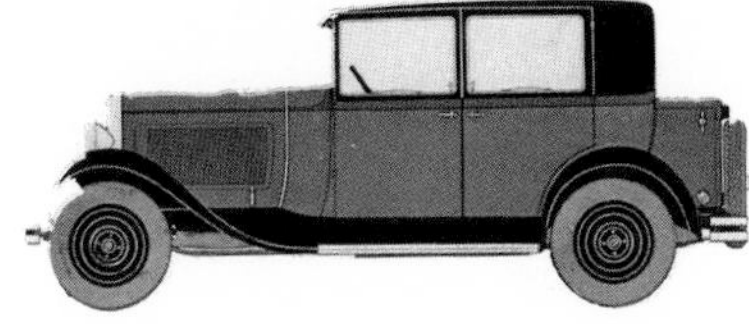

Sedan C 6 E (1929)

Family C 6 CGL (1931)

# CITROËN

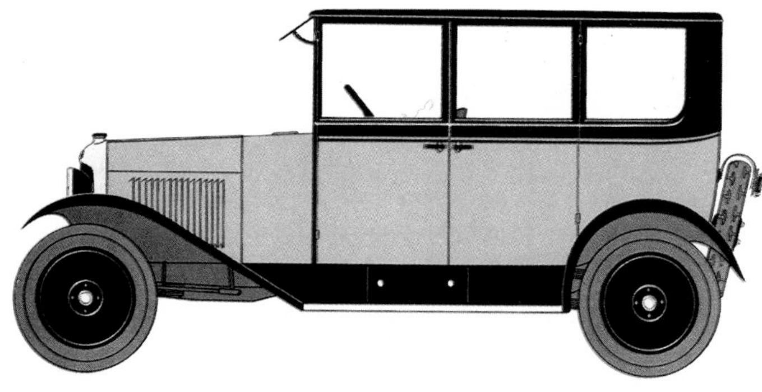

**B 12 Luxe (1924).** This was the first Citroën to have a completely metallic body.

**B 14 Landaulet Taxi (1927).** Another model on the "B 14" chassis, from 1927—a taxi that was soon to be seen all over France.

**B 14 Sedan (1927).** A four-seater with a four-cylinder, 1539 cc. 22 hp engine.

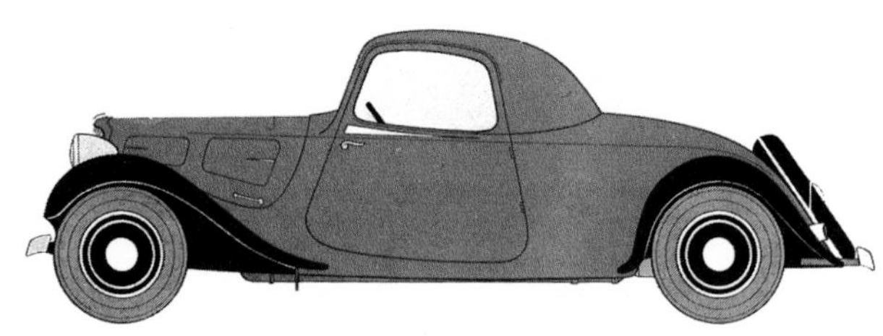

**11 CV Légère (1935).** This false cabriolet was one of the most handsome bodies set on the chassis of the famous "Traction" model. The "11 CV" was produced, with very few changes, until July 1957.

**B 14 G Cabriolet (1927).** This four-seater cabriolet could reach 80 km/h. The luggage compartment was incorporated in the body.

**Coupé 15 AL (1932)**

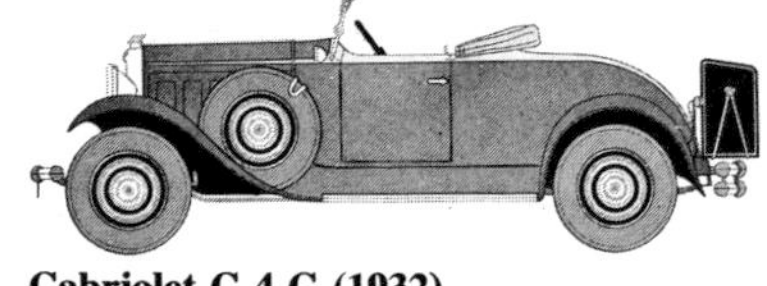

**Cabriolet C 4 G (1932)**

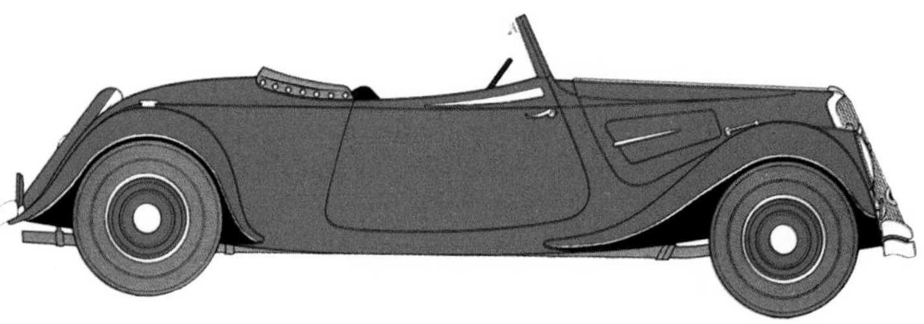

**22 CV Cabriolet (1934).** This car had an eight-cylinder V engine with 3822 cc (the largest displacement used by Citroën) and 100 hp, but was never regularly produced.

**Sedan 8 A (1932)**

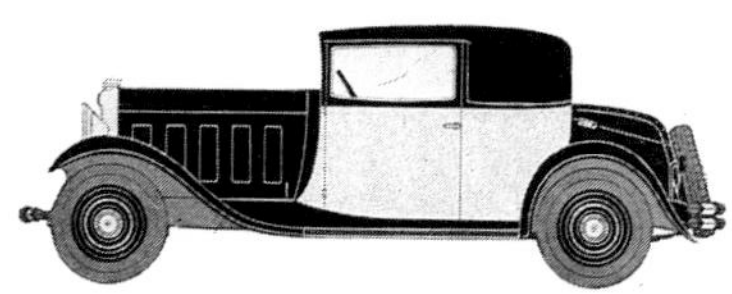

**Coupé C 6 G Sical (1932)**

# CITROËN

**5 CV, Type C (1922).** The first utility car produced by Citroën and turned out at a steady rhythm from 1922 to 1926. At first a two-seater, a third seat was later added in the rear. It had a four-aligned-cylinder, 856 cc, 11 hp engine and weighed 540 kg.

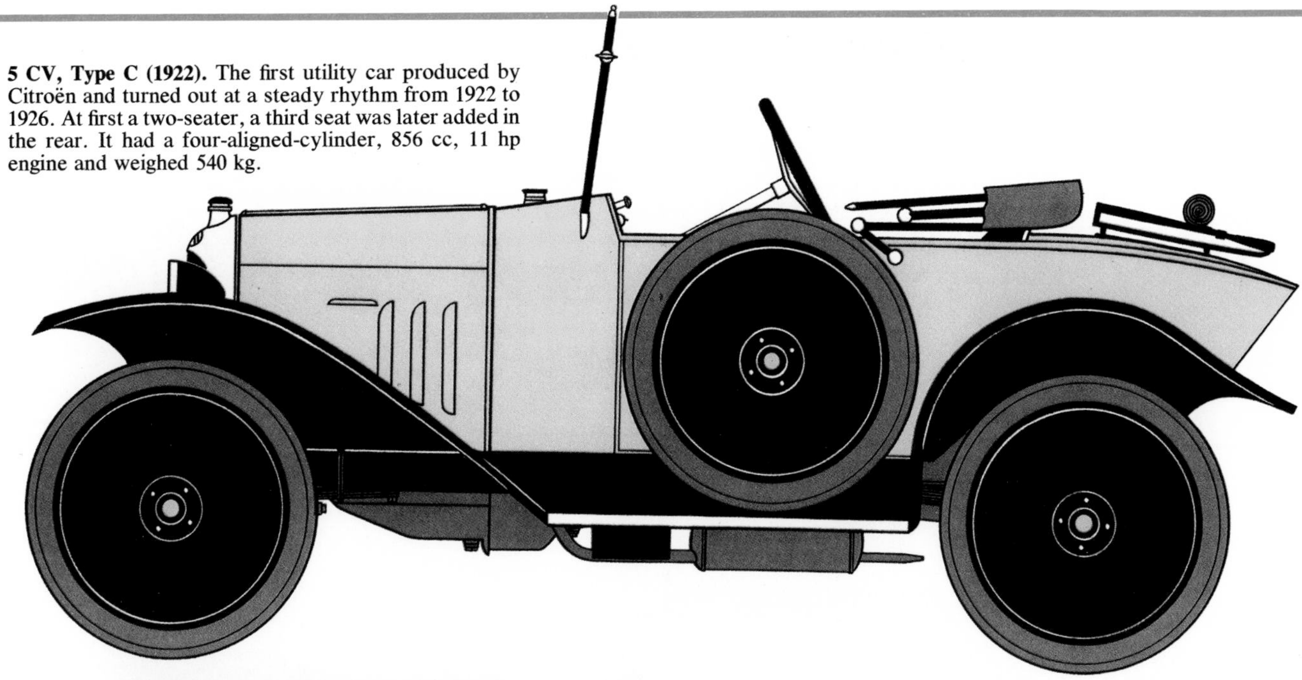

**15 CV Sedan (1939).** This vehicle, with its typical black body and yellow wheels, became famous for its superb road performance. The six-cylinder (aligned), 2867 cc, 77 hp engine allowed it to reach 130 km/h.

**C 4 (1929).** A five-seater limousine with a four-cylinder, 1628 cc engine that developed 30 hp at 3000 rpm. The maximum speed was 90 km/h.

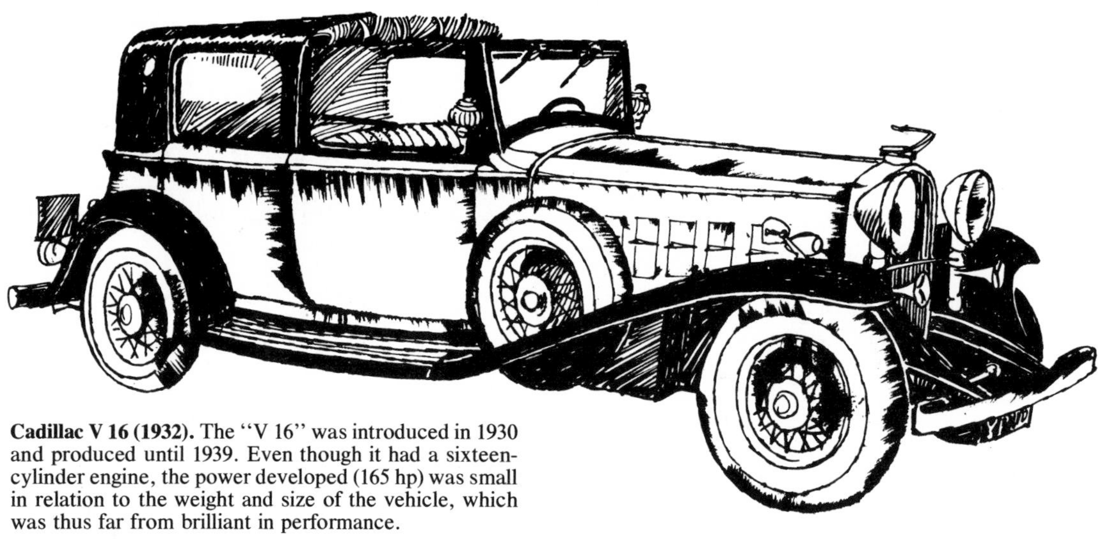

**Cadillac V 16 (1932).** The "V 16" was introduced in 1930 and produced until 1939. Even though it had a sixteen-cylinder engine, the power developed (165 hp) was small in relation to the weight and size of the vehicle, which was thus far from brilliant in performance.

**Stutz DV-32 (1933).** The "DV-32" was the last and without doubt the most handsome model of the firm founded in 1911 by Henry C. Stutz, which specialized in top-performance cars. It had a sixteen-cylinder, 5.2-liter V engine, with two overhead camshafts and four valves per cylinder.

**Opel Olympia (1935)**

**Panhard Panoramic (1934).** To guarantee total road visibility, the cars in the "Panoramic" series had the windshield enlarged by two small convex panes; the six-cylinder valve engine was available in various degrees of displacement.

**Opel Kadett (1936)**

market. But the Italian government vetoed the agreement and it fell through, even though Ford had promised not to buy out—and not even to buy into—the Milanese company. (Italian laws of the time also would have prohibited such a move by a foreign company.) So Isotta had to suspend production of automobiles and concentrate for a few years on turning out trucks and naval and airplane engines. At the Paris Salon of 1947, a prototype designed by Fabio Luigi Rapi (the author of many of the models that illustrate this book) was presented to the public; it was called the "8 C Monterosa" and was a large rear-engine car that was never produced. This was the last car made by Isotta Fraschini.

The 1930s saw the end of some of America's most famous names, a few of which went back to the days of the pioneers. Most of these failures were caused by the lack of demand for high-priced cars. Only those that had become part of great combines (like Lincoln with Ford and Cadillac with General Motors) came through, apart from Packard, the single exception among the independent firms. Packard, which was also the only one to preserve its brand name—even though it had descended in tone to a class that was not what it had once aimed for—managed to survive only because it turned out some relatively cheap models (like the "110" with just six cylinders, presented in 1936 and instantly successful) along with its cars in the high-price range, those with eight and twelve cylinders.

**Tatra 87 (1938).** Tatra, an offshoot of Nesselsdorf, is one of the oldest Czechoslovakian firms. The "87" model, with its streamlined body, had an eight-cylinder V engine, set in the rear and air-cooled, with a 3-liter displacement.

Famous firms like Marmon, Pierce-Arrow, Graham Paige, Stutz, and especially those owned by the group of financier E. L. Cord, had to close down, though. Cord not only owned the Cord brand, but also Duesenberg, Auburn, the Limousine Body plant, and the Lycoming engine factory. (Only the last was saved, to be taken over by others; today it produces engines for private planes.)

The end of Duesenberg was a great blow to the American automobile industry. Its name was known all over the world, and it was the only American car that could surpass in quality all its European competitors; its motto was quite justly "The World's Finest Motor Car." It certainly was unrivaled, both in price ($10,000 just for the chassis, up to $30,000 for the car complete with body) and in

**Maybach Zeppelin 60/200 (1936).** Maybach, formerly the partner of Gottlieb Daimler and then a manufacturer of dirigible motors, entitled this luxury car "Zeppelin" in honor of the famous dirigible builder. The "60/200" had a twelve-cylinder V, 8-liter cc, 200 hp engine, and despite its large size managed to reach a speed of 160 km/h.

**Opel 2-liter (1934).**

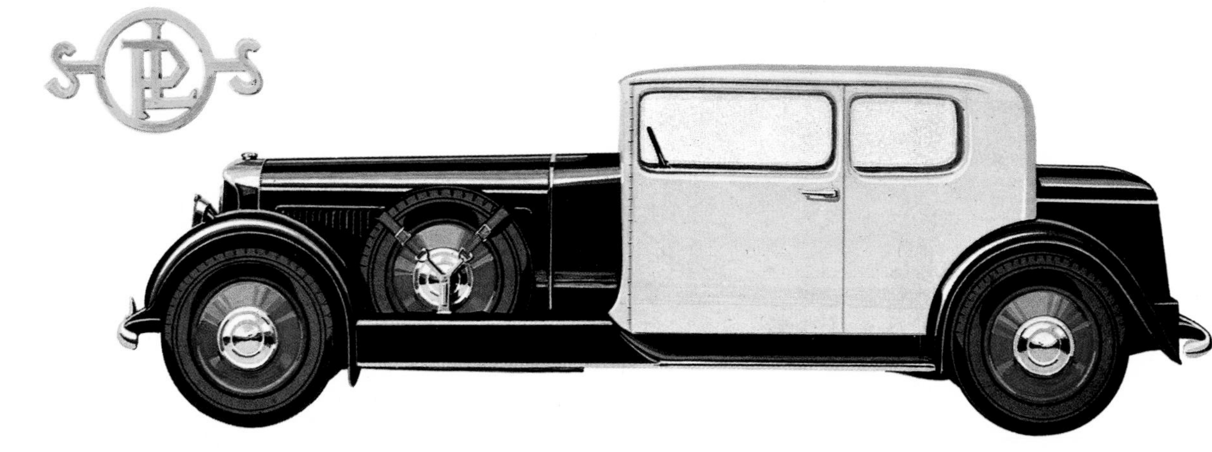

**Panhard (1933).** This coupé, with body by Million-Guiet, kept close to the line adopted by Panhard between 1920 and 1930. It had an eight-aligned-cylinder, 5-liter engine with a sheathed valve timing system, typical of the French firm's cars in those years.

**Fiat 518 L Ardita (1933).** This car had a cabriolet body by Castagna, and was fairly successful on the market; it was available in 1750 and 2000 cc, four-aligned-cylinder models and had hydraulic brakes on all four wheels.

**Mercedes Benz 380 (1935).** .This cabriolet, presented in 1933, had 90 hp that increased to 140 when a supercharger was inserted. It could do 130 km/h.

**Chrysler Airflow Sedan (1935).** The rather too bold lines of the body made the ''Airflow'' a commercial failure, and Chrysler stopped producing it after four years. But this car had the merit of introducing aerodynamic design into mass-produced models.

**Chrysler (1931)**

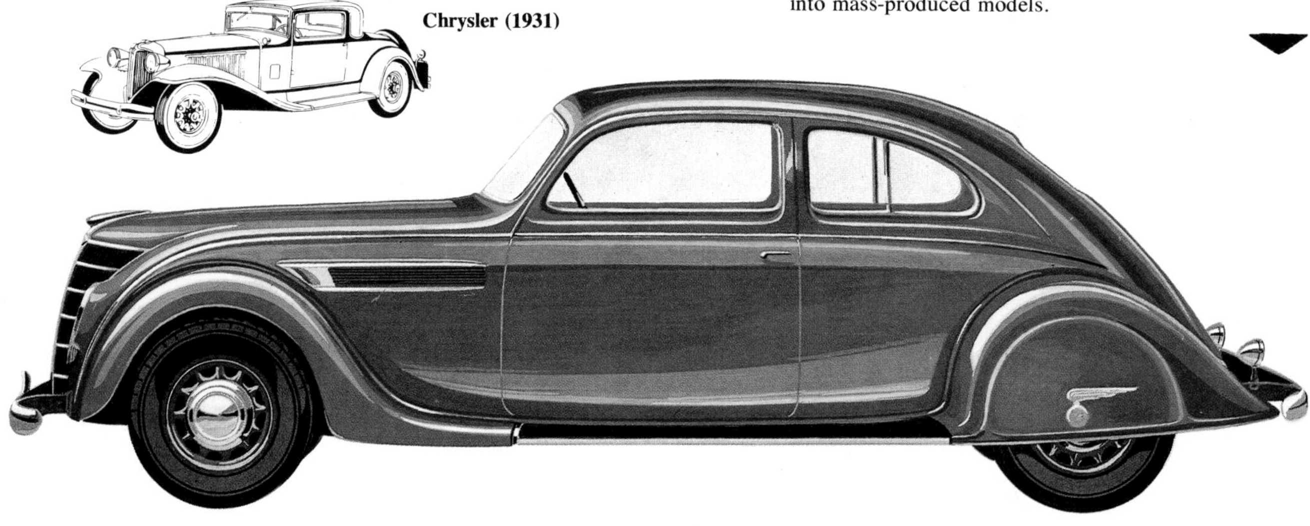

performance (the "SJ" could reach 210 km/h, despite its weight of 2,500 kg).

Enterprising Errett Lobban Cord had bought Auburn and Duesenberg and quickly enhanced their reputations, giving them a new public image. He made the first into a fast-car firm, which produced machines that were refined but fairly cheap, and the second into the world's—and America's—most exclusive car maker, which turned out extremely fast cars. If we may make the comparison, the Auburn became something like today's Alfa Romeo, the Duesenberg like today's Rolls-Royce—but with a lot more life to it. This transformation soon paid off well, and Cord made use of the experience he had gained to put on the market a new car in the price range between the Auburn and the Duesenberg. Thus the Cord L-29 was born; and, like everything born from the brain of that ingenious businessman, it was exceptional, not only for its front-wheel drive, but also because of its fine performance and class.

Despite their initial success on the market, however, Cord's cars soon fell victim to the Depression; unavoidable, in their case, since they were more or less luxury vehicles. It was even remarkable that some of his cars—like the 1936–1937 Cord, with its "810" and "812" models—managed to survive almost to the eve of the Second World War and made, before the firm closed down,

**Horch, Type 853 (1937).** The Horch became part of Auto Union in 1932 and put into its catalogue, at the end of the 1930s, this heavy sports cabriolet, with an eight-cylinder, 5-liter, 100 hp engine.

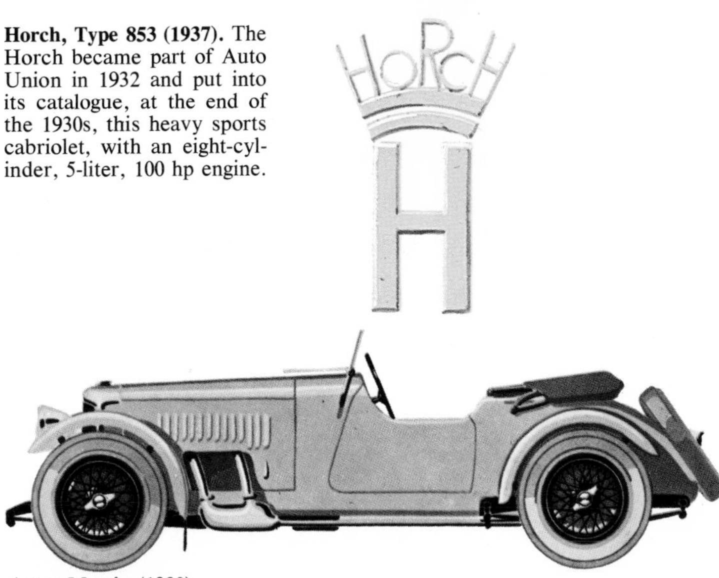


**Aston Martin (1932)**

**SS 100 (1931).** The first car—a 2-liter, six-cylinder model—produced by SS, a body and sidecar factory founded by William Lyons in 1932. It was the forerunner of the Jaguar. The SS marked the firm's first cars, but in 1936, after the birth of the Jaguar model, it was changed to SS Jaguar, and right after the war, to Jaguar.

**Cord L-29 (1931).** This impressive and elegant cabriolet had—like all the other Cord models—front-wheel drive and a Lycoming engine with eight aligned cylinders.

**Fiat 1500 (1935).** This first streamlined Fiat had a six-cylinder, 1495 cc engine derived from that of the "Balilla"; it also had independent front wheels and a central-shaft chassis.

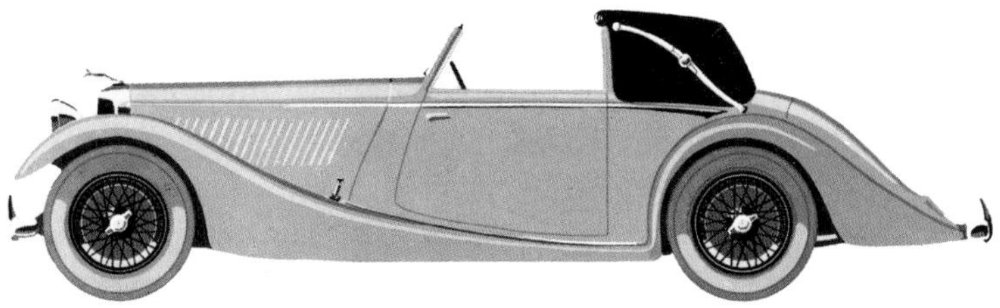

**Jaguar SS Sedanca (1939).** This Jaguar, with a Hooper body, had a typically English line.

**Alfa Romeo 6 C 2500 SS (1939).** This Touring Cabriolet, capable of a superb performance, had a six-aligned-cylinder, 110 hp engine, and could do 170 km/h.

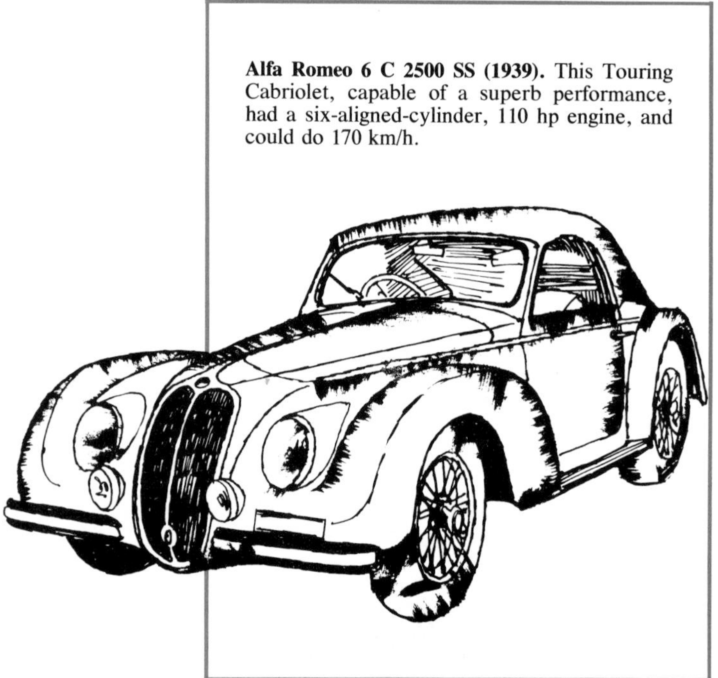

some of the most important cars in the American production of those years.

In a certain sense, Errett Lobban Cord was responsible for the premature end of some of the finest American cars. When the fabulous Duesenberg "J" was offered to the public in 1928, it was a hard blow for the other American luxury-car manufacturers; they tried to remedy it as quickly as possible by launching on the market—one right after the other—monstrous but superbly imaginative sixteen-cylinder models (the "J," fast as it was, had only eight); such was the case with Cadillac in 1930, followed by Marmon in 1931, and Peerless in 1932. The Depression was certainly the worst possible time to produce such large cars, but the ruthless laws of competition demanded that the luxury firms counter the success of the Duesenberg "J" with equally splendid cars.

Other firms, apart from the American, suffered the effects of the great crisis. In France and Germany too, the 1930s marked the end of many luxury trade names. In Germany, there folded up, one after another, Mannesmann, Brennabor, NAG, Maybach (founded by Daimler's pupil in 1921, to close just before the war after having produced for some years the fabulous "Zeppelin" with its twelve-cylinder V, 8-liter engine), Horch, and Wanderer. (The last two were owned by Auto Union and, like Maybach, were doomed to vanish just before the Second World War.)

The same fate was shared by some of the greatest names in the French automobile world. Even though Bugatti survived the war years somehow (the "real" Bugattis came out before the war, though, and the postwar models were simply copies of the earlier model "57"), Bucciali closed down in 1933, Hispano-Suiza in 1938, Berliet's passenger car division in 1939, and Voisin in 1939. Dela-

**Opel Admiral (1938)**

**Opel Kapitän (1939)**

haye and Delage, two other luxury cars on the French market, practically vanished before the war, even though some models appeared afterward with slight success.

The situation in Great Britain was different; her brands succeeded in coming through almost intact—and there were many of them—including the luxury cars. The real crisis in the British automobile industry was to begin in 1950.

**Cord 812 (1937).** This car, taken from the "810" model of 1936 caused a sensation with its bold body line (it even had vanishing headlights). It was designed by the well-known American stylist Gordon M. Buehring. The engine, an eight-cylinder V of 4729 cc, was brought to 190 hp in the 1937 version with supercharger, called "812.".

**Delahaye V 12, type 145 (1937).** This excellent French machine had a twelve-cylinder V, 4.5-liter engine of 160 hp, which rose to 238 in the sports version and let the car do 260 km/h.

**Packard Light Eight (1939).** This luxurious false cabriolet had an eight-cylinder, 4620 cc, 120 hp engine.

# MERCEDES-BENZ

## THE THREE-POINTED STAR

June 26, 1926, is an important date in the history of the automobile. On that day the Daimler Motoren Gesellschaft and Benz & Company—the world's oldest automobile factories—merged to create the Daimler-Benz AG, better known as Mercedes, the name taken by Daimler models at the start of the century. The new trademark was formed by the Daimler three-pointed star surrounded by the laurel that encircled the name Benz in that firm's former trademark.

It was really an incorporation of Benz into Daimler, rather than a merger. The models produced by Daimler-Benz were called Mercedes, and from the beginning the executive staff of Daimler dominated that of Benz. Among the designers of the Daimler was Ferdinand Porsche, who created a series of sports models, equipped with supercharger (the "S," "SS," "SSK" and "SSKL" models). These cars were a sensation at the time, both in races and in showrooms. Porsche's independent nature led him to leave Mercedes in 1929, spend a short time with Steyr, and then open his own studio in Stuttgart.

But despite the loss of Porsche, Mercedes remained—true to its tradition—in the avant-garde of technical progress. The 1930s marked an important moment in the life of the German company: its entrance into the middle-range utility field, even if with high-class models. Model "170," the firm's first car with independent wheels, and equipped with a six-cylinder, 1692 cc engine, dates from 1931. But it was with the introduction of the "130 H," with its 1.3-liter rear engine, that Mercedes produced the vehicle with the smallest displacement in its history, apart from the first V engines designed by Gottlieb Daimler. The "130 H" (all four wheels of which were independent) was followed by the "150 H" and the "170 H," of the same type but with higher displacement. The first car equipped with a Diesel engine, the "260 D," was presented in 1935; and the Stuttgart firm has always been one of the leaders in this sector. Those years also saw the birth of the "Grosser Mercedes" with an eight-cylinder, 7.7-liter engine developing 150 hp (220 with supercharger), which was produced from 1930 to 1937.

After the war, Mercedes reappeared with a smaller range of models, concentrated mainly on the "170" with front engine, a prewar car, then offered with either a gasoline or diesel motor; this was followed by models "220" and "300." From 1954 on, with the "180," Mercedes adopted, for the first time, a load-bearing body, remaining faithful to this kind of structure even in larger models.

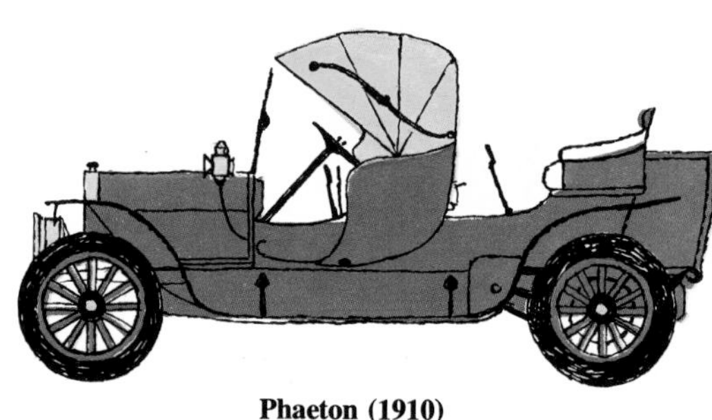

**Phaeton (1910)**

**SS 38/250 (1928).** Three famous names are associated with this powerful cabriolet: the body was by Hibbard & Darrin, the engine was designed by Ferdinand Porsche, and it was used in racing by the famous German pilot Rudolf Caracciola. The six-cylinder, 7069 cc engine had 140 hp which permitted it to exceed 180 km/h.

# MERCEDES-BENZ

**Grosser Mercedes (1937).** The first "Grosser Mercedes" dates from 1930. The Emperor of Japan used two of them for a long time. The 1937 model (the last year of production) had an eight-cylinder V engine, force-fed and with 230 hp.

**Touring car (1911)**

**Touring Car (1922)**

**Type SS (1928)**

**Stuttgart 200 (1926)**

**Type 130 (1933)**

**Type 260 D (1935)**

**Cabriolet, Type 170 V (1935)**

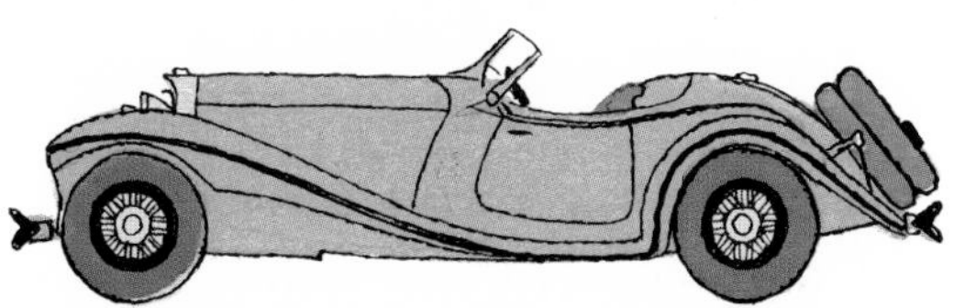

**Type 540 K (1936)**

# LANCIA

## AN ITALIAN TRADITION

In English, Lancia means "arrow" or "lance"—a fitting name for cars that are fast, streamlined, and silent, as Lancias have always been.

Vincenzo Lancia made a significant contribution to motorization all over the world, and to that of Italy in particular. A precise, scrupulous, and quiet man, like the cars he made, and like them he was also full of fantasy—as well as being a non-conformist. Probably no other creation in the world of the automobile has reflected its designer as faithfully as the Lancia, except, perhaps, the cars of two other imaginative but sometimes bizarre Italians: Ettore Bugatti and Enzo Ferrari, whose cars—like the Lancia—seem to mirror their personalities.

Vincenzo Lancia was born in Fobello, a town in the Vercelli area, in 1881. When only seventeen he entered the workshop of Giovanni Battista Ceirano in a vaguely defined job, which meant hard labor for twelve or more hours a day—an "apprenticeship." Young Vincenzo soon showed a passion for mechanical problems, and that helped his career move forward rapidly. In 1899, when the Ceirano firm was taken over in toto by the newly born Fiat company—including the employees—Lancia was already head warehouseman.

Once in Fiat, Vincenzo Lancia revealed his qualities as an excellent test driver, and when Fiat—at little more than a year from its founding—set up an official team for sports racing, Lancia was called on to take part in it with Nazzaro and Storero. He soon became the coach of the team, and under his guidance it went from triumph to triumph, in both Europe and the United States. Vincenzo Lancia was certainly one of the most successful car racers of the second decade of this century.

Then in November 1906, along with Claudio Fogolin, he too a former Fiat driver, Vincenzo Lancia

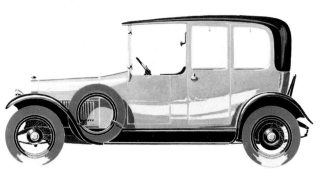

**Theta Limousine (1913).** The first European car with a mass produced electric system incorporated into it. It had a four-cylinder, 4940 cc, 70 hp engine; and its speed was exceptional for that time: a maximum of 120 km/h.

**Lambda Torpedo (1923).** The masterpiece of Vincenzo Lancia and an innovative car in both its mechanical setup and its body. The latter was a forerunner of the load-bearing body and helped to greatly reduce the height of all cars to come. It had a four-cylinder, closed-V engine, with 2120 cc and 49 hp.

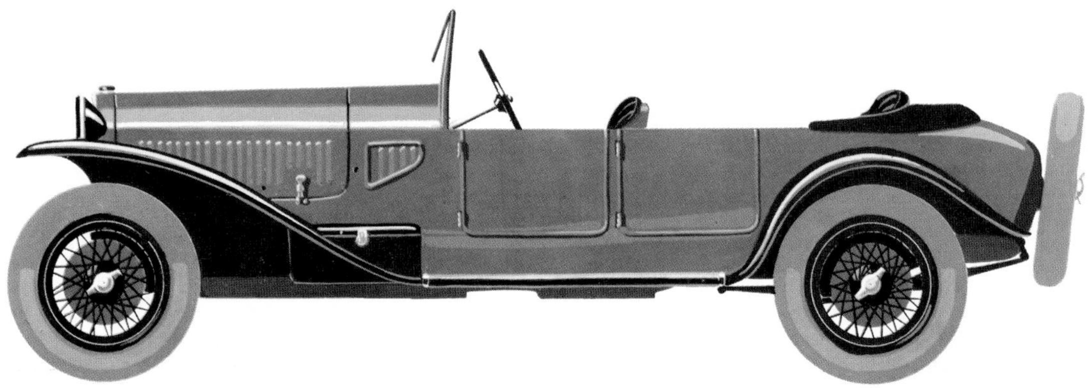

# LANCIA

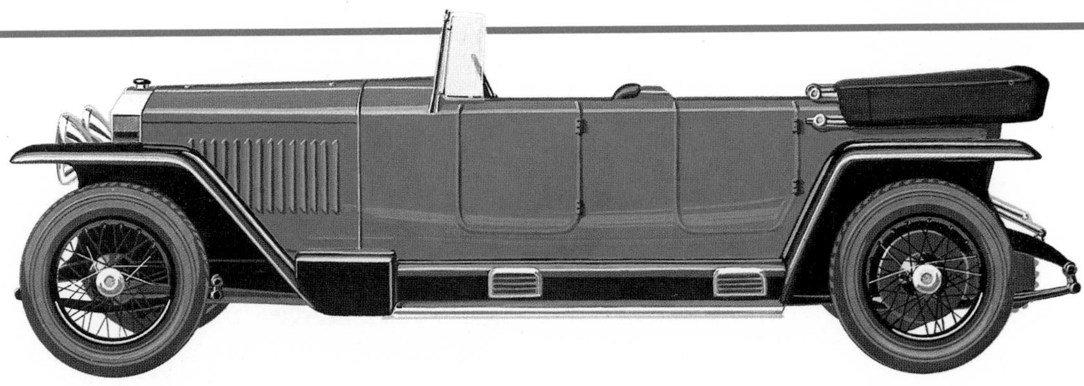

**Trikappa Torpedo (1922).** This vehicle had an eight-cylinder, 4594 cc. 98 hp engine and could reach 130 km/h.

founded in Turin the company that still bears his name: the Fabbrica di Automobili Lancia & C. It got off to a bad start when a fire destroyed the new factory and delayed the introduction of its first car, the "Alpha," which did not come out until 1908. This first model was highly advanced: it had cardanic transmission, a high rpm rate, a fair amount of power (28 hp at 1800 rpm with 2543 cc displacement), and an exceptional top speed of 90 km/h, partly aue to the light weight of the chassis. The "Alpha" contained many of the characteristics that were to mark the Lancia automobile in the future.

In 1911, Vincenzo Lancia took over the Brasier plant in Via Monginevro, Turin, and transferred his factory there. He then produced a large number of modern cars (one, the "Theta," was the first European car to boast of an incorporated electrical system), until he officially introduced, in 1923, what is usually considered his masterpiece: the revolutionary "Lambda." It was the world's first vehicle to foreshadow the load-bearing body (its brilliant designer later said: "I simply made use of the experience of ships"). It was also the first mass-produced car to have independent front suspension (with the characteristic telescopic system incorporating the spiral spring and the shock absorber) and a four-cylinder, closed-V engine.

The "Lambda"—an extremely fast car which could do from 115 to 125 km/h, depending on the model—was produced until 1930 in nine successive series, with more than 13,000 cars in all. The "Lambda" was followed by other fine models, such as the "Augusta" (the first Lancia equipped with hydraulic brakes, after thorough tests made by Lancia himself), the "Artena," and the elegant "Astura," a silent, eight-cylinder, V engine with only 2600 cc displacement.

But it was with the "Aprilia"—it is said that Henry Ford stood speechless the first time he saw it and even stretched out on the ground for a better look at its

**Augusta (1933).** The first utility car of the firm, as well as the first Lancia with hydraulic brakes and an all-steel body. A light, fast, and at the same time economical car, it had a four-cylinder, closed-V engine, with only 1196 cc displacement. Its 35 hp easily let it go beyond 100 km/h.

# LANCIA

**Dilambda Faux Cabriolet** by Farina **(1933).** The "Dilambda," which came out in 1928, had an eight-cylinder V engine, with 3960 cc and 100 hp.

highly original independent-rear-wheel back suspension—that Vincenzo Lancia brought to a close his brilliant career as a car designer. The "Aprilia" was a fast, streamlined car which had a four-cylinder, closed-V engine with only 1351 cc (later raised to 1486 cc) and with 48 hp. Vincenzo Lancia died on February 15, 1937, a few weeks before regular production of his "Aprilia" began.

**Aprilia (1937).** This car (epoch-making, like all the Lancias) was low and streamlined and could do 130 km/h with a four-cylinder V engine of only 1351 cc. All four wheels were independent.

Another excellent body by Farina on a Lancia Astura chassis.

# PACKARD

## AN AMERICAN LEGEND

Some ads for Packard that came out about 1930 in America's most exclusive magazines. There was always some reference to the more refined artisan techniques of the past, which—according to the firm—could still be found in Packard production methods. The advertising always ended with the same phrase: "Ask the Man Who Owns One."

Packard—one of the oldest automobile manufacturers in America—established an indisputable first in a nation of firsts: that of the world's largest producer of luxury cars. The firm turned out about 50 percent of the prestige models built throughout the world, up until the 1950s. In 1937 alone, Packard's assembly line finished 122,593 cars, putting the company in fifth place among American car makers for that year. The fact is all the more exceptional when we remember that at that time the great luxury car manufacturers, and especially the American ones, were closing down one after another owing to the lack of demand. But there was a demand for Packard, even in the darkest moments.

Packard knew how to keep up with the times. During the Depression years, nine tenths of the American market was concentrated on cars that cost less than $750, and of course Packard did not make such cars. In 1936, the firm therefore decided to launch a "small" car (small, that is, by American standards)—a six-cylinder, 100 hp model that retained all of the typical Packard refinements (luxury interior, accurate production, and comfortable driving) while attracting a low-cost market. It was the "110" model, which in its cheapest version, the "Business Coupé," cost no more than $795; more luxurious models cost $910. Thus, for a few dollars more, the American driver could afford a "real" Packard. The new model was successful, and 65,400 cars were sold in one year.

The firm, founded in 1890 by James Ward Packard, and called the Packard Electric Company, turned out its first gasoline-engine car in 1899. The design for this car had been ready since 1893, but was put aside because of economic difficulties.

In 1913, the company made the world's first six-cylinder model with an electrical system, including electric ignition. During the First World War, Packard produced a series of engines for the "Liberty" planes. After the war, it concentrated on prestige cars, thanks to a famous twelve-cylinder V engine (production of which had already begun in 1915; the first twelve-cylinder built in America). After its success in the 1930s and its great contribution to the war effort of the United States (with the famous Packard Merlin plane engines used in the "Mustang"), Packard began to decline in the 1950s, and was finally taken over by Studebaker in 1957. Studebaker only turned out cars with the Packard name for a couple of years—and they were really Studebakers with a Packard grill. The last Packard left the Studebaker plant in 1958, a year in which only 1745 cars bearing that glorious name were produced.

**Twelve Phaeton (1936).** The most famous Packard, with a twelve-cylinder V, 175 hp engine and a body by the American designer Le Baron.

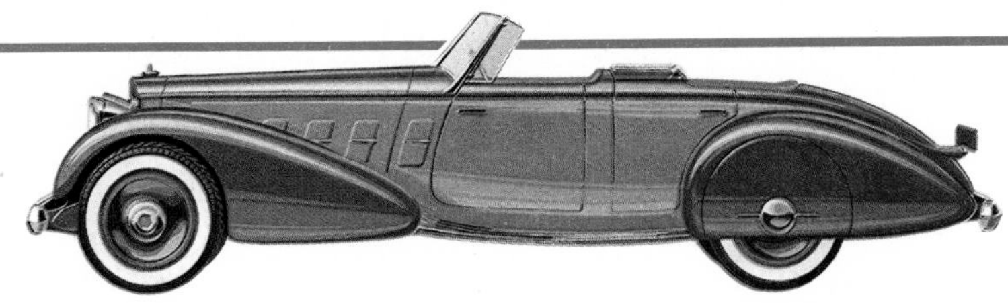

# ROLLS-ROYCE

## THE DOUBLE "R"

From the start, Rolls-Royce adopted the famous slogan "The Best Car in the World" and kept its standards tuned to that height over the years.

The brand was the result of the meeting of two pioneers of motorization in England: aristocrat Charles Stewart Rolls and humble, but talented, Henry Royce (later made a baronet). Rolls was one of the founding members of the Automobile Club of England and Ireland, as well as one of the great sportsmen of the turn of the century. And he shared with Royce a love for anything mechanical—anything of quality, that is; Rolls was also one of Royce's first customers, a customer so enthusiastic that he determined at all costs to go into business with Royce. Rolls brought the capital needed to develop the company and many financial contacts; Royce devoted his attention to the designing and production of the cars.

The combination was perfect, but all too brief: in fact, Rolls died at only thirty-five in a plane crash, in 1910. But Rolls-Royce continued its long line of successes, and the legend has survived. The legend for instance, of

The classic Rolls-Royce radiator grill, in the form of a Greek temple, topped by the famous statuette of a Winged Victory. This grill was adopted by the firm in 1907 for the "Silver Ghost." That of earlier models was similar in shape but much lower. In some cases—like the 1905–06 "V 8 invisible engine" model—there was no radiator grill at all.

The Bentley radiator grill of the 1920s, before the firm was taken over by Rolls-Royce in 1933. Up until the 1950s, Bentley preserved—in regard to the Rolls—its own "sports" identity; but from 1955 on, the two firms standardized their range of models, and only the design of its radiator grill now distinguishes the Bentley from the Rolls-Royce.

**Phantom I Doctor's Coupé (1925).** With body by Hooper.

**Phantom I Continental (1925).** The body was by Barker.

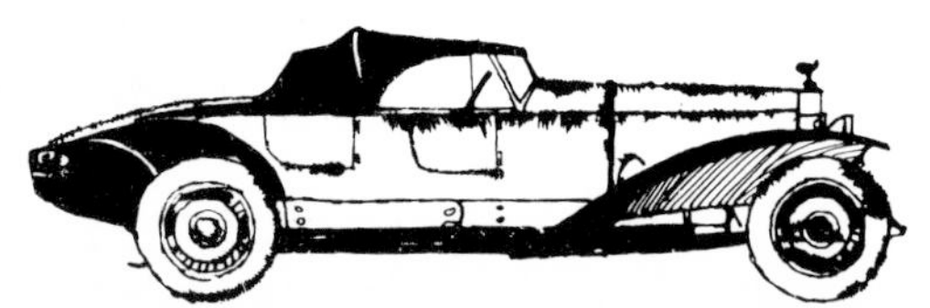

# ROLLS-ROYCE

the most quiet of cars (customers supposedly complained about the ticking of the clock, which could be heard clearly at a speed of 100 km/h), as well as that of the most perfectly serviced car (a mechanic with a suitcase was ready to leave for any place in the world). The famous English firm never denied the truth of these legends.

The strong competition from other great brands, such as Hispano, Pierce-Arrow, Bugatti, and Duesenberg, did not diminish the fame of the Rolls-Royce over the years. Not even Duesenberg—a truly exceptional car in every respect—managed to do so; it had to use the slogans "The Mightiest Car in the World" and "The World's Finest Car" to even compete.

Henry Royce dedicated his life to his company; he died in 1933, at the age of seventy. From that moment, the two famous superimposed "R's" on the Greek-temple radiator grills of the Rolls-Royce changed color, from red to black. It was a last tribute offered by the great company to the man who created its glory.

**Phantom III Coupé de Ville (1939).** The first "Phantom III" left the Rolls-Royce plant in 1936. It had a twelve-cylinder V, 7340 cc engine. The car was produced until 1939, for a total of 710 vehicles.

The classic statuette of the Winged Victory that stands on every Rolls-Royce radiator grill.

Another "Phantom III" coupé de ville with body by Mulliner. This was the first Rolls-Royce with independent front suspension, made on a General Motors patent; the brakes were mechanically controlled through a brake booster. Rolls-Royce used these brakes till the postwar period.

**Phantom I Special Salamanca (1927).** Produced in Springfield with a Brewster body.

**Phantom I Sport Touring (1928).** The body was by Brewster.

# GENERAL MOTORS:

# IN UNION THERE IS STRENGTH

**Buick Model C (1905).** Equipped with a two-counter-posed-cylinder, water-cooled, 22 hp engine, this car even had overhead valves. It cost $1200. Buick was the first name incorporated into GM, in 1908.

When William Crapo Durant founded General Motors on September 16, 1908, Henry Ford had yet to introduce his famous Model T, the car that was to literally put America on wheels in the space of a few years. In 1908 Ford was just another American car manufacturer, although one of the more important; but he was still not "the" manufacturer. In fact, that year Ford produced only 10,202 cars of the 65,000 made in the United States—not even a sixth of the overall output.

Durant, on the other hand, was on top with his Buick, to the point of asking—in 1908—the other major builders of the era (Ford, Oldsmobile, Briscoe, Perkins, etc.) to merge with him and found a great automobile "trust." But negotiations were inconclusive, since neither Henry Ford nor Ransom E. Olds had any intention of merging with Durant; at the most, they were prepared to sell him their companies. And thus it was that Durant founded alone, and with a capital of no more

# GENERAL MOTORS

**Oakland Colonial Coupé (1912).** This elegant coupé, with a robust four-cylinder engine, could be turned into a runabout.

**Buick Model 10 Single Rumble (1908).** This Buick had a four-cylinder, 18 hp engine, transmission with epicyclic gears and an additional back seat.

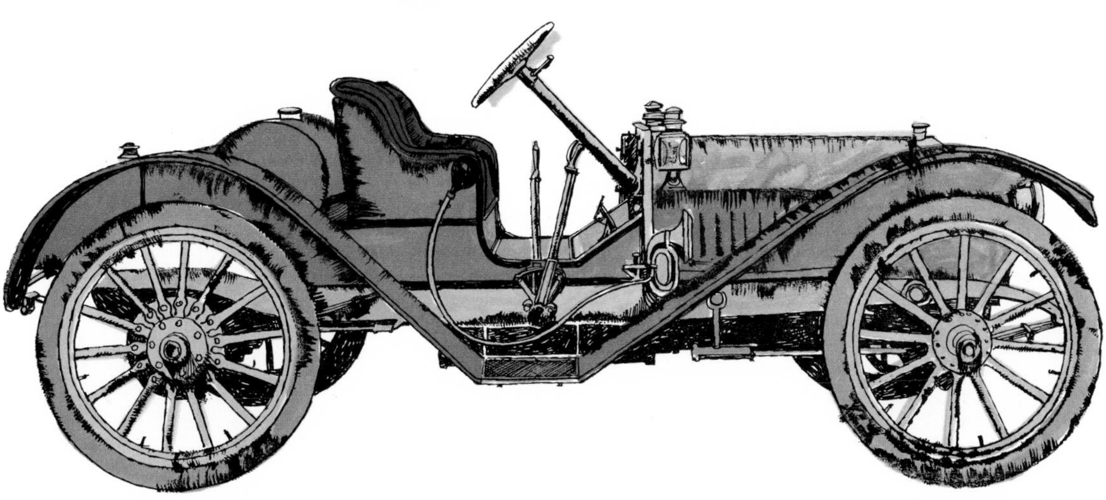

**Oldsmobile Limited Roadster (1910).** Oldsmobile became part of General Motors in 1908, and had in its catalogue various types of sports cars as well, such as this roadster, sold for $4600.

**Chevrolet Royal Mail Roadster (1914).** Founded in 1911 by William C. Durant, who had left General Motors, Chevrolet took its name from the racing driver of Swiss origin, Louis Chevrolet. The car turned in a good performance, despite its low price; this "Royal Mail" cost $750.

**Chevrolet Classic Six (1911).** The first car produced by the Chevrolet factory in Detroit. This firm became part of GM in 1918.

**Chevrolet model 490 (1916).** The name comes from the selling price of $490. It had a four-cylinder, 22 hp engine.

**Oldsmobile Sportsman's Roadster (1922).** Mass produced with numerous accessories; note the external sunshade, the step that replaces the running board, and the outside golf bag.

**Oakland (1924).** This four-seater coupé had a six-cylinder engine and brakes on all four wheels. It cost $1395.

**Buick model 50 (1924).** A seven-seater, middle-range sedan with a six-cylinder, 70 hp engine. It cost $2285.

**Pontiac (1926).** This was the first Pontiac made by Oakland. It was a six-cylinder model and cost only $825.

than $2000, the General Motors Company. It was a challenge to the automobile industry of that time, and one that was to pay off. A few days after GM was founded, its capital was brought up to 12.5 million dollars, which made it easier to buy Buick for $4 million. General Motors is not only the greatest automobile manufacturer in the world, with a production that exceeds 7 million vehicles in its various plants scattered on five continents, but is also the world's largest employer (about 800,000 employees) and sales proceeds that amply exceed the national budget of Italy.

This colossus had rather a hard time getting started, even though Durant's frenzy for buying out large and small plants brought him within a stone's throw of absorbing even Ford. The GM board of directors had approved the purchase of Ford for $8 million, but the banks dashed Durant's hopes and refused to lend him the sum needed. The deal fell through.

That didn't stop Durant from continuing his buying spree, though. In 1908, after Buick, he took over Stewart; and at the end of that same year, Oldsmobile

fell for $3 million; at the beginning of 1909, Oakland was swallowed up; then came Cadillac which cost $4.5 million, plus a few hundred thousand GM shares.

Thanks to Durant's aggressive action, GM was the owner of about thirty brands in a couple of years, as well as the founder of new trade names, such as AC, for producing electrical parts for cars. The last firm came from Albert Champion's transfer to GM (he was the founder of the company that produced Champion sparkplugs). Since Champion did not own the firm that bore his name, it was fairly easy for Durant to talk him into founding a new one, the name of which would come from his initials, AC.

But in 1910, GM suddenly found itself facing a sales crisis, accompanied by a serious lack of liquid cash. The latter problem was quickly resolved, but the new backers demanded, if not the withdrawal of Durant, at least a change in the top echelon of the company. Durant regained the presidency of the company in 1916, and brought in Chevrolet (which he had founded in 1911); in another decade, that name was to mark the best-selling car in America—from 1927, to be exact, the year in which GM surpassed the Ford sales record for the first time.

But despite the Chevrolet exploit, Durant's decline was inevitable. A sudden and very serious collapse in GM shares on the market in 1920 led to his withdrawal from the firm, definitely this time. At the same time, it marked the rise of a young engineer who up to then had headed one department in the great organization: Alfred P. Sloan, Jr.

**Chevrolet (1929).** The first six-cylinder Chevrolet.

**La Salle (1929).** The Cadillac of the poor. It cost $2495.

**Cadillac (1928).** The world's first car with a synchronized gear box.

**Buick (1936).** The cars by that name were completely changed that year.

**Chevrolet Suburban (1936).** The first all-metal station wagon.

Sloan reorganized GM from the bottom up, and in a short time made it into the great, homogeneous, and powerful complex it is today. His policy—simple and complicated at the same time—was at first to put order into the confused heap of makes and models competing with one another within the firm. As he himself wrote in his book, *My Years with General Motors,* GM "was to produce cars of such quality that they could compete both with low-cost cars, by attracting those customers who were ready to pay a bit more for added quality, and with higher-priced machines, winning over customers

**Oldsmobile (1940).** The first car with completely automatic gear shifting.

# GENERAL MOTORS

**Cadillac V 16 Fleetwood Town Brougham (1931).** The "V 16," brought out in 1930, created the American firm's reputation for extremely luxurious cars—nothing new for this company, which for years had turned out luxury machines. It had a sixteen-cylinder V engine of 165 hp, which used quite a lot of gasoline: about 50 liters every 100 kilometers.

**Chevrolet Sport Roadster (1932).** Chevrolet became the best-selling American car from 1927 on; it owed a lot of its success to an efficient engine with six aligned cylinders (produced from 1929 to 1953), which in this version developed 60 hp.

**Pontiac Convertible Coupé (1933).** Pontiac had instant success with American drivers, and soon "killed" the house that had given it birth, Oakland; and in 1931 it turned from a type of model into an actual company. The car illustrated here was well designed and had a strong engine with eight aligned cylinders.

**Chevrolet Master Town Sedan (1940)**

# GENERAL MOTORS

who preferred to spend a little less and still have the quality of costly cars. This policy meant quality competition with cars below a certain price level, and price competition with cars above that level."

The situation inherited by Sloan was chaotic, to say the least; it suffices to note that in 1921 Ford still had 60 percent of the American market, while Chevrolet had only 4 percent, and that the cheapest Chevrolet then cost $820, as against the $335 of the basic version of the Ford Model T. But Sloan's policy, accompanied by an upheaval at the summit and in the administration of the company, soon had its effect: Chevrolet quickly became the best-selling car in America and beat Ford once and for all.

Indeed, at a certain point the opposite problem was posed—that of selling less! To avoid being hit by severe antitrust laws, General Motors was often forced to close down its factories for short periods and send the workers on vacation. This kept the production level below that set by law for the market and spared the company substantial fines. To give an example from recent years, in 1972 General Motors alone produced 50.7 percent of the 11,000,310 vehicles built in the United States that year.

**Chevrolet Master Sport Sedan (1936)**

**Chevrolet Master Town Sedan (1938)**

**GMC Fire-truck (1912).** GMC, one of GM's first brand names, was created exclusively for the construction of industrial vehicles. This fire-truck used the chassis of GMC's model "V," equipped with a four-cylinder gasoline engine and with solid rubber tires.

**Chevrolet Special Cabriolet (1942)**

# JAPAN

**Takuri (1907).** With a rather advanced conception for the era, this machine had a horizontal engine set under the floor. Eighteen in all were built.

## THE ASCENT OF THE RISING SUN

**Mitsubishi A (1918)**

**Ohta OS (1921)**

**Ales M (1924)**

**Datsun Road Star (1931)**

Because of its isolation from the Western world and the social and economic conditions that prevailed there at the start of the nineteenth century, Japan came to motorization rather late. Its first self-propelled vehicle appeared in 1899, when a Yokohama business man imported an electric car. The first real motor-driven car built in Japan was made in 1902. A very enterprising importer, Shintaro Yoshida, who had seen and studied cars in the United States, went into partnership with a technician, Komanosuke Uchiyama. They turned out a four-seater with a 12 hp engine; then they built a second machine with an 18 hp engine that could carry twelve people. Two years later, in 1904, an attempt was made to build a steam-driven car, but it was not successful.

In 1907, Yoshida and Uchiyama produced a new car with a horizontal engine beneath the floor; eighteen of them were built. This car was called "Takuri." That same year saw Japan's first automobile race, wherein ten competitors did about 50 kilometers. After many experiments on the artisan level, and after an attempt at truck building by the army (four were made in the Osaka arsenal), Tokyo saw the birth of the "Dat Car," a four-seater utility model with a two-cylinder engine and three-speed gear box. The "Dat Car" was turned out in fairly large numbers in the small body shop of Masagiro Hashimoto. But for Japan the automobile continued to

# JAPAN

**Ohta Cabriolet (1937)**

**Toyota AB (1936).** The Toyota Motor Co. began producing cars in 1935, with prototype A-1. Successive models AA and AB were directly derived from that prototype.

**Nissan 70 (1937).** Nissan is one of the most famous Japanese names; the "Model 70," built with the technical assistance of the American Graham Paige company, had a six-cylinder, 85 hp engine.

**Sumida H (1933).** The Sumida model H (Sumida came from the river of the same name that crossed Tokyo) was an impressive sedan that looked a bit like the General Motors La Salle.

**Chiyoda H (1935).** One of the rare civilian models turned out by Chiyoda, which mainly produced military vehicles.

be a phenomenon that interested a very small number of people due to the low standard of living.

The first automobile factory was founded in 1922, by Masaya Toyokawa, who set up the Hakayosha company in Tokyo. One hundred and fifty cars were built a year—a small car with an air-cooled engine, the "Otomo." In the meantime, American firms had realized that the Japanese market had prospects. And under the pressure of competition, Toyokawa's small plant closed down in 1927. It is interesting to note that widespread motorization in Japan coincided with the terrible earthquake that destroyed Tokyo and Yokohama; on that occasion, people realized that cars could maintain essential contacts when all other means of communication, such as trains and trams, were eliminated. In 1939, when a law controlling international trade was passed in Japan, the American firms had to pack up and leave. This favored the rise of those national concerns that had managed to resist the ruthless competition of Japan Ford Motors and of General Motors. But war was close at hand, and the Japanese automobile industry had to switch to a military basis for production. Then, too, the lack of raw materials made car production impossible. In 1945, at the end of the war, the annual production of industrial vehicles stood at 10,000 units; that of passenger cars stood at zero.

# The

# automobile in the army

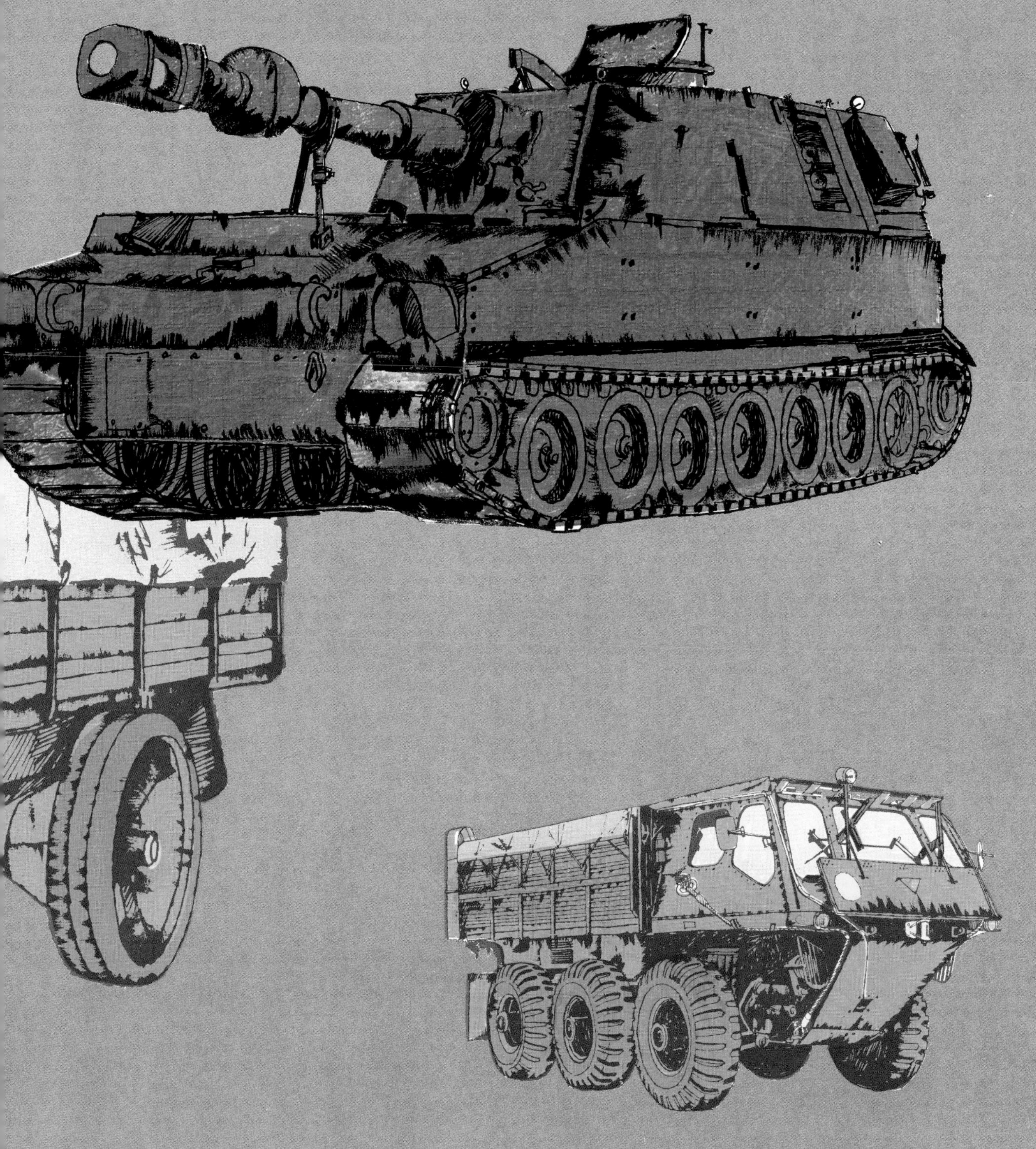

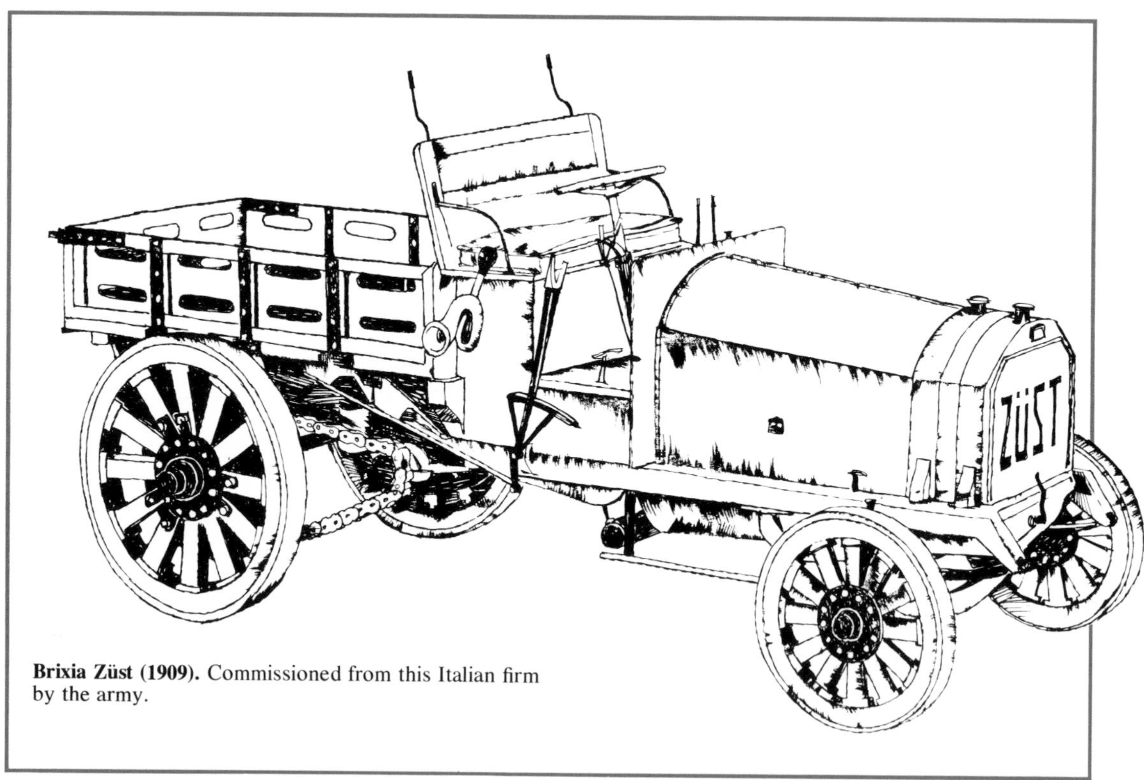


**Brixia Züst (1909).** Commissioned from this Italian firm by the army.

**Fiat 18 BL (1914).** This military truck saw great use during the First World War; it had a four-cylinder, 5650 cc engine.

# The automobile in the army

The first example of a cross-country, or "off-the-road," vehicle dates from the year 1770. In that year, Englishman Richard Lovell Edgeworth patented his "portable track," which could be applied to any kind of cart. The invention was probably destined for use in mines, where there were already in use wagons that the men pushed along tracks. Edgeworth's idea would evidently have spared the company the high cost of laying down rails, which also used up time and delayed exploitation of the mine. Richard Lovell Edgeworth's patent application states: "The invention consists of building a portable track around the cart-wheel. Many pieces of wood, directly attached to one another, are shifted in regular succession, so as to constantly supply a piece of track to the advancing wheel."

It is clear from his description that the various pieces of wood bound to one another were really a kind of track. The vagueness of Edgeworth's description, however, does not permit us to award him paternity of the invention of tracklaying wheels linked to one another—as in present-day tanks—but only that of

the tracklaying wheel not linked to the other wheels of the vehicle. In 1821, however, another Englishman, John Richard Barry, patented what is called a "full track"—that is, tracklaying wheels linked to one another.

Unfortunately, we have no trace of either Edgeworth's or Barry's inventions, apart from what they deposited at the patent office. We also have reasons for doubting that the two inventors gave a practical realization to their ideas.

We do know for sure that the vehicle designed by Guillaume Fender of Buenos Aires was made by Englishman John Clayton Newburn, who even patented it in 1882. The

(*continued on page 186*)

**GMC Columbia (1928).** The first military ambulances date from the Crimean War. This is a General Motors ambulance, made in America.

# JEEP

# THE AUTOMOBILE FOR EVERYWHERE

In 1940, during the Second World War, the United States Army held a competition for the construction of a vehicle with four-wheel drive that could serve for various tasks. Thus the name "Jeep" came from "*ge*neral *p*urpose" vehicle.

The American Bantam Company, the Willys Overland Motor Company, and the Ford Motor Company took part in the competition, and Willys won. An advance order of 1500 was produced, and after 1941 the vehicle was mass produced with the aid of Ford. Even before the end of the war in July 1945, Willys began producing the civilian version of the Jeep. It was called the "Universal" and was very similar to the military model, except for certain details such as larger headlights and a slightly different body. Production was then licensed abroad—for example, to Hotchkiss in France and to Mitsubishi in Japan.

Here are the technical details of the first Jeep. It had a four-aligned-cylinder engine, water-cooled and with 2193.53 cc displacement (a bore and stroke of 79.37 and 111.12 mm); it developed 60 hp at 4000 rpm and a maximum torque capacity of 14.5 kgm at 1800–2000 rpm; it had a side-valve timing system, a compression ratio of 6.48, forced lubrication and forced water cooling by means of a pump and fan, regulated by a thermostat. The oil pan held 3.78 liters (4.73 including the cartridge filter); mechanical single-plate clutch; three-speed gear box, with synchronized second and third, and central gear control on the transmission tunnel. Next to the gear box were the small levers for inserting front-wheel drive and the reducer (with a ratio of 1.97 : 1); counterbalanced crankshaft on three journal boxes; rigid-axle suspension with semi-elliptical, end-play leaf springs and telescopic shock absorbers in both front and rear; 6-volt electrical system with 116 A/h battery; disk brakes with hydraulic four-wheel control, and with a 750 cm² braking surface. The body rested on a strong chassis of boxed sheet steel and was very simple, of the torpedo type without doors; the bare weight was 964 kg (1050 kg when driven)—far above that set by the specifications of the offer, but Willys managed to get it through. The body was 3.37 meters long, 1.57 wide and 1.32 high with the top down, 1.77 with the top up; it had a 2.03 meter wheel base; the turning diameter was 10.70 meters and the height from the ground 22 cm.

As for the performance of the Jeep, it could reach 38 km/h.in first, 65 in second, and 96 km/h in third. Speed was cut in half in low gear.

The maximum slope the Jeep could climb was a sixty percent grade; the fording height, 54 centimeters; and it could tow 450 kg.

# JEEP

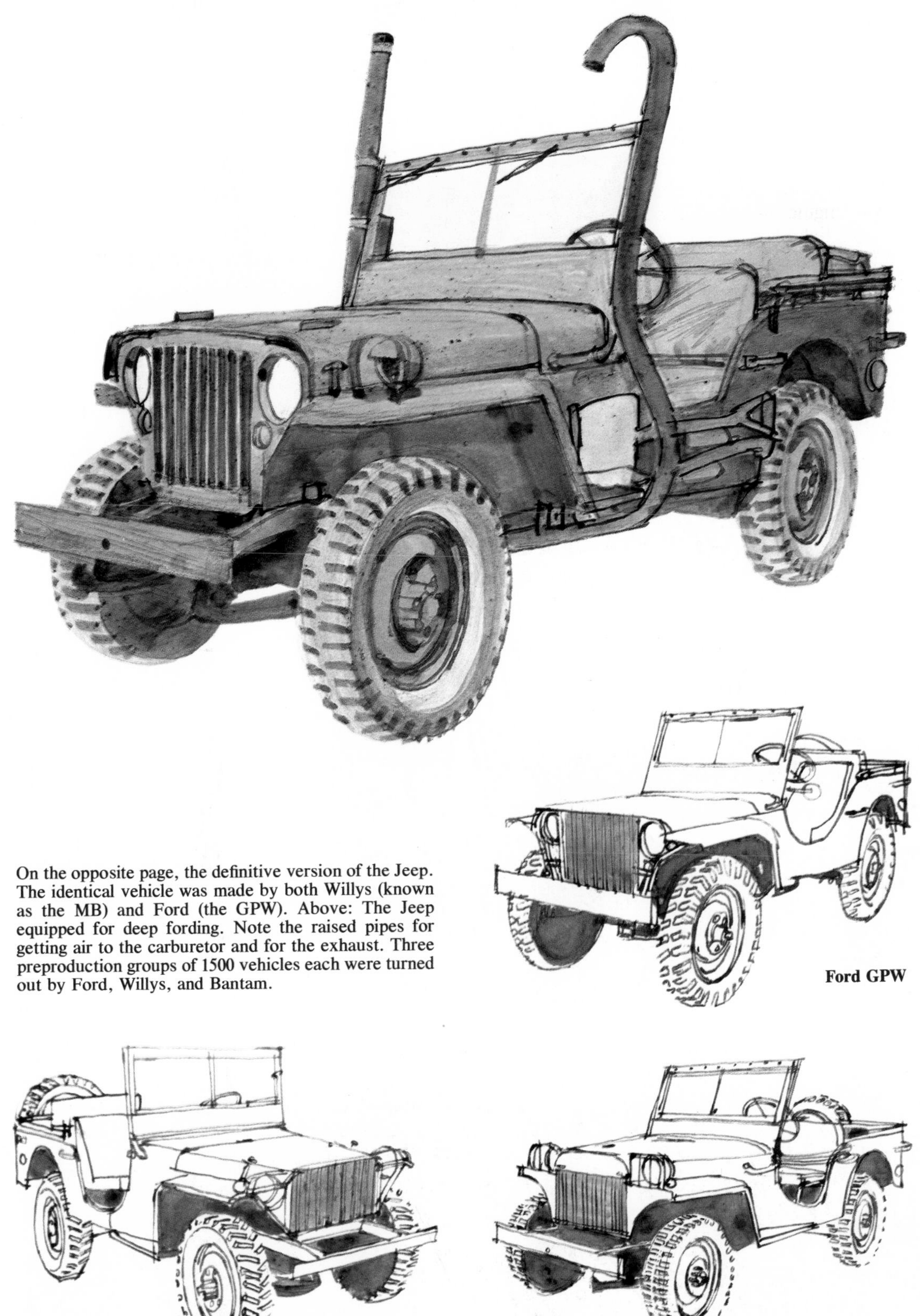

On the opposite page, the definitive version of the Jeep. The identical vehicle was made by both Willys (known as the MB) and Ford (the GPW). Above: The Jeep equipped for deep fording. Note the raised pipes for getting air to the carburetor and for the exhaust. Three preproduction groups of 1500 vehicles each were turned out by Ford, Willys, and Bantam.

**Ford GPW**

**Bantam BRC**

**Willys MA**

tracks functioned the way they do today, apart from a steering mechanism, which did not exist. Since the vehicle had to be drawn by horses, the animals had the sizable task of steering the vehicle.

A partial solution for the problem of steering a tracklaying vehicle was found by Americans Batter and Evans, who, about 1890, patented a tracked vehicle driven by a steam engine; to steer it, there were two front wheels linked to a bar. We find the same solution a few decades later on the tracklaying armored car with front steering wheels.

The Englishman Dunlop also dedicated his attention to this problem. Apart from dealing with pneumatic tires, Dunlop adored anything mechanical, and in 1861 and 1874 he patented a complex steering mechanism for tracklaying vehicles, but it was not successful.

Only with the very first tanks—on the eve of the First World War—was the perennial problem resolved. In fact, it sufficed to give the vehicle a differential gear, and endow the right and left tracks with independent brakes, to let the machine make all the curves it desired. But at this point we must leave tracklaying vehicles to their destiny (one could write a volume on them alone) and deal with cross-country vehicles that move on wheels.

Even though the need for a cross-country vehicle was deeply felt at the turn of the century—for the simple reason that there were few roads, and those in existence were in poor condition—it was only in 1903 that the Dutch firm of Spyker presented the first four-wheel drive vehicle and in 1905 that Austro-Daimler offered the first armored car, also with four-wheel drive. But only in 1910 did there appear an efficient cross-country machine with four-wheel drive; the light "Quad" truck built by the American Jeffery firm. (This firm merged in 1917 with Nash.)

Jeffery was a great producer of industrial vehicles—in fact, the greatest in the world. The "Quad" made first the fortune of Jeffery and then that of Nash, which sold thousands of them to the American army and, when the First World War broke out, to the French and English armies. By the end of the war, in 1918, Nash had become—mainly due to the "Quad"—the world's most important producer of industrial vehicles, with a production that year of 11,490 machines. The Nash cross-country vehicle was both simple and strong. Practically without a body, it could carry about a ton and had solid rubber tires, which usually had chains to make cross-country driving easier.

Although its performance was not great, this cross-country truck was the best the science of the time could offer and was unrivaled for years. The United States enjoyed the fame of the "Quad" for years, and it was not dethroned until 1940, when the Jeep was born.

In Italy, in 1923, the War Ministry announced a competition for the national

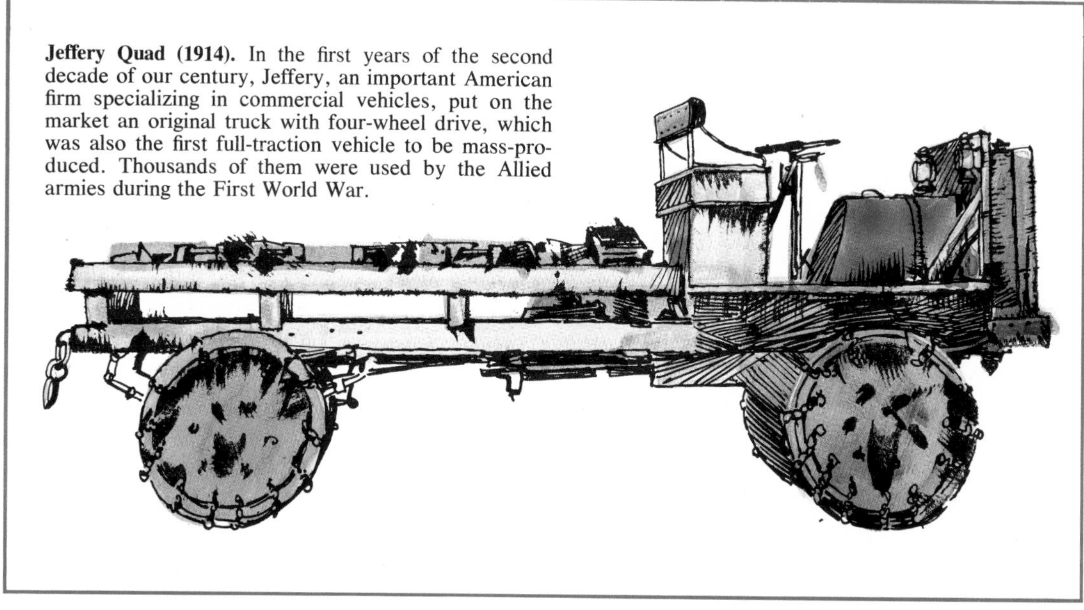

**Jeffery Quad (1914).** In the first years of the second decade of our century, Jeffery, an important American firm specializing in commercial vehicles, put on the market an original truck with four-wheel drive, which was also the first full-traction vehicle to be mass-produced. Thousands of them were used by the Allied armies during the First World War.

automobile industry, for the production of a heavy tractor *with total adhesion,* for pulling artillery pieces over any kind of terrain.

A year later, only the Motomeccanica company of Milan offered examples of tractors, which only differed from one another in the use of a varying type of electrical system. The War Ministry then ordered forty-five of these tractors, which were designed by engineer Cesare Pavesi, from Motomeccanica. These tractors were ordered for testing; a larger order was to follow if they were shown to be satisfactory. The tests showed that the machines were excellent, and the Ministry decided to turn to a larger factory to secure at least 1000 of these vehicles. Fiat was chosen, and it passed the order to its SPA works. Thus the Pavesi "Model 26" tractor was born, the first cross-country vehicle produced in Italy.

A few years later, the same Ministry set up another competition for producing a small mountain truck to be used—even on mule tracks—for reaching high altitudes. Fiat presented a highly original plan for a vehicle called "Autocarretta 1014"—which deserved a better fate than it met with. The vehicle was the forerunner of the most advanced American projects of thirty years later, such as the "Gama Goat." The Autocarretta 1014 was a six-wheeled vehicle, jointed in the center; the front part consisted of a body with two directional wheels in front and two driving wheels behind; the rear, of a one-axle wagon with two driving wheels. The wagon was linked to the front section by a ball-bearing joint and, with respect to that section, could take any vertical angle up to 30 degrees, both up and down, as well as any transverse inclination up to a variation in level between the two wheels of 40 cm.

The entire vehicle turned within a diameter of 4 meters, so as to be able to face the narrowest turns in the mule tracks; and its narrow width and wheeltrack (1.38 and 1.20 meters, respectively) let it pass anywhere without difficulty. This vehicle had the same

**Fiat Autocarretta 1014 (1930).** An original vehicle with six cross-country wheels, which never got beyond the prototype stage. It made use of the mechanical setup of the "514" (four cylinders, 1.5 liters), and the four rear wheels supplied the traction. The small trailer was completely flexible.

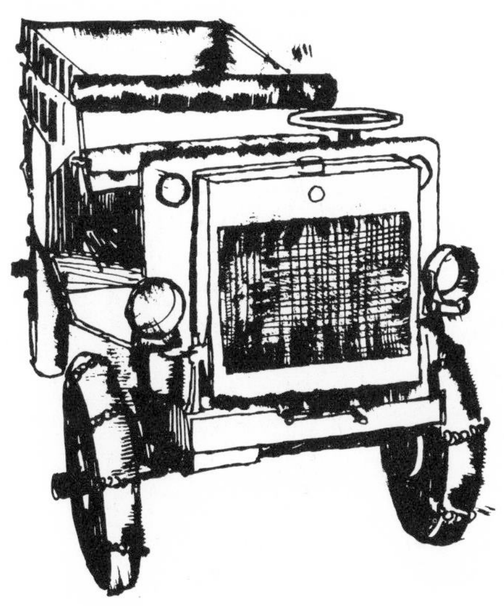

**Jeffery Quad (1915).** The first mass-produced four-wheel drive vehicle was without a body.

**Volkswagen, Type 166 (1942).** From 1941 to the end of the war, the VW was built in an amphibious version. The "166" model had a 1131 cc, 25 hp engine and a rear propeller.

four-cylinder, 1438 cc engine as the Fiat 514, with 28 hp.

But the Ministry's competition for a small mountain truck was won by a project, prepared by engineer Cappa of Ansaldo, for a vehicle whose four wheels could both steer and drive at the same time. Sanctioned in 1932, with the name of "Autocarretta Model 32," it was mass produced by OM in Brescia as part of the Fiat group, since the Ansaldo company no longer produced vehicles by the time the project was approved.

This vehicle too had some interesting features. The engine, with four aligned cylinders, had forced-air cooling, 1616 cc displacement, and the low power of 21 hp at 2400 rpm. In fact, the only defect of this interesting vehicle was its lack of power, which allowed it to reach a speed of only 23 km/h.

In the meantime, Europe showed little interest in cross-country vehicles, apart from the tracklaying machines of Citroën and, above all, the heavy vehicles—usually six-wheeled, with four-wheel drive—made by Germany in that period (Mercedes, Hanomag, Horch, Ford, etc.).

The cross-country vehicles were generally adapted from normal mass-produced cars and were almost always without four-wheel drive. Let us note, from that era, the Austin Pram, used as a reconnaissance vehicle by the British army, and derived directly from the very popular "Seven" of 757 cc, the only difference being the cross-country tires and reinforced suspension.

Only at the start of the Second World War was an efficient cross-country machine with four-wheel drive created. We are referring to the Volkswagen "Type 166" of 1942, an amphibious vehicle which followed the "Type 82" of 1940 with two-wheel drive. The Type 82 had worked well, but the fact that it had no complete transmission and no low

**Willys Overland Jeepster (1950).** The classic "city" Jeep had a four- or six-cylinder engine and rear-wheel drive only.

**Land-Rover 88 Regular (1958).** Rover's first cross-country vehicle was presented at the Amsterdam Automobile Show in 1948. It soon became famous and was used all over the world.

gears greatly limited its possibilities in cross-country driving. On the other hand, it did have a differential gear that could be blocked.

Both these vehicles were designed by the engineer Ferdinand Porsche, who modified the chassis platform and part of the mechanical setup of the Volkswagen he had already designed. In December 1939, the project for Type 82 was ready; mass production began the next year and ended in 1945, when 52,018 machines had been built.

Even though it had only two-wheel drive, the Type 82 proved useful in Africa, too.

The Type 166 went into production in 1942 and continued to the summer of 1944, during which time 14,267 vehicles were built. This machine was amphibious, with a tail propeller directly linked to the engine. The front wheels acted as a rudder in navigation. The body, with its typical hull shape, was completely watertight and without doors.

As for America, as we already noted, after the Quad no other cross-country vehicles were produced in the United States for a long time. Still, the American army experimented with various models in prototype at Aberdeen, Maryland, as far back as 1920. Some of these had highly original features. There was an amphibious one, for instance, that had to be "guided" by a soldier who followed the vehicle; the virtue of being amphibious was clearly proportional to the swimming ability of the driver.

Many other prototypes used the chassis of the very popular Ford Model T. Some of these had been given front-wheel drive; others had airplane wheels instead of normal tires; and still others used tracks. And finally there was a curious reconnaissance vehicle designed by an officer in the American army and called "flat-belly," because the two occupants had to lie flat on their stomachs inside it.

Some of the prototypes studied by the army at Aberdeen, like the small Ford 1936 truck turned into a four-wheel drive vehicle, helped to decide the famous rules for the competition announced on June 27, 1940, by the American army for the designing and pro-

**Alfa Romeo AR 51 (1951).** Nicknamed "Matta" (wild) because it performed well on all kinds of terrain.

duction of a light cross-country vehicle, called "Truck 1/4 Ton 4 × 4." In those years, the United States Army was carrying out a rearmament program that foreshadowed, among other things, the unification of means of transportation. It was decided, in particular, to reduce the chassis to six basic types, on which not more than sixteen different bodies could be mounted (ambulances, radio cars, trucks, etc.). The vehicles were then to be classified according to their load capacity, that is: ¼, ½, 1½, 2½, 4, and 6 tons. Many details were reduced to a minimum, such as batteries (from eight to two), dynamos (from eight to one), fanbelts (from twenty-one to six), door handles (from eight to one), etc. Unification was to make production faster and easier and to reduce the stock of spare parts, with advantages that are easily imagined, especially in wartime.

We thus come to that fatal June 27, 1940, the date on which the Truck 1/4 Ton 4 × 4 competition was announced. No fewer than 135 automobile industries were invited to participate; but since the period set for sending in the projects was very brief, because of the pressure of war in Europe, only two firms replied: the American Bantam Company and the Willys Overland Motors.

The competition foresaw the construction, within seventy-five days, of seventy prototypes of a light cross-country vehicle with the following qualifications: four-wheel drive; a load capacity of 270 kg; a weight of vehicle in motion within 680 kg, so as to permit its transport by air; a wheelbase and a wheeltrack not more than 2.04 and 1.20 meters, respectively; and an engine with a torque capacity of at least 12 kgm.

Since the seventy-five days set by the rules were far too few to allow for one building of a preproduction group of 70 vehicles, Willys requested at least four months for the completion of the prototypes. The Defense Department rejected this request and gave the contract to Bantam. And, in that summer in 1940, one of the smallest American automo-

**Fiat "Campagnola" (1960).** The best-selling Italian cross-country vehicle. It was presented in 1951 with a four-cylinder gasoline engine; later a Diesel version was added.

**International Scout 800 (1961).** Larger than the Jeep, it had a four-cylinder, 2.5-liter, 93 hp engine.

**Morris Mini Moke (1963).** Nicknamed the "Moke" or "Donkey" because it had all the mechanical parts of the English utility car. It thus had only front-wheel drive.

**Toyota Land Cruiser Station Wagon (1962).** The most popular Japanese cross-country vehicle; it had a six-aligned-cylinder, 3.8-liter, 145 hp engine.

bile companies began working on a project that would later help the Allies win the Second World War.

Bantam was really too small a company for such a task. The firm was born in 1931 in Butler, Pennsylvania, with the purpose of assembling on the spot the English Austin Seven car, sold in the United States under the name of "American Bantam." Bantam was soon in economic difficulty, given the lack of success of its car, wrong for the American market. Even though the American Bantam cost only $425 and had an attractive two-seater sports car body (far more striking than the original), few models were sold, and in 1939 the firm had a net loss of about $750,000. Obviously the small firm had staked all its hopes on the new cross-country vehicle for the army, even though it had limited experience in production.

Despite all this, Bantam prepared and consigned in time the first batch of seventy vehicles for the American army. Although the prototypes had their defects, they made an excellent impression on the commission set up to examine them. This convinced Willys to get back in the competition. It built a prototype at its own expense—not at the army's request—to submit to the commission for judgment, sure that it could do better than Bantam, which was known to be without

*(continued on page 196)*

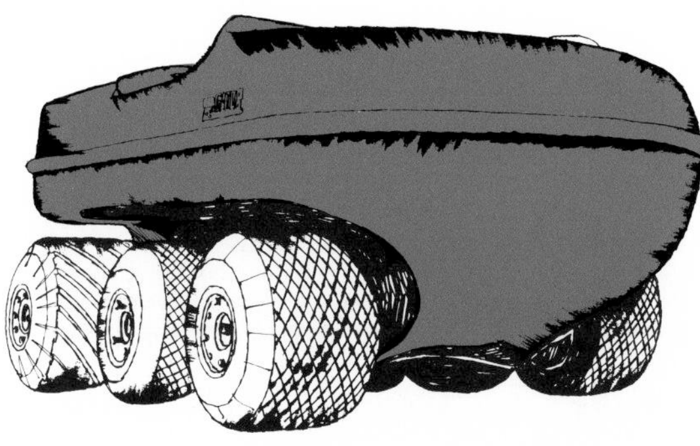

**A.T.V. (All Terrain Vehicles).** The trademark of all recent American vehicles with plastic bodies and six or more low-pressure wheels, able to cross even a water course.

**Citroën Sahara (1958).** The French firm put two engines of 425 cc each on the "2 CV" body (one on the fore carriage and one on the rear carriage), thus creating this remarkable 27 hp cross-country vehicle.

# ARMORED CARS

## ARMORED WHEELS

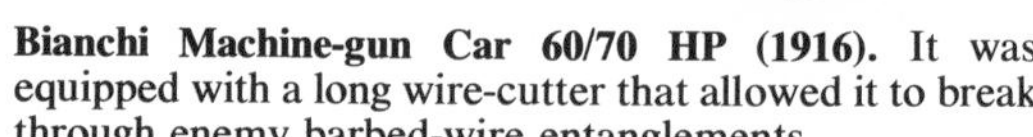

**Bianchi Machine-gun Car 60/70 HP (1916).** It was equipped with a long wire-cutter that allowed it to break through enemy barbed-wire entanglements.

**Austro-Daimler (1904).** Austrian-built and considered to be the first armored car in history. It had four-wheel drive—in 1904.

**Rolls-Royce A.T.P. (1914).** Developed from a car, it had one-axle drive only.

At the start of this century, there was a lot of science fiction conjecture as to the automobile's future. The Englishman Simms dreamed up (and built) in 1899 a De Dion quadricycle armed with a machine-gun which was protected by a metal shield. He didn't know that he had invented the armored car. Taking the hint, in 1902 the French firm of Charron Girardot and Vaigt mounted a machine-gun on one of its normal 40 hp cars, which was then endowed with a revolving turret in 1906. In 1903–1904, Austro-Daimler put a real armored car on the road; it was completely covered with armor, and had a revolving gun turret and four-wheel drive. But the first nation to make use of the armored car in an actual war was Italy, during the Libyan War, using Fiat and Bianchi chassis, thoroughly armor-plated and armed. The most famous armored car of the First World War was the German Ehrhard model (1915), with both front and back steering wheels so as to go backward without turning, four forward and reverse speeds, an 85 hp engine, space for an eight- or nine-man crew, and three or four machine-guns. It weighed eight tons.

When the Second World War broke out, all those involved had highly maneuverable armored cars. The main ones were the English two-seater Scout, the three-ton Daimler, the Italian "AB 41" with four independent directional wheels, and the German "Puma" with a 30 mm armored plate covering.

Today there is a tendency to use these armored vehicles mainly for police and antiguerilla purposes. The most interesting at the moment are the French Panhard EBR, with central retractable wheels, the English Saladin, and the Russian BTR 40 P, which is amphibious (with jet propulsion in the water) and armed with missiles.

# ARMORED CARS

**Büssing Nag Puma (1945).** Built in Germany, this vehicle had eight wheels to bear its enormous weight.

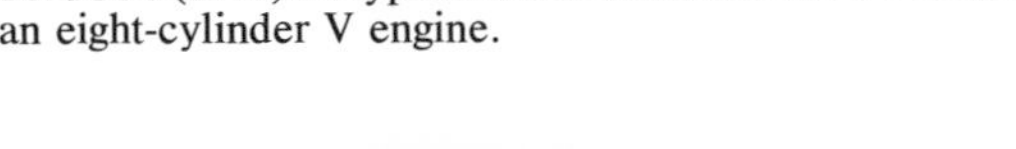

**Ford M 8 (1943).** A typical American armored car. It had an eight-cylinder V engine.

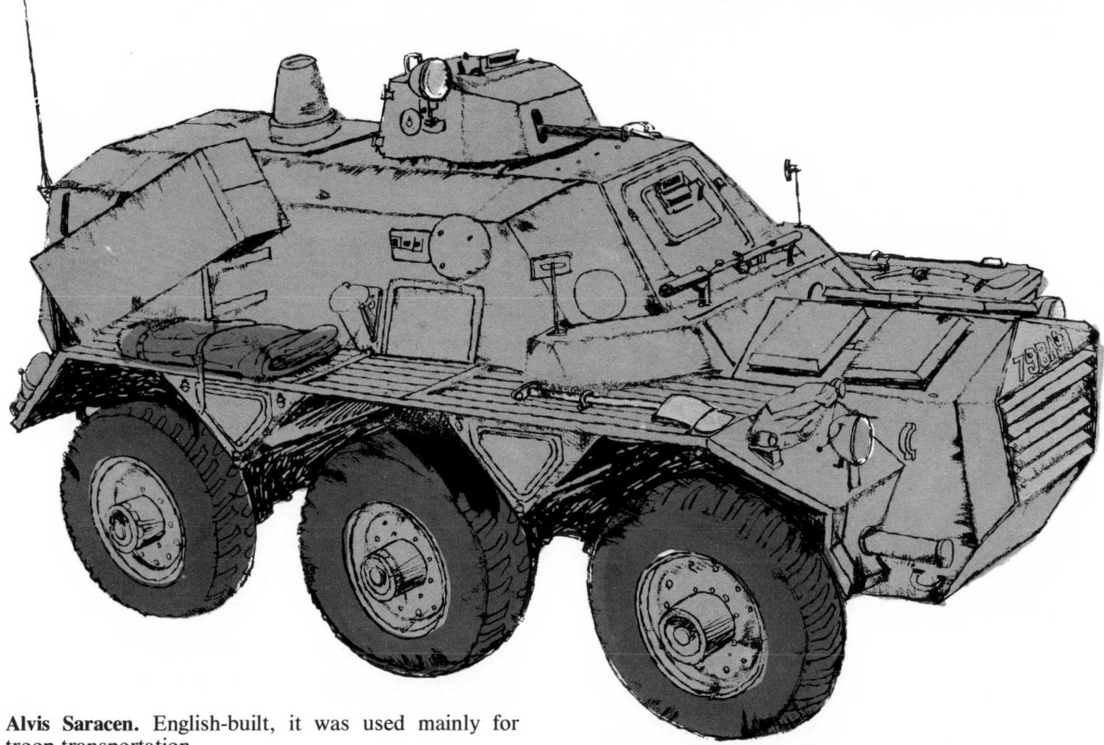

**Alvis Saracen.** English-built, it was used mainly for troop transportation.

**Alvis Saladin.** It had a Rolls-Royce engine and six-wheel drive.

**Auto Union DKW "Munga" (1954).** Winner of a German Army competition for a military vehicle prototype, it was produced in a civilian version as well, until 1968. It had a two-stroke, 1-liter engine.

experience in the field and without adequate production facilities.

The Willys prototype was tested in November 1940. It was considered so interesting that the army asked Willys to enter the competition and try out for the definitive vehicle. But at the same time the American Defense Department convinced Ford to present its own cross-country design. Ford's immense production capacity fascinated American military leaders.

So at the end of 1940 the army signed a contract with Bantam, Willys, and Ford for a preproduction series of 1500 vehicles each, to be delivered in the shortest possible time. This large number of vehicles was simply to help decide, after thorough testing in all types of climate and on all kinds of terrain, which of the three prototypes was best for the American army.

Bantam's vehicle had a Continental engine (since the firm itself was unable to produce many engines), with 1835 cc and air cooling; Ford's had a four-cylinder V, 1940 cc engine which had been used before on one of the firm's small tractors; and, last, the Willys prototype had a four-aligned-cylinder, 2193 cc, water-cooled engine. The first two engines developed 45 hp, the third 60 hp. All three had a fairly similar body, not too different from the Jeep.

The army chose the Willys prototype, with some minor variants, and promptly ordered from that firm a first batch of 16,000 vehicles. Since the Willys production capacity was insufficient for the government order, Ford entered the picture; it turned out, in the years that followed, a few hundred thousand Jeeps exactly like those of Willys (except that the Ford name was stamped on them instead of Willys). Bantam's task ended with the consignment of the preproduction series of 1500 vehicles, and the firm closed down in 1941 once and for all. By the time the war was over, Willys and Ford together had produced 639,245 Jeeps (277,806 by Willys, 361,439 by Ford).

As for the name given to the vehicle—the military name was "MA 1/4 ton 4 × 4 truck," and the next model was to become the "MB"—the word "Jeep" supposedly came from the words "*ge*neral *p*urpose."

**Alvis Stalwart (1966).** A large military vehicle with six-wheel drive that could be adapted to various uses: troop transportation, the carrying and launching of missiles, artillery tractor, and radar vehicle.

# TANKS

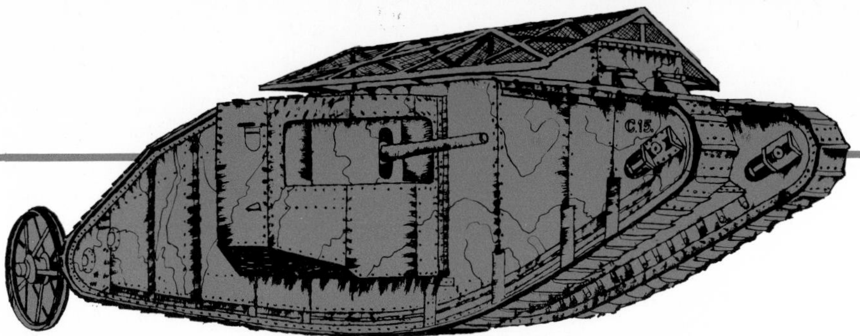

**Mark I (1916).** British-built. It had a typical rhomboid form and two side cannons.

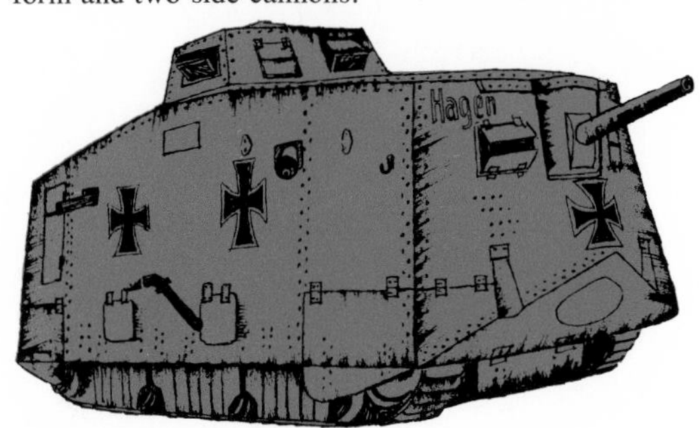


**A 7 V (1917).** German-built. It had a very compact line and had one cannon and six machine-guns.

**Renault F.T. (1918).** French-built. It had a revolving turret holding the cannon.

**Churchill (1943).** British-built. It was planned for landing operations and thus functioned in water as well as on land. The air intake and exhaust pipes were therefore set in the upper part of the tank.

The tank was born in the First World War and made its debut in the Somme region in France on September 15, 1916; it was the monstrous English "Mark 1," a rhomboid encircled by tracks, eight meters long, weighing twenty-nine tons, with two cannons (57 mm) on two gun turrets, a 105 hp engine, and space for a crew of eight men.

Its German adversary came too late—in 1918. It was the forty-five-ton A 7 V, with six machine-guns, a crew of 18, and 30 mm armored plate (the Mark had 15 mm plate, which the Germans easily perforated). The A 7 V had two engines of 130 hp each.

The French put on the field in 1916 their Schneider, a 41-ton tank with a 200 hp Renault engine, a 35-mm plate covering, a 105 mm (and 75) cannon, and two machine-guns.

Italy, for its part, had its Fiat 2000: 38 tons, a 65 mm cannon, seven machine-guns, space for ten men, and a 240 hp engine.

In the Second World War, the PKW IV was the weapon of the Panzerdivisionen; it weighed from 17.3 to 25 tons, had plate of from 20 to 80 mm, a 75 mm cannon, an engine of from 250 to 300 hp, could do a little less than 400 km/h and had a fuel capacity of up to 300 kilometers. The PKW's main obstacle was the Russian T 34 (especially the last 1943 series) of 32 tons, with 75 mm plate, and an 85 mm cannon. To face the threat, in 1942 the Germans built the famous Tiger tank, of 50 tons, and a year later the Panzer (46 tons) with 120 mm plate and a 75 mm cannon.

But the tank that triumphed in armored warfare in the West was the American Sherman tank (M4) which was first produced in 1942. The last version weighed 33 tons, had plate of from 76 to 100 mm, engine power of from 353 to 450 hp, and could do more than 40 km/h.

The main postwar versions are the American M 47 (115 mm plate, 810 hp, speed 60 km/h and weight 44 tons); the Russian T 10 (50 tons, 200 mm plate, 122 mm cannon, 700 hp, speed 45 km/h); and the German Leopard (also used by the British Army) of 39.5 tons, with an English 105 mm cannon, 830 hp, and a speed of 63 km/h.

**PKW IV (1943)**

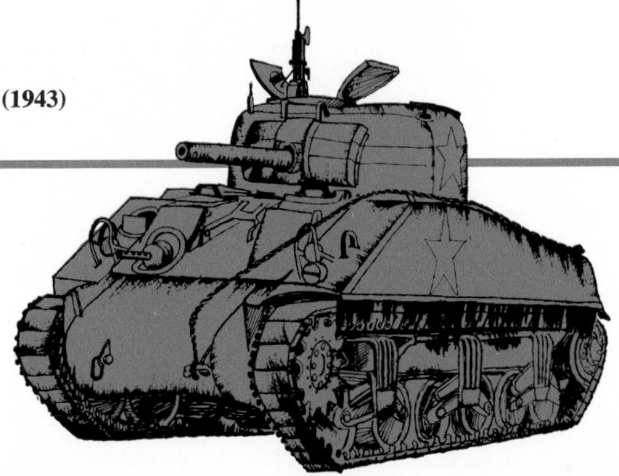

**Sherman (1943)**

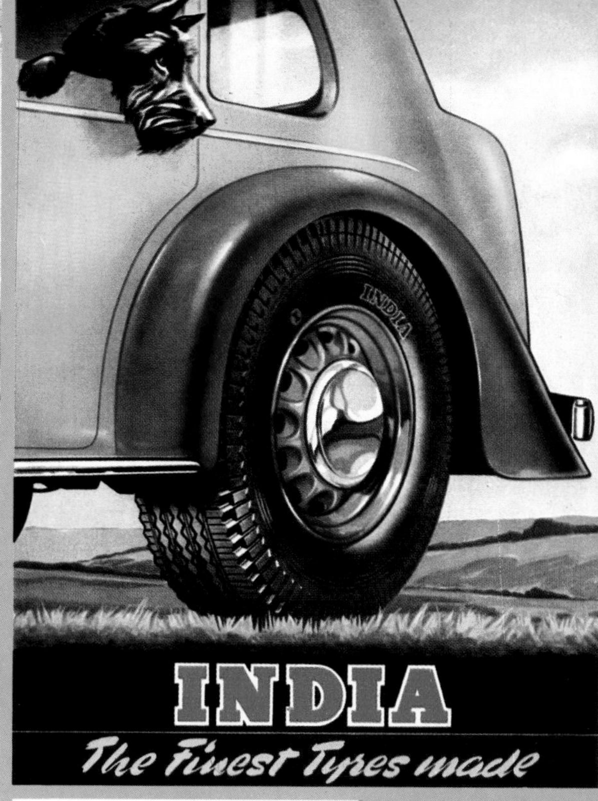

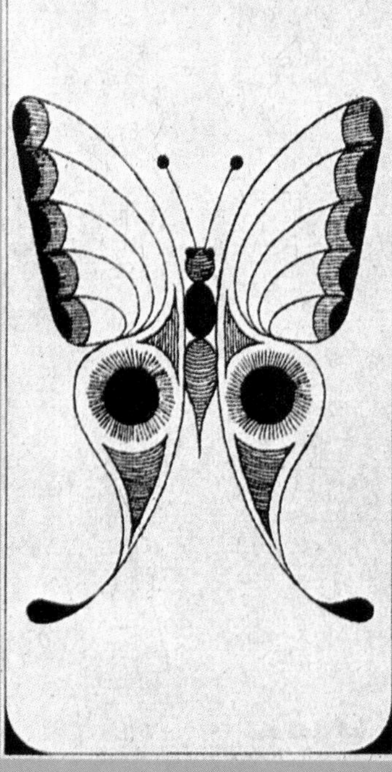

*Retrouver les sentiers du soleil et la piste des forêts oubliées, l'issue de tant d'encombrements, la sortie de secours : tout le monde en rêve, embarrassé de voisinages et de promiscuités obligatoires. Cette évasion, cette libération est à la portée de tous : écartant les roseaux d'une plage inconnue ou croisant sur le sable rose d'une Camargue secrète, la 2 CV va surprendre les merveilles dans leurs dernières cachettes. Elle va et vient, explore, frôle les broussailles des garrigues, contourne les calvaires romans et promène nonchalamment des rocs à la mer les vacances familiales. En tout confort, en toute sécurité : la 2 CV fait corps avec la route, elle règne sur les virages, les bosses et les ornières, les terrains glissants, les prairies ou les plages. En voyage ou en promenade, quelle que soit la saison, quel que soit le temps, faites confiance à la 2 CV, lisez vos cartes et laissez-la faire le reste. Sur tous les chemins du monde, la 2 CV transporte la joie de vivre. Dans son coffre, avec tous les bagages, on trouve les traces successives de tous les heureux voyages de l'année,*

# Rebirth of the automobile

**Morris Eight, Series E (1946).** Right after the war, British automobile manufacturers began to turn out once again the models produced before the war, with amazing rapidity and very slight modifications. Such was the case with the Morris utility car, offered at a basic price of £270 in the two-door version and of 300 in the four-door model. The "Series E," derived from the "Minor" of the 1930s, was the first English utility car with hydraulic brakes. (During the postwar period there were many cars circulating in Great Britain with mechanical brakes, even high-priced models.)

**Morris Minor (1949).** The "Minor," the first truly modern English car built after the war, was entirely designed by Alec Issigonis, who was later to create the "Mini." Here he made use of a load-bearing body and front independent suspension with torsion bars. When it was first presented—at a basic price of £299—the "Minor" used the same engine as the "Series E," then replaced (after 1950) with a more modern overhead valve motor. The car was produced until 1970.

**Tucker Torpedo (1948).** Despite the great publicity campaign that preceded its appearance, the Tucker was only turned out in a preproduction series of 100 cars. It had a rear engine with six counterposed cylinders, closed-circuit water cooling, 9.7-liter displacement, and 150 hp. The car also had disk brakes on all four wheels, shock-absorbing steering wheel, an ejectable windshield, and a third, revolving, central headlight.

**Triumph 1800 (1946)**

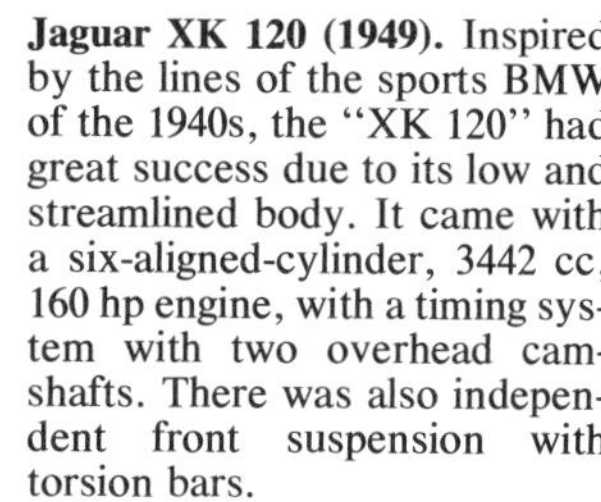

**Jaguar XK 120 (1949).** Inspired by the lines of the sports BMW of the 1940s, the "XK 120" had great success due to its low and streamlined body. It came with a six-aligned-cylinder, 3442 cc, 160 hp engine, with a timing system with two overhead camshafts. There was also independent front suspension with torsion bars.

# Rebirth of the automobile

On November 21, 1945, a long strike began in the American plants of the General Motors Company. The war had ended not long before, on August 14, with the surrender of Japan following on that of Germany on May 8.

The only automobile factories to come out of the war untouched were those of the United States, on which not a bomb had fallen. Those factories had been hastily converted to the production of war matériel in December 1941, when the war with Japan broke out, and then been reconverted to automobile production even before fighting ended. In fact, on May 11, 1945—three days after Germany surrendered, and while the war in Asia still continued—the War Production Board, which planned and controlled armament production in America, announced that from the first of July of that year the production of civilian automobiles would begin again, while from May 22 the car manufacturers had already started making spare parts.

On July 3, 1945, the first Ford model for 1946 (and the first American car made after the war) left the assembly line of the factory in Detroit. It was driven by Henry Ford II, the twenty-seven-year-old grandson of the founder of that automobile empire. The car was really a 1942 model with a slightly modified body and certain new details; but the country was starved for automobiles and was ready to accept anything on wheels, as long as it had an engine, a steering wheel, and brakes!

**Jaguar 6-Cylinder (1947).** Basically similar to the models produced before the war, the Jaguar of the early postwar years could use either a four-aligned-cylinder, 1775 cc, or six-cylinder, 2664 or 3485 cc engine, with overhead valve timing. The most powerful version (125 hp) could reach a speed of 145 km/h. It had rigid-axle front suspension.

People were tired of seeing Ford turn out planes (the "Liberators"), tanks, Jeeps, and other military vehicles; of seeing General Motors produce plane engines, bombs, helmets, and trucks of all types; of knowing that Packard was busy making plane engines (the twelve-cylinder V "Merlins" used on the "Mustangs"); and of expecting from Kaiser

**Peugeot 203 (1948).** The first Peugeot planned after the war. It had a four-aligned-cylinder, overhead valve, 1290 cc engine with 49 hp and a maximum speed of 115 km/h.

**Alfa Romeo 6C 2500 Sport (1947).** Right after the war, Alfa Romeo began production again on a small scale with its "Freccia D'Oro" (golden arrow) coupé; it had a famous six-aligned-cylinder, 2443 cc, 90 hp engine with a double overhead camshaft.

only small cruisers and transport ships (the famous "Liberty ships").

Here are some statistics that illustrate the contribution made by the American automobile industry to the Allied war effort. Apart from almost all military trucks and other vehicles, the car factories also turned out during the war 87% of the airplane bombs made in the United States; 85% of the helmets; 75% of the plane engines; 57% of the tanks; 56% of the carbine rifles; 50% of the Diesel engines; 47% of the machine guns; 10% of the planes—and so on, for a total value of almost $30 billion of that time, a sum that no other nation at war could possibly equal.

And yet that first year of automobile production after the end of the war was a tough one. On the one hand, there was a good market that would take any car offered it; on the other, industries weakened by strikes, by a lack of skilled labor and raw material, and above all by the difficulty in reconverting the plants from a wartime basis to the production of civilian cars.

A year after the start of civilian produc-

**Renault 4 CV (1947).** The first real utility car built in France after the war. The "4 CV" soon became very popular; it had a four-cylinder, 748cc (17 hp) rear engine and independent four-wheel suspension.

**Renault Juvaquatre (1946).** First offered in 1937, and introduced again after the war, slightly altered, this first Renault with a load-bearing body had a four-aligned-cylinder, water-cooled, 1003 cc engine that let it reach a speed of 100 km/h.

**Lancia Ardea (1948).** Presented in 1939 as a Lancia utility car, and equipped with a four-cylinder engine with only 903 cc, this model was offered again after the war in an improved version with, among other things, a five-speed gear box.

**Studebaker Champion (1950).** The oldest American firm (it produced horse carts as far back as the middle of the nineteenth century, before turning out cars) revolutionized postwar styling by entrusting designer Raymond Loewy—famous for the Coca-Cola bottle, among other things—with the design of its cars; the results were seen in 1946 in this futuristic line with its rounded shape, wide use of glass, and wrap-around windows.

tion, a million cars had still not been turned out, too little for a nation used to building an average of five million cars a year. Then in the second half of 1946, there was a remarkable recovery; within that very year, the American automobile industry turned out 3,090,000 cars—that is, the majority of the 3,798,000 cars produced all over the world (81.4 percent of the total).

Of the 708,000 cars built in the rest of the world, 365,000—more than 51 percent—were produced in Great Britain, despite the great damage inflicted on its automobile industry, especially in the Coventry area. (For instance, Jaguar had been almost completely destroyed by a violent bombing raid.) Despite all that, the rebirth of the automobile in Great Britain was exceptional and, proportionally, even greater than that of the United

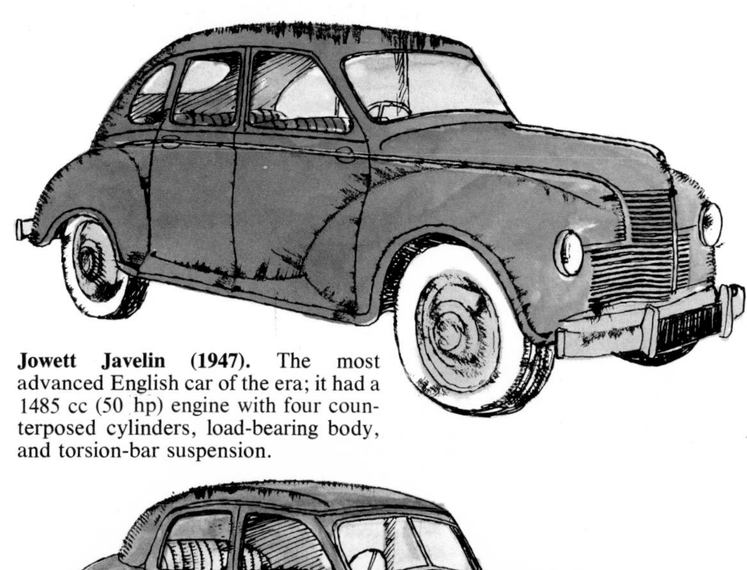

**Jowett Javelin (1947).** The most advanced English car of the era; it had a 1485 cc (50 hp) engine with four counterposed cylinders, load-bearing body, and torsion-bar suspension.

**Riley 1 1/2-liter (1947).** One of the most handsome and most classic English cars of the postwar period, with a four-cylinder, 1496 cc, 55 hp engine.

**Ford Anglia (1947).** The "Anglia" had a four-cylinder, side-valve engine with 933 cc and 23 hp, as well as mechanical brakes and rigid-axle suspension.

**Fiat 1400 (1950).** The first completely new Fiat of the postwar period, and the first car by that firm with a load-bearing body. The motor was a four-aligned-cylinder, with 1395 cc and 44 hp, and the maximum speed was 120 km/h.

**Lanchester Ten (1947)**

# VOLKSWAGEN

# THE PEOPLE'S CAR

**Prototype (1935).** Part of a small preproduction series destined for the testing of the future Volkswagen.

When, in autumn of 1933, Adolf Hitler summoned Ferdinand Porsche—owner of a successful car-designing studio in Stuttgart—to come to Berlin and asked him to design a popular four-seater car with a maximum speed of 100 km/h, to sell for not more than 1,000 marks (the price of an average motorcycle at that time), Porsche replied that such a project was impossible. That seemed to end the matter, but a few months later, the German car manufacturers' association renewed the request, and Porsche finally accepted.

But costs were too high, and the brilliant inventor went to America for a personal look at how its car makers, especially Ford, managed to keep costs so low. So the Kdf (later to be called Volkswagen) was born. It was a blend of European genius—Porsche was Austrian—and American production methods. The first prototypes were made by Mercedes in 1934. Production was started in 1939 (and almost instantly blocked by the war), owing to an original advance-payment installment plan that permitted the German government to collect the necessary capital even before a single brick for the factory was laid.

Production began again right after the war, due to the initiative of Heinz Nordhoff, who was already turning out 1785 cars in 1945, which grew to 280,000 in 1955 and 1,091,000 in 1965. The VW quickly invaded all the important markets and, on February 17, 1972, even won the title of the World's most-produced car; that day it beat the famous 15,007,033 quota reached forty-five years earlier by the Ford Model T.

Since July 1970, when its "K 70" was presented, Volkswagen seems to have been won over to front-wheel drive, while continuing to produce its rear-engine car designed by Porsche. The "K 70" was in fact followed by the "Passat," the "Scirocco," and the "Golf," all with front-wheel drive engines.

Although Ferdinand Porsche was a well-known

**1939.** The first vehicle mass-produced, if only for a short time, before the war. It had a 985 cc engine with four counterposed cylinders.

**VW 1302 (1970).** The up-to-date version of the VW, with the engine raised to 1285 or 1584 cc, a larger luggage compartment, and new front suspension.

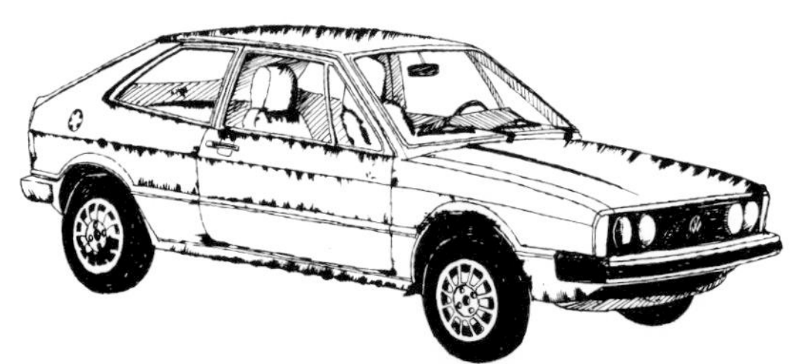

**VW Scirocco (1974)**

# PORSCHE

The first car designed by Porsche, in 1901.

**Porsche (1948).** The first car to bear the name of Ferdinand Porsche; it was produced in a limited series in Austria and then in Germany (in Stuttgart). It had a four-counterposed-cylinder engine derived from that of the Volkswagen.

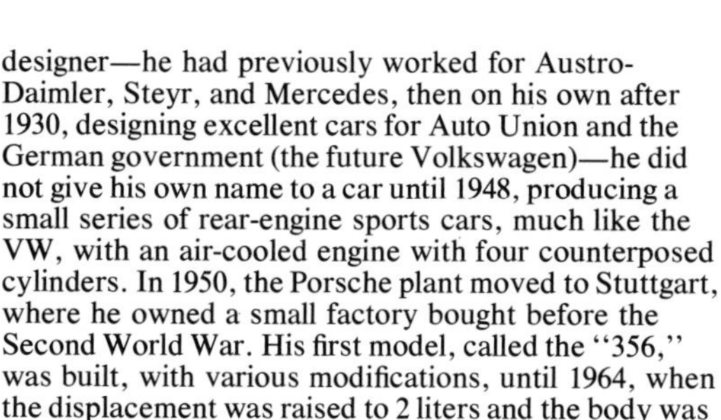

designer—he had previously worked for Austro-Daimler, Steyr, and Mercedes, then on his own after 1930, designing excellent cars for Auto Union and the German government (the future Volkswagen)—he did not give his own name to a car until 1948, producing a small series of rear-engine sports cars, much like the VW, with an air-cooled engine with four counterposed cylinders. In 1950, the Porsche plant moved to Stuttgart, where he owned a small factory bought before the Second World War. His first model, called the "356," was built, with various modifications, until 1964, when the displacement was raised to 2 liters and the body was thoroughly revised, while still preserving the round line typical of the brand.

From the beginning, the Porsche has always been considered an excellent racing car and has won countless victories in all types of competition. This has allowed the firm, originally quite small, to expand greatly, and adopt a rhythm of production truly exceptional for a car with the class and performance of the Porsche. The Stuttgart company has had spectacular success on the export market, especially in the United States, which absorbs most of its production. In 1969, Porsche and Volkswagen set up a separate organization, the VW-Porsche, for the manufacture of the "914," a central-engine car with a Volkswagen motor. This vehicle has had a rather limited success up to now.

**356 B/1600 (1961).** The same postwar Porsche, with improved details and a more powerful 1582 cc, 60 hp engine. It could do 160 km/h.

**911 Targa (1965).** The "911" had a new six-cylinder, 1991 cc, 130 hp engine, and a maximum speed of 210 km/h. Characteristic features of this "Targa" were the "roll-bar" and the removable roof.

**"Kdf" Berlin-Rome (1938)**

**Porsche (1948)**

# FIAT

# ITALY ON WHEELS

In a country that was poor, especially in customers, Giovanni Agnelli made "his" Fiat Company into Italy's—and soon Europe's—largest producer of utility cars. In the 1920s, Italy seemed to produce nothing but luxury cars, which it exported in great numbers (almost two thirds of its total production between 1922 and 1927).

It seemed almost certain that Italy—as opposed to the United States, Great Britain, and France—would never enter the utility car field, an area that involved a far greater financial and technological commitment than the production of luxury cars. But such was not the case. The first Fiat, with its two-cylinder engine with only 679 cc (in an era when displacement was usually far different, because of the low specific power obtainable) was already a utility car. When it came out in 1899, it cost only 4200 lire—the cost of ten bicycles. Even the models that followed the first—the "6/8 HP" and the "8HP"—had only 1082 cc displacement and also used a two-cylinder engine.

But it was with the "Zero" type of 1912, produced until 1915 with more than 2000 made, that Fiat faced for the first time the large-scale production of a car that, if not exactly a utility model, was at least very close to it. The "Zero" had a monobloc engine with four aligned cylinders, 1844 cc, and 19 hp and could do 70 km/h. It was available with just one kind of body, the torpedo, so that production could be standardized.

Ironically, the "501" Fiat—which was the firm's first mass produced and really popular car—was designed by a lawyer. It was built to incorporate characteristics that had already had success in America; the assembly line had finally reached Italy. The "501" was produced for eight years. There was also a similar model called the "502," and more than 76,000 were turned out, an exceptional amount for a European firm. It had a four-aligned-cylinder engine with 1460 cc and 23 hp; originally only the rear wheels had brakes.

But the "501" was still not a utility car in a true sense; it was the most popular Fiat and cheap to run but

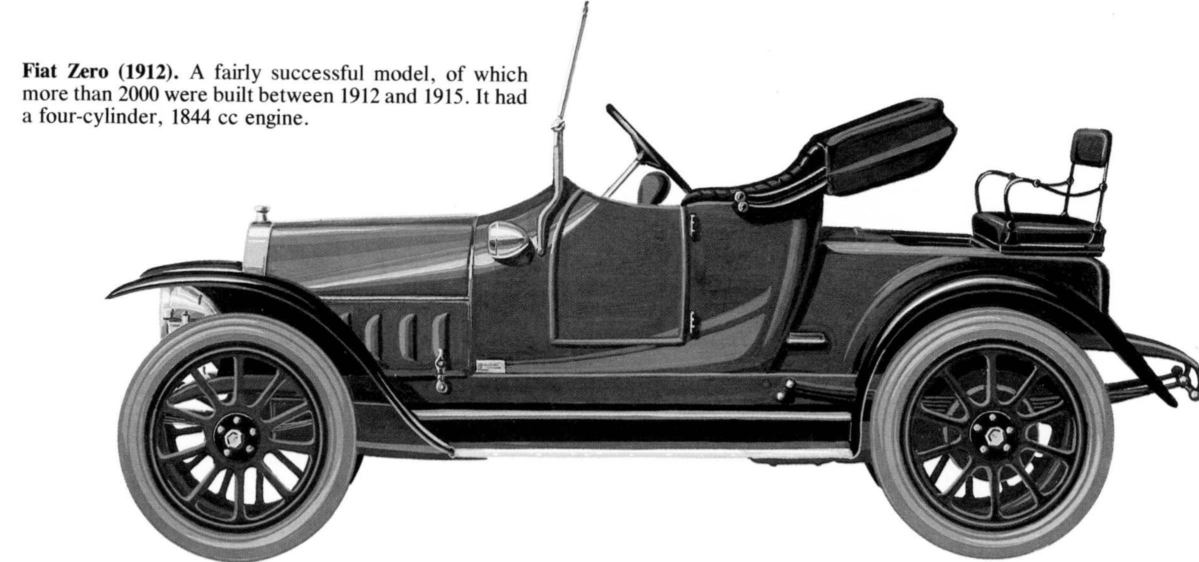

**Fiat Zero (1912).** A fairly successful model, of which more than 2000 were built between 1912 and 1915. It had a four-cylinder, 1844 cc engine.

# FIAT

**508 Spider (1932)**

**508 Coupé by Castagna (1933)**

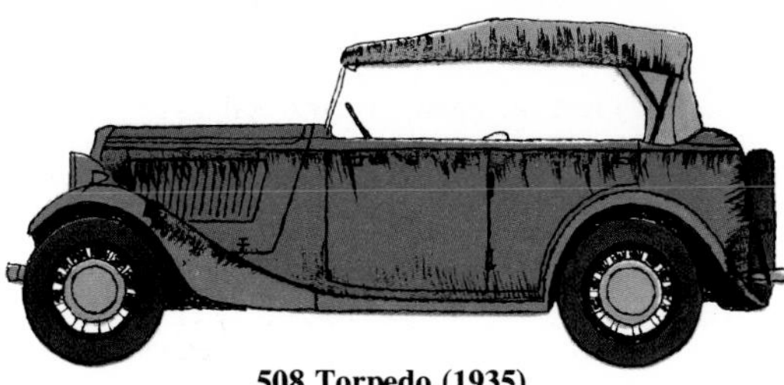

**508 Torpedo (1935)**

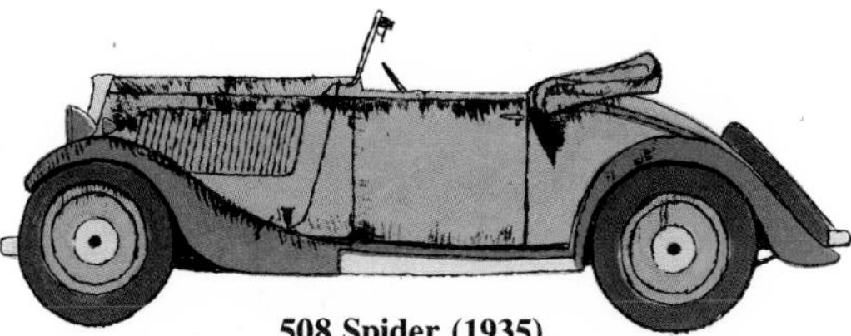

**508 Spider (1935)**

**508 Sedan (1935)**

**508 S Mille Miglia (1935)**

The poster designed by Dudovich for launching the 1932 Balilla.

it certainly was not cheap to buy. Fiat only dealt with the utility car problem with the "509," presented in 1925 and produced until 1929. During this time 92,000 cars were made. This small four-cylinder car (with 990 cc and 22 hp) also introduced installment plan payments into Italy for the first time, in the automobile trade. The "509" was a modern car: we need only note that it had an overhead valve timing system and that the power per liter ratio was very high for the time. It was also fairly fast for a utility model: it could do 80 km an hour. Fiat's next utility car, the "508 Balilla," had the same displacement as the "509," and quickly became popular, due to the enormous amount of publicity it received not only from the manufacturer but also from the regime in power. But despite its high-sounding name, only 124,000 "Balillas" were produced in five years (from 1932 to 1937). Even if its engine was more classic in conception than that of the "509" (with side-valve timing), the "Balilla" had hydraulic brakes on all four wheels and was quite robust.

Although Fiat had decided back in 1919 to put on the market a small, two-cylinder, ½-liter car, the project never materialized and it was not until 1939 that a popular utility car was launched. It was only a two-seater, but the Italians soon learned to squeeze a family of five into it. The "500" was soon nicknamed "Topolino," or "little mouse," by an enthusiastic nation.

The Topolino had a four-aligned-cylinder, 569 cc,

**514 Spider Sport, Type CA (1931)**

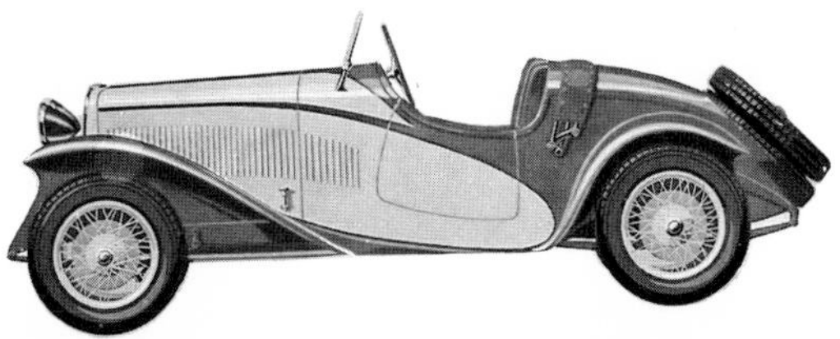

# FIAT

**508 C (1937).** Better known as the "Balilla 1100," this was one of Fiat's most successful models. It was made until 1939; after that year, it was modified by a new front grill and was simply called the "1100." It had a four-aligned-cylinder, 1089 cc, 32 hp engine, consumed about 9 liters of fuel every 100 km and could reach a speed of 110 km/h.

**500 Topolino (1936–48).** It was the world's smallest automobile to be mass produced in those years. Its size led the public to nickname it "Topolino" or "little mouse."

13 hp engine with side valves set forward; the transmission was rear-wheel, even though the engineer Giacosa, who designed it with the engineer Fessia, would have liked to have made it a front-drive machine. But Giovanni Agnelli opposed that plan, since in his opinion the Italian market was still not mature enough for such a technical device. The Topolino was also the first Fiat produced on a really large scale: 520,000 from 1936 to 1954 (of which 122,000 were of the first type, called "A," and built, except for the war years, from 1936 to 1948).

In the 1950s, two more small cars, both with rear engines, literally put Italy on wheels: the "600," which was presented in 155 and of which 2,600,000 were built until 1970, and the "New 500," introduced in 1957 and of which more than 4 million have been produced to date.

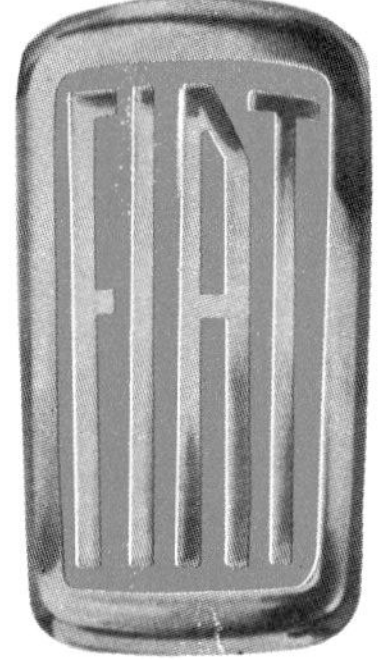

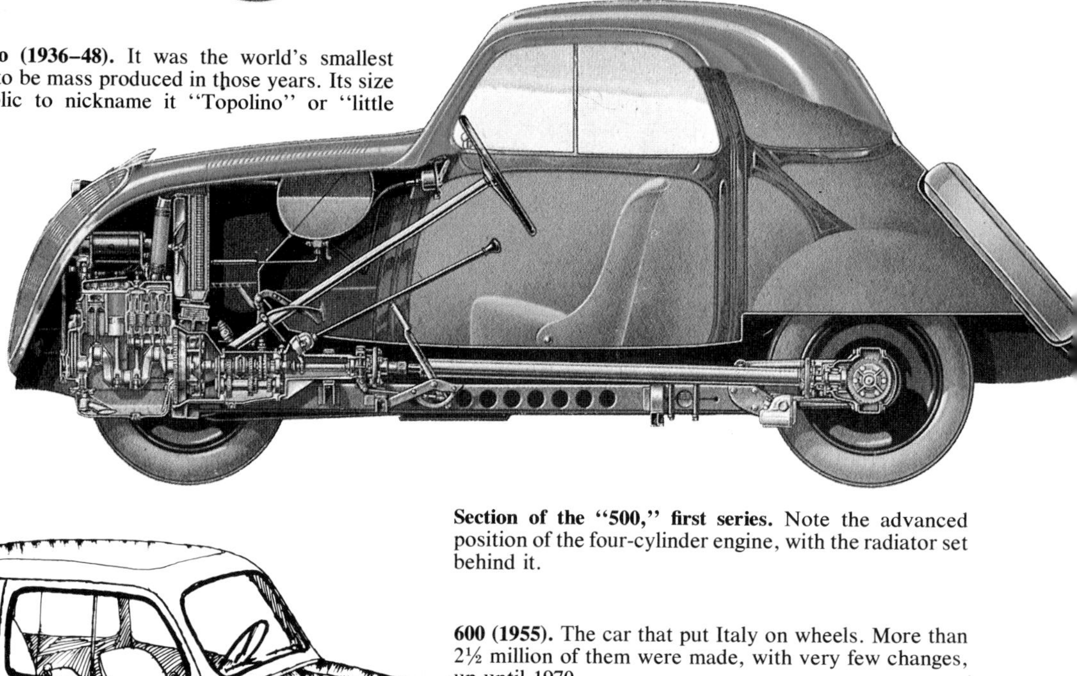

**Section of the "500," first series.** Note the advanced position of the four-cylinder engine, with the radiator set behind it.

**600 (1955).** The car that put Italy on wheels. More than 2½ million of them were made, with very few changes, up until 1970.

# SMALL BUT "BIG"

The first Chrysler (1924)

A poster from the golden age of Chrysler.

Plymouth (1938)

Chrysler Windsor Sedan (1941)

Chrysler is the smallest of the three "bigs" of the American automobile industry. For instance, in America alone it produced, in 1973, 1,700,000 cars, as against the almost 6 million of General Motors and the more than 3 million of Ford. But when we add the production of its Canadian plants (almost 300,000 cars), of Chrysler France (more than half a million), and of Chrysler U.K. (almost 300,000), we see that this American firm stands in third place among the world's car manufacturers, well above those of Europe and Japan.

Walter Percy Chrysler's story is a fairly recent one. After a number of years spent in important executive positions in an American railroad company, he concluded that his vocation lay with the automobile and in 1912, at the age of thirty-seven, he joined the Buick company of which he soon became vice-president. He had planned to retire from business in 1919, but—as a result of the competence he demonstrated with Buick—he was called in to completely reorganize Willys Overland and then Maxwell and Chalmers. In 1922, he started his own company and, with the help of some former Studebaker designers, his first car was launched in 1924. It was a modern vehicle, low and streamlined, with a six-aligned-cylinder engine and the driving shaft on seven journal boxes, and had hydraulic brakes on all four wheels. It was successful in America, despite its relatively high price of $1,526. In the following years he founded De Soto, Plymouth, and Fargo (the last exclusively for industrial vehicles). Finally, in 1928, he bought out Dodge Brothers, a well-known American name that had first introduced—in 1917—the all-steel body. Thus the Chrysler empire took on its own image, which has remained intact down to today, even if enlarged by the purchase of Simca in France, of Rootes in Great Britain, and of Barreiros in Spain.

**Citroën 2 CV (1948).** Shown in preview at the 1948 Automobile Salon in Paris, it caused a sensation with its highly original technical features: from its tiny two-cylinder engine (with only 375 cc and barely 9 hp), which nevertheless contained semicircular combustion chambers, to its revolutionary suspension, completely independent but balanced between the front and rear wheels, to its highly practical body. It had a four-speed gear box with overdrive on fourth gear, a maximum speed of slightly more than 60 km/h, and very low fuel consumption (about 4 liters per 100 km). The body was very light (490 kg) but had a strong platform chassis; the brakes were hydraulic. Like all Citroëns, it had front-wheel drive.

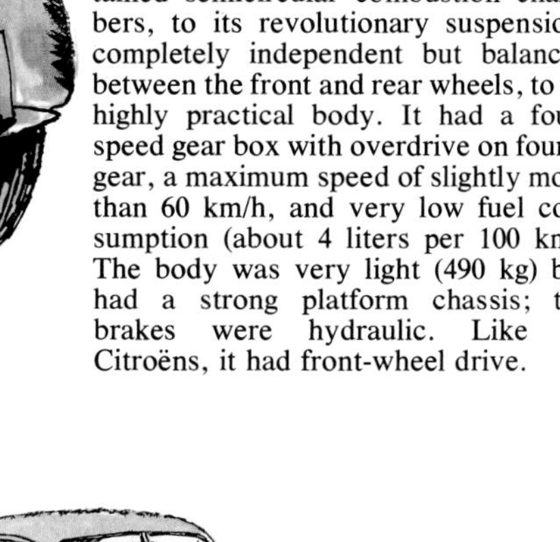

**Triumph TR 2 (1953).** Similar mechanically to the famous "1800" of the immediate postwar period, this car was an immediate success. It had a four-cylinder, 1991 cc. 80 hp engine and a maximum speed of 160 km/h.

**Standard Vanguard (1951).** This car, with many modern features, was produced for fifteen years, starting from 1947. It had a four-aligned-cylinder, water-cooled, 2088 cc engine with 68 hp; the timing system was of the overhead valve type.

**Gaz Pobieda (1949).** The first postwar car entirely designed in the Soviet Union. The motor, with four aligned cylinders of 2.1 liters, was derived from that of the Jeep; the vehicle had a load-bearing body.

**Skoda 1101 (1948)**

**BMW 501 (1953).** The Munich firm came back on the market again in the 1950s with this six-aligned-cylinder, 2-liter model, which was followed in 1955 by the "502," equipped with an 8V, 3.2-liter engine on the same body. The "501" developed 65 hp and could do 138 km/h.

**Nissan Datsun (1948)**

**DKW Meisterklasse (1952)**

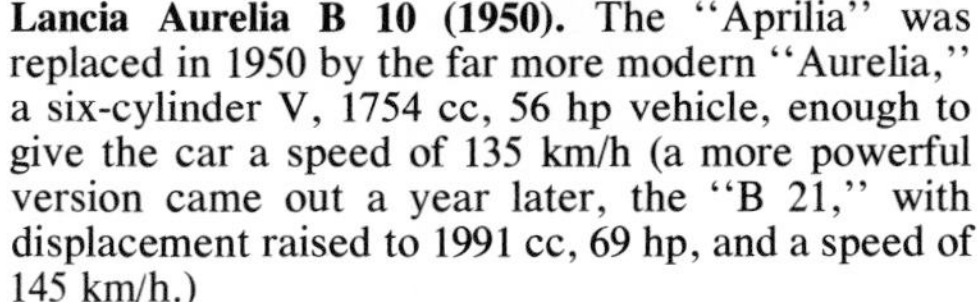

**Lancia Aurelia B 10 (1950).** The "Aprilia" was replaced in 1950 by the far more modern "Aurelia," a six-cylinder V, 1754 cc, 56 hp vehicle, enough to give the car a speed of 135 km/h (a more powerful version came out a year later, the "B 21," with displacement raised to 1991 cc, 69 hp, and a speed of 145 km/h.)

**Lancia Aurelia GT B 20 (1951).** Derived mechanically from the "21," but with power raised to 80 hp, the "Aurelia GT" was the darling of Italian fast-car drivers in the 1950s. It had, in fact, superb acceleration and a maximum speed of 162 km/h. Like the sedan from which it was copied, it had a rear axle with independent wheels, and with gear box and brakes set in the center of the axle.

States. In 1947, for example, English manufacturers equaled the production of a good year for cars like 1938; and in 1948 they reached for the first time the level of half a million vehicles produced. Too, it is significant that, in the first decade of the postwar period, Great Britain led all the automobile-producing nations in exports, preceding even the United States after 1949. (America held the title in 1946, 1947, and 1948.)

The threat offered by a strong German automobile industry was still in the future. The immediate postwar period was dramatic for Germany: her factories were either destroyed or dismantled. A good number of the plants were in the Russian occupation zone and the Russians literally took to pieces and carried off to Moscow the entire assembly line of the Opel Kadett, which was reborn in a Soviet version entitled "Moskvitch." Germany had no way of finding raw material; labor had been swallowed up by the war; and there was a tremendous energy shortage. All these factors kept German automobile production at a very low level right after the war. Barely 23,900 cars were turned out in 1946 (as against the 357,000 of 1938), and only 23,300 left the factories in 1947. The organizing abil-

**Bentley Continental (1953).** This version, marked by its "fastback" rear, continued the Bentley tradition of prestige with a sports flavor. The six-cylinder, 4566 cc engine was that of the Rolls-Royce Silver Dawn, but more powerful.

**Rolls-Royce Silver Wraith** sedan by Mulliner (1950).

**Jaguar Mk V Cabriolet (1948).** One of the English cars with greatest prestige of the late 1940s, as well as the first modern Jaguar (it had hydraulic brakes and front independent torsion-bar suspension). It also had a six-aligned-cylinder, 3485 cc, 125 hp engine.

**Simca 9 Aronde (1951).** The first Simca car to differ completely from the Fiat models. It had a four-aligned-cylinder, 1221 cc, 45 hp engine.

**Hudson Custom Commodore (1950).** The new line of the Hudson was presented in 1948 and was well-received. It was the lowest American car of the time as well as that with the best road-holding ability. It had an eight-aligned-cylinder, 128 hp engine.

**Henry J (1950).** The new trademark of the Kaiser-Frazer group was one of the first American "compacts." It had the same four- or six-cylinder engine as the Jeep, with a maximum of 75 hp. It did not have much success, despite the fact that it was sold by mail-order by Sears, Roebuck.

**Frazer Manhattan (1950).** In 1946, the American automobile industry was enriched with two new names, those of Kaiser and Frazer, both firms founded by steel magnate Henry J. Kaiser—and both firms closed down before 1955. The "Manhattan" had a 3.7-liter, 112 hp engine with six aligned cylinders with side valves.

**Ford Custom (1949).** The first newly designed Ford in almost twenty years; the rigid front axle was finally given up.

**Kaiser (1950).** It used the same six-cylinder engine as the Frazer, with power reduced to 100 hp.

**Plymouth Suburban (1950).** The first all-metal station wagon made by Chrysler, which that year adopted key ignition. It had a 97 hp engine with six aligned cylinders with side valves.

**Chrysler Windsor Newport (1950)**

ity of Heinz Nordhoff enabled him to make the Volkswagen from next to nothing—and against the will of the Allies—by starting mass production of the prewar model designed by Porsche. Also, American interests involved with German Ford and Opel (the property of General Motors since the twenties) helped to get things moving a bit and gradually brought production back to prewar levels—and (after 1951) surpassed them, thus threatening Great Britain's supremacy in Europe. England's supremacy was far from immune: apart from the fact that almost all her models were outdated even before the war (most of them still had mechanical brakes, rigid-axle front suspension, and side-valve timing), were repeated right after the war, and were modified only to some degree in 1948–1949, she had great problems in production. So a very promising postwar start in 1946–1950 was soon followed by a slowdown and then by regression (the 783,700 cars of 1950 became 733,900 in 1951 and 689,700 in 1952) which affected the British automotive industry for a long time. At the same time, this halt coincided with the rebirth of the German car industry, which went from 306,100 cars in 1950 to 428,400 in 1952, 680,600 in 1954, and 1,075,600 in 1956. That last year was a historic one for the automobile industry in the German Federal Republic, not only because it produced more than a million cars in one year for the first time, but also because—apart from the early years of motorization—Germany had never turned out more cars than Great Britain until that moment. Britain was, of course, going

**Alfa Romeo 1900 (1950).** The first car produced at a certain rhythm by Alfa Romeo, and the vehicle that quickly turned the firm into a great company. It had a four-cylinder engine with two overhead camshafts, with 1884 cc and 90 hp.

**Renault Fregate (1951).** The first nonutility type Renault made after the war by the French firm. This vehicle had a 1997 cc, 56 hp engine with four aligned cylinders and independent four-wheel suspension.

**Fiat 500 C Giardiniera (1950).** Fiat put into production, in 1949, and on the chassis of the "500" (better known as the "Topolino"), a four-seater station wagon with a large luggage compartment and a body of masonite and wood.

**Moskvitch 401 (1951).** Produced in the Moscow automobile factory, this car appeared right after the war—when the Opel Kadett assembly line was transferred from Germany to Russia.

**De Soto Suburban (1950)**

**Plymouth Coupé (1950)**

**Dodge Coronet (1950)**

**MG Midget TF (1953).** The last of the successful "Midget" series, production of which began before the war. After the war, the firm turned out—with the same 1250 cc, 54 hp engine—the "TC," the "TD," (with front independent wheels) and finally the "TF," with displacement raised to 1466 cc, and power to 64 hp. The maximum speed of this last model was 140 km/h.

**MG A (1955).** This vehicle adopted, with some changes, the motor of the last "Midget," but with power raised to 69 hp. Its highly streamlined body allowed it to reach 152 km/h with superb acceleration. It was extremely popular with young fast-car drivers in the 1950s. More than 100,000 were turned out in the six years of production.

**Rover 75 (1950)**

**Lancia Appia (1953).** Created to replace the "Ardea," the "Appia" had a four-cylinder, closed-V, 1089 cc, 37 hp engine that allowed it to reach a speed of 120 km/h. There was also a four-speed gear box.

**Standard 8 (1953).** Originally too simple, the "8" was soon better finished and sales increased. The four-aligned-cylinder, 803 cc, 26 hp engine permitted a speed of 100 km/h.

through one of her recurrent production crises; in fact, only a year before she had managed to build 233,000 cars more than the 1,004,500 produced in that year of 1956. Nor was the year that followed much better, with an increase of 145,000 cars produced as against the 1,212,200 turned out by Germany—a total the English automobile industry could never again reach. Also in 1956 the Germans managed to win another first in their history, apart from those they had won in the earliest years of the motor car: now they held first place among those nations that exported cars, beating out Britain by a narrow margin (484,600 cars as against 462,100). Another first place the English were never to hold again, but that the Japanese are trying hard to take over from the Germans.

Many factors contributed to the fast and exceptional success of the German automobile industry after the Second World War: a product generally of high quality, well-finished and carefully constructed; design less afflicted by "tradition" than British design (tradition is a quality that is useful in building

**Panhard Dyna (1956).** One of the most original utility cars of the 1950s. It was large inside (with five or six seats plus a large luggage compartment), and it had a small two-opposed-cylinder engine, air-cooled, with 850 cc and 42 hp. There was a four-speed gear box with fourth in overdrive and a maximum speed of 130 km/h.

Bentley Sports Saloon (1953). Equipped with the same six-aligned-cylinder, 4566 cc engine adopted by the Rolls-Royce, this car reached a top speed of about 160 km/h.

**Chevrolet Corvette (1953).** The first American postwar sports car. It had a very light body mounted on a steel chassis and was originally equipped with a Chevrolet six-cylinder motor with three carburetors (from 1955 on, with an eight-cylinder V 4.3 liter motor).

but not in designing); a near-total lack of union agitation; and, last but not least, a complete line of models built by many firms in close competition.

Top place in this large range of types was held by small, and even tiny, cars, characteristic of German car-manufacturing in the 1950s. This type of production had its famous forerunners, though, in the large series of small utility cars turned out at the end of the twenties and beginning of the thirties (the Goliath Pioneer with 200 cc, 1926; the BMW Dixie, 1928; the Opel Laubfrosch, 1924; the Hanomag Kommissbrot with a one-cylinder engine, 1925; the Hansa 500, 1934, et al.). Even more complete was the range of utility cars and microcars designed and produced—with very scarce commercial profit for some—in the early 1950s. The unquestionable skill of the Germans in this field managed to assure a certain market for models built on foreign concession (like the BMW Isetta, built with the permission of the Italians from the Iso after 1956), models that had been com-

**Oldsmobile 88 Super (1955).** The fashion of panoramic windshields quickly swept the United States, and in 1955 almost all cars had them. This Oldsmobile had an eight-cylinder V, 5314 cc, 187 hp engine and a maximum speed of 165 km/h.

**Mercedes 300 S Coupé (1953).**

**Mercedes 300 SL (1954).** This sports car caused a sensation when it appeared, not only because of the original way its doors opened (like a seagull's wings) but also for its excellent performance. It had a powerful (240 hp) engine with six aligned cylinders, with 2996 cc, derived from the "300" sedan of 1951. The "300 SL" could in fact reach a speed of 260 km/h.

# FERRARI

# THE PRANCING HORSE

166 S

342 America

250 GT

500 Superfast

The name of Ferrari, a small company that turns out a few hundred cars a year, is perhaps the most famous in the world of the automobile and always evokes images of magnificent racing cars and of fast and luxurious touring cars. The firm, located in Emilia, has won worldwide respect with a long series of legendary racing triumphs that have taken the prancing horse motif (the same escutcheon used on the plane of World War I ace Francesco Baracca) to every continent. Among the hundreds of car trademarks in existence, Ferrari is possibly the only one that has achieved commercial status through racing victories—that is, it has created a market for its product because of the speed and power of its racing cars.

This firm, which in 1960 took the name SEFAC (Società Esercizio Fabbriche Automobili e Corse), began its activity in 1929 as the Scuderia Ferrari ("Ferrari team"). In those days, though, the company did not build racing cars; it simply prepared the cars of Alfa Romeo for racing, for which Enzo Ferrari also worked as a driver.

The first car built by Ferrari dates from 1940 and was the "815" (eight cylinders, 1500 cc) which could not be called a Ferrari because of the preexisting contract with Alfa. The first actual Ferrari was produced in 1946, in the new plant Enzo Ferrari had built at Maranello, near Modena. It was the "125 GT," then followed by the "125 S," which made its debut at Placenza in a race on May 11, 1947, driven by Franco Cortese. That year, the car won the Gran Premio Roma on the Caracalla circuit, the first in a long series of successes.

Ferrari continued to build racing cars of all types, because the founder thought that the firm's technical knowledge should extend to various sectors without limitation; so, along with the sports model, there appeared the Formula 2 one-seater. And the history of Ferrari also includes cars specially made for uphill meets and for the extremely fast Can–Am race. The greatest champions of all time have driven and won for Ferrari: Alberto Ascari, Fangio, Moss, Graham Hill, Surtees, Phil Hill, the Rodriquez brothers, Peterson, Ickx, and Andretti. Even today, drivers consider racing in a Ferrari one of the high points of a sports career.

# FERRARI

212 Export

340 S

250 Europa

410 Superamerica

400 Superamerica

250 LM

275 GTS

365 GTC 4

# FERRARI

125 S

125 F1

375 MM

625 F1

246 F1

250 TRS

158 F1

330 P2

# FERRARI

375 F1

500 F2

750 Monza

290 MM

156 F1

246 P

206 Dino

312 B

# U.S.A.

## THE AMERICAN COMPACT

**Nash Rambler (1950).** The forerunner of the American "compact car." It had a six-aligned-cylinder, 2.8-liter engine, and a load-bearing body.

**Chevrolet Corvair (1965)**

Due mainly to the increasing popularity of the Volkswagen—nicknamed the "Beetle"—the importation of foreign cars into the United States increased to the point where in 1959 it represented 10.3 percent of all cars sold there (719,000 cars from a total of 6,983,000), as compared with 8.5 percent in 1958 and barely 4 percent in 1957.

But 1959 also represented the peak year for the importation of foreign vehicles into the United States; not until 1966 was that year's record broken. Just what had happened?

The three most important American car makers (with respect to the number of vehicles produced: General Motors, Ford, and Chrysler) had decided to fight the foreigners on their own ground, that is, small cars at low cost. So at the end of 1959 the "compact cars" were introduced. Even though they were compact, these cars were definitely larger in both size and power than their imported rivals, while selling for more or less the same price (usually less than $2,000). For the same price, American cars offered more, and the American driver has always, and quite justly, been receptive to such an appeal—even though, when all was said and done, cars more "compact" than American "compacts" were perhaps more suitable for big-city traffic.

The Chevrolet Corvair (the first American car to be mass produced with a rear engine—and air-cooled as well), the Ford Falcon and the Plymouth Valiant were an immediate and complete success. They became a third of all cars sold in those years and reduced sales of foreign cars in 1960 from 719,000 to 495,000, and in 1961 to only 298,000. But the "compacts" had their ancestors, too, in America: Kaiser's Nash Rambler and "Henry J" in 1950, and the Studebaker Lark in 1958. None of these had the success that later smiled on the Corvair, the Falcon, and the Valiant.

**Plymouth Valiant (1963)**

# U.S.A.

**Chevrolet Corvair and Chevrolet Impala (1959).** The "Corvair" was the first mass-produced American car with a rear, air-cooled motor. Above: The "Corvair" shown above a "classic" Chevrolet; there is almost a meter's difference in length.

**Ford Falcon (1959).** Unlike the "Corvair," the Ford compact was "classic" in style and technique: a front engine with six aligned cylinders and almost 2½ liters displacement, air cooling, and rear-wheel drive. The only novelty for Ford was the load-bearing body.

**Studebaker Lark (1958).** Another compact, which came out just before those made by the "big three" of Detroit. It had a six-aligned-cylinder, 2.8-liter engine.

**Renault Dauphine (1956).** Similar in idea to the widespread "4CV," but with a completely different body, larger and more modern in design and equipped with a much larger luggage compartment. This vehicle had a four-aligned-cylinder, 845 cc, 30 hp engine; the four wheels were independent and the gear box had only three speeds, as in the "4 CV." Because of its light weight (610 kg), it could easily do more than 110 km/h, despite its good-sized body (3.94 meters long and 1.52 wide). Millions of these cars were produced, in France and in various other countries, such as Italy and Brazil.

plete failures in their home country. After 1957, the BMW Isetta was joined by an original four-seater car, the "600" taken directly from the Isetta apart from the additional second row of seats and another door, set on the right side (thus there were only two doors: a front one, as on the Isetta, and one on the right side). The Zündapp Janus of 1956 was even more original and was built by a firm that up to then had specialized exclusively in motorcycles. The Janus, which hardly sold at all, was a four-seater car with two facing rows of seats reached by means of two doors, one in the front and one in the rear of the vehicle; the motor, derived from the motorcycle, was a one-cylinder, 248 cc type, set in the center of the car beneath the seats. Another strange vehicle that aroused little but curiosity was the FMR, better known as the Messerschmitt; it had two tandem seats and a plastic dome like the kind on small planes.

Success smiled, on the other hand, on the tiny "Goggomobil," produced by Glas starting in 1954. At first there was only one model, with a two-cylinder, two-stroke, 200 cc rear engine; this was followed by a more advanced

**Dodge Royal (1954).** It had an eight-cylinder V, 3.9-liter, 150 hp engine, with automatic Power-Flite transmission and power steering.

**Fiat 600 Multipla (1956).** A year after the sedan came out, Fiat presented an original station wagon in two models: a four-to-five seater, plus a large luggage compartment, and a six-seater with reclining seats, to accommodate large pieces of luggage.

**Vespa 400 (1957)**

400 cc coupé, the "TS 400." Despite its small size, the "Goggomobil" included a small rear seat, which barely held two children.

Another German microcar of the 1950s that sold quite well was the Lloyd LP 300, a front-wheel drive vehicle with a two-cylinder, two-stroke, 386 cc engine, presented in 1951 and soon made more powerful in the "LP 400" and "LP 600" models. The latter, especially, was successful, due to its four comfortable seats, its ample luggage compartment, and, above all, its low cost of operation.

Since 1929 Lloyd had belonged to Bremen manufacturer Carl Friedrich-Wilhelm Borgward, who had taken it over from Hansa-Lloyd to enlarge his automobile industry. He owned the Goliath Werke Borgward, famous for its "Pioneer" utility car, a three-wheeler, with two seats plus two extra places, and with a one-cylinder, two-stroke engine with only 200 cc. With the purchase of Hansa-Lloyd, business seemed to flourish due to the changes in production carried out by Carl Borgward, who in 1938 changed the name of the firm to Carl F.-W. Borgward Automobilwerke. The firm produced, under the Hansa name, cars with exceptional technical traits, even though their displacement was fairly low. The names of Lloyd and Goliath marked the production of industrial vehicles and trucks. Despite war damage, Borgward began production again in 1948, with a 1½-liter displacement vehicle, the Hansa 1500, followed in 1953 by an 1800 cc diesel-engine version. In the meantime, the Goliath was presented in 1950 (with a two-cylinder, two-stroke, 688 cc engine and front-wheel drive), along with the already mentioned Lloyd utility car. The Borgward Isabella came out in 1955. It was a fine modern car with six seats, 1½-liter dis-

**Jaguar XK-SS (1957).** The forerunner of the famous "E" presented in 1951. It was basically a "toned-down" version of the Jaguar "D," a racing car that had had excellent results in competition. It had the usual six-cylinder, 3.4-liter engine with power raised to 250 hp; it could do 225 km/h.

**Ford Anglia (1955).** It used the old prewar engine with a long stroke and side valves, with 1172 cc and 36 hp; the top speed was 115 km/h.

**Ford Thunderbird (1955).** Designed by Alex Tremulis (designer of the Tucker), the Thunderbird was Ford's answer to the Corvette of General Motors: a two-seater with a sporting look. It had an eight-cylinder V, 4785 cc, 190 hp engine, and a maximum speed of 195 km/h.

**Chevrolet Bel Air (1958).** This model had a completely new design as compared with that of the preceding year; four headlights were mounted on it, and it had an eight-cylinder V, 4.6-liter motor that varied between 185 and 250 hp, depending on the model.

**Rolls-Royce Phantom V (1960).**

**Rolls-Royce Silver Cloud Long Wheelbase (1959)**

**Citroën DS 19 (1955).** This car was the hit of the 1955 Paris Salon, and aroused considerable interest. It was an original machine in every respect, except for the engine, which was simply the old four-aligned-cylinder, 1911 cc motor of the "Traction," raised to 75 hp to guarantee a speed of 140 km/h. It had a hydraulic control center that worked the suspension, the brakes, the steering wheel, the clutch, and the gear level. It was also the first mass-produced car with disk brakes (on the front wheels). The body—streamlined and with a platform chassis—was quite large. The "DS" was joined, two years later, by the "ID," a model with simplified hydraulic controls.

**Peugeot 403 (1955).** Until the "403" was built, Peugeot had only one model in its catalogue: the 1290 cc "203." The new "403," the first car designed for the firm by Pininfarina, had a four-aligned-cylinder, 1468 cc, 58 hp engine and a maximum speed of 130 km/h. The four-speed gear box had fourth in overdrive and the transmission made use—in the Peugeot tradition—of an endless screw. The "403" was one of the French firm's greatest commercial successes.

**Glas Isaria Goggomobil (1955).** A tiny German utility car that sold quite well in the second half of the 1950s. It had a two-cylinder, two-stroke engine, with air-cooling, 293 cc and 17 hp. The maximum speed was 95 km/h.

**Daimler Conquest Cabriolet (1955).** Its mechanical system came from the "Conquest" sedan, of which it used the six-aligned-cylinder, 2433 cc engine, raised to 100 hp. The maximum speed was about 160 km/h. The original design for the body caused a certain amount of perplexity.

**Alvis TC 108 with body by Graber (1956).** A firm known for its quality production (and for its excellent military vehicles) which left the car-manufacturing field in the mid-1960s. The "TC 108" had a six-aligned-cylinder, 104 hp engine and its maximum speed was more than 160 km/h.

placement, a front engine with four aligned cylinders, and transmission on the independent rear wheels. Nevertheless—despite the success of the Isabella, of the Goliath 1100 (always with front-wheel drive but, after 1957, with a four-stroke engine), and of the Lloyd Arabella, and despite the industrial vehicles with original Borgward diesel engines—the small empire of the autocratic and despotic German industrialist collapsed—to everyone's astonishment—at the beginning of 1962. This totally unexpected end aroused a lot of clamor because the debacle could have been avoided if Carl Borgward, who apparently had been short of liquid cash, had asked for credit from the banks, which would have been more than ready to open their purse strings to him. His cars would have been a good investment risk: for instance, there was the Borgward 2300 (never mass produced), which had many fine technical advances, such as self-leveling suspension; its assembly line was bought en masse by Mexico, where the car was produced for many years.

The Borgward affair was a kind of "stain" on the remarkable rise of the German automobile industry of those years; and after the bankruptcy of that firm, the others made an effort to define their structure. Some trade names, smaller than Borgward, were incorpo-

**Jaguar 2.4-liter (1955).** The first car turned out by this company with a load-bearing body, and the first sedan by Jaguar to be streamlined. Its six-aligned-cylinder engine, with double overhead camshaft, was derived from the 3.4-liter used in the other models. With 2483 cc displacement and 114 hp, it could do 160 km/h.

**Alfa Romeo 1900 C (1952)**

**Alfa Romeo Giulietta Sedan (1955)**

**Alfa Romeo Giulietta Spring Spider (1956)**

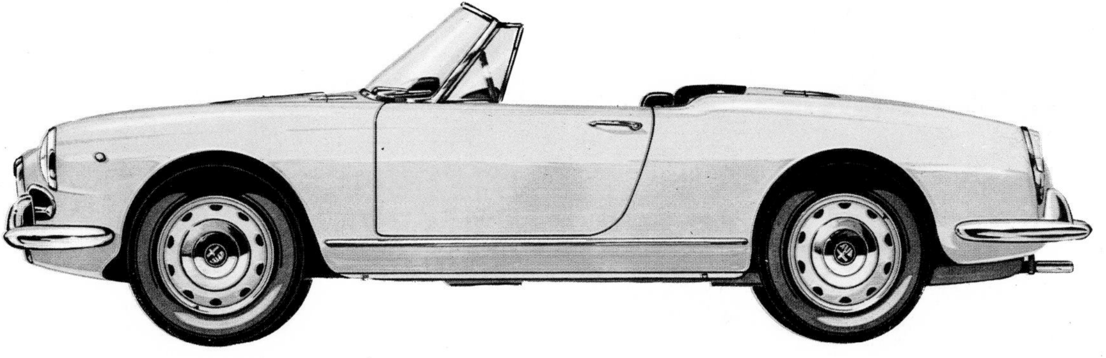

**Renault 4 L (1962).** One of the best-selling products of this French firm, which gradually converted to front-wheel drive from this car on; it was presented at the end of 1961 to replace the "4 CV," production of which ended that year. Originally offered in a 603 cc version as well ("R 3"), after 1962 it came with just two motors: 747 cc for the French and 845 cc for the foreign market.

**Morris Mini-Motor (1959).** The masterpiece of Alec Issigonis, who had already designed the 1949 Morris Minor. This car set the fashion for transverse engines with front-wheel drive and complete exploitation of the seating area. Barely 3.05 meters long, it was a comfortable four-seater, with an 848 cc, 34.5 hp engine and a top speed of 115 km/h.

**Opel Kapitän (1958).** The "Kapitän" had a completely new body design that echoed the lines of the "Rekord," presented the year before; it had the usual six-cylinder, 2473 cc. 80 hp engine and could reach a speed of 142 km/h.

rated by others. (Auto Union went from Daimler-Benz to Volkswagen; Glas Isaria was absorbed by BMW; and NSU was taken over by Volkswagen in 1969.)

But the collapse of Borgward was nothing compared with the bankruptcy of Tucker in the United States in 1949. It all began with the desire of the American government to favor small manufacturers over large ones in the reconversion of the plants used for the production of war matériel during the war. So the Securities Exchange Commission, the federal organization responsible for reconverting factories used by the nation during the war, decided to aid an enterprising designer, Preston Tucker, and granted him the plant used by Dodge in Chicago for making plane engines.

Tucker had presented to the S.E.C. an exciting design for a new car: a highly advanced vehicle in every way, with innovative safety features, superb body design, and an original mechanical setup. The motor was in the rear; it was a six-cylinder opposed or "flat" 9.7-liter engine with sealed-circuit cooling (the next sealed-circuit car after this was

**Austin A 40 (1958).** This utility car was very popular in Italy too, where it was made on license by Innocenti; with a four-cylinder, 948 cc, 34 hp engine, it could reach 116 km/h.

**Mercedes 190 SL Roadster (1962).** Presented in 1955 in the coupé version and derived from the "180" sedan in its mechanical setup, this car had a four-cylinder, 1897 cc (105 hp) engine. The same motor, with less power, was used in 1956 in the "190" sedan. It had a top speed of 175 km/h.

**FMR Tiger 500 (1959)**

**Ford Taunus 17 M (1957).** A new group of models by the German Ford Company which were added to the "12 M" and "15 M," already in production. The spacious body had an original design, and there was a four-aligned-cylinder, 1698 cc, 60 hp engine, with a maximum speed of 125 km/h.

**Ford Taunus 17 M (1961).** With a completely redesigned and slightly enlarged body—the rounded line was highly successful—this was the largest of the German Fords. It had the same mechanical setup as the previous model, but was also available with a 1498 cc, 55 hp engine inherited from the defunct "15 M." There was a maximum speed of 130 or 135 km/h, according to the version.

to be the Renault 4, created in 1961) and with hydraulic valve control. This last system permitted the creation of a perfectly hemispherical combustion chamber but caused some problems in starting—the hydraulic pump that controlled the valves did not go under pressure at once. There was direct transmission through a torque convertor for each of the rear wheels, without the intervention of gear box and differential. The independent suspension on all four wheels used elastic, rubber-block elements (like those to be used thirteen years later on the "Mini"), while for the first time in an automobile—and ten years before Jaguar and Citroën—the brakes were disk brakes of the aeronautical type, which were slightly different from those of today, though the principle was the same. As for safety features, the Tucker could count on a third directional headlight controlled by the steering mechanism itself—twenty years before Citroën's movable headlights on the DS—and on a windshield ejectable upon a certain internal pressure. Too, there was a shock-absorbing steering-wheel shaft and

**MG Magnette (1956).** Basically a sports car with a classic look, this vehicle sold quite well, due to its fine performance and excellent finishing. It had a four-aligned-cylinder, 1489 cc, 60 hp engine.

**Renault Floride (1959).** Using the mechanical system and chassis of the "Dauphine Gordini" (845 cc, 34 hp), Renault offered the public in 1958 the prototype of a car with a sporting look, available with a coupé, convertible or hardtop body; this prototype went into production a year later. The top speed was 125 km/h. In the United States, the car was sold under the name "Caravelle" rather than "Floride."

**Autonacional Voisin Biscuter (1956).** A small, front-wheel drive car quite popular in Spain in the 1950s. It was designed by French industrialist Gabriel Voisin. The vehicle had a two-stroke, one-cylinder, 197 cc, 9 hp engine, weighed only 228 kg, seated three, and had a top speed of 76 km/h.

**NSU Prinz Sport (1960)**

**Simca 1000 (1961).** Designed by Fiat—when the Italian company still owned Simca, which later went to Chrysler—this car was the French firm's best-selling model, and about 1.5 million of them were built. The rear engine, with four aligned cylinders, water cooling, and 955 cc, had 35 hp later raised to 44 hp (and even to 82 in the 1972 "Rallye 2"). Top speed in the original version was 120 km/h.

thick padding all over the inside, especially on the dashboard. Preston Tucker would also have liked to install safety belts on all models, but the sales department of his new plant advised him not to, in order to avoid scaring off eventual buyers.

And when, on June 19, 1947, the prototype was shown in Chicago, buyers fought to lay down a cash deposit and order a car that still did not have a firm to produce it! The mass of advance orders and the equally great success in selling shares in the company were a blow to the Detroit experts who wanted to keep the American market anchored to tradition and far from bold novelties. But, after all, wasn't the famous Model T of forty years before a very modern car for its time, a total break with the past? At any rate, although Tucker went out of business even before he produced on a large scale (only fifty prototypes, many still preserved, were built in the former Dodge factory), the cause was certainly not the lack, or lack of support, of a market. The firm failed only because Preston Tucker was unable to act and circulate in the world of high finance. A project as revolutionary as his needed more than the right men. (Apart from Tucker, an expert in engines, there was Alex Tremulis, who designed the revolutionary streamlined body and who, eight years later, also designed the Ford

**Fiat 850 (1964).** Mechanically adapted from the "600," this car had great success, due to its performance and its roomy interior. It had a four-cylinder, water-cooled engine, with 843 cc and 37 hp. The maximum speed was 125 km/h.

**Trabant (1960).** The most popular car made in East Germany from the late 1950s on. It had a plastic body, even in the station wagon model, and a two-cylinder, two-stroke, air-cooled, 500 cc, 18 hp engine; top speed was 100 km/h.

**Simca Ariane 4 (1960).** Born in 1957 from the union of the very roomy "Vedette" (with an 8 V, 2.3-liter engine), and the mechanical system of the "Aronde" (1290 cc and 49 hp), this machine was made until 1963. It was a six-seater and could do 125 km/h.

**Simca Aronde P. 60 Montlhéry (1959).** This vehicle performed brilliantly with its new "Rush" engine with five journal boxes (1290 cc and 56 hp); it could reach 140 km/h.

# AUSTRALIA'S TURN

**Pioneer (1898).** The first vehicle produced in Australia by the Australian Horseless Carriage Syndicate. It had a kerosene engine.

Even though the first Australian car dates back to 1898—the "Pioneer," inspired by the American "buggy" of the time, with its high wheels typical of the horse-drawn carriage—real production of automobiles only began in that country in 1948, with the inauguration of a General Motors associate, the Holden company, which launched that year a strong six-aligned-cylinder, 2170 cc car. Until then, production had been limited to a few factories which assembled English and American cars.

The start of production by Holden naturally encouraged other American and British firms to set up or enlarge factories, basing production on typically Australian standards; that is, cars that were robust and trustworthy, standing quite high above the ground so that they could be used on local roads which were often mere paths. So production rose from the 20,190 cars built in 1950 to the 61,888 turned out in 1955, and to the 181,000 of 1960, to finally reach a total of 447,266 cars in 1970. Present overall production—including both cars and industrial vehicles—is about half a million or a bit more, almost all built on the spot and no longer simply assembled as in the past.

In 1973, Australian British Leyland presented a model completely designed for that market, the "P 76," a car equipped with an eight-cylinder V, 4.4-liter engine; at the same time, both Ford and Chrysler put new models into production, the first the "Fairmont," the second the "Valiant," rather different from the same models made in the United States. There was also the "Mini-Moke," an Australian car with a strong body and with large wheels, perfect for local roads.

**Holden (1948).** The first completely Australian car to be mass produced. It had a strong six-cylinder, 2170 cc engine.

**Holden Statesman (1974).** The most luxurious of the Australian-built cars; it has an eight-cylinder V, 5-liter, 240 hp engine (available on request in a 5.7-liter, 270 hp version).

**Ford Fairmont (1974).** Redesigned and built entirely on the spot, this is the Australian version of the American Ford "Falcon," no longer produced in the States. It has a six-aligned-cylinder, 4.1-liter, 155 hp engine.

**Leyland P 76 (1973).** Designed by Italian stylist Giovanni Michelotti, it offers the customer a choice of a six-aligned-cylinder, 123 hp or eight-cylinder V (derived from the 3.5-liter of the Rover) with 4.4 liters and 195 hp.

**Chrysler Valiant (1974).** This is a car assembled in Australia, making use of parts from South African Chrysler, and with very little in common with the U.S. version. There is a six-cylinder, 3.7-liter engine.

# DUNE BUGGY

## A ROAD OF SAND

The **dune buggies,** created by a young man in America, reached technical perfection when they began to be turned out on the assembly line. Here are some of the many models of these buggies; the only common denominator is the Volkswagen mechanical system.

The "dune buggy," born in 1960, was the result of an attempt to develop new ideas for amusement. The United States, undisputed homeland of free time, has enormous sandy stretches in the California and Arizona deserts. A young Californian decided to make use of the sand dunes for a new kind of motorized amusement; with homemade tools he built a vehicle without a body, using the wrecks of a couple of Volkswagen "Beetles."

So the "dune buggy" was created for a specific purpose, and the idea was so successful that in a short time many young people in California had built their own, a cross between a regular car and a cross-country vehicle. The "buggy" is almost always made out of the mechanical parts and platform-chassis of a Volkswagen. The artisans who build them (and who are well-paid for their trouble, since the vehicle is much in demand) discovered that it was very easy to take the body off a "Beetle"; the major change is the shortening of the platform base to about two meters to guarantee the necessary driving ease and light weight of the vehicle. The use of wide-section wheels is another important factor in making sure that the "dune buggy" keeps moving over the sand without being slowly swallowed up.

Naturally, along with the first dune buggies, extremely crude in both idea and realization, there grew up a whole group of more sophisticated vehicles built with greater means and on the whole rather unfaithful to the original idea. The dune buggies produced industrially are too well-finished and refined to preserve the informal quality that made the first so popular with young people.

Europe, too, has some industries that specialize in the manufacturing of dune buggies; the idea arrived from the United States in 1964–1965 and caught on at once in the nations with a more advanced automobile tradition, including Italy.

Thus, the dune buggy has remained a vehicle made for pure entertainment, but, at the same time, it has entered into the commercial "rounds"; it has even been "interpreted" by some body makers, who have taken it as a theme for exercises in styling.

# DRAGSTER

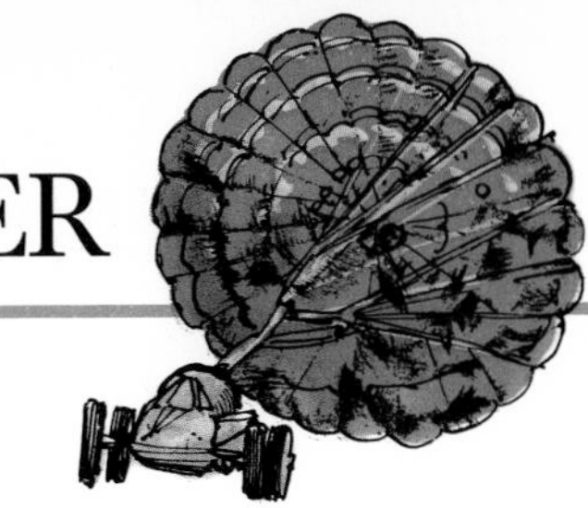

## HOT TIRES

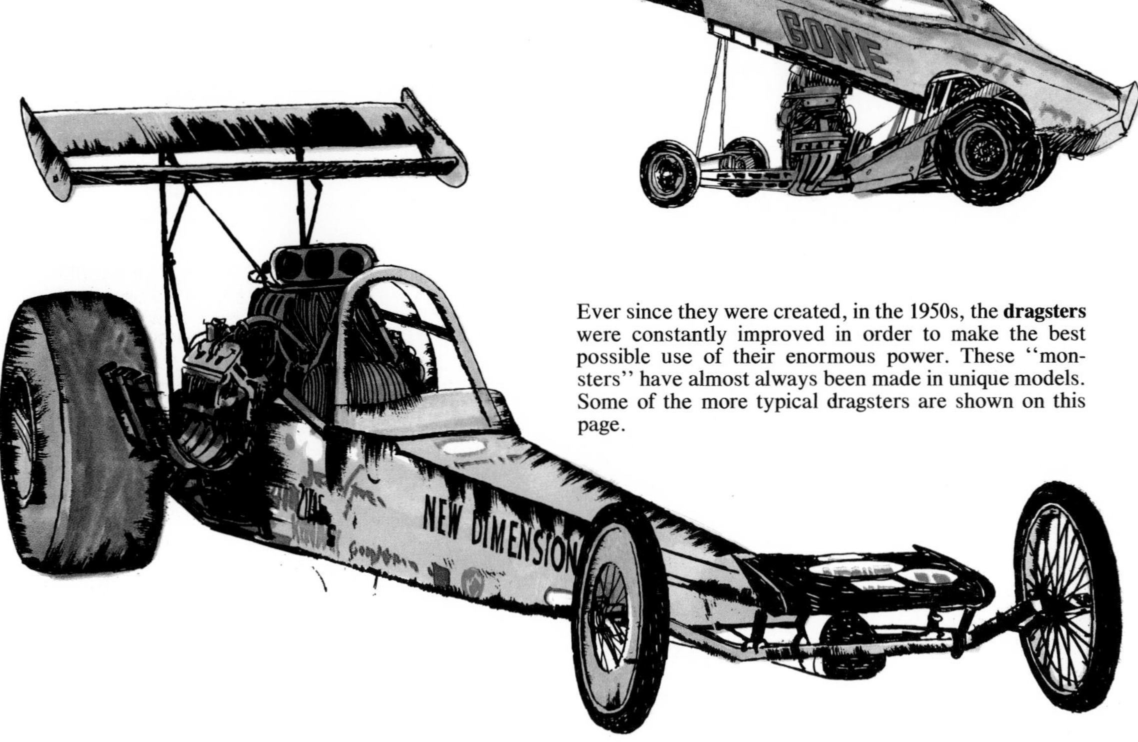


Ever since they were created, in the 1950s, the **dragsters** were constantly improved in order to make the best possible use of their enormous power. These "monsters" have almost always been made in unique models. Some of the more typical dragsters are shown on this page.

The dragsters were invented in the United States, another expression of the American love of speed, a passion that could not be fully demonstrated on the road, where the police enforced rigid speed limits. The name summons up the concept of friction and adherence on which these vehicles are based; in fact, the idea is to transmit to the ground all of the machine's power potential through a clever weight balance and appropriate use of the accelerator.

Dragsters are used mainly for racing on a quarter-mile track (1320 feet) so the vehicles must accelerate to the maximum in the shortest possible time. Of course, the tires are extremely important and are specially made; as a matter of fact, the exhaust is directed at the tires in order to soften them with its heat so they adhere even more firmly to the asphalt track.

These tracks are designed for the acceleration tests. A tar strip about 1½ kilometers long is needed to permit the machines to leave the starting line and accelerate to speeds that sometimes exceed 350 km/h and then slow down through the use of large parachutes. The race takes place as follows: two dragsters line up side by side in front of a traffic signal with seven lights (which sports fans call "the Christmas tree")—one red light, five yellow ones and a green one. The lights mark the seconds before the start, which begins when the green light goes on. The race is over in seven or eight seconds, and two more cars take their place at the starting line. Dragster races attract huge crowds, and the owners of the tracks profit.

The first races took place in 1948 and the first dragster championships (a series of elimination races with the cars divided into displacement categories) were organized in Great Bend, Kansas, in 1955. All kinds of machines were admitted in the beginning; then criteria were established that gave rise to specially built dragsters. Other machines which originated from vehicles already built were called "hot rods."

Dragsters have an extremely simple structure, devoid of all excess elements, since weight is the enemy of acceleration. The engines come from mass-produced ones and at times reach 1200 hp. They are normally without cooling and, to keep the machine light during the short race, there is gearless transmission.

# THE BODY

# A DRESS FOR THE AUTOMOBILE

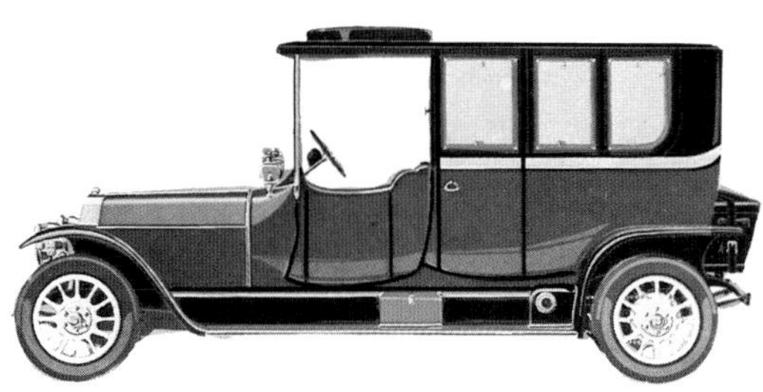

Some Fiats from the early years of this century. Most of them had a solid wood chassis strengthened with steel corners. As in all the cars of that time, the body too had a wooden framework.

The history of the car body—the part of an automobile that houses and protects the mechanical parts and the passengers—naturally began with the birth of the automobile itself; but it developed more slowly than the mechanical system, which got more attention from the early pioneers of motorization.

The car body is also called the coach, because the first mechanical groups were mounted on coaches, and it was the coach makers who built the first cars, made especially for traction supplied by an internal combustion engine or any other kind of propulsion apart from animal power.

The first cars were completely open, and this "philosophy" of driving dominated until the 1920s, even though the 1894 Benz and the 1899 Renault had "inside driving."

As the years passed, the body took on shapes and sizes closely linked to the needs of production, as was inevitable. The first car body to have a personality of its own was the "Torpedo," a convertible that linked the "nose" of the car to the "tail" in a straight line; it was designed by a Frenchman, Lamplugh (1908). Thanks to the Ford Model T, the year 1913 saw the beginning of assembly-line body production. The first all-metal body dates from 1914 and was made by the Budd Manufacturing Company of Philadelphia for John and Horace Dodge. In Italy, in 1922, Vincenzo Lancia began to use American methods, anticipating the load-bearing body with his famous "Lambda."

As we go on with our mini-history of the car body, we find, in 1925, the first European car with an all-steel body: the "Tout Acier B 12," offered by André Citroën.

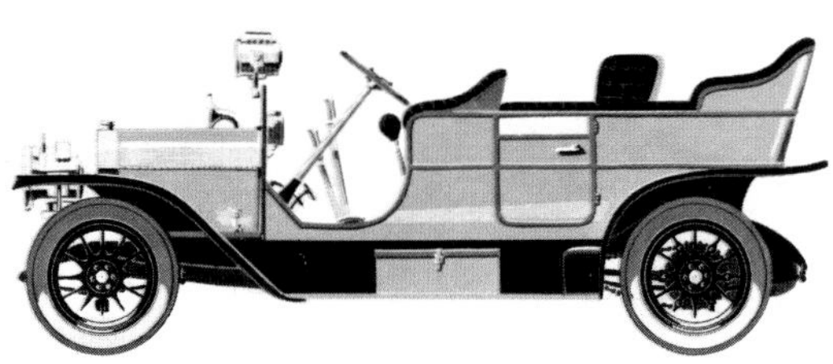

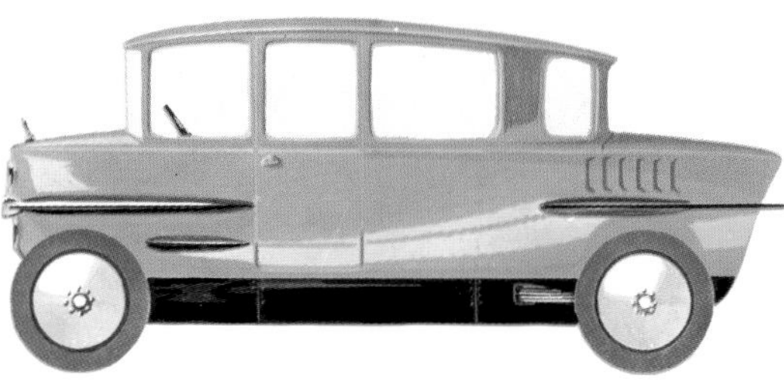

**Rumpler Tropfenwagen (1921).** The first German experiment with a streamlined car; it had a six-cylinder, 2.6-liter rear engine. Its designer, Edmund Rumpler, stopped making cars in a limited production series in 1926.

# THE BODY

Among the various firsts of Vincenzo Lancia, there was an anticipation of the load-bearing body with his 1923 "Lambda" (right). This was not a true load-bearing body, however, but a kind of skeleton that bore both the body and the mechanical parts; at any rate, the old chassis with side-members and cross-bars had been replaced by a more modern way of building machines. Not all the Lancias that came after the "Lambda" were without a chassis, though. Below: A handsome Farina body on a Lancia "Astura" mechanical system.

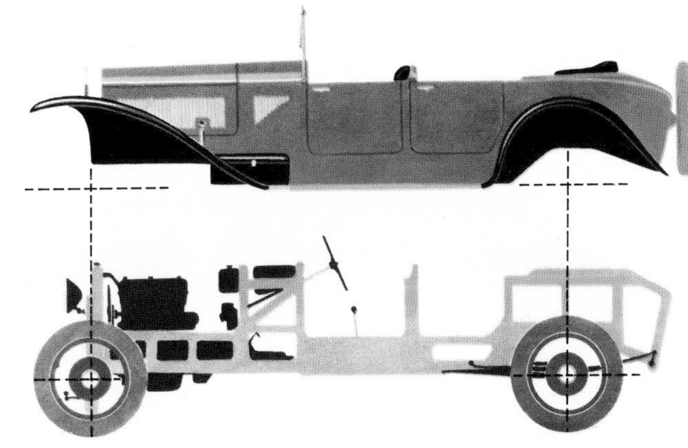

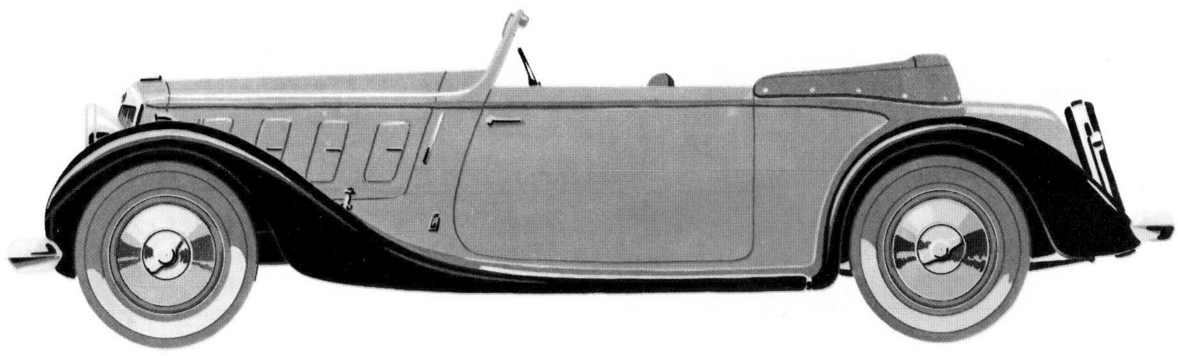

It was made of stamped plate and was also called "the car with the one-piece body." In 1930, at Cowley in England, the Pressed Steel Company began producing bodies for Morris.

In the meantime, as the years went by, new needs arose from a desire to make the product more personal by having it "signed" by talented designers who could interpret the needs of a motor vehicle objectively. The

Two Duesenbergs of the 1930s, a "J" (above) and an "SJ." The latter is one of the rare cars of this firm with body by Weymann. The "J" shown above was made with a body by the Belgian D'Ieterens. Very few Duesenbergs had bodies made outside the United States.

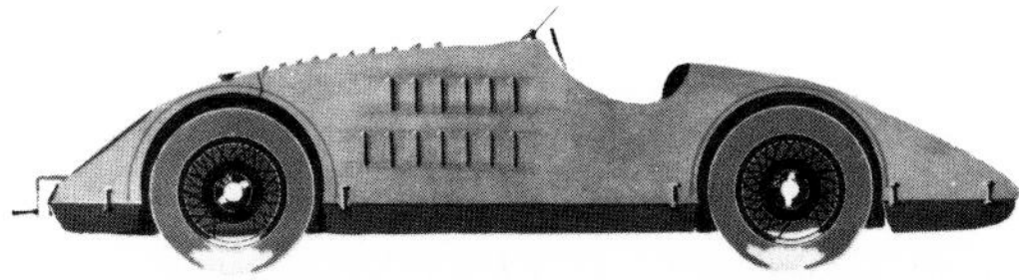

**Bugatti Grand Prix (1924)**

**Mercedes Benz** for breaking records.

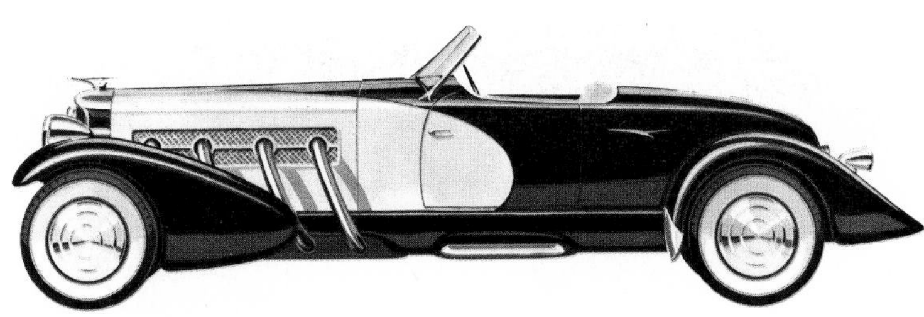

# THE BODY

**Adler** with a streamlined body by **Jaray (1936)**

**Grégoire (1910).** Another car with an avant-garde body. This was the first automobile in history to be given an aerodynamic test in a wind tunnel. The spare wheel was enclosed in the strange kind of cradle in the rear of the car. The door was set in the middle of the body—a feature characteristic of American cars of the day.

Italians are experts in this field; they were already famous before the Second World War, and found full expression for their ability at the end of the 1940s. A classic example of automobile styling is the 1948 Cisitalia, with body by Pininfarina; 485 of them were made, one of which is in the Museum of Modern Art in New York as a specimen of fine form.

The Italians were the forerunners in this aspect of automobile making, continually devising new solutions that were often applied to mass production. In the postwar years, while the manufacturers turned out more and more cars with a classic sedan body, the task of giving a special personality to the same mechanical system went to the body-makers; thus two-seaters, coupés, and station wagons were created. Italian styling was considered the best and eventually influenced all of European car production. Then, slowly, faced with the need of capturing a market that had become increasingly demanding, the great automobile companies began to mass produce special models as well, and body makers could only become industrialized themselves if they were to go on. Thus, they made the transition from creating new lines to supplying bodies for big business.

**Alfa Romeo streamlined Castagna (1913).** Count Mario Ricotti commissioned a sports-type vehicle from body maker Castagna. The result was this torpedo-shaped model, with one curved rectangular door and four "port-holes" on each side, and with seating for six people. The curved windshield took up the entire front of the car. This streamlined body, and an Alfa, four-cylinder, bi-block engine with about 4000 cc, let Ricotti reach a speed of 139 km/h.

**Alfa Romeo 6 C 1500 two-seater sports car (1928)**

A small experimental sedan made by **Zagato (1935)**

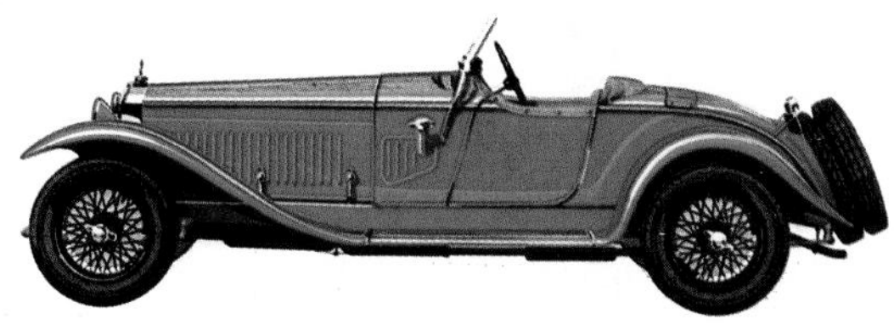

**Alfa Romeo 6 C 1750 two-seater sports car (1933)**

# THE BODY

**Fiat 8V, small sedan (1953)**

**Cadillac (1949).** The first American car to adopt the rear fins that had such an effect on car styling in later years—and not only in America.

But Italian style still has its validity and continues to point out the aesthetic paths of the future. Designers who specialize in planning car bodies find other fields in which to express their talent; so famous names known for having designed such and such a car create other products, such as helmets, or ski boots. These new efforts confirm the native skill that has put them at the top in automobile design.

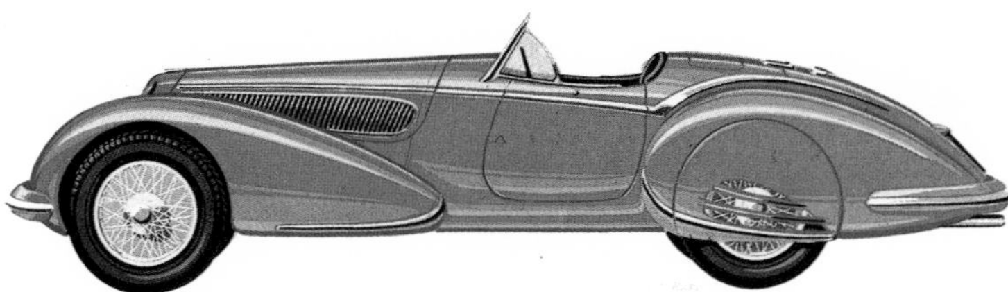

**Alfa Romeo 8 C 2900 B two-seater sports car** by Touring **(1938)**

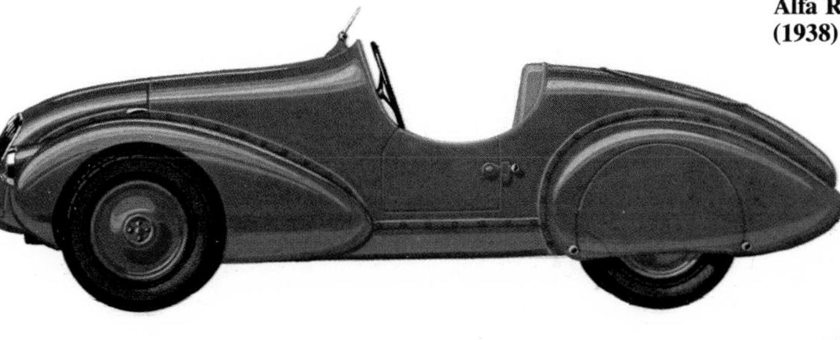

**Fiat 500** with body by **Zagato (1937)**

**Lancia Aprilia** with body by Pininfarina **(1944)**

**Cisitalia 202 (1948).** One of the finest examples of styling in the history of the automobile. In fact, one of these cars is preserved in the Museum of Modern Art in New York. It was designed by Pininfarina right after the war and its rational lines influenced car design in the years that followed. It had a four-aligned-cylinder, 1089 cc engine derived from that of the Fiat 1100, with 50 hp. This car's fine performance was partly due to its streamlined body as well; top speed was 160 km/h.

**Alfa Romeo Giulia TI (1962).** This was a powerful car; the 1570 cc, 92 hp engine—derived from that of the "Giulietta"—had a double overhead camshaft, and the new and rather streamlined body ended with a truncated back. There was a five-speed gear box, and the top speed was 165 km/h.

**Ford Mustang (1964).** A great commercial success, thanks to its sports-car look. The six-cylinder, 122 hp engine with only 3.3-liter displacement helped too. It was also available with 8 V, 4.7-liter engines. Maximum speed, according to the model chosen, was between 150 and 200 km/h.

**Plymouth Barracuda (1964).** Offered the same year as the "Mustang," this car did not have the latter's success, even though it had original styling with a long "fast-back." Mechanically, it was taken from the "Valiant," and the buyer had a choice between a six-aligned-cylinder engine with 3.7 liters or an 8 V with 4.5 liters.

**Oldsmobile Toronado (1966).** The return of front-wheel drive to American luxury cars after the experience of the Cords in the 1930s. There was an 8 V, 7-liter, 390 hp engine, and top speed was 200 km/h.

Thunderbird, a great sales success thanks mainly to its lines; Fred Rockelman, former president of Plymouth; and Ben Parsons, the famous designer of car and plane engines, plus others.) It needed capital above all: in fact, the slight amount of aid from the Federal Commission and the money collected from unknown buyers and small shareholders was just not enough. If the Tucker plan had succeeded—it did not, and Preston Tucker was tried and acquitted after the collapse of his project—American car building could have taught the European automobile industry something in the technical realm as well.

Such was not the case; and although it depended on the American automobile industry heavily for financial support, Europe experienced in the 1950s and 1960s—and still is going through—a period of great creativity that lets it act as the "trainer" for all the other car manufacturers of the world.

The creative genius of traditionalist England—where the Americans control more than 50 percent of the market, through English Ford, Chrysler U.K., and Vauxhall-Bedford, which belongs to General Motors—has been Alec Issigonis. Issigonis is a kind of prophet of the small-outside-but-big-inside car, a wholly European characteristic that was only later to be copied by the Japanese (whose interiors are not as large as that of similar European cars, though).

**Cadillac Fleetwood Eldorado (1967).** This and the Oldsmobile "Toronado" were the only American cars with front-wheel drive. It had an eight-cylinder V, 7-liter 345 hp engine, as well as self-leveling suspension.

**Citroën Dyane (1967).** Derived directly from the "2 CV," from which it borrowed the platform chassis and the two-cylinder, 425 cc engine (made slightly more powerful), this model was later joined by a 602 cc version.

We might say that, along with the designers of Jaguar and Rover, Alec Issigonis is the man who modernized the British automobile industry, the one who has always kept competition on its technical toes. He began his brilliant career as a designer with the utility cars of Morris—where he remained until he retired—planning the revolutionary 1948 "Minor," a car with a lot of room and a large luggage compartment, far superior to the obsolete prewar "Minor E," which was also produced in the early postwar years. The new model had a pleasantly modern body and was produced, with very few changes, up to the end of 1970.

Issigonis's first "Minor" still had the old side-valve, 918 cc motor and the rudimental gear box of the earlier model, so as to get the car on the market sooner. But a new engine soon appeared. It had less displacement but was far more brilliant in performance because it had overhead valves; designed by Issigonis himself, this engine also had a new gear box

**Volvo 144 (1966).** Originally equipped with the same 1778 cc, 75 hp engine as the "121," which it replaced, this model was later increased to 2 liters and also furnished with injection feeding.

**Daf 44 (1966).** Taken in its mechanical aspect from the "33," but with a larger body designed by Italian stylist Giovanni Michelotti; it had a two-counterposed-cylinder, air-cooled, 844 cc, 34 hp motor, and like all Dafs used "Variomatic" automatic belt transmission.

**Daf Daffodil (1962).** After 1968, this car became the "33"; it had a two-cylinder, 746 cc, 26 hp engine and a top speed of 105 km/h. Earlier Dafs used the same air-cooled, two-cylinder motor as the "Daffodil," but with 590 cc and 19 hp.

**Fiat 124 (1966).** One of Fiat's best-selling models, produced on license in other countries too (VAZ in the U.S.S.R, Seat in Spain, etc.). It had a four-aligned-cylinder, 1197 cc, 60 hp engine and a top speed of 140 km/h. In Italy, production lasted until 1974.

**Fiat 125 (1967).** The first Fiat sedan to have a double overhead camshaft. Partially taken from the "124," it was a comfortable five-seater with fine performance on the road; there was a 1608 cc, 90 hp engine and a maximum speed of 160 km/h.

**Wartburg 1000 (1967).** A new body for the best-known car made in East Germany, with a two-stroke, three-aligned-cylinder, water-cooled engine with 992 cc and 45 hp; front-wheel drive and a top speed of 127 km/h.

with four synchronized speeds. Issigonis's Minor was the first British car to be mass produced with a load-bearing unit-body construction and was, as well, one of the first English utility cars with independent front suspension, here accomplished with torsion bars.

But the masterpiece of Issigonis will always be the "Mini," a car that introduced a new philosophy into automobile design. For the Mini, he thought up the idea of "building" the car around its interior—or, to be more exact, around the space found to be essential for four people. The car was to be as small as possible, without an inch of space wasted inside or outside. The result was the only car in the world—unequaled since it was put on the market in autumn 1959—which contained very comfortably in a length of three meters, four adults and a small amount of luggage. The concept of small-outside-big-inside opened new prospects to all European car

**Wolseley 1100 (1966).** A new model on the Austin-Morris 1100 chassis (presented in 1963). An engine with four transverse cylinders, 1098 cc and power raised to 56 hp; Hydrolastic-type suspension and a top speed of 142 km/h.

**Rolls-Royce Silver Shadow (1966).** The first car produced by this famous firm to have a load-bearing body (but equipped with two small extra chassis for the engine and the suspension) and independent front and rear suspension with automatic level regulation. Triple-circuit disk brakes on all four wheels; an eight-cylinder V, 6230 cc engine with power not stated (as is the firm's tradition) and a maximum speed of 190 km/h.

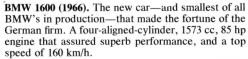

**Peugeot 204 (1965).** The first Peugeot with front-wheel drive. Four aligned transverse cylinders, overhead camshaft, 1130 cc, and 53 hp. Maximum speed: 138 km/h. The "304" was originated from the "204" in 1969.

**Lancia Fulvia Sport 1.3 (1966).** A light-alloy body by Zagato, and the same mechanical system as the Rallye Coupé 1.3; top speed of 175 km/h.

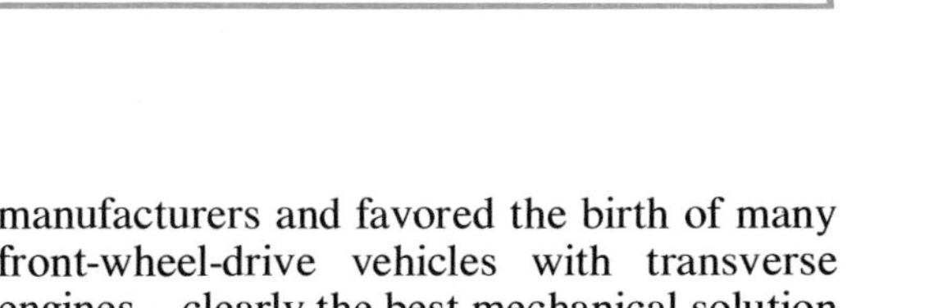

manufacturers and favored the birth of many front-wheel-drive vehicles with transverse engines—clearly the best mechanical solution for making good use of all available space.

The overwhelming success of the Mini fits into the framework of the great, even triumphant, success of front-wheel drive in France (where almost nine cars out of ten produced today use it: all Citroëns and Renaults, almost all Peugeots, and most Chryslers) and in Italy, which uses it in about two thirds of its cars (most Fiats, all Lancias and Autobianchis, and almost half of all Alfa Romeos). Front-wheel drive has had a cooler reception in Germany and in Great Britain, where, despite the great success of the Mini, the Euro-American firms—which represent half the market there—seem rather hostile to this technical solution. Still, Volkswagen in Germany, which also includes Audi-NSU, went directly from "all behind" to "all in front" in its more recent models.

**Volkswagen 1600 TL (1965).** With a brand-new body design featuring the typical "fast-back," and with an engine—still with four counterposed cylinders and air cooling—raised to 1584 cc (54 hp), this model helped to renew the top series of Volkswagen cars until the launching of the "411."

**Fiat 500 L (1968).** The luxury version of the "500" presented eleven years after the small utility car first appeared. Mechanical setup unchanged, with a two-cylinder, 499 cc, 18 hp engine and a top speed of 100 km/h.

**BMW 1600 (1966).** The new car—and smallest of all BMW's in production—that made the fortune of the German firm. A four-aligned-cylinder, 1573 cc, 85 hp engine that assured superb performance, and a top speed of 160 km/h.

**Citroën GS (1970).** This vehicle, equipped with hydropneumatic suspension and a streamlined body that started a new trend, revolutionized the middle-range automobiles in Europe. It originally had a four-counterposed-cylinder, air-cooled engine with only 1015 cc (55 hp), but from 1972 on was available with a 1220 cc (60 hp) engine.

**Fiat 128 Special 1300 (1974).** After having produced more than two million "128's" in about five years, Fiat added another model of its popular, 1116 cc to its catalogue—and one with more elaborate finishings and with a larger engine was available upon request (1290 cc and 60 hp).

**Renault 6 (1968).** Basically the luxury version of the "R 4," with a larger body; it used the 845 cc motor of the "R 4" with power raised to 34 hp and a speed of 120 km/h. In 1970, it was joined by the "6 TL" with 1108 cc and 45 hp.

But apart from the truly brilliant talent of Alec Issigonis, the present-day history of the automobile no longer concerns single personalities, but rather deals with concentrations of what used to be separate firms. For instance, if we exclude the American companies, which alone represent more than 50 percent of the British market and a little less than that in Germany, the top automobile makers in Europe today can be classified as follows: Renault and Peugeot-Citroën in France (apart from the American Chrysler France); British Leyland and Rolls-Royce in Great Britain (apart from the three powerful American "bigs"); Fiat (with Autobianchi and Lancia)

**Lancia Stratos (1973)**

**Mercedes 240 D 3.0 (1974).** This German firm was the first in the world—in 1936, with the "260 D," to be exact: four cylinders, with 2545 cc and 45 hp—to mass produce a car equipped with a diesel engine. And it was also the first—in 1974, with this "240 D 3.0"—to turn out one with a five-cylinder engine. It has 80 hp and a top speed of 143 km/h.

**Lamborghini Espada (1968).** Derived from the "400 GT" 2 + 2 of which it used the mechanical system, it had a twelve-cylinder V, 3929 cc, 350 hp engine and could reach a top speed of 250 km/h.

**Maserati Ghibli (1971)**

**Opel GT (1969)**

**Alfa Romeo 1750 (1968).** Taken from the "Giulia," but with a longer body completely redesigned by Bertone; it had the well-known four-cylinder engine with double overhead camshaft, with displacement raised to 1779 cc, and 132 hp. It could do 180 km/h.

**Lancia Fulvia Coupé (1965).** Introduced after the sedan, it had—unlike the latter—commercial success, despite the small seating space in the rear. It had a four-cylinder V engine, originally 1.2 liters, then raised to 1.6 liters.

and Alfa Romeo in Italy; Volkswagen (with Audi-NSU), Daimler-Benz, and BMW in Germany (plus the American Opel and Ford); Daf (a branch of Volvo) in Holland; and Seat (a Fiat associate) in Spain.

It is obvious that such a picture does not offer much on the horizon for the future. Even the Japanese have become associated with the three great American companies (Isuzu with General Motors, Toyo Kogyo with Ford, and Mitsubishi with Chrysler) or have joined one another so as to increase even further their already exceptional capacity for penetrating foreign markets. Will the Japanese be able to change the present world of the automobile?

**Renault 5 TL (1972).** This car soon became the best-selling French vehicle. It combined the qualities of a city car (only 3.50 meters long with retractable plastic bumpers) with those of a touring car, as well as ample seating and trunk space, and good performance (a speed of 140 km/h). There was a choice of two models: "L" (782 cc and 33 hp, later raised to 845 cc and 36 hp) and "TL" (956 cc and 46 hp).

**Citroën CX (1974).** Made to replace series "D"—the first version of which, the "DS 19," was presented in 1955. The "CX" is marked by the careful streamlining of its body, designed to reduce fuel consumption a good deal and better its speed (from 157 to 179 km/h, according to the model). This car also has fine safety features, due to the special form of the body—an original load-bearing body bolted onto a chassis with progressive shock absorption. The engine is mounted transversely on the right side of the car, and is the well-known four-cylinder of series "D," with 1985 cc (102 hp) and 2175 cc (112 hp).

# FOUR STEPS ON THE MOON

Of all the various types of motorization, that linked to the American and Russian space ventures is undoubtedly the most peculiar.

The first vehicle to move on the soil of the moon was the Soviet Lunokhod. On November 17, 1970, it was guided from earth on a lunar exploration trip. Its unusual shape led to its being nicknamed "the pot." It has a body with a diameter of 215 cm and it rests on eight wheels (diameter: 51 cm), all with drive and moved by solar batteries. It also has a ninth wheel in the rear for service functions. The Lunokhod has a wheelbase of 160 cm and its overall length is 221 cm. There are many antennae on the Soviet vehicle, which transmit images and data to earth. The top speed of the Lunokhod is 22 km/h.

The Soviet machine was the first to move on the moon, but the American one was the first to carry human beings there. The Lunar Roving Vehicle (LRV) was the result of a competition set up by NASA in the 1960s and was won by Delco, a division of General Motors, and by Boeing, the plane manufacturer. The Delco-Boeing car's wheels touched the surface of the moon at the beginning of August 1971 during the Apollo 15 mission. The LRV was used by astronauts David Scott and James Irvin for a series of explorations and covered about 30 kilometers in three days; it also carried about a hundred kilograms of moon rocks.

The Lunar Roving Vehicle is basically a chassis 310 cm long, with a 230 cm wheelbase, a wheeltrack of 183 cm, and a height of 113 cm. It has four wheels—all directional, due to the use of a small 1-hp motor. Each wheel has an electric motor with 0.25 hp at 9200 rpm. The motors are fed by two silver-zinc batteries with potassium hydroxide as electrolyte.

The wheels of the LRV are not made of rubber, but have a metallic structure. The body of the tire is made of zinc-plated steel wire (800 wires, each 1 mm wide and 81 cm long), and the tread is formed of small sheets of titanium arranged in a V-shape. Each wheel has a diameter of 82 cm. The turning radius is 3.05 meters. The vehicle has drum brakes. Empty, the LRV weighs 209 kg; full, 600 kg. Its maximum speed is 15 km/h. In addition to the two astronauts, the LRV holds a large amount of delicate equipment and some cameras. In 1972, an up-to-date version of the Lunar Roving Vehicle was used for other lunar missions.

**Lunar Roving Vehicle (1971).** Built by Delco (a division of General Motors) in collaboration with Boeing, this was the first lunar vehicle driven by man. It had four small electric motors—each linked to a wheel and with a total of 1 hp—which permitted a maximum speed of 15 km/h.

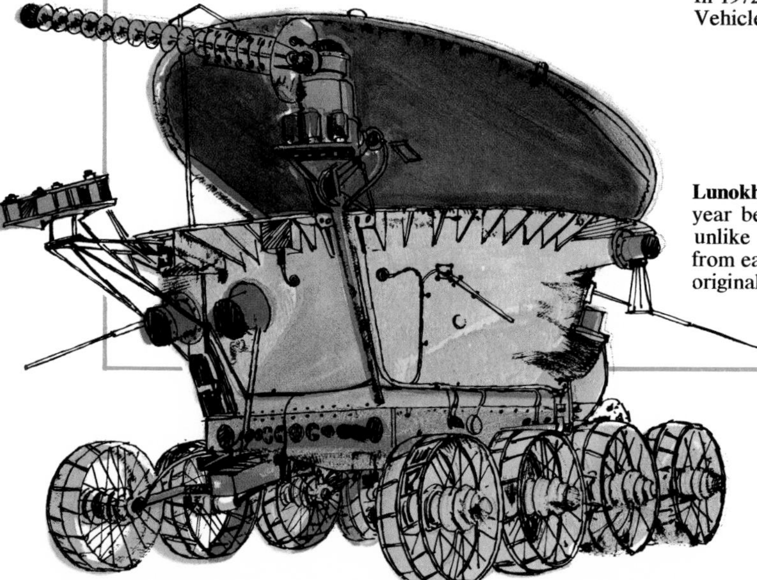

**Lunokhod (1970).** Even though it was created about a year before the American LRV, this Soviet vehicle—unlike the LRV—was not manned, but was controlled from earth by a team of five men. The Lunokhod had an original "pot" shape and could do 22 km/h.

# Acknowledgments

The texts: "Dust and Glory," "A Four-leaf Clover to Win," "The Prancing Horse," and "The Ascent of the Rising Sun" were written by **Tommaso Tommasi**

**Coordinator and Art Director**

Adriano Zannino

**Editorial Director and Research**

Serenella Genoese Zerbi

**Make-up**

Ovidio Ricci
Paolo Buonarrivo

**Designers**

Vincenzo Cosentino
Fabio Luigi Rapi
Pino dell'Orco ("The Cart Becomes a Carriage," "The Automobile for Everywhere")
Emilio Ferraboschi ("The Prancing Horse")
Domenico Nardiello ("A Four-leaf Clover to Win")

Special thanks are due to the automobile manufacturers who gave us access to their files.

A LEA (L'Editrice dell'Automobile) creation, Rome 1974.

# APPENDIX

# THE AUTOMOBILE IN NUMBERS

## THE EVOLUTION OF THE GASOLINE ENGINE

| page | Inventor | Type | Year of make | Velocity | | Number of cylinders | Weight | |
|---|---|---|---|---|---|---|---|---|
| | | | | km/h | mph | | kg | lb |
| 14 | Valturio | Muscle (*) | 1472 | — | — | — | — | — |
| 14 | Valturio | Wind-driven car (*) | 1472 | — | — | — | — | — |
| 14 | Verbiest | Turbine cart | 1672 | — | — | — | — | — |
| 14 | Leonardo | Tortoise (*) | 1500 circa | — | — | — | — | — |
| 15 | Leonardo | Spring-powered cart (*) | 1500 circa | — | — | — | — | — |
| 15 | Ramelli | Amphibian armored cart (*) | 1588 | — | — | — | — | — |
| 16 | Dürer | Triumphal cart (*) | 1510 | — | — | — | — | — |
| 17 | Newton | Jet-driven vehicle | 1680 | — | — | — | — | — |
| 17 | Hautsch | Spring-powered vehicle | 1649 | — | — | — | — | — |
| 22 | Cugnot | Steam cart | 1769 | 3,5-5 | 2-3 | 2 | 5.000 | 11.000 |
| 22 | Papin | Steam car | 1690 | — | — | — | — | — |
| 22 | Newcomen | Steam-pressure-driven car | | — | — | — | — | — |
| 22 | Watt | Steam car | 1769 | — | — | — | — | — |
| 23 | Goldsworthy Gurney | Steam stagecoach | 1825 | 20 | 12 | 1 | 3.000 | 6.615 |
| 24 | Trevithick | Steam vehicle | 1802 | — | — | — | — | — |
| 24 | Hill | Steam coach | 1839 | 20 | 12 | — | — | — |
| 24 | — | English "Velocifero" | 1830 | — | — | — | — | — |
| 25 | Hancock | Enterprise Era Automathon | | — | — | — | — | — |
| 25 | Bordino | Steam coach | 1854 | 8 | 5 | 2 | — | — |
| 26 | Pecori | Steam tricycle | 1891 | — | — | — | — | — |
| 27 | Bollée Amédée | L'Obéissante | 1873 | 40 | 25 | — | 4.500 | 10.000 |
| 27 | Bollée Amédée | La Mancelle | 1878 | 35 | 22 | 2 | 2.500 | 5.500 |

(*) Reconstructed from sketches and manuscripts.

## THE BEGINNING OF THE GASOLINE ENGINE

| page | Designer | Characteristics | Year of make | Number of cylinders | Power hp |
|---|---|---|---|---|---|
| 32 | De Cristoforis | Igneous-pneumatic machine | 1841 | 1 | — |
| 32 | Barsanti-Matteucci | Motor with two opposed pistons | 1858 | 1 | 20 |
| 32 | Lenoir | Uncompressed direct-acting engine | 1858 | 1 | — |
| 34 | Marcus | Gasoline automobile | 1874 | 1 | 4 |
| 35 | Otto-Langen | Four-cycle engine | 1876 | 1 | 8 |
| 35 | Daimler-Maybach | V engine | 1889 | 2 | 3,35 |
| 37 | Delamarre Deboutteville | Break | 1884 | 2 | — |
| 37 | Benz | Velocipede | 1886 | 1 | 0,98 |

# FROM DAIMLER MOTOR TO ASSEMBLY-LINE PRODUCTION

| page | Make & type | International Registration Letter* | Year of make | Number of cylinders | Displacement | Power hp | rpm | Bore & stroke | | Velocity | | Engine position | Weight | |
|---|---|---|---|---|---|---|---|---|---|---|---|---|---|---|
| | | | | | | | | mm | inches | km/h | mph | | kg | lb |
| **38** | Daimler Motorkutsche | D | 1886 | 1 | 0,46 | 1,1 | 750 | 70 x 120 | 2,76 x 4,72 | 15 | 9 | r | 600 | 1.323 |
| **38** | Lanchester Phaeton | GB | 1897 | 2 | 3,46 | 10 | 1.250 | 127 x 136 | 5,00 x 5,37 | 32 | 20 | r | | |
| **39** | Benz Victoria | D | 1893 | 1 | 1,73 | 3 | 400 | 130 x 130 | 5,12 x 5,12 | | | r | | |
| **39** | Nesselsdorf Präsident | CS | 1897 | 2 | | 5 | | | | | | r | | |
| **39** | Benz Ideal | D | 1898 | 1 | 1,10 | | | | | | | f | | |
| **40** | Bernardi Motorcycle | I | 1893 | 1 | 0,26 | 1 | 500 | 65 x 80 | 2,56 x 3,15 | | | r | | |
| **40** | Bernardi Tricycle | I | 1896 | 1 | 0,62 | 4 | 800 | 85 x 110 | 3,35 x 4,33 | | | r | 300 | 662 |
| **41** | Benz Velo | D | 1898 | 1 | 1,14 | 3 | 400 | 110 x 120 | 4,33 x 4,72 | 25 | 16 | r | 300 | 662 |
| **41** | Woods (Electric Vehicle) | USA | 1899 | | | | | | | | | r | | |
| **42** | Daimler Motorcycle | D | 1885 | 1 | 0,46 | 1,1 | | 70 x 120 | 2,76 x 4,72 | | | c | | |
| **47** | Panhard Dog-Cart | F | 1894 | 2 | 1,11 | 4 | 800 | 80 x 120 | 3,15 x 4,72 | 30 | 19 | f | | |
| **48** | Panhard Dos-à-dos | F | 1891 | 2 | | 3 | | 70 x 110 | 2,76 x 4,33 | | | c | | |
| **48** | Peugeot 2-seat Quadricycle | F | 1891 | 2 | 0,56 | 2 | 1.000 | 60 x 100 | 2,36 x 3,94 | 18 | 11 | r | 400 | 882 |
| **48** | Peugeot Vis-à-vis | F | 1891 | 2 | 0,56 | 2 | 1.000 | 60 x 100 | 2,36 x 3,94 | 16 | 10 | r | 530 | 1.169 |
| **48** | Panhard Enclosed Cab | F | 1894 | 2 | 1,22 | 4 | 800 | 80 x 120 | 3,15 x 4,72 | 30 | 19 | f | | |
| **48** | Peugeot 2-seat Quadricycle | F | 1894 | 2 | 0,56 | 2 | 1.000 | 60 x 100 | 2,36 x 3,94 | 18 | 11 | r | 400 | 882 |
| **49** | Peugeot 2½ HP | F | 1894 | 2 | 0,56 | 2 | 1.000 | 60 x 100 | 2,36 x 3,94 | 18 | 11 | r | 500 | 1.103 |
| **49** | Peugeot Vis-à-vis | F | 1892 | 2 | | 3¾ | 1.018 | 72 x 125 | 2,83 x 4,92 | 25 | 16 | r | 520 | 1.147 |
| **49** | Panhard Tonneau | F | 1899 | 2 | 1,11 | 4 | 800 | 80 x 120 | 3,15 x 4,72 | 30 | 19 | f | | |
| **50** | Peugeot Double Phaeton | F | 1903 | 4 | 3,63 | 18 | 1.200 | 105 x 105 | 4,13 x 4,13 | 80 | 50 | f | | |
| **51** | Léon Bollée Tricycle | F | 1896 | 1 | 0,65 | 3 | 750 | 85 x 145 | 3,35 x 5,71 | | | r | | |
| **51** | Delahaye Break | F | 1896 | 2 | | 6-8 | 700 | 110 x 140 | 4,33 x 5,51 | 30 | 19 | r | 700 | 1.544 |
| **52** | Décauville 3½ HP | F | 1898 | 2 | 0,49 | 3½ | | 66 x 76 | 2,60 x 2,99 | | | r | 200 | 441 |
| **53** | De Dion Tricycle | F | 1896 | 1 | | 3½ | 1.500 | | | 32 | 20 | r | 250 | 551 |
| **53** | De Dion Coupé Docteur | F | 1900 | 1 | 0,49 | 4,5 | 1.500 | 84 x 90 | 3,31 x 3,54 | 30 | 19 | r | 500 | 1.103 |
| **54** | De Dion Bouton Populaire | F | 1903 | 1 | 0,69 | 6 | | 100 x 120 | 3,94 x 4,72 | 50 | 31 | f | 350 | 772 |
| **54** | Renault 3½ HP | F | 1899 | 1 | | 3½ | 1.500 | | | 32 | 20 | f | | |
| **55** | Renault Enclosed Cab | F | 1899 | 1 | | 1¾ | 1.500 | | | 20 | 12 | f | | |
| **56** | Darracq Type N | F | 1901 | 1 | 0,64 | 9 | 1.500 | 90 x 100 | 3,54 x 3,94 | 50 | 31 | f | 600 | 1.323 |
| **56** | Darracq 9½ HP | F | 1902 | 1 | 1,28 | 9 | 1.200 | 112 x 130 | 4,41 x 5,12 | 40 | 25 | f | 600 | 1.323 |
| **57** | Bollée Limousine | F | 1901 | 2 | 3,04 | 9 | 1.000 | 110 x 160 | 4,33 x 6,30 | | | f | 1.800 | 3.969 |
| **57** | Bugatti 12 CV | F | 1901 | 4 | 3 | 12 | | | | 60 | 37 | f | 650 | 1.433 |
| **58** | De Dion Bouton Vis-à-vis | F | 1898 | 1 | | 3½ | 1.500 | | | | | r | | |
| **62** | Duryea Buggy | USA | 1893 | 2 | | 5 | | 101 x 114 | 4,00 x 4,50 | 16 | 10 | r | | |
| **62** | Duryea Dos-à-dos | USA | 1896 | | | | | | | | | c | | |
| **62** | Columbia | USA | 1901 | 1 | | 5 | | | | 45 | 28 | f | | |
| **63** | Oldsmobile | USA | 1897 | | | | | | | 30 | 19 | r | | |
| **64** | Oldsmobile Curved Dash | USA | 1901 | 1 | 1,56 | 5 | 700 | 114 x 152 | 4,49 x 5,98 | 30 | 19 | r | 270 | 595 |
| **65** | Cadillac Model A | USA | 1902 | 1 | 1,64 | 9,7 | 800 | 127 x 127 | 5,00 x 5,00 | 40 | 25 | f | 600 | 1.323 |
| **66** | Oakland | USA | 1908 | 2 | 2,5 | 20 | | | | | | f | | |
| **66** | Pope (Electric Vehicle) | USA | 1905 | | | | | | | | | r | | |
| **66** | Buick Model A | USA | 1903 | 2 | | 22 | | | | | | r | | |
| **66** | Buick Model D | USA | 1907 | 2 | | 22 | | | | | | f | | |
| **67** | Daimler Wagonette | D | 1900 | 2 | 1,50 | | | | | | | f | | |
| **67** | Daimler Open Tourer | D | 1907 | 4 | 10,60 | | | | | | | f | | |
| **67** | Daimler Open Tourer | D | 1910 | 4 | | 38 | | | | | | f | | |
| **67** | Wolseley 6 HP | GB | 1904 | 1 | 1,30 | 6 | 800 | 114 x 127 | 4,50 x 5,00 | 32 | 20 | f | | |
| **68** | Rover 8 HP | GB | 1904 | 1 | | 8 | | | | | | f | | |
| **68** | Rolls Royce Silver Ghost | GB | 1907 | 6 | 7,05 | 50 | 1.250 | 114 x 114 | 4,50 x 4,50 | 100 | 62 | f | | |

*International Registration Letters used in this book:

| | | | | | | | | | |
|---|---|---|---|---|---|---|---|---|---|
| A | Austria | CH | Switzerland | E | Spain | I | Italy | S | Sweden |
| AUS | Australia | CS | Czechoslovakia | F | France | J | Japan | SU | USSR |
| B | Belgium | D | Germany | GB | Great Britain | NL | Netherlands | USA | United States of America |

# THE AUTOMOBILE IN NUMBERS

| page | Make & type | International Registration Letter* | Year of make | Number of cylinders | Displacement | Power hp | rpm | Bore & stroke | | Velocity | | Engine position | Weight | |
|---|---|---|---|---|---|---|---|---|---|---|---|---|---|---|
| | | | | | | | | mm | inches | km/h | mph | | kg | lb |
| **68** | Auburn | GB | 1903 | 2 | | 6 | | | | | | f | | |
| **68** | Auburn | GB | 1907 | 4 | | 24 | | | | | | f | | |
| **69** | Benz Coupé Milord | D | 1897 | 2 | 1,36 | 9 | 900 | 120 x 120 | 4,72 x 4,72 | 40 | 25 | r | | |
| **69** | Ayax Landaulet | CH | 1908 | 4 | 2,27 | 16-20 | | 85 x 100 | 3,35 x 3,94 | 60 | 37 | f | 1.400 | 3.087 |
| **69** | Studebaker (Electric Vehicle) | USA | 1902 | | | | | | | 20 | 12 | c | | |
| **69** | Studebaker Garford | USA | 1904 | 2 | | 16 | | | | | | f | | |
| **70** | Lutzmann 4 HP | D | 1895 | | | 4 | | | | | | r | | |
| **70** | Opel 4 HP | D | 1898 | 1 | | 4 | | | | 23 | 14 | r | | |
| **70** | Opel Darracq | D | 1908 | 1 | | 9 | 1.200 | | | | | f | | |
| **70** | OM Züst | I | 1908 | 3 | | 10 | | | | | | f | | |
| **71** | Popp 7 HP | CH | 1898 | 2 | 1,60 | 7 | | 92 x 120 | 3,62 x 4,72 | | | r | | |
| **71** | Pierce-Arrow Motorette | USA | 1901 | 1 | | 2¾ | | | | | | r | | |
| **71** | Pierce-Arrow Great Arrow | USA | 1907 | 6 | | 40 | | | | | | f | | |
| **72** | Mercedes Simplex | D | 1902 | 4 | 6,79 | 44 | 1.300 | 120 x 150 | 4,72 x 5,91 | 75 | 46 | f | 600 | 1.323 |
| **72** | Isotta Fraschini type fenc | I | 1906 | 4 | 1,33 | 17 | 2.500 | 65 x 100 | 2,56 x 3,94 | | | f | | |
| **72** | Isotta Fraschini 40 HP | I | 1906 | 4 | 7,96 | 50 | 1.200 | 130 x 150 | 5,12 x 4,72 | 120 | 75 | f | | |
| **72** | Welleyes 3 CV | I | 1899 | | | 3 | | | | | | r | | |
| **73** | Fiat 3½ HP | I | 1899 | 2 | 0,67 | 4,7 | 800 | 65 x 99 | 2,56 x 3,90 | 35 | 22 | r | 420 | 926 |
| **73** | Fiat 16/24 HP | I | 1903 | 4 | 4,50 | 24 | 1.400 | 105 x 130 | 4,13 x 5,12 | 75 | 47 | f | 1.300 | 2.867 |
| **73** | Fiat 24/32 HP | I | 1903 | 4 | 6,37 | 32 | 1.200 | 130 x 120 | 5,12 x 4,72 | 75 | 47 | f | 1.700 | 3.749 |
| **74** | Ceirano 5 HP | I | 1901 | 1 | 0,63 | 5 | | | | | | f | | |
| **74** | Duesenberg Mason | USA | 1906 | | | 24 | | | | | | f | | |
| **75** | Marchand 12/16 HP | I | 1904 | 4 | | 16 | | | | | | f | 1.397 | 3.080 |
| **75** | Austin Baby | GB | 1909 | 1 | | 7 | | 105 x 127 | 4,13 x 5,00 | 24 | 15 | f | | |
| **75** | Itala 35/45 HP | I | 1909 | 4 | 7,43 | 45 | | | | | | f | | |
| **75** | Packard 12 HP Model F | USA | 1902 | 1 | | | | | | | | c | | |
| **75** | Maxwell 14 HP | USA | 1908 | | | | | | | | | f | | |
| **78** | Amédée Bollée | F | 1898 | 2 | 3,04 | | | 110 x 160 | 4,33 x 6,30 | | | f | | |
| **78** | Jeantaud | F | 1899 | | | 36 | | | | | | f | 1.400 | 3.087 |
| **78** | Serpollet | F | 1903 | 4 | | 40 | | | | | | r | | |
| **78** | Wolseley | GB | 1904 | 4 | 11,89 | 96 | | 152 x 165 | 6,00 x 6,50 | | | f | | |
| **78** | Mors | F | 1904 | 4 | 10,08 | 60 | | 140 x 150 | 5,51 x 5,91 | 124 | 77 | f | | |
| **79** | Itala 35/45 HP | I | 1907 | 4 | 7,43 | 45 | 1.500 | 130 x 140 | 5,12 x 5,51 | 71 | 44 | f | 2.235 | 4.928 |
| **80** | Dufaux | F | 1904 | 8 | 12,76 | 90 | 1.300 | 125 x 130 | 4,92 x 5,12 | 71 | 44 | f | | |
| **80** | Thomas Flyer type 35 | USA | 1907 | 4 | 9,36 | 70 | | 146 x 139 | 5,75 x 5,50 | 96 | 60 | f | 1.818 | 4.010 |
| **80** | Peugeot | F | 1912 | 4 | 7,6 | 130 | 2.200 | 110 x 200 | 4,33 x 7,87 | 160 | 100 | f | 1.422 | 3.136 |
| **80** | Fiat Grand Prix | I | 1907 | 4 | 16,28 | 130 | 1.600 | 180 x 160 | 7,09 x 6,30 | 157 | 98 | f | 1.371 | 3.023 |
| **81** | Fiat 75 HP | I | 1904 | 4 | 14,11 | 76 | 1.200 | 165 x 165 | 6,50 x 6,50 | 160 | 100 | f | 800 | 1.764 |
| **81** | Fiat 100 HP racer | I | 1905 | 4 | 16,28 | 100 | 1.100 | 180 x 160 | 7,09 x 6,30 | 160 | 100 | f | 780 | 1.720 |
| **81** | Fiat S 74 racer | I | 1911 | 4 | 14,13 | 190 | 1.600 | 150 x 200 | 5,91 x 7,87 | 165 | 103 | f | 1.250 | 2.756 |
| **81** | Fiat S 57/14B racer | I | 1914 | 4 | 4,49 | 135 | 3.000 | 100 x 143 | 3,94 x 5,63 | 145 | 90 | f | 1.150 | 2.536 |
| **81** | Fiat Grand Prix type 804 | I | 1922 | 6 | 1,99 | 112 | 5.000 | 65 x 100 | 2,56 x 3,94 | 170 | 106 | f | 650 | 1.433 |
| **81** | Fiat S 76 | I | 1911 | 4 | 28,35 | 290 | 1.900 | 190 x 250 | 7,48 x 9,84 | | | f | 1.650 | 3.638 |
| **82** | Vauxhall | GB | 1910 | | 3 | | | | | 160 | 100 | f | | |
| **82** | Sizaire-Naudin | F | 1912 | 4 | 2,96 | 95 | | 78 x 156 | 3,07 x 6,14 | 153 | 95 | f | | |
| **83** | Hispano-Suiza | E | 1913 | 4 | 3,62 | 64 | | 80 x 180 | 3,15 x 7,09 | 124 | 77 | f | | |
| **83** | Delage | F | 1913 | 4 | 6,2 | 105 | 2.300 | 105 x 180 | 4,13 x 7,09 | 160 | 100 | f | 1.371 | 3.023 |
| **83** | Vauxhall | GB | 1914 | 4 | 4,00 | 75 | | 95 x 140 | 3,74 x 5,51 | 136 | 85 | f | | |

# THE AUTOMOBILE IN NUMBERS

| page | Make & type | International Registration Letter* | Year of make | Number of cylinders | Displacement | Power hp | rpm | Bore & stroke | | Velocity | | Engine position | Weight | |
|---|---|---|---|---|---|---|---|---|---|---|---|---|---|---|
| | | | | | | | | mm | inches | km/h | mph | | kg | lb |
| 83 | Aston Martin | GB | 1922 | 4 | 1,48 | | | | | | | f | | |
| 84 | Fiat Grand Prix | I | 1924 | 8 | 2,00 | 130 | 5.500 | 60 x 87 | 2,36 x 3,44 | 220 | 137 | f | 680 | 1.499 |
| 84 | Maserati type 26 | I | 1926 | 8 | 1,50 | | | | | 150 | 93 | f | | |
| 84 | Bugatti type 35 | F | 1927 | 8 | 2,01 | 105 | | 60 x 88 | 2,36 x 3,49 | | | f | | |
| 85 | Mercedes type W 25 | D | 1934 | 8 | 3,36 | 302 | 5.800 | 78 x 88 | 3,07 x 3,46 | 270 | 168 | f | 820 | 1.808 |
| 85 | Citroën Petite Rosalie | F | 1933 | 6 | | | | 75 x 100 | 2,95 x 3,94 | | | f | | |
| 86 | Alfa Romeo 24 HP | I | 1911 | 4 | 4,08 | 42 | 2.200 | 100 x 130 | 3,94 x 5,12 | 100 | 62 | f | 1.000 | 2.205 |
| 86 | Alfa Romeo 40/60 HP | I | 1921 | 4 | 6,08 | 82 | 2.400 | 110 x 160 | 4,33 x 6,30 | 150 | 93 | f | 1.100 | 2.426 |
| 86 | Alfa Romeo 20/30 ES | I | 1921 | 4 | 4,25 | 67 | 2.600 | 102 x 130 | 4,02 x 5,12 | 140 | 87 | f | 1.050 | 2.315 |
| 86 | Alfa Romeo RL SS | I | 1925 | 6 | 2,99 | 83 | 3.600 | 76 x 110 | 2,99 x 4,33 | 130 | 80 | f | 1.600 | 3.528 |
| 87 | Alfa Romeo RL Targa Florio | I | 1924 | 6 | 3,15 | 95 | 3.800 | 78 x 110 | 3,07 x 4,33 | 160 | 100 | f | 980 | 2.161 |
| 87 | Alfa Romeo 6C 1500 SS | I | 1928 | 6 | 1,48 | 76 | 4.800 | 62 x 82 | 2,44 x 3,23 | 140 | 87 | f | 860 | 1.896 |
| 88 | Alfa Romeo Gran Premio P2 | I | 1930 | 8 | 2,00 | 175 | 5.500 | 61 x 85 | 2,42 x 3,35 | 225 | 140 | f | 780 | 1.720 |
| 88 | Alfa Romeo Gran Premio type BP3 | I | 1932 | 8 | 2,65 | 215 | 5.600 | 65 x 100 | 2,56 x 3,94 | 230 | 143 | f | 700 | 1.544 |
| 88 | Alfa Romeo Gran Premio P2 | I | 1924 | 8 | 1,98 | 140 | 5.500 | 61 x 85 | 2,40 x 3,35 | 225 | 140 | f | 720 | 1.588 |
| 89 | Alfa Romeo 6C 1750 Gran Sport | I | 1930 | 6 | 1,75 | 85 | 4.500 | 65 x 88 | 2,56 x 3,46 | 145 | 90 | f | 920 | 2.029 |
| 89 | Alfa Romeo 8C 2300 | I | 1931 | 8 | 2,33 | 142 | 5.400 | 65 x 88 | 2,56 x 3,46 | 170 | 106 | f | 1.000 | 2.205 |
| 89 | Alfa Romeo Gran Premio type A | I | 1931 | 12 | 3,50 | 230 | | 65 x 88 | 2,56 x 3,46 | 240 | 150 | f | 930 | 2.051 |
| 89 | Alfa Romeo GP 8C 2300 Monza | I | 1931 | 8 | 2,33 | 165 | 5.400 | 65 x 88 | 2,56 x 3,46 | 210 | 130 | f | 920 | 2.029 |
| 89 | Alfa Romeo type 158 | I | 1938 | 8 | 1,47 | 195 | 7.200 | 58 x 70 | 2,28 x 2,76 | 230 | 145 | f | 620 | 1.367 |
| 90 | Tracta Gephi | F | 1927 | | | | | | | | | f | | |
| 90 | Invicta | GB | 1930 | 6 | 4,46 | 120 | | 85 x 120 | 3,37 x 4,72 | 160 | 100 | f | | |
| 90 | Delahaye Competition | F | 1936 | 6 | 3,55 | 160 | 4.200 | 84 x 107 | 3,31 x 4,21 | | | f | | |
| 91 | Delage Competition | F | 1937 | 6 | 3,0 | | | | | | | f | | |
| 91 | Auto Union | D | 1937 | 16 | 4,4 | 295 | 4.500 | 68 x 75 | 2,68 x 2,95 | 265 | 165 | r | 1.092 | 2.408 |
| 92 | Cooper Mark IV | GB | 1950 | 1 | 0,49 | 45 | 6.000 | 80 x 99 | 3,15 x 3,90 | | | r | 236 | 518 |
| 93 | Jaguar XK-120 tipo C | GB | 1951 | 6 | 3,44 | 160 | 5.200 | 83 x 106 | 3,27 x 4,17 | | | f | 460 | 1.015 |
| 94 | Cooper-Climax | GB | 1959 | 4 | 2,5 | 240 | 6.750 | 94 x 89 | 3,70 x 3,54 | | | r | | |
| 94 | Ferrari 246 | I | 1960 | 6 | 2,5 | 280 | 8.500 | 85 x 71 | 3,35 x 2,80 | 270 | 168 | f | 560 | 1.235 |
| 94 | Lotus 25 | GB | 1962 | 8 | 1,5 | 200 | 10.000 | 67 x 51 | 2,64 x 2,01 | | | r | 453 | 1.000 |
| 94 | Ford GT 40 | USA | 1966 | 8 | 4,7 | 390 | 7.000 | 101 x 72 | 3,98 x 2,83 | | | r | | |
| 94 | Lotus 49 | GB | 1970 | 8 | 3,0 | 410 | 9.000 | 85 x 64 | 3,37 x 2,55 | | | r | 580 | 1.280 |
| 94 | Lotus 72 | GB | 1972 | 8 | 3,0 | 450 | 11.000 | 85 x 64 | 3,37 x 2,55 | | | r | 550 | 1.214 |
| 95 | Brabham F1 | GB | 1969 | 8 | 3,0 | 450 | 10.500 | 85 x 64 | 3,37 x 2,55 | | | r | 530 | 1.169 |
| 95 | Brabham F1 | GB | 1970 | 8 | 3,0 | 450 | 10.500 | 85 x 64 | 3,37 x 2,55 | | | r | 530 | 1.169 |
| 96 | Chaparral | USA | 1967 | 8 | 7,0 | 575 | 7.500 | 107 x 95 | 4,21 x 3,76 | 325 | 215 | r | | |
| 96 | Porsche 917 | D | 1969 | 12 | 4,5 | 580 | 8.400 | 86 x 66 | 3,35 x 2,60 | | | r | 800 | 1.763 |
| 96 | Gulf Mirage | GB | 1973 | 8 | 3,0 | 440 | 10.000 | 85 x 64 | 3,37 x 2,55 | | | r | 680 | 1.499 |
| 97 | Tyrrel | GB | 1972 | 8 | 3,0 | 450 | 10.500 | 85 x 64 | 3,37 x 2,55 | | | r | 540 | 1.192 |
| 97 | Alfa Romeo 33/3 | I | 1971 | 8 | 3,0 | 430 | 9.200 | 86 x 64 | 3,39 x 2,54 | | | r | 625 | 1.378 |
| 97 | Ferrari 312 | I | 1972 | 12 | 3,0 | 450 | 10.800 | 78 x 51 | 3,09 x 2,03 | 300 | 186 | r | 550 | 1.213 |
| 102 | Jamais Contente | F | 1899 | | | 24 | 1.000 | | | 112 | 70 | r | 998 | 2.200 |
| 102 | Ford 999 | USA | 1903 | 4 | 16,8 | 72 | 800 | 179 x 179 | 7,05 x 7,05 | 145 | 90 | f | | |
| 103 | Sunbeam 350 HP | GB | 1924 | 12 | 18,3 | 350 | | 120 x 135 | 4,72 x 5,31 | | | f | | |
| 103 | Fiat | I | 1924 | 12 | 10,7 | 350 | | 90 x 140 | 3,54 x 5,51 | | | f | 950 | 2.095 |
| 103 | Sunbeam | GB | 1926 | 12 | 4,0 | 306 | | | | | | f | | |
| 103 | Higham Special «Babs» | GB | 1926 | 12 | 27,0 | 500 | | 127 x 177 | 5,00 x 6,97 | | | f | 2.000 | 4.410 |
| 104 | White Triplex | USA | 1928 | 12 | 26,9 | 400 | | | | | | f | | |

# THE AUTOMOBILE IN NUMBERS

| page | Make & type | International Registration Letter* | Year of make | Number of cylinders | Displacement | Power hp | rpm | Bore & stroke | | Velocity | | Engine position | Weight | |
|---|---|---|---|---|---|---|---|---|---|---|---|---|---|---|
| | | | | | | | | mm | inches | km/h | mph | | kg | lb |
| **104** | Irving Napier Golden Arrow | GB | 1929 | 12 | 23,9 | 930 | 3.500 | 139 x 130 | 5,50 x 5,13 | | | f | 3.000 | 6.615 |
| **104** | Bluebird | GB | 1935 | 12 | 36,5 | | 2.300 | | | | | f | | |
| **105** | Thunderbolt | GB | 1937 | 24 | 73,2 | | 5.000 | 157 x 167 | 6,18 x 6,57 | | | c | 7.000 | 15.435 |
| **105** | Green Monster | USA | 1964 | | | 17.500 | | | | | | f | | |
| **108** | Ford A | USA | 1903 | 2 | 1,72 | 8 | 1.000 | | | | | c | | |
| **109** | Ford Quadricycle | USA | 1896 | 2 | 0,97 | | | 63 x 152 | 2,50 x 6,00 | 28 | 17 | r | | |
| **110** | Ford Model T | USA | 1908 | 4 | 2,89 | 21 | 1.500 | 95 x 102 | 3,74 x 4,02 | 65 | 40 | f | 650 | 1.433 |
| **115** | Ford Model A | USA | 1928 | 4 | 3,28 | 40 | 2.200 | 98 x 108 | 3,87 x 4,25 | 150 | 65 | f | 1.075 | 2.370 |
| **118** | White Steamer type O | USA | 1909 | 2 | | | | 63 x 76 | 2,50 x 3,00 | | | f | | |
| **118** | Le Zebre type A | F | 1909 | 1 | 0,61 | 6 | | 86 x 106 | 3,39 x 4,17 | 45 | 28 | f | 350 | 772 |
| **119** | Brixia Züst 10 HP | I | 1909 | 3 | | 10 | 1.000 | 70 x 120 | 2,76 x 4,72 | 50 | 31 | f | | |
| **120** | Austin 18/24 | GB | 1911 | 4 | | 45 | | 111 x 127 | 4,37 x 5,00 | 80 | 50 | f | | |
| **120** | Berliet | F | 1910 | 4 | 2,4 | | | 80 x 120 | 3,15 x 4,72 | | | f | | |
| **120** | Studebaker 20 | USA | 1911 | 4 | | 30 | | | | | | f | | |
| **120** | Chevrolet Baby Grand | USA | 1912 | 4 | | | | | | | | f | | |
| **121** | Mercer 35 T Raceabout | USA | 1911 | 4 | 4,78 | 55 | 1.650 | 110 x 126 | 4,33 x 4,96 | 120 | 75 | f | | |
| **121** | White | USA | 1912 | 6 | | | | | | | | f | | |
| **121** | Buick Roadster | USA | 1910 | 4 | | | | | | | | f | | |
| **121** | Oldsmobile Autocrat | USA | 1912 | 6 | | | | | | | | f | | |
| **121** | Packard Six | USA | 1912 | 6 | | 105 | | | | | | f | 2.041 | 4.500 |
| **122** | Panhard & Levassor X 17 SS | F | 1912 | 4 | 2,61 | 15 | 1.200 | 80 x 130 | 3,15 x 5,12 | 50 | 31 | f | 1.250 | 2.756 |
| **122** | Vauxhall Prince Henry | GB | 1913 | | 3,96 | 75 | 2.500 | 95 x 140 | 3,74 x 5,51 | 120 | 75 | f | 1.100 | 2.426 |
| **122** | Studebaker Custom Roadster | USA | 1913 | 4 | | | | | | | | f | | |
| **123** | Lancia Theta | I | 1914 | 4 | 4,94 | 70 | 2.200 | 110 x 130 | 4,33 x 5,12 | 120 | 75 | f | | |
| **123** | Hispano-Suiza Alfonso XIII | F | 1912 | 4 | 2,5 | 60 | 2.300 | 80 x 180 | 3,15 x 7,09 | 120 | 75 | f | | |
| **123** | Peugeot Bebé | F | 1912 | 4 | 0,85 | 6 | | 55 x 90 | 2,17 x 3,54 | 65 | 40 | f | | |
| **123** | Daimler 20 HP | D | 1915 | | | 20 | | | | | | f | | |
| **124** | Renault voiturette type A | F | 1899 | 1 | 0,27 | 1,75 | 1.500 | 66 x 70 | 2,60 x 2,76 | 36 | 22 | f | 200 | 441 |
| **124** | Renault voiturette type C | F | 1900 | 1 | | 3,5 | 1.600 | 50 x 90 | 1,97 x 3,54 | | | f | | |
| **125** | Renault Fiacre type AG | F | 1906 | 2 | 1,20 | 8 | | 80 x 120 | 3,15 x 4,72 | 60 | 37 | f | | |
| **125** | Renault VB | F | 1907 | 4 | 4,40 | 20 | 1.200 | 100 x 140 | 3,94 x 5,51 | 60 | 37 | f | 900 | 1.984 |
| **126** | Renault Grand Prix | F | 1906 | 4 | 13,20 | 90 | | 166 x 150 | 6,54 x 5,91 | 130 | 81 | f | 1.000 | 2.205 |
| **126** | Renault Parigi-Vienna | F | 1902 | 4 | 3,77 | 14 | | 100 x 120 | 3,94 x 4,72 | 125 | 78 | f | 600 | 1.325 |
| **126** | Coupé «12 CV» | F | 1921 | 4 | 2,81 | | | 80 x 140 | 3,15 x 5,51 | 80 | 50 | f | 1.500 | 3.307 |
| **127** | Renault Reinastella | F | 1929 | 8 | 7,12 | | | 90 x 140 | 3,54 x 5,51 | 145 | 90 | f | 2.700 | 5.953 |
| **127** | Renault Nervasport | F | 1932 | 8 | 4,24 | | | 75 x 120 | 2,95 x 4,72 | 135 | 84 | f | 2.250 | 4.961 |
| **127** | Renault Nerva Grand Sport | F | 1937 | 8 | 5,45 | | | 85 x 120 | 3,35 x 4,72 | 140 | 87 | f | 2.450 | 5.402 |
| **128** | Panhard & Levassor Sport Skiff | F | 1913 | 4 | 4,39 | | | 100 x 140 | 3,94 x 5,51 | | | f | | |
| **128** | Oldsmobile 45 A | USA | 1918 | 8 | | | | | | | | f | | |
| **128** | Packard Twin Six | USA | 1916 | 12 | | 85 | | | | | | f | 2.086 | 4.600 |
| **128** | Opel | D | 1917 | | | | | | | | | f | | |
| **128** | Studebaker Light 6 | USA | 1921 | | | | | | | | | f | | |
| **129** | Fiat 501 | I | 1919 | 4 | 1,46 | 23 | 2.600 | 65 x 110 | 2,56 x 4,35 | 70 | 43 | f | 1.000 | 2.205 |
| **129** | Crane Simplex Model 5 | USA | 1918 | 6 | 9,9 | 46 | | 112 x 153 | 4,41 x 6,02 | | | f | | |
| **129** | Itala 25/35 HP | I | 1912 | 4 | | 35 | | 90 x 110 | 3,54 x 4,33 | | | f | | |
| **129** | Super-Fiat | I | 1921 | 12 | 6,80 | 90 | 2.000 | 85 x 100 | 3,35 x 3,94 | 120 | 75 | f | 1.850 | 4.080 |
| **130** | Isotta Fraschini type 8 | I | 1920 | 8 | 5,90 | 80 | 2.200 | 85 x 130 | 3,35 x 5,12 | 113 | 70 | f | 1.676 | 3.700 |

# THE AUTOMOBILE IN NUMBERS

| page | Make & type | International Registration Letter* | Year of make | Number of cylinders | Displacement | Power hp | rpm | Bore & stroke mm | Bore & stroke inches | Velocity km/h | Velocity mph | Engine position | Weight kg | Weight lb |
|---|---|---|---|---|---|---|---|---|---|---|---|---|---|---|
| 130 | Crossley | GB | 1921 | 4 | | 19,6 | | 89 x 143 | 3,50 x 5,63 | | | f | | |
| 130 | Temperino | I | 1923 | 2 | 1,1 | 10 | 1.500 | 85 x 89 | 3,35 x 3,50 | | | f | 350 | 772 |
| 131 | Fiat 520 Coupé | I | 1927 | 6 | 2,25 | 46 | 3.400 | 68 x 103 | 2,68 x 4,06 | 90 | 56 | f | 1.280 | 2.822 |
| 131 | Darracq V8 | F | 1921 | 8 | 4,58 | 62 | | 75 x 130 | 2,95 x 5,12 | 105 | 65 | f | | |
| 131 | Chrysler Six | USA | 1924 | 6 | 3,30 | | | | | 120 | 75 | f | | |
| 131 | Bianchi S4 | I | 1925 | 4 | 1,31 | 30 | 3.000 | 64 x 100 | 2,52 x 3,94 | 90 | 56 | f | | |
| 132 | Austin Seven | GB | 1925 | 4 | 0,74 | 10,5 | 2.400 | 56 x 76 | 2,20 x 3,00 | 60 | 37 | f | 356 | 784 |
| 134 | MG | GB | 1923 | 4 | 1,55 | | | | | 125 | 78 | f | | |
| 134 | Hispano-Suiza Boulogne | E | 1924 | 6 | 8,0 | 46 | | 100 x 140 | 3,94 x 5,51 | 175 | 109 | f | | |
| 134 | Morris Bullnose | GB | 1924 | 4 | 1,55 | 26 | 2.800 | 69 x 102 | 2,74 x 4,02 | 80 | 50 | f | 750 | 1.650 |
| 134 | Alvis 12/50 | GB | 1925 | 4 | | 50 | | 68 x 110 | 2,68 x 4,33 | | | f | | |
| 134 | Chrysler Six | USA | 1925 | 6 | 1,50 | | | 76 x 121 | 2,99 x 4,76 | | | f | | |
| 135 | Frazer Nash Boulogne | GB | 1926 | 4 | 1,5 | | | 69 x 100 | 2,72 x 3,94 | | | f | | |
| 135 | Bugatti type 30 | F | 1926 | 8 | 2,0 | | | 60 x 88 | 2,36 x 3,46 | 130 | 80 | f | | |
| 135 | Bugatti type 43 | F | 1927 | 8 | 2,3 | | | 60 x 100 | 2,36 x 3,94 | 160 | 100 | f | | |
| 135 | Isotta Fraschini type A | I | 1926 | 8 | 7,4 | 45 | | 95 x 130 | 3,74 x 5,12 | | | f | | |
| 135 | Pierce-Arrow type 80 | USA | 1926 | 6 | | 30 | | 89 x 127 | 3,50 x 5,00 | | | f | | |
| 138 | Buick | USA | 1927 | 6 | 3,4 | | | 79 x 114 | 3,13 x 4,50 | | | f | | |
| 138 | Rolls Royce Phantom I | GB | 1928 | 6 | 7,6 | 100 | | 108 x 140 | 4,25 x 5,51 | | | f | | |
| 138 | Cord L-29 | USA | 1930 | 8 | | 125 | | | | 125 | 78 | f | | |
| 138 | Auburn type 8-77 | USA | 1927 | 8 | 4,5 | | | 69 x 120 | 2,75 x 4,75 | | | f | | |
| 139 | Reo Flying Cloud | USA | 1929 | 6 | 1,5 | | | 82 x 127 | 3,25 x 5,00 | 100 | 62 | f | | |
| 140 | Minerva | B | 1927 | 6 | 2,0 | | | 68 x 92 | 2,68 x 3,62 | | | f | | |
| 140 | Lincoln | USA | 1928 | 8 | 5,9 | | | 85 x 127 | 3,37 x 5,00 | | | f | | |
| 140 | Peugeot | F | 1927 | 4 | 3,8 | 75 | 1.900 | 95 x 135 | 3,74 x 5,31 | 100 | 62 | f | | |
| 141 | Stutz 8 Club Coupé | USA | 1928 | 8 | 4,9 | 96 | | 82 x 114 | 3,25 x 4,50 | | | f | | |
| 141 | Bucciali Double-Huit | F | 1932 | 16 | | 165 | | | | 201 | 125 | f | | |
| 141 | Delage D 8 | F | 1932 | 8 | 4,1 | | | | | | | f | | |
| 141 | Chrysler Imperial Coupé | USA | 1932 | 8 | 6,3 | 135 | | | | | | f | | |
| 142 | OM Alcyone | I | 1934 | 6 | 2,20 | 60 | 3.600 | 62 x 90 | 2,44 x 3,54 | | | f | 900 | 1.985 |
| 142 | Bianchi S 5 type V | I | 1932 | 4 | 1,3 | 30 | | | | | | f | | |
| 142 | Marmon 8/69 | USA | 1931 | 8 | 3,91 | | | 79 x 101 | 3,12 x 4,00 | | | f | | |
| 142 | Auburn Speedster | USA | 1935 | 8 | 4,57 | 115 | | | | 160 | 100 | f | | |
| 142 | Chevrolet Capitol | USA | 1927 | 4 | | | | 94 x 101 | 3,69 x 4,00 | | | f | | |
| 143 | NSU 7/34 PS | D | 1928 | 6 | 1,78 | 34 | 3.000 | 62 x 90 | 2,44 x 3,54 | 90 | 56 | f | 815 | 1.797 |
| 143 | Austro-Daimler type ADR 6 | A | 1933 | 6 | 3,61 | 120 | 3.600 | 82 x 115 | 3,23 x 4,53 | 145 | 90 | f | 1.200 | 2.845 |
| 143 | Pierce-Arrow Silver Arrow V12 | USA | 1933 | 12 | 7,0 | 175 | 3.400 | | | | | f | | |
| 145 | Isotta Fraschini type 8A | I | 1927 | 8 | 7,37 | 120 | 2.400 | 95 x 130 | 3,74 x 5,12 | | | f | | |
| 145 | Isotta Fraschini 8 C Monterosa | I | 1947 | 8 | 3,40 | 125 | 4.200 | | | | | r | | |
| 146 | Hispano-Suiza 6 A Victoria | E | 1928 | 6 | 3,74 | | | 85 x 110 | 3,35 x 4,33 | | | f | | |
| 146 | Hispano-Suiza Coupé | F | 1931 | 6 | 7,98 | 180 | 2.500 | 110 x 140 | 4,33 x 5,51 | 160 | 100 | f | | |
| 147 | Voisin Sport 12 cylinders | F | | 12 | 3,0 | | | 76 x 110 | 2,99 x 4,33 | | | f | | |
| 148 | Bugatti Royale Coupé | F | 1928 | 8 | 12,76 | 300 | 1.700 | 125 x 130 | 4,92 x 5,12 | 150 | 93 | f | | |
| 148 | Bugatti Coupé type 44 | F | 1927 | 8 | 3,0 | | | 69 x 100 | 2,72 x 3,94 | | | f | | |
| 149 | Bugatti Coupé type 50 T | F | 1933 | 8 | 4,97 | 200 | 4.000 | 86 x 107 | 3,39 x 4,21 | | | f | | |
| 149 | Bugatti Berlinetta Sport type 57 | F | 1934 | 8 | 3,3 | | | 72 x 100 | 2,83 x 3,94 | | | f | | |
| 150 | Duesenberg J Beverly | USA | 1931 | 8 | 6,88 | 265 | 4.250 | 95 x 120 | 3,75 x 4,75 | 175 | 109 | f | | |
| 150 | Duesenberg A | USA | 1925 | 8 | 4,26 | 90 | 3.600 | 72 x 127 | 2,87 x 5,00 | | | f | | |

# THE AUTOMOBILE IN NUMBERS

| page | Make & type | International Registration Letter* | Year of make | Number of cylinders | Displacement | Power hp | rpm | Bore & stroke | | Velocity | | Engine position | Weight | |
|---|---|---|---|---|---|---|---|---|---|---|---|---|---|---|
| | | | | | | | | mm | inches | km/h | mph | | kg | lb |
| 152 | Duesenberg J | USA | 1931 | 8 | 6,88 | 265 | 4.250 | 95 x 120 | 3,75 x 4,75 | 187 | 116 | f | 2.260 | 4.983 |
| 153 | Duesenberg SJ | USA | 1932 | 8 | 6,90 | 320 | 4.750 | 95 x 120 | 3,73 x 4,75 | 209 | 130 | f | | |
| 154 | Citroën 10 HP type A | F | 1919 | 4 | 1,4 | 18 | 2.100 | 65 x 100 | 2,56 x 3,94 | 65 | 40 | f | 810 | 1.788 |
| 154 | Citroën B 2 | F | 1922 | 4 | 1,5 | 20 | 2.100 | 68 x 100 | 2,68 x 3,94 | 70 | 43 | f | 1.010 | 2.227 |
| 154 | Citroën B 12 | F | 1926 | 4 | 1,5 | 20 | 2.100 | 68 x 100 | 2,68 x 3,94 | 75 | 47 | f | 1.000 | 2.205 |
| 154 | Citroën B 14 | F | 1927 | 4 | 1,6 | 22 | 2.300 | 70 x 100 | 2,76 x 3,94 | 80 | 50 | f | 1.150 | 2.536 |
| 155 | Citroën C 6 E | F | 1929 | 6 | 2,5 | 42 | 3.000 | 72 x 100 | 2,83 x 3,94 | 105 | 65 | f | 1.275 | 2.811 |
| 155 | Citroën C 6 C GL | F | 1931 | 6 | 2,5 | 53 | | 72 x 100 | 2,83 x 3,94 | 105 | 65 | f | 1.340 | 2.955 |
| 156 | Citroën B 14 G | F | 1927 | 4 | 1,6 | 22 | 2.300 | 70 x 100 | 2,76 x 3,94 | 80 | 50 | f | 1.360 | 3.000 |
| 156 | Citroën 15 AL | F | 1932 | 6 | 2,6 | 56 | 3.200 | 75 x 100 | 2,95 x 3,94 | 120 | 75 | f | 1.360 | 3.000 |
| 156 | Citroën C 6 G | F | 1932 | 6 | 2,6 | 50 | 3.200 | 75 x 100 | 2,95 x 3,94 | 105 | 65 | f | 1.380 | 3.043 |
| 156 | Citroën 11 AL | F | 1935 | 4 | 1,9 | 46 | 3.800 | 78 x 100 | 3,07 x 3,94 | 110 | 68 | f | 1.060 | 2.340 |
| 156 | Citroën 22 CV | F | 1934 | 8 | 3,8 | 100 | | 78 x 100 | 3,07 x 3,94 | 140 | 87 | f | 1.250 | 2.756 |
| 156 | Citroën 54 G | F | 1932 | 4 | 1,8 | 32 | 2.700 | 75 x 100 | 2,95 x 3,94 | 95 | 59 | f | 1.200 | 2.646 |
| 156 | Citroën 8 A | F | 1932 | 4 | 1,4 | 32 | 3.200 | 68 x 100 | 2,68 x 3,94 | 90 | 56 | f | 1.165 | 2.570 |
| 157 | Citroën 5 CV type C | F | 1922 | 4 | 0,86 | 11 | 2.100 | 55 x 90 | 2,17 x 3,54 | 60 | 37 | f | 543 | 1.197 |
| 157 | Citroën C 4 | F | 1929 | 4 | 1,6 | 30 | 3.000 | 72 x 100 | 2,95 x 3,94 | 90 | 56 | f | 1.180 | 2.602 |
| 157 | Citroën 15 CV | F | 1939 | 6 | 2,9 | 77 | 3.800 | 78 x 100 | 3,07 x 3,94 | 130 | 81 | f | 1.325 | 2.922 |
| 158 | Cadillac V 16 | USA | 1932 | 16 | 7,41 | 165 | 3.200 | 76 x 101 | 3,00 x 4,00 | | | f | | |
| 158 | Stutz DV-32 | USA | 1933 | 16 | 5,20 | 156 | 3.900 | 85 x 114 | 3,37 x 4,46 | 160 | 100 | f | | |
| 158 | Panhard Panoramic | F | 1933 | 6 | | | | | | | | f | | |
| 158 | Opel Kadett | D | 1936 | 4 | 1,07 | 23 | 3.545 | 67 x 75 | 2,66 x 2,35 | 92 | 57 | f | 755 | 1.655 |
| 158 | Opel Olympia | D | 1935 | 4 | 1,27 | 24 | 3.200 | 67 x 90 | 2,66 x 3,54 | 95 | 59 | f | 820 | 1.808 |
| 158 | Delage D8 120 | F | 1937 | 8 | 4,75 | 140 | 4.000 | 80 x 107 | 3,15 x 4,21 | 145 | 90 | f | 1.769 | 3.900 |
| 159 | Tatra 87 | CH | 1938 | 8 | 3,0 | 72 | 3.600 | 75 x 84 | 2,95 x 3,31 | | | r | | |
| 159 | Maybach Zeppelin 60/200 | D | 1936 | 12 | 7,97 | 200 | 2.000 | 92 x 100 | 3,62 x 3,94 | 160 | 100 | f | 2.090 | 4.608 |
| 160 | Panhard | F | 1933 | 8 | 5,0 | | | | | | | f | | |
| 160 | Fiat 518 L Ardita | I | 1933 | 4 | 1,95 | 54 | 3.800 | 82 x 92 | 3,23 x 3,62 | 115 | 71 | f | 1.185 | 2.613 |
| 160 | Mercedes Benz 380 | D | 1933 | 8 | 3,80 | 90 | 3.400 | 78 x 100 | 3,07 x 3,94 | 130 | 80 | f | 1.280 | 2.820 |
| 160 | Chrysler Airflow Sedan | USA | 1935 | 8 | 5,30 | 130 | | 82 x 123 | 3,25 x 4,84 | | | f | | |
| 161 | Cord L-29 | USA | 1931 | 8 | 4,93 | 125 | 3.500 | 82 x 114 | 3,25 x 4,50 | 145 | 90 | f | | |
| 161 | Horch type 853 | D | 1937 | 8 | 5,0 | 100 | 3.200 | 87 x 104 | 3,43 x 4,09 | | | f | | |
| 161 | Aston Martin | GB | 1932 | 4 | 1,50 | 80 | 4.750 | 69 x 99 | 2,72 x 3,90 | 140 | 87 | f | | |
| 161 | SS 100 | GB | 1931 | 6 | 3,48 | 125 | 4.250 | 82 x 110 | 3,23 x 4,33 | 96 | 60 | f | | |
| 162 | Opel Admiral | D | 1938 | 6 | 3,62 | 75 | 3.200 | 90 x 95 | 3,54 x 3,74 | 130 | 80 | f | 1.600 | 3.528 |
| 162 | Opel Kapitän | D | 1939 | 6 | 2,47 | 55 | 3.500 | 80 x 82 | 3,15 x 3,23 | 125 | 78 | f | 1.180 | 2.602 |
| 162 | Fiat 1500 | I | 1935 | 6 | 1,49 | 45 | 4.400 | 65 x 75 | 2,56 x 2,95 | 115 | 71 | f | 1.070 | 2.359 |
| 162 | Jaguar SS Sedanca | GB | 1938 | 4 | 1,78 | 75 | 4.500 | 75 x 106 | 2,95 x 4,17 | | | f | 1.320 | 2.911 |
| 162 | Alfa Romeo 6 C 2500 SS | I | 1939 | 6 | 2,50 | 110 | 4.800 | 72 x 100 | 2,83 x 3,94 | 170 | 106 | f | 1.270 | 2.800 |
| 163 | Cord 812 | USA | 1937 | 8 | 4,73 | 190 | 4.200 | 89 x 95 | 3,50 x 3,75 | 161 | 100 | f | 1.656 | 3.650 |
| 163 | Packard Light Eight | USA | 1939 | 8 | 4,62 | 120 | 3.200 | 81 x 127 | 3,19 x 5,00 | | | f | | |
| 163 | Delahaye V 12 type 145 | F | 1937 | 12 | 4,50 | 160 | 4.500 | 75 x 84 | 2,95 x 3,33 | 180 | 112 | f | | |
| 163 | Standard Flying Twenty | GB | 1935 | 6 | 2,60 | 20 | | 73 x 106 | 2,87 x 4,17 | | | f | | |
| 164 | Mercedes Benz SS 38/250 | D | 1928 | 6 | 7,0 | 140 | 3.200 | 100 x 150 | 3,94 x 5,91 | 180 | 112 | f | 1.270 | 2.800 |
| 165 | Grosser Mercedes | D | 1937 | 8 | 7,7 | 230 | 2.800 | 95 x 135 | 3,74 x 5,31 | 160 | 100 | f | 1.980 | 4.366 |
| 165 | Mercedes Benz Stuttgart 200 | D | 1926 | 6 | 1,98 | 38 | 3.200 | 65 x 100 | 2,56 x 3,94 | 80 | 50 | f | 800 | 1.764 |
| 165 | Mercedes Benz type 130 H | D | 1933 | 4 | 1,30 | 26 | 3.200 | 70 x 85 | 2,76 x 3,35 | 92 | 57 | r | 880 | 1.940 |
| 165 | Mercedes Benz type 260 D | D | 1935 | 4 | 2,55 | 45 | 3.000 | 90 x 100 | 3,54 x 3,94 | 100 | 62 | f | 1.620 | 3.572 |

# THE AUTOMOBILE IN NUMBERS

| page | Make & type | International Registration Letter* | Year of make | Number of cylinders | Displacement | Power hp | rpm | Bore & stroke | | Velocity | | Engine position | Weight | |
|---|---|---|---|---|---|---|---|---|---|---|---|---|---|---|
| | | | | | | | | mm | inches | km/h | mph | | kg | lb |
| 165 | Mercedes Benz type 170 V | D | 1935 | 4 | 1,70 | 38 | 3.400 | 73 x 100 | 2,89 x 3,94 | 108 | 67 | f | 760 | 1.676 |
| 165 | Mercedes Benz 540 K | D | 1936 | 8 | 5,4 | 180 | 3.300 | 88 x 111 | 3,46 x 4,37 | 160 | 100 | f | | |
| 166 | Lancia Theta | I | 1913 | 4 | 4,94 | 70 | 2.200 | 110 x 130 | 4,33 x 5,12 | 120 | 75 | f | | |
| 166 | Lancia Lambda | I | 1923 | 4 | 2,12 | 49 | 3.250 | 75 x 120 | 2,95 x 4,72 | 115 | 71 | f | | |
| 167 | Lancia Trikappa | I | 1922 | 8 | 4,60 | 98 | 2.500 | 75 x 130 | 2,95 x 5,12 | 130 | 80 | f | | |
| 167 | Lancia Augusta | I | 1933 | 4 | 11,20 | 35 | 4.000 | 69 x 78 | 2,75 x 3,07 | 102 | 63 | f | | |
| 168 | Lancia Dilambda | I | 1933 | 8 | 3,96 | 100 | 3.800 | 79 x 100 | 3,12 x 3,94 | 120 | 75 | f | | |
| 168 | Lancia Aprilia | I | 1937 | 4 | 1,35 | 47 | 4.300 | 72 x 83 | 2,83 x 3,27 | 127 | 79 | f | | |
| 168 | Lancia Astura | I | 1937 | 8 | 2,97 | 82 | 4.000 | 74 x 85 | 2,94 x 3,35 | 128 | 80 | f | | |
| 169 | Packard Twelve | USA | 1936 | 12 | 7,3 | 175 | 3.200 | 87 x 101 | 3,44 x 3,98 | 169 | 105 | f | 2.134 | 4.712 |
| 170 | Rolls Royce Phantom I | GB | 1925 | 6 | 7,66 | 95 | | 108 x 139 | 4,25 x 5,47 | 120 | 75 | f | | |
| 171 | Rolls Royce Phantom III | GB | 1939 | 12 | 7,34 | 165 | 3.000 | 82 x 114 | 3,25 x 4,49 | 160 | 100 | f | | |
| 172 | Buick Model C | USA | 1922 | 2 | | 22 | | 114 x 127 | 4,50 x 5,00 | | | f | 790 | 1.740 |
| 173 | Oakland | USA | 1912 | 4 | 5,44 | 45 | | | | | | f | | |
| 173 | Buick Model 10 | USA | 1908 | 4 | 1 | 18 | | 95 x 95 | 3,75 x 3,75 | | | f | | |
| 173 | Oldsmobile | USA | 1910 | 4 | 4,54 | 40 | | | | | | f | | |
| 173 | Chevrolet Royal Mail | USA | 1914 | 6 | 2,80 | 24 | | | | | | f | 1.010 | 2.225 |
| 174 | Chevrolet Classic Six | USA | 1911 | | | | | | | | | f | | |
| 174 | Chevrolet Model 490 | USA | 1916 | 4 | 2,70 | 22 | | 94 x 102 | 3,69 x 4,00 | | | f | | |
| 174 | Oldsmobile | USA | 1922 | | | | | | | | | f | | |
| 174 | Oakland | USA | 1924 | 6 | | 44 | | 71 x 121 | 2,81 x 4,75 | | | f | | |
| 174 | Buick Model 50 | USA | 1924 | 6 | 4,17 | 70 | | 85 x 120 | 3,37 x 4,75 | 110 | 68 | f | | |
| 174 | Pontiac | USA | 1926 | 6 | | | | 82 x 95 | 3,25 x 3,75 | | | f | | |
| 175 | Chevrolet | USA | 1929 | 6 | 3,18 | | | 84 x 95 | 3,31 x 3,75 | | | f | 1.173 | 2.585 |
| 175 | La Salle | USA | 1929 | 8 | 5,57 | 91 | 3.500 | 84 x 125 | 3,31 x 4,92 | 130 | 80 | f | | |
| 175 | Cadillac | USA | 1928 | 8 | 5,57 | 91 | 3.500 | 84 x 125 | 3,31 x 4,92 | 130 | 80 | f | | |
| 175 | Buick | USA | 1936 | 8 | 3,77 | | | 74 x 108 | 2,94 x 4,25 | | | f | | |
| 175 | Chevrolet Suburban | USA | 1936 | 6 | 4,26 | | | 71 x 102 | 3,31 x 4,00 | | | f | 1.410 | 3.110 |
| 175 | Oldsmobile | USA | 1940 | 8 | | 110 | | | | | | f | | |
| 176 | Cadillac V 16 Fleetwood | USA | 1931 | 16 | 7,41 | 165 | 3.200 | 76 x 101 | 3,00 x 4,00 | | | f | | |
| 176 | Chevrolet Sport | USA | 1932 | 6 | 3,18 | 60 | | 84 x 95 | 3,31 x 3,75 | | | f | 1.247 | 2.750 |
| 176 | Pontiac | USA | 1933 | 8 | 3,66 | 84 | 3.800 | 81 x 88 | 3,19 x 3,46 | 130 | 80 | f | | |
| 176 | Chevrolet Cabriolet | USA | 1942 | 6 | 3,54 | | | 89 x 95 | 3,50 x 3,75 | | | f | 1.433 | 3.160 |
| 177 | Chevrolet Muster | USA | 1940 | 6 | 3,54 | | | 89 x 95 | 3,50 x 3,75 | | | f | 1.342 | 2.960 |
| 177 | Chevrolet Muster | USA | 1936 | 6 | 3,18 | | | 84 x 102 | 3,31 x 4,00 | | | f | 1.410 | 3.110 |
| 177 | Chevrolet Muster | USA | 1938 | 6 | 3,54 | | | 89 x 95 | 3,50 x 3,75 | | | f | 1.290 | 2.845 |
| 178 | Toyota B | J | 1936 | 6 | | 85 | | | | | | f | | |
| 178 | Ohta cabriolet | J | 1937 | | | | | | | | | f | | |
| 179 | Sumida H | J | 1933 | | | | | | | | | f | | |
| 179 | Chiyoda H | J | 1935 | | | | | | | | | f | | |
| 179 | Nissan 70 | J | 1937 | 6 | | 85 | | | | 120 | 75 | f | | |
| 182 | Fiat 18 BL | I | 1914 | 4 | 5,65 | 30 | 1.200 | 100 x 180 | 3,94 x 7,09 | | | f | | |
| 185 | Jeep | USA | 1941 | 4 | 2,19 | 60 | 4.000 | 79 x 111 | 3,12 x 4,38 | 96 | 60 | f | 964 | 2.126 |
| 187 | Fiat Autocarretta 1014 | I | 1930 | 4 | 1,44 | 28 | 3.400 | 67 x 102 | 2,64 x 4,02 | | | f | | |
| 188 | Volkswagen type 166 | D | 1942 | 4 | 1,13 | 25 | 3.000 | 75 x 64 | 2,95 x 2,52 | 80 | 50 | r | | |
| 188 | Willy Jeepster | USA | 1950 | 6 | 2,19 | 72 | 4.000 | 79 x 111 | 3,12 x 4,38 | 105 | 64 | f | 1.180 | 2.602 |
| 189 | Land-Rover 88 Regular | GB | 1949 | 4 | 2,29 | 78 | 4.250 | 90 x 88 | 3,56 x 3,50 | 105 | 64 | f | 1.315 | 2.900 |
| 190 | Alfa Romeo AR 51 | I | 1954 | 4 | 1,88 | 70 | 4.400 | 82 x 88 | 3,25 x 3,46 | 105 | 64 | f | 1.250 | 2.756 |

# THE AUTOMOBILE IN NUMBERS

| page | Make & type | International Registration Letter* | Year of make | Number of cylinders | Displacement | Power hp | rpm | Bore & stroke | | Velocity | | Engine position | Weight | |
|---|---|---|---|---|---|---|---|---|---|---|---|---|---|---|
| | | | | | | | | mm | inches | km/h | mph | | kg | lb |
| **190** | Fiat Campagnola | I | 1960 | 4 | 1,90 | 61 | 4.000 | 80 x 90 | 3,15 x 3,54 | 110 | 68 | f | 1.290 | 2.846 |
| **190** | International Scout 800 | USA | 1961 | 4 | 2,50 | 93 | 4.400 | 98 x 81 | 3,87 x 3,22 | 100 | 62 | f | 1.450 | 3.197 |
| **191** | Morris Mini-Moke | GB | 1963 | 4 | 0,85 | 34 | 5.500 | 62 x 68 | 2,48 x 2,69 | 100 | 62 | f | | |
| **191** | Toyota Land Cruiser | J | 1962 | 6 | 3,88 | 135 | 3.800 | 90 x 101 | 3,54 x 4,00 | 135 | 84 | f | 1.480 | 3.263 |
| **191** | Citroën Sahara | F | 1958 | 2+2 | 0,85 | 25 | 4.200 | 66 x 62 | 2,60 x 2,44 | 100 | 62 | f–r | 640 | 1.411 |
| **194** | Auto Union DKW Munga | D | 1954 | 3 | 0,98 | 44 | 4.250 | 76 x 74 | 3,00 x 2,91 | 98 | 61 | f | 1.085 | 2.395 |
| **194** | Alvis Stalwart | GB | 1966 | 8 | 6,51 | 220 | 4.000 | 95 x 114 | 3,75 x 4,50 | 64 | 40 | c | 13.500 | 29.813 |
| **198** | Morris Eight Series E | GB | 1946 | 4 | 0,92 | 37 | 4.600 | 57 x 90 | 2,24 x 3,54 | 100 | 62 | f | 775 | 1.708 |
| **198** | Morris Minor | GB | 1949 | 4 | 0,92 | 37 | 4.600 | 57 x 90 | 2,24 x 3,54 | | | f | 760 | 1.675 |
| **198** | Tucker Torpedo | USA | 1948 | 6 | 9,75 | 150 | 3.000 | 127 x 127 | 5,00 x 5,00 | 195 | 122 | r | 1.920 | 4.235 |
| **198** | Triumph 1800 | GB | 1946 | 4 | 1,78 | 65 | 4.500 | 73 x 106 | 2,87 x 4,17 | | | f | 1.219 | 2.688 |
| **198** | Jaguar XK 120 | GB | 1949 | 6 | 3,44 | 160 | 5.200 | 83 x 106 | 3,27 x 4,17 | 193 | 120 | f | 1.120 | 2.470 |
| **199** | Jaguar 6 cylinders | GB | 1947 | 6 | 3,48 | 125 | 4.250 | 82 x 110 | 3,23 x 4,33 | 145 | 90 | f | 1.626 | 3.585 |
| **200** | Renault 4 CV | F | 1947 | 4 | 0,75 | 18 | 4.000 | 54 x 80 | 2,15 x 3,15 | 95 | 59 | r | 560 | 1.235 |
| **200** | Renault Juvaquatre | F | 1946 | 4 | 1,00 | | | | | 100 | 62 | f | 1.450 | 3.197 |
| **200** | Alfa Romeo 2500 Sport | I | 1947 | 6 | 2,44 | 90 | 4.600 | 72 x 100 | 2,83 x 3,94 | 155 | 96 | f | 1.550 | 3.418 |
| **200** | Peugeot 203 | F | 1948 | 4 | 1,29 | 49 | 4.500 | 75 x 73 | 2,95 x 2,87 | 115 | 71 | f | 920 | 2.029 |
| **200** | Lancia Ardea | I | 1948 | 4 | 0,90 | 29 | 4.600 | 65 x 68 | 2,56 x 2,68 | 108 | 67 | f | 750 | 1.653 |
| **201** | Studebaker Champion | USA | 1950 | 6 | 2,78 | 85 | 4.000 | 76 x 101 | 2,97 x 4,00 | | | f | 1.250 | 2.780 |
| **201** | Ford Anglia | GB | 1947 | 4 | 0,93 | 23 | 4.000 | 56 x 92 | 2,23 x 3,64 | | | f | 747 | 1.647 |
| **201** | Jowett Javelin | GB | 1947 | 4 | 1,49 | 50 | 4.250 | 72 x 90 | 2,85 x 3,54 | 125 | 78 | f | 1.016 | 2.240 |
| **201** | Riley 1½ litre | GB | 1947 | 4 | 1,50 | 55 | 4.500 | 69 x 100 | 2,72 x 3,94 | 125 | 78 | f | 1.232 | 2.716 |
| **201** | Fiat 1400 | I | 1950 | 4 | 1,39 | 44 | 4.400 | 82 x 66 | 3,23 x 2,60 | 120 | 75 | f | 1.130 | 2.492 |
| **201** | Lanchester Ten | GB | 1947 | 4 | 1,29 | 40 | 4.200 | 63 x 101 | 2,50 x 4,00 | | | f | 1.118 | 2.465 |
| **202** | Kdf | D | 1939 | 4 | 0,98 | 22 | 3.000 | 70 x 64 | 2,76 x 2,52 | 100 | 62 | r | 650 | 1.430 |
| **202** | Volkswagen 1302 | D | 1970 | 4 | 1,28 | 44 | 4.400 | 77 x 69 | 3,03 x 2,72 | 125 | 78 | r | 870 | 1.918 |
| **202** | Volkswagen Scirocco | D | 1974 | 4 | 1,09 | 50 | 6.000 | 69 x 72 | 2,74 x 2,83 | 144 | 89 | f | 775 | 1.708 |
| **203** | Porsche | D | 1948 | 4 | 1,13 | 40 | 4.000 | 75 x 64 | 2,95 x 2,52 | 150 | 93 | r | | |
| **203** | Porsche 356 B/1600 | D | 1961 | 4 | 1,58 | 60 | 4.500 | 82 x 74 | 3,25 x 2,91 | 160 | 100 | r | 900 | 1.984 |
| **203** | Porsche 911 Targa | D | 1965 | 6 | 1,99 | 130 | 6.100 | 80 x 66 | 3,15 x 2,60 | 210 | 131 | r | 1.080 | 2.381 |
| **204** | Fiat Zero | I | 1912 | 4 | 1,85 | 19 | 2.000 | 70 x 120 | 2,76 x 4,72 | 62 | 39 | f | 900 | 1.984 |
| **205** | Fiat 508 Balilla Sedan | I | 1932 | 4 | 0,99 | 20 | 3.400 | 65 x 75 | 2,56 x 2,95 | 85 | 53 | f | 685 | 1.510 |
| **205** | Fiat 508 S Mille Miglia Coupé | I | 1935 | 4 | 0,99 | 36 | 4.400 | 65 x 75 | 2,56 x 2,95 | 110 | 68 | f | 625 | 1.378 |
| **205** | Fiat 514 Spider Sport CA | I | 1931 | 4 | 1,44 | 34 | 3.500 | 67 x 102 | 2,64 x 4,02 | 112 | 70 | f | 875 | 1.929 |
| **206** | Fiat 508 C | I | 1937 | 4 | 1,09 | 32 | 4.000 | 68 x 75 | 2,68 x 2,95 | 110 | 68 | f | 850 | 1.874 |
| **206** | Fiat 500 Topolino | I | 1936 | 4 | 0,57 | 13 | 4.000 | 52 x 67 | 2,05 x 2,64 | 85 | 53 | f | 535 | 1.180 |
| **206** | Fiat 600 | I | 1955 | 4 | 0,63 | 222 | 4.600 | 60 x 56 | 2,36 x 2,20 | 100 | 62 | r | 585 | 1.290 |
| **207** | Chrysler Windsor Sedan | USA | 1941 | 6 | 4,11 | 120 | 3.600 | 87 x 114 | 3,43 x 4,49 | 145 | 90 | f | | |
| **207** | Plymouth Tourer | USA | 1938 | 6 | 3,30 | 82 | 3.600 | | | | | f | | |
| **208** | Triumph TR 2 | GB | 1953 | 4 | 1,99 | 80 | 4.300 | 83 x 92 | 3,27 x 3,62 | 160 | 100 | f | 840 | 1.852 |
| **208** | Gaz Pobieda | URSS | 1949 | 4 | 2,12 | 52 | 3.600 | 82 x 100 | 3,23 x 3,94 | 110 | 68 | f | 1.350 | 2.977 |
| **208** | Citroën 2 CV | F | 1948 | 2 | 0,37 | 9 | 3.800 | 62 x 62 | 2,44 x 2,44 | 60 | 37 | f | 490 | 1.080 |
| **208** | Nissan Datsun | J | 1948 | | | | | | | | | f | | |
| **208** | Skoda 1101 | CS | 1948 | 4 | 1,09 | 32 | 4.400 | 68 x 65 | 2,68 x 2,56 | 100 | 92 | f | | |
| **208** | Standard Vanguard | GB | 1951 | 4 | 2,09 | 68 | 4.000 | 85 x 92 | 3,35 x 3,62 | 120 | 75 | f | 1.250 | 2.756 |
| **208** | BMW 501 | D | 1953 | 6 | 1,97 | 65 | 4.400 | 66 x 96 | 2,60 x 3,78 | 138 | 86 | f | 1.235 | 2.723 |
| **208** | DKW Meisterklasse | D | 1952 | 2 | 0,68 | 23 | 4.500 | 76 x 76 | 2,99 x 2,99 | 100 | 62 | f | 790 | 1.741 |
| **209** | Lancia Aurelia B 10 | I | 1950 | 6 | 1,75 | 56 | 4.000 | 70 x 76 | 2,76 x 2,99 | 135 | 115 | f | 1.100 | 2.425 |

# THE AUTOMOBILE IN NUMBERS

| page | Make & type | International Registration Letter* | Year of make | Number of cylinders | Displacement | Power hp | rpm | Bore & stroke | | Velocity | | Engine position | Weight | |
|---|---|---|---|---|---|---|---|---|---|---|---|---|---|---|
| | | | | | | | | mm | inches | km/h | mph | | kg | lb |
| 209 | Lancia Aurelia GT B 20 | I | 1951 | 6 | 1,99 | 80 | 4.700 | 72 x 81 | 2,83 x 3,21 | 162 | 101 | f | 1.040 | 2.293 |
| 209 | Jaguar Mk V Cabriolet | GB | 1948 | 6 | 3,49 | 125 | 4.250 | 82 x 110 | 3,23 x 4,33 | | | f | 1.730 | 2.814 |
| 209 | Bentley Continental | USA | 1952 | 6 | 4,57 | | | 92 x 114 | 3,62 x 4,50 | 190 | 118 | f | 1.640 | 3.616 |
| 209 | Simca 9 Aronde | F | 1951 | 4 | 1,22 | 45 | 4.500 | 72 x 75 | 2,83 x 2,95 | 120 | 75 | f | 930 | 2.051 |
| 209 | Rolls Royce Silver Wraith | GB | 1950 | 6 | 4,26 | | | 89 x 114 | 3,50 x 4,49 | | | f | | |
| 210 | Hudson Custom Commodore | USA | 1950 | 8 | 4,16 | 128 | 4.200 | 76 x 114 | 3,00 x 4,50 | | | f | 1.667 | 3.675 |
| 210 | Henry J | USA | 1950 | 4 | 2,20 | 64 | 4.500 | 76 x 117 | 3,00 x 4,63 | | | f | 1.300 | 2.866 |
| 210 | Frazer Manhattan | USA | 1950 | 6 | 3,70 | 112 | 3.600 | 84 x 111 | 3,31 x 4,37 | | | f | 1.800 | 3.969 |
| 210 | Ford Custom | USA | 1949 | 6 | 3,70 | 95 | 3.300 | 83 x 111 | 3,30 x 4,39 | | | f | 1.380 | 3.043 |
| 210 | Kaiser | USA | 1950 | 6 | 3,70 | 100 | 3.600 | 84 x 111 | 3,31 x 4,37 | | | f | 1.500 | 3.310 |
| 210 | Plymouth Suburban | USA | 1950 | 6 | 3,57 | 97 | 3.600 | 82 x 111 | 3,25 x 4,37 | | | f | 1.500 | 3.307 |
| 210 | Chrysler Windsor Newport | USA | 1950 | 8 | 5,42 | 180 | 4.000 | 96 x 92 | 3,81 x 3,62 | | | f | 1.900 | 4.189 |
| 211 | Alfa Romeo 1900 | I | 1950 | 4 | 1,88 | 90 | 5.200 | 82 x 88 | 3,25 x 3,46 | 150 | 93 | f | 1.100 | 2.425 |
| 211 | Moskvitch 401 | SU | 1951 | 4 | 1,07 | 23 | 4.000 | | | 90 | 54 | f | 845 | 1.863 |
| 211 | Renault Fregate | F | 1951 | 4 | 2,00 | 56 | 3.800 | 85 x 88 | 3,35 x 3,46 | 130 | 80 | f | 1.210 | 2.668 |
| 211 | Fiat 500 C Giardiniera | I | 1950 | 4 | 0,57 | 16 | 4.400 | 52 x 67 | 2,05 x 2,64 | 90 | 54 | f | 610 | 1.345 |
| 211 | De Soto Suburban | USA | 1950 | 6 | 4,11 | 116 | 3.600 | 87 x 114 | 3,43 x 4,49 | | | f | 1.500 | 3.307 |
| 211 | Plymouth Coupé | USA | 1950 | 6 | 3,57 | 97 | 3.600 | 82 x 111 | 3,25 x 4,37 | | | f | 1.430 | 3.153 |
| 211 | Dodge Coronet | USA | 1950 | 6 | 3,87 | 103 | 3.600 | 82 x 117 | 3,25 x 4,63 | | | f | 1.550 | 3.418 |
| 212 | Lancia Appia | I | 1953 | 4 | 1,09 | 37 | 4.800 | 68 x 75 | 2,68 x 2,95 | 120 | 75 | f | 820 | 1.808 |
| 212 | Standard 8 | GB | 1953 | 4 | 0,80 | 26 | 4.500 | 58 x 76 | 2,28 x 2,99 | 100 | 62 | f | 675 | 1.488 |
| 212 | Panhard Dyna | F | 1956 | 2 | 0,85 | 42 | 5.000 | 85 x 75 | 3,35 x 2,95 | 130 | 81 | f | 780 | 1.719 |
| 212 | MG Midget TF | GB | 1953 | 4 | 1,49 | 64 | | 73 x 88 | 2,88 x 3,50 | 140 | 87 | f | | |
| 212 | MG A | GB | 1955 | 4 | 1,49 | 69 | 5.500 | 73 x 88 | 2,88 x 3,50 | 152 | 95 | f | 890 | 1.962 |
| 212 | Rover 75 | GB | 1950 | 6 | 2,10 | 75 | 4.200 | 65 x 105 | 2,57 x 4,13 | 130 | 81 | f | 1.450 | 3.197 |
| 213 | Oldsmobile 88 Super | USA | 1955 | 8 | 5,31 | 188 | | 98 x 87 | 3,87 x 3,44 | 165 | 103 | f | 1.900 | 4.189 |
| 213 | Mercedes 300 SL | D | 1954 | 6 | 3,00 | 240 | 6.100 | 85 x 88 | 3,35 x 3,46 | 260 | 162 | f | 1.160 | 2.558 |
| 213 | Chevrolet Corvette | USA | 1955 | 8 | 4,34 | 228 | 5.200 | 95 x 76 | 3,75 x 3,00 | 200 | 125 | f | 1.230 | 2.712 |
| 213 | Bentley Sport Saloon | USA | 1953 | 6 | 4,57 | | | 92 x 114 | 3,62 x 4,50 | 160 | 100 | f | 1.800 | 3.969 |
| 214 | Ferrari 166 S | I | 1948 | 12 | 1,20 | 150 | 7.000 | 60 x 58 | 2,36 x 2,31 | 190 | 118 | f | 800 | 1.764 |
| 214 | Ferrari 342 America | I | 1952 | 12 | 4,10 | 200 | 5.000 | 80 x 68 | 3,15 x 2,68 | 186 | 116 | f | 1.200 | 2.646 |
| 214 | Ferrari 250 GT | I | 1963 | 12 | 2,96 | 220 | 7.000 | 73 x 58 | 2,87 x 2,31 | 220 | 137 | f | 1.050 | 2.315 |
| 214 | Ferrari 500 Superfast | I | 1964 | 12 | 4,96 | 400 | 6.500 | 88 x 68 | 3,46 x 2,68 | 280 | 174 | f | 1.400 | 3.087 |
| 215 | Ferrari 212 Export | I | 1951 | 12 | 2,56 | 150 | 6.500 | 68 x 58 | 2,68 x 2,31 | 196 | 122 | f | 1.000 | 2.205 |
| 215 | Ferrari 340 S | I | 1953 | 12 | 4,10 | 280 | 6.600 | 80 x 68 | 3,15 x 2,68 | 270 | 168 | f | 850 | 1.874 |
| 215 | Ferrari 250 Europa | I | 1952 | 12 | 2,96 | 200 | 6.300 | 68 x 68 | 2,68 x 2,68 | 218 | 136 | f | 1.150 | 2.536 |
| 215 | Ferrari 410 Superamerica | I | 1958 | 12 | 4,96 | 340 | 6.000 | 88 x 68 | 3,46 x 2,68 | 260 | 162 | f | 1.200 | 2.646 |
| 215 | Ferrari 400 Superamerica | I | 1960 | 12 | 3,97 | 400 | 7.000 | 77 x 71 | 3,03 x 2,80 | 300 | 187 | f | 1.200 | 2.646 |
| 215 | Ferrari 250 LM | I | 1964 | 12 | 2,95 | 300 | 7.500 | 73 x 58 | 2,87 x 2,31 | 290 | 181 | f | 850 | 1.874 |
| 215 | Ferrari 275 GT S | I | 1964 | 12 | 3,28 | 260 | 7.000 | 77 x 58 | 3,03 x 2,31 | 240 | 150 | f | 1.150 | 2.536 |
| 215 | Ferrari 365 GT C | I | 1969 | 12 | 4,39 | 320 | 6.600 | 81 x 71 | 3,19 x 2,80 | 245 | 153 | f | 1.350 | 2.977 |
| 216 | Ferrari 125 S | I | 1947 | 12 | 1,50 | 118 | 7.000 | 55 x 52 | 2,17 x 2,07 | 170 | 106 | f | 750 | 1.653 |
| 216 | Ferrari 125 F 1 | I | 1948 | 12 | 1,50 | 230 | 7.000 | 55 x 52 | 2,17 x 2,07 | 240 | 150 | f | 700 | 1.543 |
| 216 | Ferrari 375 MM | I | 1953 | 12 | 4,52 | 340 | 7.000 | 84 x 68 | 3,31 x 2,68 | 290 | 180 | f | 900 | 1.984 |
| 216 | Ferrari 625 F 1 | I | 1953 | 4 | 2,50 | 240 | 7.000 | 94 x 90 | 3,70 x 3,54 | 270 | 168 | f | 600 | 1.323 |
| 216 | Ferrari 246 F 1 | I | 1958 | 6 | 2,42 | 270 | 8.300 | 85 x 71 | 3,35 x 2,80 | 270 | 168 | f | 560 | 1.235 |
| 216 | Ferrari 250 TRS | I | 1958 | 12 | 2,95 | 300 | 7.200 | 73 x 58 | 2,87 x 2,31 | 270 | 168 | f | 800 | 1.764 |

# THE AUTOMOBILE IN NUMBERS

| page | Make & type | International Registration Letter* | Year of make | Number of cylinders | Displacement | Power hp | rpm | Bore & stroke mm | Bore & stroke inches | Velocity km/h | Velocity mph | Engine position | Weight kg | Weight lb |
|---|---|---|---|---|---|---|---|---|---|---|---|---|---|---|
| 216 | Ferrari 158 F 1 | I | 1964 | 8 | 1,40 | 200 | 10.500 | 67 x 52 | 2,64 x 2,08 | 260 | 162 | r | 460 | 1.014 |
| 216 | Ferrari 330 P2 | I | 1965 | 12 | 3,97 | 410 | 8.200 | 77 x 71 | 3,03 x 2,80 | 320 | 199 | r | 885 | 1.951 |
| 217 | Ferrari 375 F 1 | I | 1951 | 12 | 4,50 | 384 | 7.500 | 80 x 74 | 3,15 x 2,93 | 300 | 188 | f | 720 | 1.587 |
| 217 | Ferrari 500 F 2 | I | 1951 | 4 | 1,99 | 170 | 7.000 | 90 x 78 | 3,54 x 3,07 | 240 | 150 | f | 560 | 1.235 |
| 217 | Ferrari 750 Monza | I | 1954 | 4 | 3,00 | 250 | 6.000 | 103 x 90 | 4,06 x 3,54 | 264 | 165 | f | 760 | 1.675 |
| 217 | Ferrari 290 MM | I | 1956 | 12 | 3,50 | 320 | 6.800 | 73 x 69 | 2,87 x 2,74 | 280 | 174 | f | 880 | 1.940 |
| 217 | Ferrari 156 F 1 | I | 1961 | 6 | 1,48 | 190 | 9.400 | 73 x 59 | 2,87 x 2,32 | 240 | 150 | r | 460 | 1.014 |
| 217 | Ferrari 246 P | I | 1961 | 6 | 2,42 | 270 | 8.000 | 85 x 71 | 3,35 x 2,80 | 260 | 162 | r | 590 | 1.301 |
| 217 | Ferrari Dino 206 S | I | 1966 | 6 | 1,99 | 218 | 9.000 | 86 x 57 | 3,39 x 2,24 | 260 | 162 | r | 580 | 1.279 |
| 217 | Ferrari 312 B F 1 | I | 1971 | 12 | 2,99 | 480 | 11.500 | 78 x 51 | 3,09 x 2,03 | 300 | 188 | r | 534 | 1.177 |
| 218 | Nash Rambler | USA | 1950 | 6 | 2,83 | 82 | 3.800 | 79 x 101 | 3,13 x 4,00 | 130 | 81 | f | 1.100 | 2.425 |
| 218 | Plymouth Valiant | USA | 1963 | 6 | 2,79 | 102 | 4.400 | 86 x 79 | 3,40 x 3,12 | 140 | 87 | f | 1.210 | 2.668 |
| 219 | Chevrolet Corvair | USA | 1959 | 6 | 2,29 | 81 | 4.400 | 85 x 66 | 3,37 x 2,60 | 135 | 84 | r | 1.100 | 2.425 |
| 219 | Chevrolet Impala | USA | 1959 | 8 | 5,69 | 253 | 4.400 | 104 x 82 | 4,12 x 3,25 | 170 | 106 | f | 1.820 | 4.013 |
| 219 | Ford Falcon | USA | 1959 | 6 | 2,36 | 91 | 4.200 | 88 x 63 | 3,50 x 2,49 | 130 | 81 | f | 1.070 | 2.359 |
| 219 | Studebaker Lark | USA | 1958 | 6 | 2,78 | 91 | 4.000 | 76 x 101 | 3,00 x 4,00 | 130 | 81 | f | 1.200 | 2.646 |
| 220 | Renault Dauphine | F | 1956 | 4 | 0,84 | 30 | 4.250 | 58 x 80 | 2,28 x 3,15 | 110 | 68 | r | 610 | 1.345 |
| 220 | Dodge Royal | USA | 1954 | 8 | 3,95 | 150 | 4.400 | 87 x 82 | 3,44 x 3,25 | 150 | 93 | f | | |
| 220 | Fiat 600 Multipla | I | 1956 | 4 | 0,63 | 21 | 4.600 | 60 x 56 | 2,46 x 2,20 | 90 | 56 | r | 700 | 1.543 |
| 220 | Vespa 400 | F | 1957 | 2 | 0,39 | 14 | 4.350 | 63 x 63 | 2,48 x 2,48 | 90 | 56 | r | 360 | 794 |
| 221 | Ford Thunderbird | USA | 1955 | 8 | 4,78 | 190 | 4.600 | 92 x 83 | 3,63 x 3,30 | 195 | 122 | f | 1.600 | 3.528 |
| 221 | Ford Anglia | GB | 1955 | 4 | 1,17 | 36 | 4.500 | 63 x 92 | 2,50 x 3,64 | 115 | 71 | f | 710 | 1.565 |
| 221 | Chevrolet Bel Air | USA | 1958 | 8 | 4,64 | 188 | 4.600 | 98 x 72 | 3,87 x 2,84 | 160 | 100 | f | 1.820 | 4.013 |
| 221 | Rolls Royce Phantom V | GB | 1960 | 8 | 6,23 | | | 104 x 91 | 4,10 x 3,60 | 160 | 100 | f | | |
| 221 | Rolls Royce Silver Cloud | GB | 1959 | 8 | 6,23 | | | 104 x 91 | 4,10 x 3,60 | 170 | 106 | f | 2.035 | 4.487 |
| 221 | Mercedes 300 S Coupé | D | 1953 | 6 | 3,00 | 150 | 4.850 | 85 x 88 | 3,35 x 3,46 | 175 | 109 | f | 1.680 | 3.704 |
| 221 | Jaguar XK-SS | GB | 1957 | 6 | 3,44 | 250 | | 83 x 106 | 3,27 x 4,17 | 225 | 141 | f | 1.180 | 2.602 |
| 222 | Glas Isaria Goggomobil | D | 1955 | 2 | 0,29 | 17 | 4.800 | 58 x 56 | 2,28 x 2,20 | 95 | 59 | r | 386 | 851 |
| 222 | Citroën DS 19 | F | 1955 | 4 | 1,91 | 75 | 4.500 | 78 x 100 | 3,07 x 3,94 | 140 | 87 | f | 1.110 | 2.447 |
| 222 | Alvis TC 108 | GB | 1956 | 6 | 2,99 | 104 | 4.000 | 84 x 90 | 3,31 x 3,54 | 160 | 100 | f | 1.300 | 2.866 |
| 222 | Peugeot 403 | F | 1955 | 4 | 1,47 | 58 | 4.900 | 80 x 73 | 3,15 x 2,87 | 130 | 81 | f | 1.025 | 2.260 |
| 222 | Daimler Conquest Cabriolet | D | 1955 | 6 | 2,43 | 100 | 4.400 | 76 x 88 | 3,00 x 3,50 | 160 | 100 | f | 1.220 | 2.690 |
| 223 | Alfa Romeo Sprint 1900 | I | 1952 | 4 | 1,88 | 100 | 5.500 | 82 x 88 | 3,25 x 3,46 | 180 | 112 | f | 1.100 | 2.425 |
| 223 | Alfa Romeo Giulietta Sprint Spider | I | 1956 | 4 | 1,29 | 65 | 6.000 | 74 x 75 | 2,91 x 2,95 | 160 | 100 | f | 820 | 1.808 |
| 223 | Alfa Romeo Giulietta Sedan | I | 1955 | 4 | 1,29 | 53 | 5.500 | 74 x 75 | 2,91 x 2,95 | 135 | 86 | f | 870 | 1.918 |
| 223 | Jaguar 2,4 litre | GB | 1955 | 6 | 2,48 | 114 | 5.750 | 83 x 76 | 3,27 x 3,01 | 160 | 100 | f | 1.270 | 2.800 |
| 224 | Renault 4 L | F | 1962 | 4 | 0,84 | 32 | 4.700 | 58 x 80 | 2,28 x 3,15 | 110 | 69 | f | 570 | 1.257 |
| 224 | Morris Mini-Minor | GB | 1959 | 4 | 0,85 | 34,5 | 5.500 | 62 x 68 | 2,48 x 2,69 | 115 | 71 | f | 570 | 1.257 |
| 224 | Opel Kapitän | D | 1958 | 6 | 2,47 | 80 | 4.100 | 80 x 82 | 3,15 x 3,23 | 142 | 88 | f | 1.260 | 2.778 |
| 224 | Austin A 40 | GB | 1958 | 4 | 0,95 | 34 | 4.750 | 62 x 76 | 2,48 x 3,00 | 115 | 71 | f | 725 | 1.598 |
| 224 | FMR Tiger 500 | D | 1959 | 2 | 0,49 | 20 | 5.000 | 67 x 70 | 2,74 x 2,76 | 130 | 81 | r | 350 | 772 |
| 224 | Mercedes 190 SL Roadster | D | 1962 | 4 | 1,90 | 105 | 5.700 | 85 x 83 | 3,35 x 3,29 | 175 | 109 | f | 1.100 | 2.447 |
| 225 | Ford Taunus 17 M | D | 1957 | 4 | 1,70 | 60 | 4.250 | 84 x 76 | 3,31 x 3,02 | 125 | 78 | f | 973 | 2.145 |
| 225 | Renault Floride | F | 1959 | 4 | 0,84 | 35 | 5.000 | 58 x 80 | 2,28 x 3,15 | 125 | 78 | r | 730 | 1.609 |
| 225 | MG Magnette | GB | 1956 | 4 | 1,49 | 60 | 4.600 | 73 x 88 | 2,87 x 3,50 | 135 | 84 | f | 1.090 | 2.403 |
| 225 | Autonacional Biscuter | E | 1956 | 1 | 0,20 | 9 | 4.800 | 59 x 72 | 2,32 x 2,83 | 76 | 47 | f | 228 | 502 |
| 225 | NSU Prinz Sport | D | 1960 | 2 | 0,58 | 30 | 5.500 | 75 x 66 | 2,95 x 2,60 | 130 | 81 | r | 535 | 1.180 |
| 226 | Simca 1000 | F | 1961 | 4 | 0,94 | 35 | 4.800 | 68 x 65 | 2,68 x 2,56 | 120 | 75 | r | 698 | 1.539 |

# THE AUTOMOBILE IN NUMBERS

| page | Make & type | International Registration Letter* | Year of make | Number of cylinders | Displacement | Power hp | rpm | Bore & stroke | | Velocity | | Engine position | Weight | |
|---|---|---|---|---|---|---|---|---|---|---|---|---|---|---|
| | | | | | | | | mm | inches | km/h | mph | | kg | lb |
| 226 | Fiat 850 | I | 1964 | 4 | 0,84 | 37 | 5.000 | 65 x 63 | 2,56 x 2,50 | 126 | 78 | r | 670 | 1.477 |
| 226 | Trabant | D | 1960 | 2 | 0,50 | 18 | 3.750 | 66 x 73 | 2,60 x 2,87 | 100 | 62 | f | 620 | 1.367 |
| 226 | Simca Ariane 4 | F | 1960 | 4 | 1,29 | 49 | 4.800 | 74 x 75 | 2,91 x 2,95 | 127 | 79 | f | 1.050 | 2.315 |
| 226 | Simca Aronde P 60 Montlhéry | F | 1959 | 4 | 1,29 | 56 | 5.000 | 74 x 75 | 2,91 x 2,95 | 140 | 87 | f | 940 | 2.073 |
| 227 | Holden | AUS | 1948 | 6 | 2,17 | 60 | 3.800 | 76 x 79 | 3,00 x 3,13 | 125 | 78 | f | 970 | 2.139 |
| 227 | Holden Statesman | AUS | 1974 | 8 | 5,00 | 240 | 4.800 | 101 x 77 | 4,00 x 3,06 | | | f | 1.375 | 3.032 |
| 227 | Ford Fairmont | USA | 1974 | 6 | 4,09 | 155 | 4.000 | 93 x 99 | 3,68 x 3,91 | 165 | 103 | f | 1.480 | 3.263 |
| 227 | Leyland P 76 | GB | 1973 | 8 | 4,42 | 195 | 4.250 | 88 x 88 | 3,50 x 3,50 | 170 | 106 | f | 1.300 | 2.866 |
| 227 | Chrysler Valiant | USA | 1974 | 6 | 3,68 | 105 | 3.600 | 86 x 104 | 3,40 x 4,12 | 160 | 100 | f | | |
| 230 | Rumpler Tropfenwagen DA 104 | D | 1921 | 6 | 2,60 | 36 | 2.000 | 74 x 100 | 2,91 x 3,94 | 110 | 70 | r | 1.050 | 2.315 |
| 232 | Grégoire | F | 1910 | 4 | 3,22 | | | 80 x 160 | 3,15 x 6,30 | 80 | 50 | f | | |
| 232 | Alfa Romeo 6 C 1500 Sport | I | 1928 | 6 | 1,49 | 54 | 4.500 | 62 x 82 | 2,44 x 3,23 | 125 | 78 | f | 960 | 2.117 |
| 232 | Alfa Romeo 6 C 1750 SS | I | 1933 | 6 | 1,75 | 85 | 4.500 | 65 x 88 | 2,56 x 3,46 | 145 | 90 | f | 920 | 2.029 |
| 233 | Cisitalia 202 | I | 1948 | 4 | 1,09 | 50 | 5.500 | 68 x 75 | 2,68 x 2,95 | 160 | 100 | f | 875 | 1.929 |
| 233 | Cadillac | USA | 1949 | 8 | 5,42 | 162 | 3.600 | 96 x 92 | 3,81 x 3,62 | | | f | 2.000 | 4.410 |
| 233 | Fiat 8V Sedan | I | 1953 | 8 | 2,00 | 105 | 6.000 | 72 x 61 | 2,83 x 2,41 | 190 | 119 | f | 997 | 2.198 |
| 233 | Alfa Romeo 8 C 2900 B Spider | I | 1938 | 8 | 2,90 | 180 | 5.200 | 68 x 100 | 2,68 x 3,94 | 185 | 115 | f | 1.150 | 2.536 |
| 234 | Alfa Romeo Giulia TI | I | 1962 | 4 | 1,57 | 92 | 6.000 | 78 x 82 | 3,07 x 3,23 | 165 | 103 | f | 1.060 | 2.337 |
| 234 | Ford Mustang | USA | 1964 | 6 | 3,27 | 122 | 4.000 | 93 x 79 | 3,68 x 3,13 | 160 | 100 | f | 1.250 | 2.756 |
| 234 | Plymouth Barracuda | USA | 1964 | 6 | 3,68 | 147 | 4.000 | 86 x 104 | 3,40 x 4,12 | 160 | 100 | f | 1.310 | 2.888 |
| 234 | Oldsmobile Toronado | USA | 1965 | 8 | 6,96 | 390 | 4.800 | 104 x 100 | 4,12 x 3,97 | 200 | 125 | f | 2.040 | 4.498 |
| 235 | Daf 44 | NL | 1966 | 2 | 0,84 | 34 | 4.500 | 85 x 73 | 3,37 x 2,87 | 123 | 77 | f | 725 | 1.598 |
| 235 | Daf Daffodil | NL | 1962 | 2 | 0,75 | 26 | 4.000 | 85 x 65 | 3,37 x 2,56 | 105 | 66 | f | 665 | 1.466 |
| 235 | Citroën Dyane | F | 1967 | 2 | 0,42 | 18 | 4.750 | 66 x 62 | 2,60 x 2,44 | 100 | 62 | f | 590 | 1.301 |
| 235 | Cadillac Fleetwood Eldorado | USA | 1967 | 8 | 7,02 | 345 | 4.600 | 104 x 101 | 4,13 x 4,00 | 190 | 119 | f | 2.130 | 4.697 |
| 235 | Volvo 144 | S | 1966 | 4 | 1,78 | 75 | 4.700 | 84 x 80 | 3,31 x 3,15 | 150 | 94 | f | 1.170 | 2.580 |
| 236 | Fiat 124 | I | 1966 | 4 | 1,20 | 60 | 5.600 | 73 x 71 | 2,87 x 2,81 | 140 | 87 | f | 910 | 2.006 |
| 236 | Fiat 125 | I | 1967 | 4 | 1,61 | 90 | 5.600 | 80 x 80 | 3,15 x 3,15 | 160 | 100 | f | 1.000 | 2.205 |
| 236 | Wartburg 1000 | D | 1967 | 3 | 0,99 | 45 | 4.200 | 73 x 78 | 2,89 x 3,07 | 127 | 79 | f | 900 | 1.984 |
| 236 | Wolseley 1100 | GB | 1966 | 4 | 1,10 | 56 | 5.500 | 64 x 83 | 2,54 x 3,30 | 142 | 89 | f | 830 | 1.837 |
| 236 | Rolls Royce Silver Shadow | GB | 1966 | 8 | 6,23 | | | 104 x 91 | 4,10 x 3,60 | 190 | 118 | f | 2.100 | 4.630 |
| 237 | Peugeot 204 | F | 1965 | 4 | 1,13 | 53 | 5.800 | 75 x 64 | 2,95 x 2,52 | 138 | 86 | f | 850 | 1.874 |
| 237 | Volkswagen 1600 TL | D | 1965 | 4 | 1,58 | 54 | 4.000 | 85 x 69 | 3,37 x 2,72 | 135 | 84 | r | 920 | 2.029 |
| 237 | BMW 1600 | D | 1966 | 4 | 1,57 | 85 | 5.700 | 84 x 71 | 3,31 x 2,80 | 160 | 100 | f | 920 | 2.029 |
| 237 | Fiat 500 L | I | 1968 | 4 | 0,50 | 18 | 4.600 | 67 x 70 | 2,65 x 2,76 | 100 | 62 | r | 530 | 1.169 |
| 237 | Lancia Fulvia Sport 1,3 | I | 1966 | 4 | 1,30 | 86 | 6.000 | 77 x 69 | 3,03 x 2,74 | 175 | 109 | f | 915 | 2.017 |
| 238 | Opel GT | D | 1969 | 4 | 1,90 | 90 | 5.100 | 93 x 69 | 3,66 x 2,75 | 185 | 116 | f | 940 | 2.073 |
| 238 | Fiat 128 Special 1300 | I | 1974 | 4 | 1,29 | 60 | 6.000 | 86 x 55 | 3,39 x 2,19 | 145 | 91 | f | 825 | 1.819 |
| 238 | Mercedes 240 D 3,0 | D | 1974 | 5 | 2,97 | 80 | 4.000 | 91 x 92 | 3,58 x 3,64 | 143 | 89 | f | 1.430 | 3.153 |
| 238 | Maserati Ghibli | I | 1971 | 8 | 4,72 | 330 | 5.500 | 93 x 85 | 3,70 x 3,35 | 270 | 168 | f | 1.530 | 3.374 |
| 238 | Lancia Stratos | I | 1974 | 6 | 2,42 | 190 | 7.000 | 92 x 60 | 3,64 x 2,36 | 230 | 144 | r | 920 | 2.029 |
| 238 | Lamborghini Espada | I | 1968 | 12 | 3,93 | 350 | 7.500 | 82 x 62 | 3,23 x 2,44 | 250 | 155 | f | 1.695 | 3.737 |
| 238 | Citroën GS | F | 1970 | 4 | 1,01 | 55 | 6.500 | 74 x 59 | 2,91 x 2,32 | 149 | 93 | f | 880 | 1.940 |
| 238 | Renault 6 | F | 1968 | 4 | 0,84 | 34 | 5.000 | 58 x 80 | 2,28 x 3,15 | 120 | 75 | f | 750 | 1.653 |
| 239 | Renault 5 TL | F | 1972 | 4 | 0,96 | 46 | 5.500 | 65 x 72 | 2,56 x 2,83 | 140 | 87 | f | 760 | 1.675 |
| 239 | Citroën CX 2000 | F | 1974 | 4 | 1,98 | 102 | 5.500 | 86 x 85 | 3,39 x 3,37 | 167 | 104 | f | 1.265 | 2.789 |
| 239 | Alfa Romeo 1750 | I | 1968 | 4 | 1,78 | 132 | 5.500 | 80 x 88 | 3,15 x 3,48 | 180 | 112 | f | 1.110 | 2.447 |
| 239 | Lancia Fulvia Coupé | I | 1965 | 4 | 1,22 | 80 | 6.000 | 76 x 67 | 2,99 x 2,64 | 160 | 100 | f | 960 | 2.117 |

# THE AUTOMOBILE IN NUMBERS

## PRODUCTION (Thousands of vehicles)

| | Canada | France | Germany | Japan | Italy | U.K. | Sweden | U.S.A. | Total |
|---|---|---|---|---|---|---|---|---|---|
| 1930 | 153,4 | 230,0 | 96,0 | 0,5 | 46,4 | 236,5 | 2,2 | 3.362,8 | 4.127,8 |
| 1931 | 82,6 | 201,0 | 77,8 | 0,4 | 28,4 | 226,3 | 2,2 | 2.380,4 | 2.999,1 |
| 1932 | 60,8 | 163,0 | 51,8 | 0,9 | 29,6 | 232,7 | 2,7 | 1.331,9 | 1.873,4 |
| 1933 | 65,9 | 189,0 | 105,7 | 1,7 | 41,7 | 286,3 | 2,8 | 1.889,8 | 2.582,9 |
| 1934 | 116,9 | 181,0 | 175,4 | 2,8 | 45,4 | 342,5 | 3,2 | 2.737,1 | 3.604,3 |
| 1935 | 172,9 | 165,0 | 249,1 | 5,1 | 50,5 | 416,9 | 3,3 | 3.971,2 | 5.034,0 |
| 1936 | 162,2 | 204,0 | 303,9 | 12,2 | 53,1 | 481,5 | 4,4 | 4.461,5 | 5.682,8 |
| 1937 | 207,5 | 201,0 | 332,8 | 18,1 | 77,7 | 493,3 | 6,6 | 4.820,2 | 6.157,2 |
| 1938 | 166,1 | 224,0 | 357,0 | 24,4 | 70,8 | 444,9 | 6,9 | 2.508,4 | 3.802,5 |
| 1939-45 | ........ | ........ | ........ | ........ | ........ | ........ | ........ | ........ | ........ |
| 1946 | 171,5 | 96,1 | 23,9 | 14,9 | 29,0 | 365,3 | 7,3 | 3.089,7 | 3.797,7 |
| 1947 | 258,0 | 137,4 | 23,3 | 11,3 | 43,7 | 441,7 | 9,3 | 4.797,6 | 5.722,3 |
| 1948 | 263,8 | 198,4 | 61,3 | 20,4 | 59,9 | 508,1 | 9,5 | 5.285,5 | 6.406,9 |
| 1949 | 292,6 | 285,6 | 163,6 | 28,7 | 86,1 | 628,7 | 11,1 | 6.253,7 | 7.750,1 |
| 1950 | 390,1 | 357,6 | 306,1 | 31,6 | 127,8 | 783,7 | 17,6 | 8.003,1 | 10.017,6 |
| 1951 | 415,4 | 445,7 | 374,2 | 38,5 | 145,6 | 733,9 | 23,0 | 6.765,3 | 8.941,6 |
| 1952 | 434,1 | 499,0 | 428,4 | 39,0 | 138,4 | 689,7 | 21,2 | 5.539,0 | 7.788,8 |
| 1953 | 486,0 | 497,3 | 490,6 | 49,8 | 174,3 | 834,8 | 29,4 | 7.323,2 | 9.885,4 |
| 1954 | 352,1 | 600,0 | 680,6 | 70,1 | 216,7 | 1.037,9 | 44,7 | 6.601,1 | 9.603,2 |
| 1955 | 452,1 | 725,1 | 908,7 | 68,9 | 268,8 | 1.237,1 | 50,3 | 9.169,3 | 12.880,3 |
| 1956 | 471,4 | 827,1 | 1.075,6 | 111,1 | 315,8 | 1.004,5 | 57,3 | 6.920,6 | 10.783,4 |
| 1957 | 413,6 | 928,0 | 1.212,2 | 182,0 | 351,8 | 1.149,1 | 71,7 | 7.220,5 | 11.528,9 |
| 1958 | 356,4 | 1.127,5 | 1.495,3 | 188,3 | 403,6 | 1.364,4 | 91,2 | 5.135,1 | 10.161,8 |
| 1959 | 367,9 | 1.283,2 | 1.718,6 | 262,8 | 500,8 | 1.560,4 | 112,4 | 6.728,6 | 12.534,7 |
| 1960 | 397,7 | 1.369,2 | 2.055,1 | 481,6 | 644,6 | 1.810,7 | 128,5 | 7.869,3 | 14.756,7 |
| 1961 | 386,9 | 1.244,3 | 2.147,8 | 813,9 | 759,1 | 1.464,1 | 131,8 | 6.676,5 | 13.624,4 |
| 1962 | 505,2 | 1.536,1 | 2.356,6 | 990,7 | 946,8 | 1.674,5 | 151,6 | 8.173,4 | 16.334,9 |
| 1963 | 631,4 | 1.737,0 | 2.667,9 | 1.283,5 | 1.180,5 | 2.011,7 | 167,9 | 9.100,4 | 18.780,3 |
| 1964 | 671,0 | 1.640,8 | 2.909,7 | 1.702,5 | 1.090,1 | 2.332,4 | 184,0 | 9.292,3 | 19.822,8 |
| 1965 | 846,6 | 1.642,0 | 2.976,5 | 1.875,6 | 1.175,5 | 2.227,3 | 205,7 | 11.057,4 | 22.006,6 |
| 1966 | 872,2 | 2.024,2 | 3.050,7 | 2.286,4 | 1.365,9 | 2.042,4 | 199,9 | 10.329,4 | 22.171,1 |
| 1967 | 919,5 | 2.009,7 | 2.482,3 | 3.146,5 | 1.542,7 | 1.937,1 | 214,6 | 8.976,2 | 21.228,6 |
| 1968 | 1.150,2 | 2.075,6 | 3.106,9 | 4.085,8 | 1.663,6 | 2.225,1 | 244,8 | 10.718,2 | 25.270,2 |
| 1969 | 1.326,5 | 2.459,0 | 3.604,6 | 4.674,9 | 1.595,9 | 2.182,8 | 271,4 | 10.146,9 | 26.262,0 |
| 1970 | 1.193,6 | 2.750,1 | 3.842,2 | 5.289,2 | 1.854,3 | 2.098,5 | 310,1 | 8.239,3 | 25.577,3 |
| 1971 | 1.375,5 | 3.010,3 | 3.982,7 | 5.810,8 | 1.817,0 | 2.198,1 | 317,1 | 10.637,8 | 29.149,3 |
| 1972 | 1.464,5 | 3.328,3 | 3.816,0 | 6.294,4 | 1.839,8 | 2.329,4 | 351,0 | 11.310,7 | 30.734,1 |
| 1973 | 1.587,0 | 3.596,2 | 3.949,1 | 7.082,7 | 1.958,0 | 2.163,9 | 378,0 | 12.681,5 | 33.396,4 |

## CIRCULATION (Thousands of vehicles)

| | Canada | France | Germany (*) | Japan | Italy | U.K. | Sweden | U.S.A. |
|---|---|---|---|---|---|---|---|---|
| 1930 | 1.223,1 | 1.544,1 | 662,7 | 89,2 | 245,5 | 1.560,3 | 145,3 | 26.532,0 |
| 1931 | 1.191,0 | 1.711,0 | 688,4 | 97,8 | 251,4 | 1.588,1 | 149,4 | 25.862,0 |
| 1932 | 1.104,1 | 1.731,9 | 654,4 | 100,9 | 256,7 | 1.642,6 | 146,9 | 24.132,6 |
| 1933 | 1.073,0 | 1.855,2 | 682,5 | 100,8 | 293,6 | 1.739,0 | 143,9 | 23.876,7 |
| 1934 | 1.119,2 | 1.938,5 | 781,7 | 114,4 | 316,8 | 1.874,0 | 149,8 | 24.954,0 |
| 1935 | 1.165,6 | 2.004,9 | 1.063,0 | 125,9 | 326,1 | 2.070,7 | 159,1 | 26.229,7 |
| 1936 | 1.229,3 | 2.095,3 | 1.243,1 | 136,7 | 294,4 | 2.271,9 | 173,3 | 28.172,3 |
| 1937 | 1.308,6 | 2.171,7 | 1.460,4 | 145,5 | 353,5 | 2.461,8 | 191,9 | 29.706,2 |
| 1938 | 1.382,8 | 2.269,0 | 1.673,8 | 151,2 | 373,0 | 2.644,2 | 219,2 | 29.442,7 |
| 1939-45 | ........ | ........ | ........ | ........ | ........ | ........ | ........ | ........ |
| 1946 | 1.605,3 | 1.700,0 | 340,3 | 130,2 | 288,6 | 2.551,5 | 202,7 | 33.945,8 |
| 1947 | 1.809,8 | 1.750,0 | 399,8 | 150,5 | 373,1 | 2.861,1 | 238,1 | 37.360,5 |
| 1948 | 2.001,0 | 1.850,0 | 604,2 | 181,6 | 415,3 | 3.002,0 | 262,4 | 40.556,5 |
| 1949 | 2.250,6 | 1.950,0 | 835,5 | 206,1 | 486,2 | 3.257,1 | 281,0 | 44.140,0 |
| 1950 | 2.557,0 | 2.150,0 | 1.053,3 | 225,5 | 577,1 | 3.435,8 | 345,0 | 49.161,7 |
| 1951 | 2.829,2 | 2.289,7 | 1.347,2 | 264,2 | 675,2 | 3.602,5 | 410,4 | 51.914,0 |
| 1952 | 3.113,7 | 2.583,0 | 1.669,6 | 322,9 | 782,0 | 3.788,4 | 465,8 | 53.265,4 |
| 1953 | 3.390,5 | 2.970,0 | 1.978,6 | 379,7 | 913,9 | 4.067,5 | 542,3 | 56.221,1 |
| 1954 | 3.606,9 | 3.308,0 | 2.258,6 | 434,6 | 997,7 | 4.445,5 | 652,3 | 58.510,3 |
| 1955 | 3.912,4 | 3.700,0 | 2.584,6 | 471,3 | 1.196,4 | 4.956,0 | 754,9 | 62.688,3 |
| 1956 | 4.229,8 | 4.200,0 | 3.023,1 | 553,9 | 1.382,9 | 5.396,5 | 855,1 | 65.148,3 |
| 1957 | 4.462,2 | 4.753,0 | 3.499,8 | 682,2 | 1.595,9 | 5.742,5 | 987,0 | 67.124,9 |
| 1958 | 4.689,9 | 5.230,0 | 4.108,1 | 817,3 | 1.769,1 | 6.163,7 | 1.097,8 | 68.296,6 |
| 1959 | 4.983,5 | 5.745,0 | 4.763,2 | 1.009,1 | 2.087,8 | 6.651,0 | 1.215,9 | 71.354,4 |
| 1960 | 5.221,9 | 6.340,0 | 5.632,8 | 1.353,5 | 2.431,2 | 7.300,9 | 1.324,0 | 73.868,7 |
| 1961 | 5.482,7 | 6.993,3 | 6.613,2 | 1.963,6 | 2.952,8 | 7.825,2 | 1.438,9 | 75.958,2 |
| 1962 | 5.741,7 | 7.850,0 | 7.648,2 | 2.729,3 | 3.580,2 | 8.441,9 | 1.561,8 | 79.173,3 |
| 1963 | 6.037,5 | 8.800,0 | 8.669,9 | 3.762,4 | 4.521,6 | 9.354,5 | 1.696,7 | 82.713,7 |
| 1964 | 6.334,9 | 9.786,0 | 9.645,8 | 4.988,5 | 5.319,3 | 10.299,3 | 1.809,5 | 86.301,2 |
| 1965 | 6.624,8 | 10.815,0 | 10.714,7 | 6.300,0 | 6.137,0 | 11.024,9 | 1.934,5 | 90.360,7 |
| 1966 | 6.927,3 | 11.636,0 | 11.673,0 | 7.921,4 | 7.056,0 | 11.622,6 | 2.033,3 | 93.962,0 |
| 1967 | 7.356,3 | 12.405,0 | 12.325,1 | 10,029,0 | 8.041,7 | 12.487,3 | 2.126,1 | 96.930,9 |
| 1968 | 7.746,8 | 13.040,0 | 13.113,8 | 12.482,3 | 9.077,1 | 12.972,4 | 2.222,6 | 100.884,8 |
| 1969 | 8.115,8 | 13.710,0 | 14.297,6 | 15.126,7 | 10.043,1 | 13.405,3 | 2.349,8 | 105.096,6 |
| 1970 | 8.340,0 | 14.370,0 | 15.568,3 | 17.581,8 | 11.120,4 | 13.709,7 | 2.446,4 | 108.375,4 |
| 1971 | 8.977,0 | 15.020,0 | 16.717,4 | 19.857,9 | 12.287,6 | 14.276,7 | 2.513,1 | 112.922,4 |
| 1972 | 9.399,4 | 15.920,0 | 17.640,6 | 22.408,5 | 13.516,0 | 14.909,5 | 2.618,0 | 117.606,0 |
| 1973 | 9.620,4 | 16.720,0 | 18.383,5 | 24.999,3 | 14.507,8 | 15.325,0 | 2.666,8 | 124.478,0 |

(*) Only West Germany since 1946.

# THE AUTOMOBILE IN NUMBERS

| REGISTRATIONS (Thousands of vehicles) | | | | | | | | |
|---|---|---|---|---|---|---|---|---|
| | Canada | France | Germany | Japan | Italy | U.K. | Sweden | U.S.A. |
| 1930 | ........ | 225,6 | 97,1 | ........ | 31,1 | 225,0 | 22,2 | 3.036,7 |
| 1931 | ........ | 188,3 | 68,8 | ........ | 18,5 | 205,9 | 19,5 | 2.222,0 |
| 1932 | 45,9 | 166,1 | 48,0 | ........ | 22,8 | 210,3 | 8,0 | 1.276,8 |
| 1933 | 45,3 | 177,2 | 93,6 | ........ | 32,0 | 248,5 | 8,5 | 1.739,7 |
| 1934 | 73,4 | 176,7 | 154,4 | ........ | 34,2 | 309,4 | 15,5 | 2.292,4 |
| 1935 | 101,5 | 162,4 | 213,9 | ........ | 29,6 | 363,0 | 20,5 | 3.254,6 |
| 1936 | 113,3 | 190,2 | 258,8 | ........ | 24,6 | 411,0 | 26,1 | 4.016,1 |
| 1937 | 144,4 | 185,0 | 261,8 | ........ | 39,7 | 419,0 | 34,6 | 4.102,0 |
| 1938 | 121,2 | 205,7 | 272,7 | ........ | 45,0 | 374,8 | 43,0 | 2.256,4 |
| 1939-45 | ........ | ........ | ........ | ........ | ........ | ........ | ........ | ........ |
| 1946 | 120,0 | 67,5 | 7,3 | ........ | 22,0 | 246,8 | 19,4 | 2.440,4 |
| 1947 | 230,3 | 62,3 | 6,3 | ........ | 27,7 | 299,6 | 35,5 | 4.046,4 |
| 1948 | 221,3 | 112,4 | 26,8 | ........ | 43,9 | 246,4 | 25,4 | 4.526,1 |
| 1949 | 286,3 | 175,5 | 114,5 | ........ | 64,5 | 289,8 | 22,4 | 5.800,3 |
| 1950 | 429,7 | 238,8 | 223,9 | 25,9 | 99,7 | 250,9 | 73,2 | 7.468,7 |
| 1951 | 385,6 | 317,9 | 253,0 | 35,7 | 107,4 | 246,9 | 74,0 | 6.064,8 |
| 1952 | 400,8 | 378,5 | 281,1 | 48,5 | 110,5 | 293,5 | 63,9 | 4.970,5 |
| 1953 | 462,5 | 378,0 | 325,4 | 63,8 | 139,6 | 417,4 | 89,7 | 6.669,3 |
| 1954 | 382,6 | 443,4 | 389,4 | 74,8 | 167,6 | 525,1 | 142,1 | 6.364,6 |
| 1955 | 465,7 | 541,2 | 501,1 | 72,9 | 193,1 | 689,9 | 141,5 | 8.126,9 |
| 1956 | 499,9 | 608,1 | 589,9 | 107,1 | 231,0 | 582,6 | 145,0 | 6.849,6 |
| 1957 | 458,3 | 639,2 | 639,6 | 161,1 | 222,6 | 595,7 | 167,5 | 6.840,4 |
| 1958 | 444,8 | 697,4 | 773,8 | 171,1 | 237,5 | 758,7 | 161,0 | 5.381,2 |
| 1959 | 502,6 | 664,4 | 919,8 | 238,1 | 284,7 | 871,1 | 184,1 | 6.983,4 |
| 1960 | 523,2 | 761,7 | 1.073,4 | 408,2 | 427,8 | 1.074,4 | 174,8 | 7.520,1 |
| 1961 | 511,5 | 838,0 | 1.213,2 | 743,0 | 553,8 | 1.008,0 | 196,7 | 6.773,4 |
| 1962 | 585,2 | 1.044,9 | 1.338,9 | 933,0 | 704,5 | 1.020,3 | 212,0 | 8.007,6 |
| 1963 | 655,0 | 1.191,0 | 1.398,3 | 1.210,5 | 1.038,4 | 1.272,2 | 247,1 | 8.800,8 |
| 1964 | 725,9 | 1.211,6 | 1.473,3 | 1.494,2 | 894,0 | 1.481,4 | 275,4 | 9.426,9 |
| 1965 | 831,0 | 1.202,8 | 1.648,7 | 1.675,0 | 939,6 | 1.424,3 | 294,7 | 10.842,8 |
| 1966 | 827,4 | 1.367,8 | 1.633,4 | 2.060,1 | 1.074,7 | 1.357,1 | 226,6 | 10.618,9 |
| 1967 | 815,3 | 1.382,7 | 1.467,5 | 2.714,8 | 1.240,7 | 1.405,8 | 194,2 | 9.875,8 |
| 1968 | 889,4 | 1.406,8 | 1.547,6 | 3.308,2 | 1.254,0 | 1.414,7 | 229,9 | 11.179,5 |
| 1969 | 917,5 | 1.589,0 | 1.986,4 | 3.835,4 | 1.309,0 | 1.286,8 | 243,9 | 11.335,3 |
| 1970 | 774,2 | 1.504,4 | 2.271,8 | 4.100,4 | 1.448,2 | 1.393,3 | 222,7 | 10.178,4 |
| 1971 | 940,3 | 1.695,7 | 2.314,5 | 4.020,8 | 1.513,6 | 1.601,4 | 215,1 | 11.710,4 |
| 1972 | 1.065,4 | 1.886,7 | 2.292,0 | 4.366,5 | 1.552,5 | 2.016,0 | 236,5 | 12.244,8 |
| 1973 | 1.170,2 | 2.016,0 | 2.169,0 | 4.915,0 | 1.533,0 | 1.962,0 | 242,4 | 14.380,1 |

| EXPORTS (Thousands of vehicles) | | | | | | | | | |
|---|---|---|---|---|---|---|---|---|---|
| | Canada | France (*) | Germany (**) | Japan | Italy | U.K. | Sweden | U.S.A. | Total |
| 1930 | 44,6 | 31,1 | 5,6 | ........ | 19,2 | 30,0 | ........ | 245,2 | 375,7 |
| 1931 | 13,8 | 26,3 | 11,5 | ........ | 11,9 | 24,4 | ........ | 135,8 | 223,7 |
| 1932 | 12,5 | 19,2 | 11,3 | ........ | 6,4 | 40,3 | 1,0 | 70,1 | 160,8 |
| 1933 | 20,4 | 25,5 | 13,5 | ........ | 7,1 | 51,9 | ........ | 111,5 | 229,9 |
| 1934 | 43,4 | 25,0 | 13,4 | ........ | 9,0 | 57,9 | ........ | 242,2 | 390,9 |
| 1935 | 64,3 | 18,9 | 24,9 | ........ | 14,4 | 68,6 | 1,8 | 271,4 | 464,3 |
| 1936 | 55,6 | 21,2 | 37,4 | ........ | 15,0 | 82,3 | 2,6 | 285,8 | 499,9 |
| 1937 | 65,9 | 25,1 | 69,6 | ........ | 25,9 | 99,2 | 4,4 | 395,2 | 685,3 |
| 1938 | 57,8 | 23,8 | 79,2 | ........ | 19,4 | 83,7 | 4,6 | 276,7 | 545,2 |
| 1939-45 | ........ | ........ | ........ | ........ | ........ | ........ | ........ | ........ | ........ |
| 1946 | 68,1 | 32,8 | ........ | ........ | 3,1 | 129,4 | 2,8 | 331,1 | 567,3 |
| 1947 | 83,8 | 83,8 | ........ | ........ | 10,6 | 199,5 | 3,4 | 534,4 | 915,5 |
| 1948 | 48,2 | 73,2 | 6,8 | ........ | 14,2 | 298,3 | 2,6 | 422,7 | 866,0 |
| 1949 | 29,6 | 101,3 | 15,3 | 0,5 | 17,5 | 350,0 | 2,2 | 274,4 | 790,8 |
| 1950 | 34,3 | 117,3 | 83,5 | 1,1 | 21,9 | 541,9 | 3,3 | 251,7 | 1.055,0 |
| 1951 | 60,5 | 125,3 | 120,0 | 6,7 | 32,3 | 505,0 | 5,0 | 434,7 | 1.289,5 |
| 1952 | 79,9 | 107,1 | 136,9 | 0,9 | 26,5 | 437,1 | 6,1 | 296,5 | 1.091,0 |
| 1953 | 45,2 | 104,3 | 177,5 | 1,1 | 31,5 | 412,1 | 4,8 | 288,9 | 1.065,4 |
| 1954 | 11,0 | 131,6 | 298,2 | 1,0 | 44,1 | 490,8 | 8,2 | 358,0 | 1.342,9 |
| 1955 | 18,4 | 162,7 | 404,0 | 1,2 | 74,6 | 528,6 | 10,9 | 388,8 | 1.589,2 |
| 1956 | 19,0 | 176,6 | 484,6 | 2,4 | 87,0 | 462,1 | 17,1 | 372,4 | 1.621,2 |
| 1957 | 20,1 | 251,9 | 584,3 | 6,6 | 119,1 | 547,3 | 28,1 | 336,0 | 1.893,4 |
| 1958 | 16,4 | 359,3 | 733,4 | 10,2 | 169,3 | 596,2 | 41,7 | 269,5 | 2.196,0 |
| 1959 | 11,8 | 561,7 | 871,0 | 19,3 | 221,2 | 697,0 | 54,8 | 267,7 | 2.704,5 |
| 1960 | 20,6 | 555,9 | 982,8 | 38,8 | 203,9 | 716,0 | 62,2 | 322,5 | 2.902,7 |
| 1961 | 12,4 | 483,8 | 1.006,2 | 57,0 | 245,0 | 538,7 | 61,2 | 259,0 | 2.663,3 |
| 1962 | 15,5 | 552,9 | 1.101,9 | 66,7 | 319,1 | 694,6 | 70,4 | 232,0 | 3.053,1 |
| 1963 | 22,8 | 604,3 | 1.331,8 | 98,6 | 305,3 | 774,8 | 80,3 | 267,8 | 3.485,7 |
| 1964 | 51,9 | 577,1 | 1.499,0 | 150,4 | 331,1 | 849,1 | 95,5 | 333,0 | 3.887,1 |
| 1965 | 103,4 | 638,3 | 1.527,3 | 194,2 | 326,7 | 793,8 | 108,1 | 167,7 | 3.859,5 |
| 1966 | 297,9 | 787,4 | 1.637,4 | 255,7 | 393,6 | 722,0 | 126,8 | 256,5 | 4.477,3 |
| 1967 | 543,8 | 835,0 | 1.463,2 | 362,2 | 426,9 | 637,8 | 143,8 | 363,0 | 4.775,7 |
| 1968 | 803,0 | 958,2 | 1.919,7 | 612,4 | 587,1 | 818,6 | 157,9 | 419,2 | 6.267,1 |
| 1969 | 1.124,3 | 1.175,0 | 2.055,7 | 858,1 | 630,1 | 952,8 | 164,1 | 437,8 | 7.397,9 |
| 1970 | 928,8 | 1.525,4 | 2.103,9 | 1.086,8 | 671,0 | 862,7 | 213,1 | 379,1 | 7.770,8 |
| 1971 | 1.020,4 | 1.631,0 | 2.293,0 | 1.779,0 | 680,5 | 915,8 | 237,8 | 486,8 | 9.044,3 |
| 1972 | 1.102,5 | 1.769,3 | 2.188,1 | 1.965,4 | 699,7 | 767,4 | 221,3 | 531,0 | 9.244,8 |
| 1973 | 1.122,8 | 1.931,2 | 2.347,7 | 2.067,5 | 705,3 | 761,9 | 203,9 | 661,0 | 9.801,3 |

(*) From 1961, data have been obtained from the car manufacturers. (**) From 1946, only West Germany.

# YESTERDAY'S BODIES

Rear-entrance tonneau

Dos-à-dos

Double Phaeton

Vis-à-vis

Torpedo

Mylord

Landaulet

Duc

Coupé de Ville

# TODAY'S BODIES

Two-door sedan

Four-door sedan

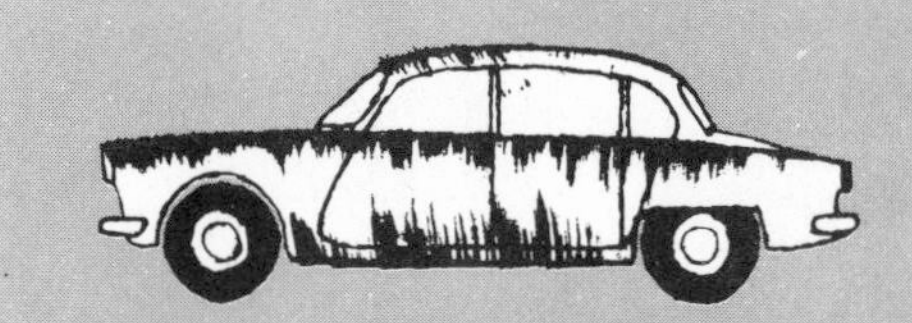
Limousine

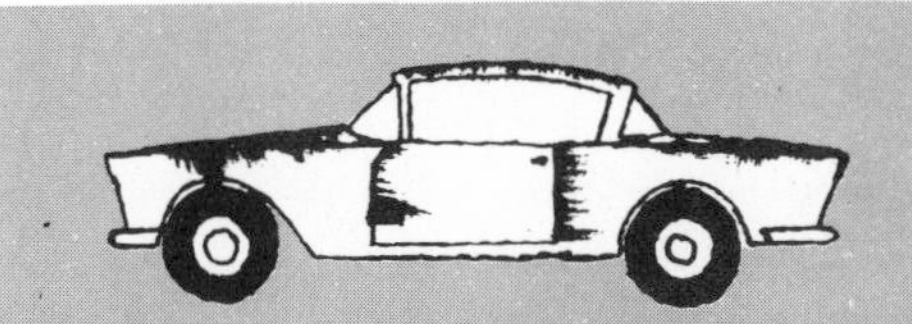
Two-door false convertible

Four-door false convertible

Convertible roadster

Station wagon

Two-seater coupé

Four-seater coupé

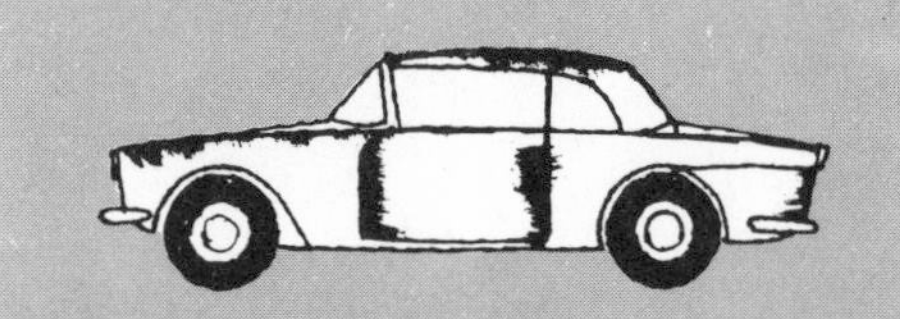
Four-seater convertible

Two-seater convertible

Roadster

Hard-top

# FROM HORSE TO HP

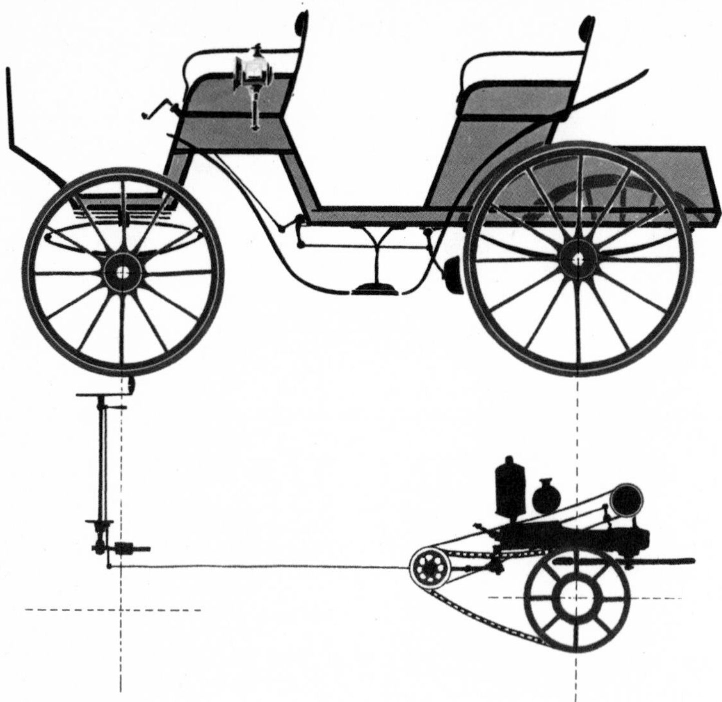

Plan of the body, steering controls, and engine group, in their first adaptation to the automobile body.

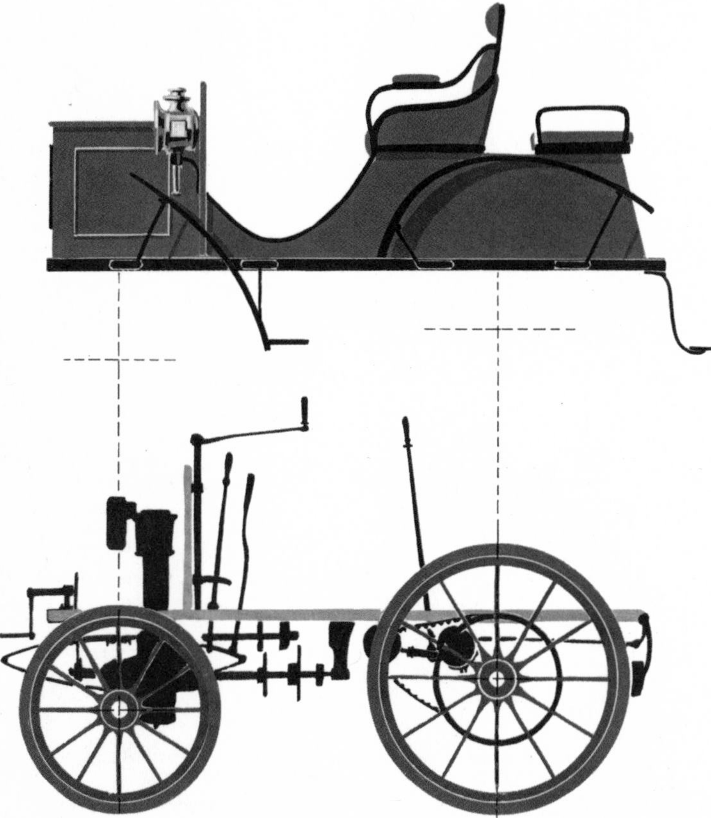

Plan of the body, chassis, and mechanical system used by most car makers in the 1900–1905 period. The word "chassis" also included the mechanical parts and was introduced and known as the "Panhard system."

# ENGINE NOMENCLATURE

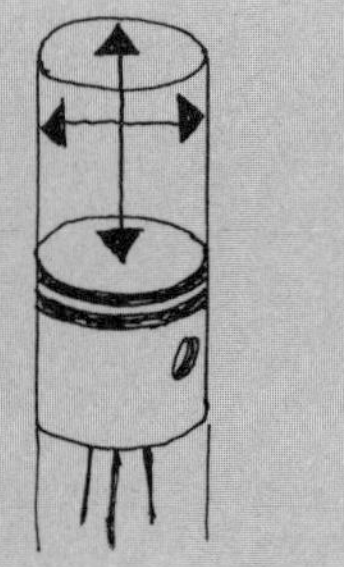

**Bore and stroke.** The first refers to the diameter of the cylinder, the second to the distance the piston goes from the bottom dead center to the top dead center.

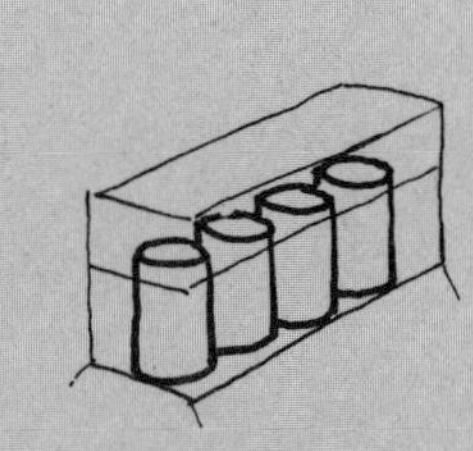

**Aligned cylinders.** Many car makers prefer the solution of cylinders set in a row because it is more economical to operate the car.

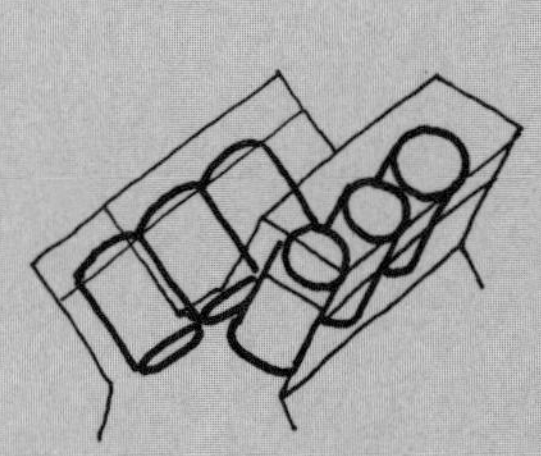

**V cylinders.** Cylinders set in the form of a V—a more costly solution, but better adapted to air-cooled engines, or even to those that are water-cooled, since it reduces the longitudinal mass of the motor.

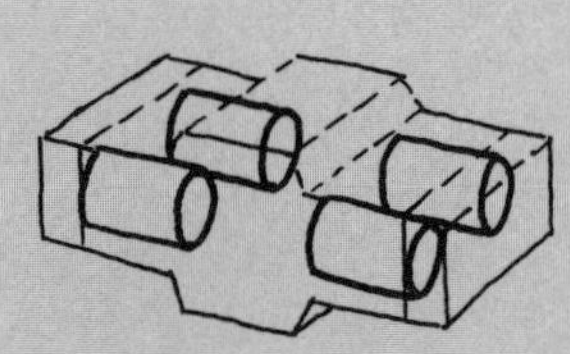

**Opposed cylinders.** The comment made for V cylinders applies here as well: even more longitudinal space is gained with opposed cylinders (while some is lost transversally). This is the ideal solution for air-cooled motors (Citroën 2 CV and GS, Volkswagen 1200–1300, Porsche, Chevrolet Corvair, etc.).

**Side valves.** An arrangement no longer in use; it was very common in the past, though. While simple in construction, it had the disadvantage of lowering engine efficiency because of the shape of the combustion chamber.

**Mixed valves.** Hardly used at all now (but still employed by the Brazilian Ford "Rural"), these were to be found on English and American motors. Valves for overhead induction and for side exhaust.

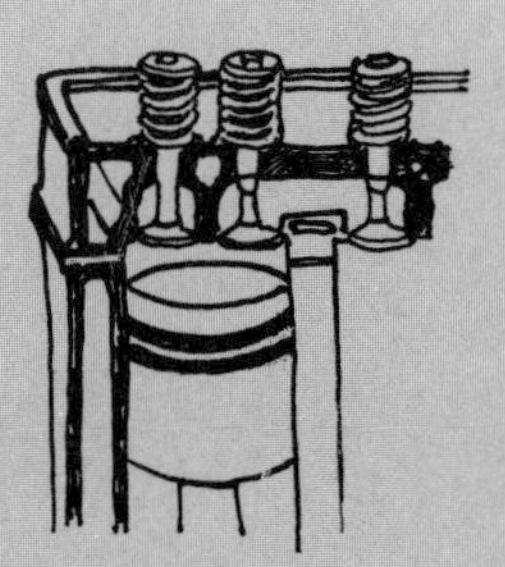

**Aligned overhead valves.** The arrangement preferred today because it is the most economical (apart from the side-valve system).

**Inclined-V valves.** The best way to obtain maximum engine efficiency, because it allows a semicircular combustion chamber. It requires, however, overhead valve control of the timing system.

**Base camshaft.** The most common solution because the most economical. The camshaft in the block works a long pushrod that in turn controls a rocker that opens and closes the valves.

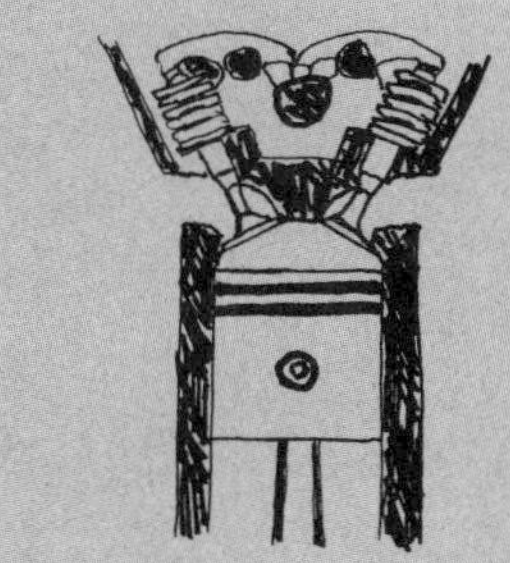

**Single overhead camshaft.** Permits a hemispherical combustion chamber, but does not do away with rocker arms. The engine can, however, reach higher peaks than can be attained with a rod and equalizer timing system.

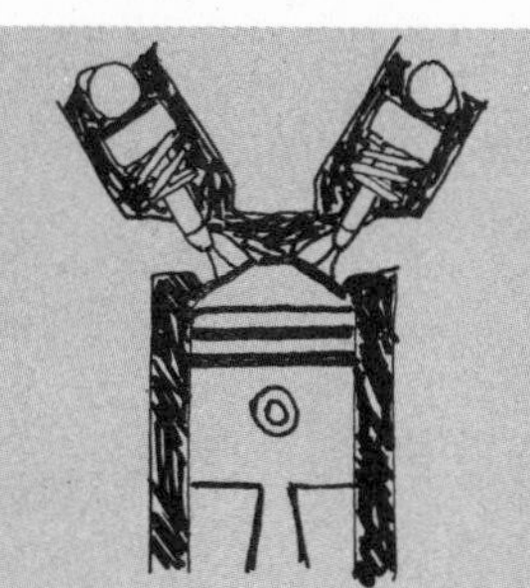

**Double overhead camshaft.** The best solution from the point of view of engine efficiency. It not only gives a hemispherical combustion chamber but also high rpm peaks; in fact, valve control is direct.

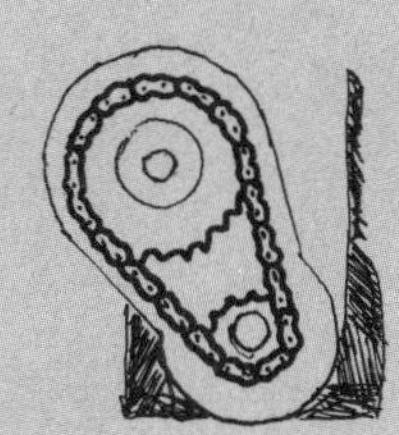

**Chain control of the timing system.** Although this is still the most widespread system, it is about to be replaced by the toothed belt, which offers the same advantages but is more quiet. It links the gears of the driving shaft to the camshaft which controls the valves.

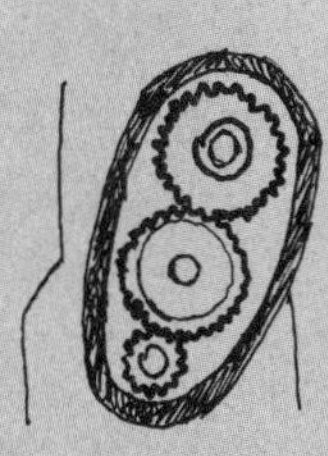

**Gear control of the timing system.** Not used very often, because it is noisy. It links the gears of the driving shaft to the camshaft by means of one or more intermediate gears.

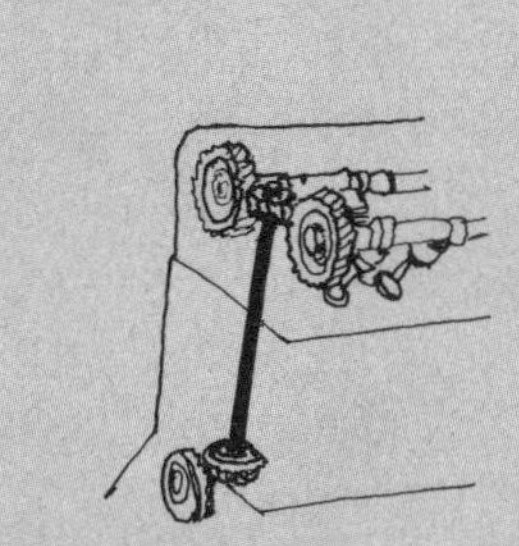

**Return shaft control of the timing system.** This has certain advantages, although rarely used. It is employed in particular for putting in motion the twin overhead camshafts.

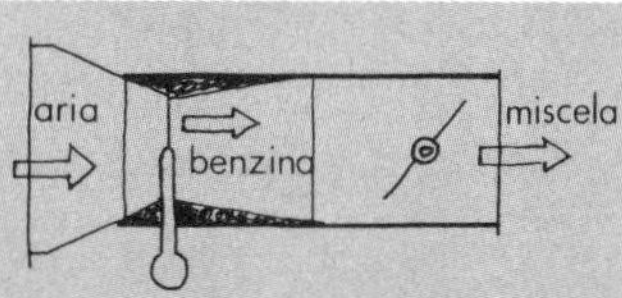


**Horizontal carburetor.** A horizontal or vertical placing of the carburetor—the device that mixes air with the gasoline and then sends it to the induction manifold—helps to classify its type. The choice of a horizontal rather than vertical carburetor is usually due only to factors of space inside the engine compartment. Naturally, in a horizontal carburetor the flow of the air–gasoline mixture is horizontal.

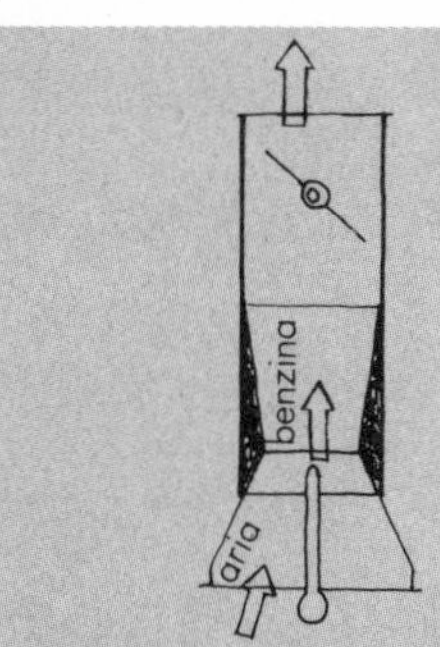


**Vertical carburetor.** The most widely used, along with the inverted carburetor (in which the air comes in from above and the gasoline jet from the side).

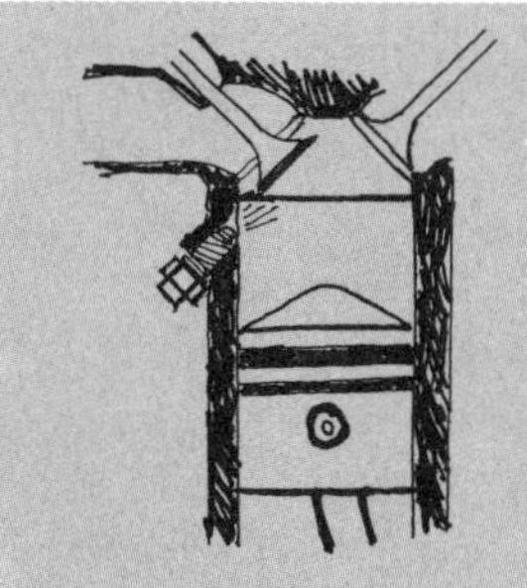

**Direct injection.** The solution that demands an injector set directly inside the combustion chamber; the suction valve then lets only air in.

**Indirect injection.** The injector is placed in the suction duct; from there it injects the fuel, mixed with air, into the combustion chamber through the suction valve.

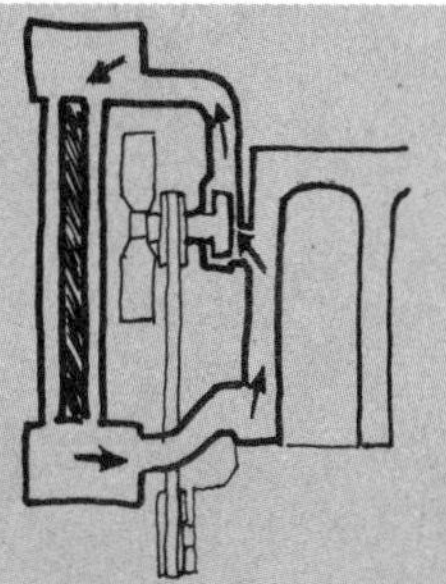

**Water cooling with forced circulation.** A pump circulates the flow of water that passes from the motor (where it absorbs heat) to the radiator (where it expels heat).

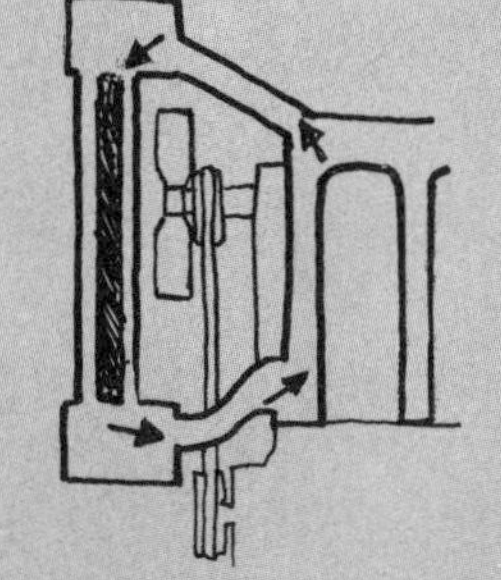

**Water cooling with radiator circulation.** Simpler than the preceding system, because without a pump. It functions according to the principle of physics that hot water rises and cold water descends.

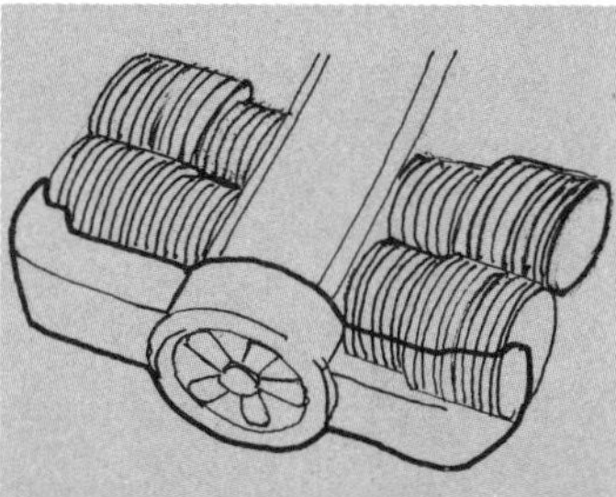

**Air cooling.** This makes use of a fan to activate air circulation (carefully directed onto the cylinders) and of fanning all over the engine to increase the surface hit by the air.

# CAR MUSEUMS OF THE WORLD

AUSTRALIA

**Gilltraps Auto Museum Pty. Ltd.**
P.O. Box 131, Coolangatta, Queensland 4225

AUSTRIA

**Technisches Museum für Industrie und Gerwerbe**
Mariahilferstrasse 212, Vienna XIV

BELGIUM

**Automobielmuseum Kelchterhoef**
3530 Houthalen

**Automobilecollection Mahy**
Garage FIAT, Lamstraat 13, 9000 Gent

DENMARK

**Aalholm Automobilmuseum-Raben Car Collection**
Aalholm Castle, 4880 Nysted

**Danmarks Tekniske Museum**
Ole Romers Vej, 3000 Helsingor

**Egeskov Veteranmuseum**
DK 5772 Kvaerndrup

**Jysk Automobilmuseum**
8883 Gjern, Jylland

BRAZIL

**Museu Paulista de Antiguidades Mecânicas**
c/o Roberto Eduardo Lee, Rua Santo Antonio 611, Sao Paulo

FRANCE

**Autobiographie Renault**
53 Champs Elysées, 75008 Parigi

**Musée Bonnal-Renaulac**
80 rue Ferdinand Buisson, Begles 22, Gironde

**Musée d'Automobiles du Forez**
Route d'Epeluy, 42 Sury le Comtal, Loire

**Musée de l'Automobile** (sezione del Musée de l'Automobile di Le Mans)
Esplanade du Paradis 65, Lourdes

**Musée de l'Automobile de Chatellerault**
3 rue Clement Krebs, 86100 Chatellerault

**Musée de l'Automobile de la Sarthe**
Circuit des 24 Heures, Les Raineries, 72101 Le Mans

**Musée de l'Automobile du Centre**
Vatan, Indre

**Musée Français de l'Automobile**
Château Rochetaillée sur Saône, Rhone

**Musée Marius Berliet**
Automobiles M. Berliet, Route d'Heyrieux, 69200 Venissieux

**Musée National de la Voiture et du Tourisme**
Palais de Compiègne 60, Compiègne

GERMANY

**BMW Museum**
Petuelring 130, Monaco

**Daimler-Benz Automobile-Museum**
Stuttgartn Untertürkheim

**Deutsches Museum von Meisterwerken der Naturwissenschaft und Technik**
Museumsinsel 1, 8 Monaco 26

**Deutsches Zweiradmuseum**
Urbanstrasse 13, 7107 Neckarsulm

**Motoren-Museum der Klockner-Humboldt-Deutz AG**
Deutz-Mülheimerstrasse 111, 5 Köln

**Verkehrsmuseum**
Augustrusstrasse 1, 801 Dresden

**Zweitakt-Motorrad-Museum**
9382 Augustusburg, Erzgeh

GREAT BRITAIN

**Bristol City Museum**
Queen's Road, Bristol BS8 IRL

**Cheddar Veteran & Vintage Car Museum**
(Cheddar Motor & Transport Museum)
Cheddar, Somerset

**Herbert Art Gallery and Museum**
Jordan Well, Coventry CV1 5QP

**Kingston Upon Hull Museum** (Transport & Archaelogy Museum)
36 High Street, Hull, Yorkshire

**Myreton Motor Museum**
Aberlady, East Lothian, Scozia

**Museum of Science and Industry**
Nexhall Street, Birmingham B3 1RZ

**Royal Armoured Corps Tank Museum and Royal Tank Regiment Museum**
Bovington Camp, Wareham, Dorset

**Royal Scottish Museum**
Chambers Street, Edinburgh 1, Scozia

**The Museum of Transport**
25 Albert Drive, Glasgow S1, Scozia

**The National Motor Museum**
Palace House, Beauhieu, Brockenhurst, Hampshire S 04 7 ZN

**The Shuttleworth Collection**
The Aereodrome Old Warden, Bedfordshire

ITALY

**Centro Storico Fiat**
Via Chiabrera 20, 10126 Torino

**Museo Alfa Romeo**
Arese, Milano

**Museo dell'Automobile Carlo Biscaretti di Ruffia**
Corso Unità d'Italia 40, 10126 Torino

**Museo Nazionale della Scienza e della Tecnica « Leonardo da Vinci »**
Via San Vittore 21, 20123 Milano

HOLLAND

**Autotron**
Drunen

**Het Nationaal Automobielmuseum**
Veursestraatweg 280, Leidschendam

PORTUGAL

**Museu do Automovel**
Caramulo

SPAIN

**Musée de la Carrosserie Française**
Puerto de Andraitx, Mallorca

UNITED STATES

**Bellm Cars and Music of Yesterday**
5500 North Tamiami Trail, Sarasota, Florida

**Boyertown Auto Body Works Collection**
Boyertown, Pennsylvania

**Briggs Cunningham Automotive Museum**
250 Baker Street, Costa Mesa, California

**Brooks Stevens Automotive Museum**
Route 141, Mequon, Wisconsin

**Elliot Museum of Vehicular Evolution**
Hutchinson Island, Stuart, Florida

**Frederick C. Crawford Auto-Aviation Museum of the Western Reserve Historical Society**
10825 East Boulevard, Cleveland, Ohio 44106

**Gene Zimmerman's Antique Car Museum**
Harrisburg, Pennsylvania

**Harold Warp's Pioneer Village**
Minden, Nebraska 68959

**Harrah's Auto Collection**
Reno, Nevada

**Henry Ford Museum and Greenfield Village**
Dearborn, Michigan

**Indianapolis Motor Speedway Museum**
Indianapolis, Indiana

**Long Island Automotive Museum**
Southampton, Long Island, New York

**Museum of Science and Industry**
Chicago, Illinois

**Museum of Speed**
P.O. Box 4157, Daytona Beach, Florida 32021

**Smithsonian Institution**
Transportation Division, Washington D.C.

**The Museum of Automobiles**
Winthrop Rockefeller Collection, Petit Jean Mountain, Arkansas

**The Carraige House**
Stony Brook, Long Island, New York

**VMCCA Antique Auto Museum**
Larz Anderson Park, Brookline, Massachusetts 02146

SWEDEN

**Skokloster's Motormuseum**
1904 Skokloster

**Tekniska Museet**
Museivagen 7, 115 27 Stoccolma

**Vatterbygdens Automobilmuseum**
Motell Vatterleden, Huskvarna

SWITZERLAND

**Swiss Transport Museum**
Swiss Institute of Transport, Communications and Longines Planetarium
Lidostrasse 5, CH-6000 Lucerna

**Musée de l'Automobile Château de Grandson**
1422 Grandson

HUNGARY

**Auto es Motorkerekpar Muzeum Haris Testverek**
Moricz Zsigmond Korter 12, Budapest XI
**Bristol Museum**

U.S.S.R.

**Polytechnical Museum**
Novaya Pl. 3/4, Mosca

# HISTORY OF MANUFACTURERS

**ABARTH** (Italy) **1949**

After Carlo Abarth left Cisitalia, he began to remodel Fiat motors and those of other companies on his own, in 1949. His production followed two main lines: the first dealt with Fiat "500" and "600" models, replacing the original driving shaft with a more rigid one, strengthening the clutch, lowering the suspension, and, from 1961 on, applying front disk brakes. The second dealt with the building of Abarth vehicles which had bodies designed by Allemano and Zagato on the "600" chassis. The Abarth took part in many international meets and from 1960 to 1964 won the Nürburgring "1000 Kilometers."

**A.C.** (Great Britain) **1908**

This company continued the Weller tradition and its first car was a version—by John Weller himself—of a three-wheeled industrial vehicle, the "auto-carrier," hence the initials "A.C." Weller's 1991 cc model is famous; it was presented at the London Auto Show in 1919—and remained in production until 1963. After 1921, the firm took part in car racing, establishing various records and winning the world record at the "24 Hours" of Montlhéry in 1925. After a period of crisis that began in 1929, A.C. began full production again in 1947, creating, among other models, the famous "Cobra."

**ALFA ROMEO** (Italy) **1910**

Founded in Milan, in the former Darracq factory at Portello, under the single name ALFA (Anonima Lombarda Fabbrica Automobili), it began its own production with cars designed by Cavalier Merosi. In 1915, the plant was taken over by industrialist Nicola Romeo, and the official name became Alfa Romeo. This name became famous in the field of auto racing because of the many victories won by the firm, among which were the Targa Florio, the "Mille Miglia," the Grand Prix of Monza, France and Germany, the G.P. des Nations at Geneva, and many others. The year 1950 marked an important change in policy: production was switched from expensive touring Alfas practically made on commission, to mass-produced touring models. Soon more than 100,000 cars a year were being turned out.

**ALPINE** (France) **1955**

A French firm for the production of racing cars, founded by Jean Rédélé, an auto-racing fanatic and the son of a Renault dealer. The first Alpine made was called the "Mille Miglia," after the owner of the firm which won the Italian race. It had a Renault "4 CV" engine and was made until 1960. Alpine single-seaters have taken part in, and won, various meets of Formula 2 and Formula 3.

**AMERICAN MOTORS**
(see Rambler)

**Abarth 124 Rally**

**AC 3000**

**Alfa Romeo Alfetta**

**FNM 2300**

**Alpine A 310**

**Audi 80 LS**

**Austin Maxi 1750**

**ASTON MARTIN** (Great Britain) **1922**

The name comes from the combination of the names of the uphill meet at Aston Clinton and of one of the firm's founders, Lionel Martin; the other founder was Robert Bamford.

The company only produced about one hundred cars in its first twenty years of activity, yet the name is one of Britain's most illustrious, due to the high quality of its automobiles—which are too well-built and personalized to be sold at competitive prices and reach a wide public. In 1947, the firm was taken over by the David Brown group; and this purchase started a new production policy aimed at a constant increase in displacement in Aston Martin engines, so as to turn out cars for an even larger international market, and not just superb racing models.

Aston Martin became an important producer of racing cars after victories in various international competitions; and in 1959 it was the first British firm to win the championship meets for sports-car manufacturers.

**AUDI** (Germany) **19[illegible]**

A company founded by August Horch, who called it Audi, the Latin translation of his last name. The immediate success of his first car was partly due to his own success in those years in the Austrian Alpine meets. In 1928, the company was absorbed by the D.K.W., which began production of two models inspired—as was common in German industry at that time—by American cars (the "Zwickau" and the "Dresden"). In 1932, this firm became part of Auto Union, along with Wanderer and Horch. It was nationalized in 1945; in 1956, Mercedes-Benz became the chief shareholder; but in 1964 the majority stockholder became Volkswagen.

**AUSTIN** (Great Britain) **1906**

Founded by Herbert Austin, this company immediately showed that its main interest was in mass production.

The "Seven," produced in 1922, was one of the most important efforts in the low-displacement field. Its sales and technical success started mass motorization in Great Britain. More than 300,000 cars were made until 1939, and the model took part in many meets, winning, among others, the "500 Miles" of the BRDC in 1930.

In 1945, control of the firm went to L. P. Lord, who increased exportation, especially to America. In 1952, Austin merged with Morris, forming the British Motor Company.

The famous "Mini," a revolutionary little car designed by Alec Issigonis, went on sale in 1960 in the Austin "Seven" and Morris "Mini-Minor" versions. This car won many races and had exceptional success on the market.

**AUSTIN-HEALEY** (Great Britain) **1953**

In 1952, David Healey presented the Healey "100" at the London Auto Show; it was a two-seater sports car with the engine of the Austin "A 90." This vehicle was renamed the Austin-Healey after an agreement made with Austin in 1953. The car then had great commercial success, captured the American market and won many meets, among them some World Championship races.

**AUTOBIANCHI** (Italy) **1955**

In 1954, engineer Ferruccio Quintavalle managed to interest Fiat and Pirelli in the future of Bianchi cars. Thus the new Autobianchi Company came into being. The first car—the "Bianchina"—came out in 1957; at the same time, the Fiat "Nuova 500" went on the market. The "Bianchina" used its mechanical parts but had greater style and all the trademarks of a luxury utility car.

**Autobianchi A 112**

**BENTLEY** (Great Britain) **1920**

When W. B. Bentley's first 3-liter model, designed by him in collaboration with H. Varley and F. T. Burgess, was presented at the London Automobile Show in 1919, he was already well known as a D.F.P. dealer, a pioneer in aluminum pistons, and an airplane engine designer. The "3-liter" model—which was produced until 1929 and was famous as the archetype of all the racing cars of the era—won many victories in long-distance races. Bentley always followed the policy of using its cars in racing to test them and make their quality known (and they really *were* indestructible). The firm went bankrupt in 1931, and Napier tried to obtain the Bentley plant; but Rolls got there first and, at the Olympia Salon of 1933, presented its own version of the Bentley, made famous by its nickname of "silent sports car." In 1951, Bentley and Rolls-Royce merged, and in the 1960s they began turning out models that are exactly alike, except for the shape of the radiator.

**Bentley Corniche**

**B.M.W.** (Germany) **1916**

Started in 1916, as the Bayerische Flugzeng-werke, it changed its name a year later and became the Bayerische Motoren Werke (B.M.W.). At first it concentrated on engines for planes, trucks, and boats. Its first motor for a motorcycle was produced in 1923.

After buying out the plant and licenses of Dixi in Eisenach, in 1928, the firm turned out a Dixi exactly like the British "Austin Seven," and the car won many victories in races; the company then began making sports cars as well.

Production came to a halt during the war, and the plant in Eisenach closed down, since it was in East Germany and was confiscated. Car production only began again in 1952, with the "501" limousine, presented at Frankfurt. For a certain period, the German firm turned out expensive and powerful cars that brought it to the verge of bankruptcy; in 1955, it bought a license from the Italian "Iso" for making the small "Isetta." The first original BMW car, the "700," designed by Michelotti, only came out in 1959 and was produced until 1965.

BMW production then continued to expand, and its touring cars have been successful in automobile races.

**BMW 1602**

**BRISTOL** (Great Britain) **1947**

After the Second World War, the Bristol Aeroplane Company opened a section for producing cars. The first was the "400," a car very similar to the BMW 438. The firm also turned out racing cars and Formula 2 motors.

The Arnolt Bristol Company was created in Chicago in 1954 to make Bristol cars for the American market. In 1960, the automobile division of the firm was sold to private interests which formed a new company in 1966.

**Bristol 411**

**BUICK** (United States) **1903**

Founded by a plumber of Scottish origin, David Dumbar Buick, this firm shortly became one of the most famous American trade names in the world, as the maker of medium-quality cars, with advanced styling, and sold at reasonable prices.

Things did not go well with Buick, and in 1908 William Crapo Durant became the head of the company; he gave it new life and put on the market a wide range of models within a very short time. On September 16 of that same year, Buick became part of General Motors, which also absorbed Oldsmobile, Cadillac, and Oakland. During those years, the Buick took part in various meets and won many prizes; there were no less than 166 victories in 1909, among them the opening race that inaugurated the new track in Indianapolis.

Just after the First World War, Buick put out two cars, a four-cylinder and a six-cylinder, which put it in fourth place among American manufacturers, right after Dodge, Ford, and Chevrolet, which produced much cheaper vehicles. In 1950, Buick turned out more than half a million cars and rose to third place on the list, after Chevrolet and Ford—a real success, given its higher prices.

**Buick Regal**

**CADILLAC** (United States) **1903**

The Cadillac trademark, which represented the most luxurious of all American cars, started quite humbly with a machine driven by a one-cylinder motor selling for $750. It was created by Henry Martyn Leland, who had worked with Henry Ford and had also produced engines for Oldsmobile.

In 1909, Cadillac became part of the General Motors group, but it always kept its own policy-making rights within that organization. It was the first firm in the world to offer—in 1928—a synchronized gear called "Synchro-Mesh." After the war, its prices rose, and it then became an international prestige symbol.

Cadillac is one of the few firms that has remained true to its original intentions and to tradition; its cars are justly called "the most reasonable high-class cars in the world."

**Cadillac Fleetwood Sixty**

**CHECKER** (United States) **1959**

A taxi maker since 1923, this company began making cars and station wagons in 1959. One of its typical models, called the "Aerobus," is a huge 8-door machine adapted for hotels and airports.

**Checker Marathon**

**CHEVROLET** (United States) **1911**

In 1911, Louis Chevrolet was asked by William Crapo Durant to create the prototype of a car to bear the former's name, a name that had become famous for Chevrolet's racing victories on the Buick team. On November 3 of that year, the Chevrolet Motor Company of Michigan was founded.

The year 1915 saw the appearance on the market of the "490," so-called because it cost only $490; it instantly became the rival of the Ford. In 1918, the firm was taken over by General Motors, and under the leadership of Alfred P. Sloan, Jr., began to turn out inexpensive cars which became the world's best-selling automobiles.

Chevrolet took part in racing, too: Juan Manuel Fangio won the very difficult Buenos Aires–Lima–Buenos Aires race with a Chevy, and he also won other victories with the same trademark in the years that followed.

In 1953, production of the "Corvette" began; it had a revolutionary fiberglass body and was the only mass-produced sports car built in the United States.

**Chevrolet Vega**

**CHRYSLER** (United States) **1923**

Chrysler owed its fortune to the business enterprise of Walter P. Chrysler (former executive of General Motors), who raised the firm to third place in the list of American car makers only three years after it was founded. His first car, the "Six," caused a sensation with its hydraulic brakes on all four wheels, its streamlined body, its modern engine, and its high top speed. It offered sports performance hitherto confined to luxury cars with engines twice as powerful—and at a price within the range of a good part of the public. One hundred thousand cars were sold in 1925. The Chrysler also won some racing victories.

In 1928, Chrysler laid the foundations for an automobile empire in competition with that of General Motors and Ford, by absorbing Dodge and launching two new series of models under the names De Soto and Plymouth. The 1960s saw the Chrysler empire stretch over to Europe, with the purchase of the majority of shares in the French Simca, the English Rootes group, and the Spanish Barreiros, as well as the enlarging of plants in Australia and South Africa.

**CHRYSLER FRANCE**
(see Simca)

**CITROËN** (France) **1919**
(see p. 155)

**DAF** (Netherlands) **1958**

D.A.F (van Doorne's Automobiel Fabrieken) was founded by two brothers, Wim and Hub van Doorne, who had some experience with industrial vehicles. The first car, which came out at the end of the 1950s, had an original transmission system called "Variomatic"—completely automatic, with belts and pulleys, and taken from the gears used by the firm on some farm machines. The Variomatic was to remain a constant feature of all DAF cars, along with practicality and simplicity. While the company prefers to use its own motors on its two-cylinder models, it turns to Renault for its four-cylinder engines.

DAF made two important business agreements in 1972: one with Volvo and the other, involving heavy machines, with the International Harvester Company of Chicago.

Even though the D.A.F. was designed as a utility car, it has done well in competition; due to the Variomatic, it has achieved excellent results in more than one meet.

**DAIHATSU** (Japan) **1954**

Founded in 1907, for the production of internal combustion engines, the firm presented its first car in 1958: the "Bee," a three-wheeled, rear-engine sedan that was mainly adopted as a taxi. In 1968, Daihatsu was taken over by the Toyota group.

**DAIMLER** (Great Britain) **1896**

The Daimler Motor Syndicate was founded in 1893 by F. R. Simms, for making use in England of the patents of the German Gottlieb Daimler.

Chrysler New Yorker

Citroën Mehari

Daf 66 1300 Marathon

Daihatsu Fellow

Daimler Double-Six 5,3

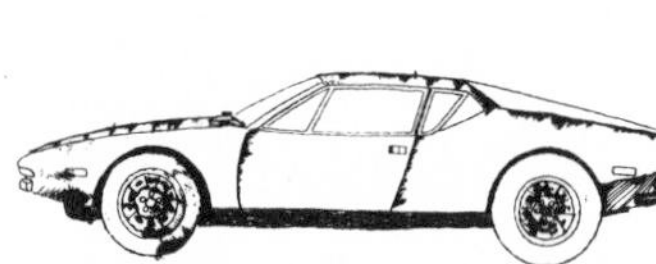

De Tomaso Pantera L

Dodge Coronet

Only in 1896 did it start turning out cars, very similar to the French Panhards and with motors imported directly from Germany. John Scott-Montagu—the first English driver to take part in an international race—participated in the Paris–Ostend race with a four-cylinder, 3-liter Daimler. And the firm won many victories with large cars in races in Europe and America, as well as in England itself.

In 1908, Daimler bought the construction rights for the double-sheathed "Silent" engines, created by Charles Yale Knight, and continued to use them in its cars for twenty-three years. Then, in 1931, it bought out Lanchester and had it build less expensive models. Daimler has been part of Jaguar since 1960 and is today one of the most important British bus factories.

**DATSUN** (Japan) **1932**

In 1926, the Kwaishinsha Motor Car Company merged with the Jitsuyo Seizo Company and formed the Dat Car Manufacturing Company of Osaka. At any rate, up until 1930 the firm concentrated exclusively on industrial vehicles. In 1931, production of the model "91" began; it was first called Datson, then changed to Datsun in 1932.

A new plant was built in Yokohama in 1933 for the production of larger sedans, and the name was changed again in 1934 to Nissan. The present production of this company includes a complete range of models; and on some markets, the larger Nissans, made by the same plant, are sold under the name of Datsun.

**DE TOMASO** (Italy) **1960**

Founded by former Argentine driver Alessandro De Tomaso. After a period of production almost exclusively aimed at the racing field—with single-seaters for Formula 1, 2, and 3 and for Junior races—with OSCA, Alfa Romeo, and Ford engines, the firm went large-scale in 1965, building mass-produced sports cars. The 1967 Torino Show was marked by the presentation of the Rowan, a small electric car for city use, the result of the collaboration between the Rowan Controller Company and the Carrozzeria Ghia, body makers. The Ford Motor Company took over De Tomaso in 1972. The company continued producing the "Pantera" in Turin (De Tomaso's latest car), and world-wide distribution was handled by Ford.

**DODGE** (United States) **1914**

The Dodge brothers, John and Horace, founded this company in July 1914 after having been Ford shareholders and executives. In November of that year, their first car left the Hamtramck plant: a torpedo model with a 12-volt electric system. This model was used as an ambulance during the First World War.

In 1916, Dodge reached fourth place in the USA in regard to the number of cars produced and by 1919 it was in second place. In 1917, this Detroit firm prepared what is considered to be the first closed car in automobile history with an all-steel body.

After taking over Graham Brothers, the company also began making industrial vehicles. But in 1928 Dodge was in turn absorbed by Chrysler, which left production as it was, except for abolishing the four-cylinder engine. Since 1959, the firm has produced both normal and "fast" cars.

**FERRARI** (Italy) **1940**
(see p. 214)

**FIAT** (Italy) **1899**
(see p. 204)

**FORD** (United States) **1903**
(see p. 109)

**F.N.M.** (Brazil) **1942**

The Brazilian firm that makes industrial vehicles and medium-price-range automobiles. In 1968, Alfa Romeo bought 85 percent of this company and is producing the 2300 sedan, designed in Italy and aesthetically very much like the "Alfetta."

**GAZ** (Soviet Union) **1932**

The first four-seater touring car to leave the Gorky factory had more than one feature in common with the Ford Model A, because the American firm gave a large contribution to the setting-up of the Russian factory. The resemblance to American models lasted until 1941. The war saw the arrival of the Gaz "67," a utility car for the armed forces, of which the "B" version is still produced. After the war, Gaz turned out the "Pobieda" (victory) and then the "Volga" and the "Chaika." The Gorky plant was at one point the largest producer of trucks in Europe and is at the moment being enlarged to face the increased demand for private vehicles. Apart from trucks, Gaz is now turning out an up-to-date version of the "Volga."

**HILLMAN** (Great Britain) **1907**

This car was originally known as the Hillman-Coatalen, since the designer of the first model was named Louis Coatalen. The first car was made expressly for the 1907 Tourist Trophy. There was a rather scarce production of large cars until 1914; a sports model took part in many races in the 1920s, and Raymond Mays served his apprenticeship in one of them. The firm joined the Rootes group in 1928, and mass production began in 1932 with the "Minx" utility car, sold for £159. This model was constantly improved and brought up-to-date and other cars were derived from it, such as the Singer "Gazelle" (also in the Rootes group), which first used its body and later its engine. The "Minx" was produced on license in Japan by Isuzu. Chrysler became the majority shareholder in the Rootes group in 1968.

**HINDUSTAN** (India) **1946**

This firm turns out just one model, derived from the Morris "Oxford" of the 1950s and aimed exclusively at the Indian market, where it is the best-selling car. During the 1950s, though, the company turned out (on license) some Studebakers, mainly the "Champion" model.

**Ford Pinto**

**Gaz Volga M 24**

**Hillman Imp**

**Hindustan Ambassador Mk II**

**Holden HQ Premier**

**Honda Civic**

**Humber Sceptre**

**Innocenti Mini Cooper 1300**

**HOLDEN** (Australia) **1948**

Holden began as body makers, and some of their production was put on Morris cars imported from England in the 1920s. After becoming part of General Motors, it began mounting American and British GM cars for the Australian market, producing "fastback" coupés back in 1938—three years before the mother plant in Detroit.

In 1948, it began producing the first entirely Australian car; the first exportation of these mass-produced vehicles to New Zealand took place in 1954, and by 1958 annual production had reached a total of 100,000 cars. Holden has been the most important Australian car manufacturer since the end of the last war.

**HONDA** (Japan) **1962**

Known above all as a motorcycle-maker, this company ended up by taking an interest in four-wheeled vehicles as well; it has produced a large amount of farm machinery, as well as Formula 1 racing cars and small trucks. Its first four-seater sedan came out in 1966. Honda won its first Formula 1 Grand Prix in Mexico in 1965, followed by John Surtees's triumph at Monza in 1967. Equipped at first only with two-cylinder engines of the motorcycle type, the latest Hondas are also produced with engines with medium displacement.

**HUMBER** (Great Britain) **1898**

Thomas Humber's bicycle factory, founded in 1868, became part of H. J. Lawson's automobile empire in 1898. The first vehicle produced there—called the "Pennington" and with three weeks—was a complete failure. Actual car production began with an experimental prototype, while production of tricycles and quadricycles continued, with motors added. This firm was the first in England to successfully market a light and cheap car: the "Humberette." For the Tourist Trophy in 1941, Humber, a great supporter of that race, entered a team of cars far from its usual style; they were exactly like the Peugeots designed for that event.

In the meantime, the firm had been taken over by Rootes in 1930; then began a general revision of Humber's traditional line. From that year on, attention was paid to the production of comfortable touring sedans.

In 1950, a Humber car, the "Super Snipe," came in second in the Monte Carlo Rally. In 1967, production of high-displacement models was suspended.

**INNOCENTI** (Italy) **1960**

This company began its activity at the end of 1960, producing on concession the small "A 40" Austin sedan, to which was added a sports version, called "950" and originated from the Austin-Healey "Sprite." The year 1963 saw the introduction of the "IM3," derived—like the later "J4"—from the Austin-Morris 1100. In 1965, the company began producing the "Mini" and in 1973 the Italian version (called "Regent") of the Austin "Allegro."

**JAGUAR** (Great Britain) **1945**

The name "Jaguar" appeared on some SS models as far back as 1936, but only became an actual trademark in 1945. The cars made between 1945 and 1948 were 1940 SS models and combined great performance with elegance and a reasonable price. In 1951 the large "Mk VII" sedan came out, with the size and comfort of American cars and the fine finishing and handling of English vehicles. An "Mk VII" won the 1956 edition of the Monte Carlo Rally and thus inaugurated Jaguar's domination of the meets reserved for large-engine sedans, a domination that lasted until 1963.

Jaguar began its official participation in racing in 1950 and won five victories in the Le Mans "24 Hours." The British firm then applied the experience acquired on the tracks to the building of its touring cars.

In 1960, Jaguar enlarged through the purchase of Daimler, of Guy (which built industrial vehicles) and of the factory that produced Coventry Climax and Meadows engines. In 1966, it merged with the British Motor Corporation to form the British Motor Holdings.

**JEEP** (see p. 184)

**JENSEN** (Great Britain) **1936**

An English company founded by Richard and Allan Jensen, two brothers who were famous car stylists in the 1930s. The plant also made bodies for the large Austin-Healeys and, at the start, for the Volvo P1800 coupé. In recent years, Jensen has specialized in limited production of top-performance cars, some with both front- and rear-wheel drive.

**LAMBORGHINI** (Italy) **1963**

In 1946, Ferruccio Lamborghini modified Fiat "500's" and in 1949 set up a tractor factory. His first farm machines were built from odd parts left over from the war. The first Lamborghini was built in 1963, to satisfy the proprietor's personal passion. The GT coupés were designed by Gian Paolo Dallara, and about 200 of them were built in 1965: that year the firm was powerful competition for Ferrari, but Lamborghini never entered the field of sports competition with his cars.

**LANCIA** (Italy) **1906**
(see p. 166)

**LINCOLN** (United States) **1920**

After leaving Cadillac in 1917, Henry M. Leland started his own company and turned out large cars called Lincolns. Henry Ford bought the firm in 1922 but kept up the original high-quality standards. Lincoln had a great name with both the American gangsters and police of that time, who used fast models that could do 130 km/h. Many American presidents used a Lincoln, and it is still the preferred presidential car. Since the firm could not keep going on prestige cars alone, in 1936 it put out a relatively cheap model: the "Zephyr," which cost $1320 and the engine of which was adopted by various Anglo-American cars of the day.

In 1952, the Lincoln won the Carrera Pan-American trophy in the touring class. From 1961 on, the firm's fortune was staked on the "Continental"; and in 1968, it introduced a new and

**Jaguar XJ6 4,2**

**Jensen Interceptor III**

**Lamborghini Urraco 250**

**Lincoln Continental**

**Lotus « + 2 S »**

**Maserati Khamsin**

**Mazda Savanna AP**

**Mercury Montego**

personalized model: the "Continental Mark III."

**LOTUS** (Great Britain) **1952**

Perhaps no one did as much as Colin Chapman, head of Lotus, to renew automobile mechanical technique in the postwar period. For not one of his many imitators had the determination, technical knowledge, open mind and business sense that made—and make—Chapman unique in his field.

In 1952, he set up a company with Michael Allen; they were joined in 1953 by Frank Costin, who had previously worked for the De Havilland plane company. A year later, Costin designed the streamlined "Mark 8."

Lotus has built cars for Formula 1, for the Junior formula, and for Formula 3. From the start, it has won many racing prizes; and in 1956 alone, it won 156 victories. By 1966, Lotus was selling so well that the firm transferred its activity to larger quarters. More than 5000 vehicles were turned out in 1967.

**MASERATI** (Italy) **1926**

This company won world fame with its racing cars rather than with its sports models. In 1925, the Maserati plant began building force-fed machines adapted from the Diatto GP; and a year later, Diatto withdrew from racing and the Maserati brothers took it over, founding the Officine Alfieri Maserati, the trademark adopted was Neptune's trident, taken from the statue standing in Piazza del Municipio in Bologna.

Alfieri, the partner, won the Targa Florio in 1926 in his own car. Production for private clients got under way, and in 1929 the legendary sixteen-cylinder model was produced; in 1930, the 2.5-liter GP won five Grand Prix in one season. Control of the company went to Ernesto Maserati in 1932, and he began turning out less powerful cars. In 1938, the firm was bought by the Orsi industrial group, which continued to produce racing cars, winning new prizes and letting Fangio triumph in the Grand Prix of Modena and of Italy in 1953. Orsi then gave up racing and concentrated on the production of expensive sports cars. In 1969, Maserati was taken over by Citroën, which uses it for the production of its own high-displacement engines ("SM").

**MATRA** (France) **1965**

Engins Matra's main activity is the production of missiles; but in 1965 it took over control of the firm of René Bonnet, which specialized in sports cars with Renault engines, and then made a good Formula 3 car. Despite the new owner, Bonnet has continued its original policy and uses Renault engines modified by Gordini.

As of 1967, the company turned out a new car, the "M 530," with a highly streamlined plastic body and a Ford V4, 1699 cc motor; this car was produced until April 1973, when the firm launched the Matra Simca "Bagheera," the first fruits of its collaboration with Chrysler France.

In 1969, a Formula 1 Matra won the World Driving Championships with Stewart.

**MAZDA** (Japan) **1960**

Originally a cork products firm, Mazda began building three-wheeled industrial vehicles in 1931. The first car, a sedan, appeared in prototype form in 1940. Only twenty years later did Mazda start actual automobile production, building mostly utility cars. It uses a Wankel engine in its machines.

**McCLAREN** (Great Britain) **1964**

Bruce McClaren followed the example of another English driver, Brabham, making his own cars and driving racing cars after leaving Cooper. Both he and Chris Amon have had good results with a car built in 1965, with an Oldsmobile engine modified by Traco. The Formula 1 single-seaters have not been as successful.

**MERCEDES BENZ** (Germany) **1926**
(see p. 164)

**MERCURY** (United States) **1938**

Mercury was created by the Lincoln Division of Ford to increase its penetration of the American market in the middle-class sector, in competition with Buick and Oldsmobile, both General Motors cars. The first vehicle turned out, a more powerful version of the Ford 138, cost $40 less than the cheapest Buick.

**M.G.** (Great Britain) **1924**

The M.G. trademark stands for sports cars, even though the original models made by the firm were not in that category. In 1922, Cecil Kimber, who ran the Morris Garages in Oxford, began modifying the "Cowley," a car no longer produced by Morris; and two years later he transformed the 1.8-liter Morris "Oxford," which he then named the "M.G. Super Sports." This car had great success and was backed by the name and sales and repair service of Morris.

The small M.G. "Midget" was the first really cheap and practical sports car to appear in Britain. From 1930 to 1935, the firm concentrated on racing and won many prizes, among them the 1933 "Mille Miglia" and the Ulster Tourist Trophy (driven by Tazio Nuvolari). The M.G. soon became *the* English sports car. After 1935, the company left the racing field and began producing more spacious and comfortable cars. The "Midget TC" was made after the last war and—along with later "Midgets"—did more than any other car to spread the cult of European sports cars in the United States.

**MITSUBISHI** (Japan) **1917–1921; 1959**

The 1917 model "A," clearly copied from Fiat, was the first Japanese car produced in a limited number. The firm then concentrated (until 1921) on experimental models, while continuing to turn out industrial vehicles. After a thorough reorganization of the company in 1959, production of private cars was begun again; and from then on, Mitsubishi has enlarged its activity in this field. The "Jeep" has also been produced on license since 1953.

**MORGAN** (Great Britain) **1910**

One of the most popular and admired three-wheeled English vehicles—and also one of the first of its kind to attract the attention of sports enthusiasts. After the First World War, Morgan continued to produce all kinds of vehicles; and in 1936 it produced its first four-wheeled vehicle, the "4/4." After the Second World War, Morgan adopted Ford engines for its less powerful cars and Triumph engines for its sports cars.

**MGB GT**

**Mitsubishi Lancer**

**Morgan Plus 8**

**Morris Marina Estate Car**

**AZLK Moskvich 427**

**Nissan Sunny**

**Oldsmobile Omega**

**MORRIS** (Great Britain) **1913**

After being a bicycle salesman, W. R. Morris (later Lord Nuffield) launched his first car—called the "Oxford"—in 1913, in the city which gave the vehicle its name. At first these cars were built with parts taken from other makes. When Morris began producing his own parts, the increase in production permitted him to lower his prices. Morris cars soon swept the market and the firm set the sales record of 54,000 cars in 1925. In 1927, Morris bought out Wolseley and, in 1938, Riley as well. In 1952, the British Motor Corporation was created from the merger of Morris and Austin; this led to a more rational process of production for the two firms.

**MOSKVICH** (Soviet Union) **1947**

The first Moskvitch was really a prewar Opel Kadett, since the assembly line of that car had been carried off lock, stock, and barrel from Germany to Russia; the 1956 model broke away from the Opel line, though; and the 1958 model "407" was highly modified, and offered in sedan, taxi, ambulance, station wagon, and delivery van versions. The 1968 model was changed even more and showed the Soviet interest in foreign markets. An unusual variant of the Moskvich was the "Scaldia" sedan, assembled in Belgium by the Sobimpex company on a Russian chassis and with a British diesel engine by Perkins.

**NISSAN** (Japan) **1934**

Set up in 1934, Nissan continued to make the Datsun, brought out when the company decided to produce more powerful models. In 1966 Nissan absorbed Prince Motors. It is the second largest Japanese firm producing automobiles, after Toyota, and in 1972 turned out 1,864,244 cars.

**NSU** (Germany) **1905**

This company began producing cars after winning a good reputation for its bicycles and motorcycles. Its first vehicle was built on license, followed a year later by that of its own designers. In 1907, NSU got interested in the production of low-displacement models; the period after the First World War saw it win many sports awards; and after the Second World War there was an important development in production with the appearance of the Wankel rotary engine, mounted for the first time on the two-seater version of the "Prinz Sport." With Audi, NSU is part of Volkswagen.

**OLDSMOBILE** (United States) **1896**

The first experimental vehicle built by Ransom Eli Olds (a three-wheeled steam machine) dates back to 1891. This was followed six years later by a one-cylinder gasoline model with a calash-type body.

After turning out some electric cars, Olds built his famous "Curved Dash" model, the world's first mass-produced car, forerunner of Henry Ford's building techniques. The prototype of the small Olds was saved from the fire that destroyed the plant in 1901 and was an immediate success. Even though it was a light two-seater for urban use, it carried out some epic runs, such as the 1903 San Francisco–New York marathon.

In time, the Oldsmobile models began to increase in power and that tendency continued after the firm went over to General Motors in 1909. After the Second World War, Oldsmobile took the lead in GM with its technical innovations, among them the famous "Hydramatic" automatic shifting.

**OPEL** (Germany) **1898**

When the Opel brothers decided to enter the field of car making, they were already famous for their bicycles and their sewing machines. Their first step was to buy the production rights of the Lutzmann Company, but the first car made was not successful. In 1902, Opel and Darracq reached an agreement that lasted until 1909; it stated that Opel was to import the chassis on which to assemble its cars in Germany. Opel was very active in sports car racing and won more than a hundred victories in 1905 alone. Until 1911, it was one of Germany's greatest automobile manufacturers, with a large range of models. In 1928, it became the largest German car manufacturer.

Between 1923 and 1924 the firm set up an assembly line to produce cars in the American way, the first German factory to do so. In 1921, General Motors became the chief shareholder in Opel. During the 1930s, the company led all others in Europe in the number of cars produced. The year 1935 saw the birth of the "Olympia," the first car with an all-steel, load-bearing body to be mass produced on a large scale. After the Second World War, the assembly line of the "Kadett" was dismantled and transferred to the Moskvich in the USSR. The new "Kadett," produced in the Bochum factory, came out in 1962.

**PEUGEOT** (France) **1889**

The Peugeot family began making bicycles in 1885 and four years later produced its first three-wheeled steam vehicle, with the collaboration of Léon Serpollet. On the suggestion of Emile Levassor, steam engines were given up for gasoline ones, and engines built on a Daimler license were employed. In 1891, a Peugeot carried out the first long race made by a gasoline-driven vehicle: the route from Beaulieu-Valentigny to Paris, and then on to Brest. The firm is also given credit for having consigned the first gasoline-engine car to a customer in France. Peugeots have always taken part in sports racing, with many successes to their credit.

A general aesthetic revolution took place in Peugeot cars from 1936 on. In 1950, the firm absorbed Chenard-Walcker and continued to produce its small van under the Peugeot name. It also held a good number of Hotchkiss shares. In 1974 it became a Citroën associate.

**PLYMOUTH** (United States) **1928**

The first Plymouth appeared in 1928, was a sedan, and cost $725. It replaced the preceding Chrysler and was a serious challenge to the hegemony of Ford and Chevrolet in the cheap car field.

**Opel Kadett Coupé**

**Peugeot 104**

**Plymouth Valiant**

**Pontiac Firebird**

**AMC Gremlin**

**AMC Matador**

**Reliant Rebel 750**

**Renault 6 TL**

After the Second World War, Plymouth evolved exactly like the other brands belonging to the Chrysler Corporation, while Buick took over its third place in the ranks of American car production. The models of the 1960s were far different from the traditional family sedans made in the past, and the firm helped launch the Chrysler group's "compacts" with its "Valiant," the lines of which showed its European inspiration. In recent years, Plymouth, like Ford and Chevrolet, for that matter, has aimed mainly at complete penetration of the low- and medium-powered market, presenting a large range of models for all tastes.

**PONTIAC** (United States) **1926**

This firm is a branch of General Motors and one of the American car makers that produces the widest range of models, from cheap cars to luxury and sports vehicles. In 1954 it replaced Plymouth in fourth place on the list of the builders with the largest production in America. After the late 1950s, it and other well-known American names, such as Plymouth and Mercury, worked at increasing the power of their products.

**PORSCHE** (Austria–Germany) **1948**
(see p. 203)

**RAMBLER** (United States) **1902–1913; 1950**

The original Rambler took its name from the bicycles made by Gormully and Jeffery, who also owned a factory at Coventry in England at the end of the last century. The first Rambler had a typically American line (1902) and its success put the firm—along with Oldsmobile—among the pioneers of automobile mass production. The Nash Motor Company, which took over from Jeffery, pulled out the name "Rambler" again in 1950 for the first American compact. Thanks to the Rambler, Nash sales increased greatly.

In 1954, after the merger that led to the creation of the American Motor Corporation, some of these cars were sold under the name of Hudson. After 1958, all the A.M.C. products were known as Ramblers, forerunners of the period of the "compacts"—and followed by Ford, Chrysler, and General Motors.

**RELIANT** (Great Britain) **1952**

This company was founded in 1935 by T. L. Williams to relaunch production of the three-wheeled Raleigh truck, which after 1939 had an Austin Seven engine modified by the firm. Its first car, the "Regal" was born in 1952. The first four-wheeled car was announced for 1962, and was designed in collaboration with Sabra Autocars of Israel. This vehicle was a two-seater sports model with a Ford Consul engine, and had a varied reception. Reliant also produced other "Sabra" models, and specialized in cheap cars made in limited numbers in developing nations.

**RENAULT** (France) **1898**
(see p. 125)

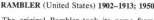

**ROLLS-ROYCE** (Great Britain) **1904**
(see. p. 170)

**ROVER** (Great Britain) **1904**

This famous bicycle factory began making conventional three-wheeled vehicles in 1903. The first four-wheeled vehicle appeared in 1904 and was driven by an interesting engine made by E. W. Lewis. In 1920, the firm again made a small, cheap car—like a cyclecar—and sales continued to increase until 1925, while the price went steadily down. It was produced in Germany on a Peter-Moritz license. Rover cars have always taken part in racing meets and won quite a few. In 1933, Rover began to produce medium-power cars of high quality, a policy it still follows. In 1950, it turned out the first car driven by a gas turbine engine, the result of research carried out during the Second World War. Rover still produces high-class cars and cross-country vehicles, the first of which, the "Land Rover," dates from 1948. The company became a branch of the British Leyland group in 1967.

**SAAB** (Sweden) **1950**

Saab began experimenting with cars during the war and presented a prototype to the press in 1947, but production did not start until 1950, with the "92," a car with a quality road holding that made it a favorite in meets held on the highways. Later models also took part in rallies. Saab has conducted experiments with sports cars and fast touring cars for many years, while continuing mass production of sedans and station wagons, all with front-wheel drive.

**SABRA** (Israel) **1960**

"Sabra" is a kind of cactus, the national emblem of Israel. This firm—officially called "Autocars," while "Sabra" is the name given to the models produced—was developed with the collaboration of the British Reliant company and at first used Ford parts. Among the first Sabras there was a sports car exactly like the British "Reliant." Today it produces vehicles with plastic bodies, partly on a Reliant license and partly on license from other companies.

**SEAT** (Spain) **1953**

The major Spanish automobile company specialized in the production of Fiat models on license. In 1974, it presented for the first time a car that differed from those made in Turin: the "133."

**SIMCA** (France) **1935**

This company was founded by Henry Pigozzi in November 1934 to produce Fiat cars on license for the French market in plants that had belonged to Donnet. Simca made a reputation for itself even outside of France, due to the success of the special versions made by Amédée Gordini, who continued building racing cars for the company until 1951. Simcas have won many rallies.

In January 1957, the firm reached a total of half a million cars sold, a figure that reached one million in 1960. Simca took over French Ford in 1954. In 1958, Chrysler became a majority shareholder in Simca, and the majority one in 1963; by 1967, the five-pointed star of Chrysler could be seen on the entire Simca output. The firm became Chrysler France in 1970. In 1968, the millionth Simca "1000" left the assembly line; in that same year, the company reached fourth place in the classification of French car producers, after Renault, Peugeot, and Citroën.

**SKODA** (Czechoslovakia) **1923**

One of the most important industrial complexes of the Austro-Hungarian empire; after the First World War it became Czech. The group made its debut in the automobile sector with production of the Hispano-Suiza on license. In 1925, it took over the Laurin & Klement plant in Mlada Boleslav, where it began turning out cars based on the earlier Laurin-Klement models. In the 1930s, the coupé version of the "Popular" won many victories in sports car races, including the Monte Carlo Rally. Skoda is one of the two automobile industries in Czechoslovakia (the other is Tatra) and also has the highest production rate. At the moment, its catalogue contains only models with a four-cylinder rear engine.

**STEYR** (Austria) **1920–1940; 1957**

After the First World War, the Steyr arms factory entered the automobile field. The first model (1920) was designed by Hans Ledwinka and had great success. In 1925, after a period in which rather large cars were turned out, Steyr set up an agreement with Austro-Daimler and thus began the production of popular cars. These inexpensive models with streamlined, load-bearing bodies sold very well. After the war, the Austrian firm did not go back to its own cars; it assembled Fiats, especially the "500," with Steyr motors for the Austrian market. Fast versions of this car, sold as Steyr-Puch, have had many triumphs on the track.

**SUBARU** (Japan) **1958**

The Fuji Heavy Industries is one of the many that developed after the war from the former Nakajima plane factory. At present, it turns out a wide range of products, such as planes, railroad equipment, buses, scooters, Subaru cars, and trucks.

**SUNBEAM** (Great Britain) **1899–1937; 1953**

John Marston's tin-goods factory first built bicycles as well, then produced its first car prototype in 1899. The first model to be mass produced was the Sunbeam-Mabley, a small car with its wheels set to form a rhombus.

Sunbeam's golden age began in 1909, when Louis Coatalen left Hillman and joined the firm. The car he designed won many races. In 1920, the company merged with Talbot and Darracq to form the S.T.D. group. At that time, Sunbeam produced sports and racing cars, and won the world ground speed title five times, from 1922 to 1927. The normal cars produced by the company at that time were well made, even if performance was not exceptional.

Rover 2200 SC

Saab 99 LE

Autocars Carmel

Seat 127

Simca 1100 Special

Skoda 110 L

Subaru Rex

Sunbeam Alpine

Rootes took it over in 1935. The Sunbeam name came to the fore again in 1953, with a two-seater sports version of the Sunbeam-Talbot "90." This car and those that followed won many racing victories. Chrysler became the major stockholder of Sunbeam in 1967.

**SUZUKI** (Japan) **1961**

Apart from its highly successful motorcycles, Suzuki also makes low-power cars. The first utility model turned out, the "Suzulite," dates from 1961. Suzuki is one of the many Japanese automobile companies that originated in the textile trade.

**TATRA** (Czechoslovakia) **1923**

Originally, Tatra was the continuation of Nesselsdorf. The first real Tatra came out in 1923 and was far different from earlier Nesselsdorfs. The "11" type, designed by Hans Ledwinka and destined for success, was based on earlier Tatra models. Even though this car and the one that followed were not planned for racing, they won first and second place in the 1925 Targa Florio. The 1934 type "77," with its typically streamlined body, was considered a classic.

After the Second World War, the plant was nationalized; and now it concentrates mainly on industrial vehicles and railroad carriages, although the catalogue still offers large rear-engine cars.

**TOYOTA** (Japan) **1936**

The prosperous Toyota textile company began to get interested in automobiles in 1935, and turned out the "A1" prototype. In the years that followed, production concentrated on a sedan and a touring car, the body of which vaguely resembled the Chrysler "Airflow" model. Toyota is at the moment Japan's most important automobile company, with a production (in 1972) of 2,087,133 cars.

**TRIUMPH** (Great Britain) **1923**

This successful motorcycle factory presented its first three-wheeled vehicle in 1903, but twenty years passed until its first four-wheeled car appeared (designed by engineer Ricardo). But Triumph made its name in England and abroad with the 1928 "Super 7." In 1936, the firm separated automobile from motorcycle production, while, from the following year on, the cars got heavier and Triumph engines replaced those of Coventry-Climax. The early 1950s saw the first successful generation of sports cars, with streamlined bodies. The "TR2" of those years had success in competition, and many Triumphs were exported to the United States. In 1961, Triumph joined the Leyland group. With its present range of models, the firm aims at the same section of the market as in the 1930s—the field of fast sports cars at competitive prices.

**VAUXHALL** (Great Britain) **1903**

This naval equipment factory, founded by Alexander Wilson, built its first American-style car in 1903. It produced racing cars as well as a cheaper model, like Sunbeam, in 1922. The last real racing Vauxhalls came out for the 1922 Tourist Trophy. Vauxhall was taken over by General Motors in 1925; the first GM-style machine appeared in 1928. After becoming part of GM, the British firm switched to the production of cheap, popular cars.

Suzuki Fronte

Tatra 613

Toyota Publica 1000

Triumph Spitfire Mk 4

Vauxhall Magnum 2300

Vauxhall Victor 2300

Volvo 144

Wolseley Six

**VOLKSWAGEN** (Germany) **1936**
(see. p. 202)

**VOLKSWAGEN-PORSCHE** (Germany) **1969**

The company founded by Volkswagen and Porsche for selling the central-engine model "914." See PORSCHE.

**VOLVO** (Sweden) **1927**

Founded under the direction of Assar Gabrielson and with the financial support of the SKF ball-bearings firm. Its first car, the "P4," while fairly low-powered, was well-built and sold well. In the 1930s, the Swedish company produced a series of solid cars for family use, not unlike the American machines of the day. In 1944, it made a small sedan, the "PV444," the first Volvo to reach a market outside of Sweden and establish the bridgehead that created the firm's reputation for solidity. It was produced in successive versions until 1965. Model "122" came out in 1956, but it was the "144" of 1967, more than any other, that strengthened Volvo's prestige throughout the world. Volvo engines have also been adopted by Facel Vega and Marcos.

**WOLSELEY** (Great Britain) **1899**

The first Wolseley prototype was made in 1895 by the firm's general manager, Herbert Austin. The first four-wheeled model came out in 1899 and took part in the 1900 "Mille Miglia"; it served as a basis for all the models that followed, and was the starting-point for all the cars designed by Austin and built by Vickers for the next six years. In 1914, the firm headed the national list for cars sold. Austin also had the Wolseley participate in racing. After he resigned from the company, the Wolseleys were designed by J. D. Siddeley and were called Wolseley-Siddeley. In 1927, the firm was taken over by Sir William Morris (Lord Nuffield) and the new owner developed the overhead valve technique, also used in the Morris and the M.G. In 1930, Wolseley produced, for the first time in England, a really cheap six-cylinder car.

The 18 hp model came out in 1937 and was also used by Scotland Yard; this was the first Wolseley to find favor with the police force, and the preference lasted through the later six-cylinder models, down to the 1960s. Morris and Austin merged in 1952, and their production was unified as a result. Wolseley is now a partner with Austin in the British Motor Corporation and produces luxury versions of the Austin and the Morris.

# INDEX

[*Numbers in boldface (***101***) refer to illustrations.*]

## A


Ackermann, 43
Adler, 53
Agajanian Special, **101**
Agajanian Willard Special, **101**
Agnelli, Giovanni, 30, **72, 73,** 204
Aintree, circuit of, 95
Albion, 69
Ales, M., **178**
Alessio, Marcello, **73**
Alfa Romeo, 57, 77, **85,** 87, 92, 95, 161, 211, 214, 237, 239
AR 51, **190**
Giulia, **234**
Giulietta, **223, 234**
GP P2, **87, 88**
GP P3, **88**
GP type A, **89**
RL Super Sport, **86**
RL Targa Florio, **87**
type 158, **88, 89**
type 159, 88
6 C 1500 Super Sport, **87**
6 C 1750 Grand Sport, **89**
6 C 2500 SS, **162**
8 C 2300, **89**
8 C 2300 Monza, **89**
8 C 2900 B, **233**
20/30 ES, **86**
24 HP, **86**
33, **88**
33/3, **97**
40/60 HP, **86**
1750, **239**
1900, **211, 223**
2500, **200**
Allison, Jim, 98
Alvis,
12/50, **134**
Saladin, 192, **193**
Saracen, **193**
Stalwart, **194**
TC 108, **222**
American Bantam Company, 184, 190, 191, 194
American Red Ball Special, **100**
Andretti, Mario, 88, 98, 214
Angeres, 104
Ansaldo, 142, 188
Apperson, **66**
Archdeacon, 80
Arfons, Art, 103, **105**
Armored cars, 192, 193
Alvis Saladin, **193**
Alvis Saracen, **193**
Austro-Daimler, **192**
Bianchi machine-gun car, **192**
Bussing Nag Puma, **193**
Ford M8, **193**
Rolls-Royce A.T.P., **192**
Argyll, 53
Ariel, 53
Armstrong-Siddeley, 69
Ascari, Alberto, 214
Ascari, Antonio, 87, 92
Aster, **74**
Aston Martin, 76, **134, 161**
1922, **83**
A.T.V., **191**
Auburn, **138,** 161, 162
Speedster, **142**
type 6-66, **68**
Audi-NSU, 239
Austin, 133
A 40, **224**
18/24, **120**
Pram, 118
Seven, 133, 188, 191
Austin, Herbert, **67, 78,** 133
Austro-Daimler, 186, 192, **192,** 203
type ADR 6, **143**
Autobianchi, 237, 239
Autonacional Voisin,
Biscuter, 225
Auto Union, 76, 88, **91,** 93, 96, **161,** 163, 203, 224
DKW "Munga", **194**
Avus, circuit of, 91


## B


Baker, 33
Bantam, 133
BRC, **185**
Baracca, Francesco, 214
Baras, 104
Barker, **138, 170**
Barreiros, 207
Barry, John Richard, 183
Barsanti, Eugenio, **32, 33,** 36, 39, 74
Batter, 186
Belanger Special, **101**
Belond AP Special, **101**
Belond Exhaust Special, **101**
Benoist, Robert, 92, 94
Bentley, 76, **90, 170**
Continental, 209
Sport Saloon, **213**
Benz, **43,** 70, 80, 230
Coupe Milord, **69**
Ideal, **39**
Parsifal, **43**
Tonneau, **43**
Touring car, **43, 71**
Velo, **41,** 43, 71
Velociped, **37,** 43
Victoria, **39**
Benz, Karl, 30, **37,** 41, 43, 47, 69
Bend und C.ie Rheinische Gasmotoren-Fabrick, 43
Berliet, **120,** 163
Bernardi, motorcycle, **40**
tricycle, **40**
Bernardi, Enrico, **40,** 41, 74
Bianchi, 53, **131,** 192
S5 type Viareggio, **142**
60/70 CV, **192**
Biondetti, 88
Birkigt, Marc, **123,** 129, 130, 146
Bleriot, 147
Bluebird, **104**
Blue Crown Spark Special, **100**
Blue Flame, 103, **105**
BMW, 133, 224, 239
Dixie, **213**
Isetta, 220
501, **208**
600, 220
1600, **237**
Bollée, Amédée, **27,** 30, 33, 51, **78**
Bollée, Léon, **51, 52,** 57, **67,** 68
Bollée,
Limousine, **57**
Bonnier, 96
Bordino, 92
Bordino, Virginio, **25**
Borgward Automobilwerke, 221
2300, 224
Isabella, 223
Borgward, Carl Friedrich-Wilhelm, 221, 223
Borzacchini, 92
Boulton, Matthew, 28
Bourmont, 80
Bouton, George, 51, 52, 58, **58**
Bowes Seal Fast Special, **99, 100**
Boyle Products Special, **99**
Boyle Special, **100, 101**
Brabham, 76
F1, **95**
1969, **95**
1970, **95**
Brabham, Jack, **92, 94,** 95, 96
Branca, Giovanni, 19
Brands Hatch, circuit of, 95
Brands Hatch, 6 Hours of, 96
Brasier, 80, 167
Breedlove, Craig, 103, **105**
Brennabor, 163
Brewster, **171**
Brilli Peri, 87, 92
Briscoe, 172
British Motor Syndicate, 68
British Leyland, 227, 239
Brivio, 87
Brixia Züst, 182
10 HP, 119
BRM, 76, **93,** 95
Brooklands Motor Course, **81,** 85, 90, **90,** 103
Brown, Samuel, **32,** 36
BTR 40 HP, 192
Bucciali, 163
Double-Huit, **141**
Buehring, Gordon M., **163**
Bugatti, 76, 92, **134,** 163, 171
Coupé type 44, **148**
Coupé type 50, 149
Gulinelli, 148
Royale, **148,** 149, 150
Sport type 57, **149**
type 30, **135**
type 35, **84, 135,** 149
type 43, **135**
1901, **57**
Bugatti, Ettore, 31, **123,** 128, 135, 148, 149, 163, 166
Bugatti, Jean, 149, **149**
Buick, 120, 121, 172, 174, 207
model C, **172**
model 10, **173**
model 50, **174**
Roadster, **121**
1903, **66**
1927, **138**
1936, **175**
Buick, David, **138**
Burd Piston Ring Special, **100**

Burgmeister, **143**
Burkhandt, **71**
Büssing Nag Puma, **193**


# C


Cadillac, 121, **140,** 159, 162, 175, **233**
  A, **65**
  Fleetwood Eldorado, **235**
  V 16, **158,** 176
  1902, **65**
  1908, **65**
  1928, **175**
Campari, Giuseppe, 87, 92
Campbell, Donald, 102, 103
Campbell, Malcom, 102, 104
Canestrini, Giovanni, 84, 92
Caracciola, Rudolf, 92, **164**
Carter, 121
Castagna, Ercole, **145, 160**
Castagneto, Renzo, 92
Caterina de' Medici, 17
Cattaneo, Giustino, 143, 144, 145
Ceirano 53, **73, 74**
  5 HP, **74**
Ceirano, Giovanni Battista, **72,** 75, 131, 166
Centro Storico Fiat, **73**
Chalmers, 207
Champion, Albert, 175
Chaparral, 77, **96**
Chapman, Colin, **94**
Chapron, **148**
Charron Girardot and Vaigt, 192
Chasseloup-Laubat, Gastone, **78, 103,** 104
Chenard Walcker, 53, **90**
Chevrolet, 98, 121, 122, 128, 155, **173, 174,** 175, **176,** 177, **177,** 213
  Baby Grand, **120**
  Bel Air, **221**
  Capitol, 142
  Classic Six, **174**
  Corvair, 218, **219**
  Corvette, **213**
  Impala, **219**
  Master, **176, 177**
  Royal Mail, **173**
  Suburban, **175**
  1929, **175**
  490, **174**
Chevrolet, Louis, **173**
Chiyoda, M, **179**
Chrysler, **150,** 210, 218, 227, 235, 237
  Airflow Sedan, **160**
  Imperial, **141**
  Roadster, **143**
  Six, **131**
  Valiant, 227, **227, 234**
  Windsor, **207, 210**
Chrysler, Walter Percy, 207
Cisitalia, 233
Citroën, 131, 155, 188, 226, 237, 238
  B 2 Cady, **154**
  B 2 Coupé de Ville, **155**
  B 2 Coupé Docteur, **154**
  B 12, **154, 156,** 223
  B 14, **154,** 155, **156**
  C 4, 155, **156, 157**
  C 6, 155, **155, 156**
  CX, **239**
  DS 19, **222,** 226
  GS, **238**
  ID, **222**
  Petite Rosalie, **85**
  Sahara, **191**
  Trèfle, 155
  2 CV, **208**
  5 CV, 127, 157
  7 CV, 155
  8 A, **156**
  10 HP type A, 154, **154,** 155
  11 CV, 155, **156**
  15 CV, 155, **157**
  15 AL, **156**
  22, 155
Citroën, Andrée, 127, 129, 131, 154, 155
City and Suburban, **62**
Clark, Jim, **94,** 98
Clermont-Ferrand, 82
Cobb, Cohn, 103, 105
Collins, Peter, **92**
Colombo, 88, **89**
Colt, 114
Columbia, **62,** 65
Consolidated Motors, 122
Cooper, 77, 92, 95
  Climax, **94,** 96
  Mark IV, 92
Cord, 159, 234
  L-29 1930, **138,** 161, **161**
  810, 162, **163**
  812, 162, **163**
Cord, Errett Lobban, **138, 152,** 153, 161, 162
Cortese, Franco, 214
Cosworth, 96, **97**
Crane, Henry M., **129**
Crane Simplex model 5, **129**
Crossley, 69
  19,6 CV, **130**
Cugnot, Nicolas-Joseph, **22,** 23, 25


# D


Daf, 239
  Daffodil, **235**
  44, **235**
Daimler, **37, 48,** 49, **49,** 50, **72,** 74, 81, 82, 150, 192
  Conquest, **222**
  Motorcycle, **42**
  Motorkutsche, **38,** 42
  Open Tourer, **67**
  Paul Daimler, **70**
  Phaeton 1897, **42**
  20 HP, **123**
  Vis-à-vis 1893, **42**
Daimler-Benz AG, 164, 224, 239
Daimler, Gottlieb, 30, 34, **38,** 41, 42, 47, 69, 70, **159,** 164
Darracq, 53, 57, 87
  9½ HP, **56**
  type N, **56**
  V8, **131**
Darracq, Alexandre, **56,** 57
Dat Car, 178
Datsun, 133, **178**
Décauville, **52,** 57
De Cristoforis, **32,** 74
De Dietrich, 135, 149
De Dion, Albert, 30, 51, 52, 55, 58, 68, 81
De Dion Bouton, 33, 51–54, **54,** 55–58, 67, 80, **124,** 192
  Coupé Docteur, **53**
  Populaire, **54,** 55
  Steam wagon, 58
  Vis-à-vis 3½ HP, 54, **58**
De Dion Bouton & Trépardoux, 58
Delage, 53, 55, 76, **99,** 163
  D8, **141**
  1913, **82**
Delahaye, 76, 163
  Break 1896, **51**
  Competition, **90**
  V 12 type 145, **163**
  1909, **51**
Delamarre-Debouttevillе, **36,** 41
De Palma, 98
De Paolo, 87
De Prandieres, 80
De Prandieres-Serpollet, 80
Derham, **151**
De Rivaz, Isaac, 35
De Rochas, Beau, 39
De Soto, 207
  Suburban, **211**
D'Ienterens, 231
Diesel, Rudolf, 30, 69
Dixie, 133
DKW Meisterklasse, **208**
Dodge, 225, 234
  Coronet, **211**
  Royal, **220**
Dodge Brothers, 230
  Dodge, Horace, 22
  Dodge, John D., 150
Doriot, 80
Dort, 122
Dragster, 229
Dubois, 80
Duckworth, Keith, 96
Duesenberg, **99, 138,** 150, **152,** 161, 162, 171
  A, **150,** 153
  J, 150, **152,** 153
  J Beverly, **150**
  Mason, **74**
  S J, 150, 153, **153**
  Special, **98, 99**
Duesenberg, August, 152
Duesenberg, Frederick, 152
Duncan, 68
Dune buggy, 228
Dunlop, John Boyd, 31, 67, 186
Durant, William C., 120–122, **121,** 128, **138,** 172, **173,** 174, 175
Duray, 103, 104
Dürer, Albrecht, 15, **18**
Duryea, **62**
Duryea, Charles Edgar, 30, **62,** 65, 66
Duryea, Frank, **62,** 65, 66


# E


Eagle, 76
Eagle-STP, **100**
Edgeworth, Richard Lovell, 183
Ehrhardt, 192
Eldin, 50
Eldridge, Ernest, **103,** 104
Electromotion, **62**
Elmore, 121
Empress, 53
Enrico, **73**
Evans, 186
Ewing, 121
Eyston, 103, 105


# F


Faccioli, Aristide, **72, 73,** 75
Fagioli, 87, 88, 92
Fangio, Juan Manuel, 88, 214
Fargo, 207
Farina, 87, 88, **168, 231**
Farman, 147
Fender, Guillaume, 186
Ferrari, 77, **89, 94,** 95, 214
  125 F1, **216**
  125 GT, 214
  125 S, 214, **216**
  156 F1, **217**
  158 F1, **216**
  166 S, **214**
  206 Dino, **217**
  212 Export, **215**
  246, **94**
  246 F1, **216**
  246 P, **217**
  250 Europa, **215**
  250 GT, **214**
  250 LM, **215**
  250 TRS, **216**
  275 GTS, **215**
  290 MM, **217**
  312, **97**
  330 P2, **216**
  340 S, **215**
  342 America, **214**
  365 GTC 4, **215**
  375 F1, **217**
  375 MM, **216**
  400 Superamerica, **215**
  410 Superamerica, **215**
  500 F2, **217**

500 Superfast, **214**
625 F1, **216**
750 Monza, **217**
Ferrari, Enzo, 87, 92, 95, 97, 166, 214
Fiat, **72, 73,** 74–76, 80, **103,** 130, **131,** 155, 166, 167, 187, 188, 192, 204, 205, 237, 239
Autocarretta 1014, 187, **187**
Campagnola, **190**
Grand Prix, **80**
Grand Prix type 804, **81**
Grand Prix 1924, **84**
Super-Fiat, **129**
Zero, 204, **204**
3½ HP, **73,** 75
6/8 HP, 204
8 HP, 204
16/24 HP, **73**
18 BL, **182**
24/32 HP, **74**
75 HP, **81**
100 HP, **81**
124, **236**
125, **236**
128, **238**
500, 206, **206, 211, 237**
501, **129,** 204
502, 204
508 Balilla, **162,** 205, **205**
508 C, **206**
508 S Mille Miglia, **205**
509, 205
514, **187,** 188, **205**
518 L Ardita, **160**
520 Coupé, **131**
600, 206, **206, 220**
850, **226**
1100, **233**
1400, **201**
1500, **162**
2000, 195
S 57/14 B, **81**
S 74, **81**
S 76 Mefistofele, **81**
Fittipaldi, Emerson, **94**
Flint, 122
Florio, Vincenzo, 83, 84
FMR Tiger 500, **224**
Fogoli, Claudio, 167
Ford, 76, 80, 96, 97, 120, 123, 128, 131, 133, 155, 159, 172, 174, 175, 177, 184, 185, 188, 191, 194, 205, 209, 218, 227, 239
A, **108,** 112, 115, **115**
Anglia, **201, 213**
Custom, **210**
Fairmont, 227, **227**
Falcon, 218, **219, 227**
Gaz A, 115
GPW, **185**
GT 40, **94**
K, **108, 112**
M8, **193**
Museum, 73
Mustang, **234**
N, 112
Quadricycle, **109**
S, 108, 112
T, **108,** 109, **110, 112,** 114, 115, 119, 128, 133, 172, 177, 189, 202, 230, 232
Taunus, **225**
Thunderbird, **221,** 234
999, **102**
Ford, Henry, 30, 51, 59, 64, 65, 66, **102, 109,** 110–114, 119, 121–123, 128, 139, **140,** 155, 172
Ford, Henry II, 96, 97, 199, 205
Ford, William, 110
Foyt, 98
Frazer Nash, **135**
Frontenac, **98**
Fuel Injection Special, **100**


# G


Gabelich, Gary, 103, **105**
Gabriel, Fernand, 82
Gallieni, 126
Gangloff, **149**
Gasmotoren-Fabrik Deutz, **35,** 42
Gautier, 80
Gaz Pobieda, **208**
General Motors, **66,** 120–122, **138,** 159, **171, 172,** 172–175, **173, 174,** 177, **179, 183,** 199, 207, 209, 215, 221, 234, 239, 240, **240**
Giacosa, 202
Giffard, Pierre, 80
Gilmore Speedway Special, **99**
Glas Isaria, 224
Goggomobil, 221, **222**
TS 400, 220
GMC, **177, 183**
Goliath Werke Borgward, 221, 223
Pioneer, 213, 221
1100, 223
Goodwood, circuit of, 95
Gordon Bennett, **80,** 82, 84, 85
Gordon Bennett, James, 82
Gordon England, **132**
Graber, 222
Graham Paige, 159
Grand Prix of France, 85, **135,** 154
Grand Prix of Italy, 94
Gray, J.S., 112
Green Monster, 103, **105**
Grégoire, **232**
Grégoire, Jean-Albert, **90**
Grimaldi, Father, 14
Guiet, **146**
Guinness, K. Lee, **103,** 104
Gulf Mirage, **96**
Gurney, Goldsworthy, **23,** 28


# H


Hakayosha, 179
Hancock, Walter, **25**
Hanomag, 188
Kommissbrot, **213**
Hansa-Lloyd, 221
Hashimoto, Masagiro, 178
Hautsch, Giovanni, 19, **19**
Haynes-Apperson, 66
Haynes, Elwood, 65, 66
H.C.S. Special, **99**
Healey, Donald, **90**
Hero of Alexandria, **12,** 13
Hewland, 96
Hibbard & Darrin, **164**
Higham Special Babs, **103**
Hill, **24**
Hill, Graham, 98, 214
Hill, Phil, **95, 96,** 214
Hillman, 69
Hispano-Suiza, 55, 129, 130, 146
Alfonso XIII, **123,** 129, 146
Boulogne, **134**
1913, **82**
6 A Victoria, **146**
Holden 90, 227, **227**
Statesman, **227**
Honda, 77
Horch, 163, 188
type 853, **161**
Hotchkiss, 184
Hourgieres, 103
Hudson, **210**
Custom Commodore, **210**
Hulme, Denny, **97**
Humber, 53, 69
Hurtu, **52,** 57
Huygens, Cristiano, 25


# I


Ickx, Jackie, 214
Indianapolis 500, 85, 90, 98
International Scout 800, **190**
Invicta, **90**
Irvin, James, 240
Irving-Napier Golden Arrow, **104**
Isotta Fraschini, 130, 142–144
type fenc, **72**
type 8, **130,** 144, 145
type 8 A, **135,** 144, 145, **145**
type 8 B, 143, 144, **144,** 145
8 C Monterosa, **145,** 159
40 HP Landaulet, **72**
Issigonis, Alec, **198,** 235, 238
Isuzu, 239
Itala, **74,** 142
35/45 HP, **79**


# J


Jaguar, 76, **199,** 209, 235
D, **221**
E, **221**
MKV, **209**
XK-SS, **221**
XK 120, **93, 198**
2,4 liter, **223**
Jamais Contente, **102,** 103
Jano, 87, **87, 89**
Jeantaud, 43, **78,** 103, 104
Jeep, 184, 187, 194
Universal, **184**
Jeffery, 186
Jellinek, Emile, 70, **72**
Jellinek, Mercedes, 70, **72**
Jenatzy, **102,** 103, 104
Jensen, 69
Johnny Lightning 500 Special, **100, 101**
John Zink Special, **100, 101**
Jowett, 69
Javelin, **201**


# K


Kaiser-Frazer, **210**
Henry J, **210,** 218
Manhattan, **210**
1950, **210**
Keech, Ray, 105
Ken Paul Special, **100**
Kimber, Cecil, **134**
Kleyer, 53
Kraeutler, 80


# L


Lagonda, 76
La Grande, **151**
La Lorraine, 76, **90**
Lamborghini,
Espada, **238**
Lanchester, **38,** 69
Ten, **201**
Lancia, 131, 166, 237, 239
Alpha, **123,** 131
Appia, **212**
Aprilia, 134, 167, 168, **168**
Ardea, **200, 212**
Artena, **123,** 134, 167
Astura, **123,** 134, 167, **168,** 231
Augusta, 134, 167, **167**
Aurelia B 10, **209**
Aurelia GT B 20, **209**
Dilambda, **168**
Fulvia, **235, 237**
Lambda, 131, 134, 166, 167, 231
Stratos, **238**

Theta, **123, 166,** 167
Trikappa, **167**
Lancia, Vincenzo, 75, 129, 131, 134, 166–168, 230, 231
Land-Rover 88 Regular, **189**
Langen, **35,** 39, 69
Lanza, Michele, 75
La Salle, **175**
Latil, 53
Lawson, 53, 68
Leader Card 500 Roadster, **100, 101**
Lea - Francis, 69
Le Baron, **151, 169**
Le Blant, Etienne, 80
Le Blant, Maurice, 80
Le Blant-Serpollet, 80
Le Brun, 80
Leland, Henry M., **65, 140**
Lemaitre, 80
Le Mans, circuit of, 90, 97
Le Mans, 24 Hours of, **85,** 90, **90,** 91, **93, 94,** 98
Lenoir, Etienne, **32,** 36
Leonardo da Vinci, **14,** 15, **15**
Letourneur and Marchand, **127**
Levassor, Emile, 47
Lewis, E. W., **68**
Leyland, **227**
Le Zebre type A, **118**
Limousine Body, 159
Lincoln, **140,** 159
Lloyd, 223
Arabella, 223
LP 300, 221
LP 400, 221
LP 600, 221
Locomobile, 85
Locomotive Rocket, 28
Loewy, Raymond, **201**
Long Island, circuit of, **81**
Lotus, 77, **94,** 95, 96
Ford, 98, **100**
25, **94**
49, **94**
72, **94**
Loughead, Malcolm, 123
Lunar Roving Vehicle, 240, **240**
Lunokhod, 240, **240**
Lutzmann, 69, **70**
4 HP, **70**
Lutzmann-Opel, **70**
Lycoming, **138, 161,** 159, **163**
Lyons, William, **161**


# M


Machaux, 80
Maggy, Aymo, 92
Malatesta, Sigismondo Pandolfo, 15
Mallory Park, circuit of, 95
Mancelle, **27**
Mannesmann, 163
Marchand, 53, **75**
12/16 HP, **75**
Marcus, Siegfried, **34,** 39
Marmon, 159, 162
Wasp, **98**
8/69, **142**
Martina, brothers, 75
Maserati, 77, **92,** 238
1500, **84**
Masetti, 87, 92
Mason, 122
Massimino, 88, **89**
Mathesius, 19
Matra, 77, 96, **96**
Matteucci, 32, 39, 74
Maxim, Hiram P., 65
Maxwell, 207
14 HP, **75**
Maxwell-Briscoe, 121
Mayadex, 80
Maybach, 163
Zeppelin, **159,** 163
Maybach, Wilhelm, **35, 38,** 42, 69, 70, **72, 159**
Marzotti, Franco, 92
McLaren, 77, 95, **97**
McLaren, Bruce, **97**
McRobic, 68
Mercedes Benz, 77, 80, **85,** 88, 92, 93, 95, 164, 188, 202
Flying Dutchman, **81**
Grosser Mercedes, 164, **165**
Simplex, 70, **72,** 73
SS 38/250, **164**
Stuttgart 200, **165**
W 25, **85**
130 H, 164, **165**
150 H, 164
170, 164
170 H, 164, **165**
180, 164, **224**
190 SL, **224**
220, 164
240 D 3.0, **238**
260 D, 164, **165, 238**
300, 164
300 S, **213**
300 SL, **213**
380, **160**
540 K, **165**
1915, **98**
Mercer 35 T, **120**
Merosi, Giuseppe, 86, 87
Merzario, 88
MG, **134**
A, **212**
Magnette, **225**
Midget TF, **212**
TC, **212**
TD, **212**
TF, **213**
Michelotti, Giovanni, **227**
Mille Miglia, 87, 92
Miller - Hartz Special, **99**
Miller Special, **99**
Million - Guiet, **126**
Minerva, **140**
Mirage, 77
Mitsubishi, 184, 239
A, **178**
Modena, circuit of, 91
Monroe, 76, **99**
Monte Carlo, Rally of, 90, **90,** 91
Montlhéry, circuit of, **85,** 91, 155
Monza, circuit of, 91
Morgan, 69
Morris, 231
Bullnose, **134**
Eight Series E, **198**
Mini, **224,** 226
Mini-Moke, **191**
Minor, **198, 235**
Morris, W. R., **134**
Mors, **78,** 82
Moskvitch, 211
401, **211**
Moss, Stirling, **92,** 94, 95, 97, 214
Mulliner, **132, 171, 209**
Murphy Special, **99**
Museo dell'Automobile, 23, **40, 54, 73**
Museo Storico della Motorizzazione Militare in Rome, **58**
Museum of Science and Industry, **40**


# N


Nag, 163
Napier, 69
Nash, 186
Rambler, 218, **218**
Nash, Charles W., 121
National, **99**
Nazzaro, Felice, 92, 166
Nesselsdorf, **39,** 159
Präsident, **39**
Neubauer, 92
Newburn, John Clayton, 186
Newby, Arthur, 98
Newcomen, Thomas, **22,** 26
Newton, Isaac, 19, **19**
Nissan
Datsun, **208**
70, **179**
Noc Out H. C., **101**
Nordhoff, Heinz, 202, 211
NSU, 224
Prinz Sport, **225**
7/34 PS, **143**
Nürburgring, circuit of, 91
Nürburgring, 1.000 Km., **96**
Nuvolari, Tazio, 87, 88, 92


# O


Oakland, **66,** 121, **173, 174,** 175, **176**
Obéissante, **27**
Ohio Electric, 33
Ohta,
Cabriolet, **179**
OS, **178**
Oldsmobile, 121, **139,** 172, **173**
Autocrat Touring Roadster, **121**
Curved Dash, 64, 66
Limited, **173**
Sportsman's, **174**
Toronado, **235**
Touring 45 A, **128**
88 Super, **213**
1940, **175**
Olds, Ransom Eli, 64, 66, **139,** 172
OM, **119,** 188
Alcyone, **142**
Autocarretta model 1014, 188
Opel, 53, 57, 80, 239
Admiral, **162**
Darracq, **70**
GT, **238**
Kadett, **158, 162, 211**
Kapitän, **162,** 224
Laubfrosh, **213**
Olympia, **158**
Rekord, **224**
Züst 10 HP, **70**
4 HP, **70**
1914, **122**
1917, **128**
1925, **131**
Otomo, 179
Otto, Nikolaus Klaus, **35,** 39, 69, 74
Oulton Park, circuit of, 95
Overland, 120


# P


Packard, 53, **128,** 159, 169, **169**
Light Eight, **163**
model C, **128**
Six, **121**
Twelve, **169**
Twin Six, **128**
12 HP, **75**
110, 159, 169
Packard, James Ward, 169
Panhard & Levassor, 34, **35,** 42, **46,** 47–50, 56, 80, 81
Covered body, **48**
Dog-Cart, 47
Dos-à-dos 1891, **48**
Dyna, **212**
EBR, 192
Panoramic, **158**
Sport Skiff, **128**
Tonneau 1899, **49**
1933, **160**
Panhard, Louis-René, 30, 47
Papin, Denis, 19, **22,** 25, 26
Parsons, Ben, 234
Pavesi, 187
Pecori, 26
Peerless, 53, 162
Périn, 47
Perkins, 172

Pescarolo, 88
Peterson, 88, **94,** 214
Peugeot, 34, **35,** 42, 49, 50, **50,** 51, 80, 81, **99, 140, 141,** 235, 238
Bebé, **123,** 135
Double Phaeton, 50
2-seat quadricycle, **48**
Vis-à-vis, **48, 49**
2½ HP, **49**
203, **200**
204, **237**
403, **222**
1912, **80**
Peugeot, Fréderic, 49
Peugeot, Jean-Pierre, 49
Phébus, 53
Pierce-Arrow, 53, 159, 171
Great Arrow, **71**
Motorette, **71**
Silver Arrow V 12, **143**
type 80, **135, 138**
Pintacuda, 87
Pioneer, **227**
Plymouth, 207, **207**
Barracuda, **234**
Coupé 1950, **211**
Suburban, **210**
Valiant, 218, **218, 227**
Pontiac, **174, 176**
Pope, 66
Pope, Albert A., 65
Popp,
7 HP, **71**
Popp, Lorenz, **71**
Porsche, 77, 95, **95,** 203, **203**
Carrera, **95**
356 B/1600, **203**
906, **95**
908, **95**
911 Targa, **203**
917, **95, 96**
Porsche, Ferdinand, 57, **91,** 164, **164,** 189, 202, 203, **203**
Prinetti & Stucchi, 135, 148

# Q

Quad, 186, 187

# R

Radley, **129**
Ramelli, **15**
Rameses II, 13
Rapi, Fabio Luigi, **145,** 159
Ravel, Joseph, 36
Renault, 53, 56, 83, 195, 230, 237, 238
Dauphine, **220, 225**
Floride, **225**
Fregate, 211
F.T., **195**
Juvaquatre, **200**
Marne taxi, **125**
Monaquatre, **127**
Monastella, **127**
Nerva Gran Sport, **127**
Nervasport, **127**
type A, **124**
type C, **124**
Torpedo, **125**
Touring Sedan, **125**
3, **224**
3½ HP, **54**
4, **200, 220,** 225
4 L, **224**
5 TL, **239**
6, **238**
40 CV, 56
Renault, Louis, 31, **54, 55,** 55–57, 125, 127
Reo, 121, **139**
Flying Cloud, **139**
Resta, 98
Revson, Peter, **97**
Ricordi, 53
Rigoulot, 80
Riley, **201**
Rindt, **94**
Ring Free Special, **99**
Rislone Special, **101**
Roochet, 53
Rockelman, Fred, 234
Rodriguez, 214
Roger-Benz, 69
Roger, Emile, **37,** 80
Rolls Royce, **68,** 135, **138,** 150, 161, 170, 171, **171,** 239
A.T.P., **192**
Continental, **129**
Phantom I, **138,** 170, **170, 171**
Phantom III, **171**
Phantom V, **221**
Silver Cloud, **221**
Silver Ghost, **68,** 135, **170**
Silver Shadow, **236**
Silver Wraith, **209**
Rolls, Charles Stewart, **68,** 134, 135, 170
Rollston, **151, 153**
Rootes, 207
Rose, 98
Rosemeyer, 92
Rosengart, 133
Rover, **68,** 69, 227, 235
8 HP, **68**
75, **212**
Royce, F. Henry, **68,** 128, 134, 135, 170, 171
Rumpler,
Tropfenwagen, **230**
Rumpler, Edmund, **230**

# S

Saab, 239
Sala, Cesare, **130, 144**
Salamano, 92
Salomons, David, 57, 68
Sanesi, 88
Sarazin, Edouard, 47
Satta, 88
Savery, Thomas, **22,** 26
Scat, **74**
Scott, David, 240
Scotte, 80
Seat, 239
Segrave, Henry, 103, **103,** 105
Selden, George B., 59, 63, 65, 112, 113
Serpollet, 33, 49, **78,** 80, 104
Shaw, 98
Shaw-Gilmore Special, **100**
Sheraton-Thompson Special, **100,** 101
Silverstone, circuit of, 95
Simca, 209
Ariane, **226**
Aronde, **209, 226**
Rallye 2, **226**
Vedette, **226**
1000, **226**
Simms, 192
Simplex Piston Ring Special, **98**
Sivocci, 87, 92
Sizaire-Naudin, **82**
Skoda 1101, **208**
Skriner, 53
Sloan, Alfred P., 122, 128, 175, 177
Société des Voiturettes Système Léon Bollée, 57
Sommer, 88
Snetterton, circuit of, 95
Spirit of America, 103, **105**
Spyker, 186
SS 100, **161**
Standard, **212**
Vanguard, **208**
8, **212**
Stanley, 33
Stars, 122
Stewart, Jackie, **97**
Steyr, 164, 203
Storero, 166
STP Oil Treatment Special, **101**
Stuart, Lewis-Evans, **92**
Stuck, 92
Studebaker, 169, 207
Champion, **201**
Electric, **69**
Garford, **69**
Lark, 218, **219**
20, **120**
Stutz, **141,** 159
DV-32, **158**
8 Club Coupé, **141**
Stutz, Henry C., **158**
Sumida, 179
H, **179**
Sunbeam, **103**
350 HP, **103**
Sunoco-McLaren, **100**
Surtees, John, 95, 214
Swallow Sidecars, **133**
Szisz, 83

# T

Takuri, 178, **178**
Talbot, 57, 77
Talbot-Darracq, 76
Tanks, 195
A7V, **195**
Churchill, **195**
Mark I, **195**
PKW, **195**
Renault F.T., **195**
Sherman, **195**
Targa Florio, 83, 87, 98
Tatra, 39
87, **159**
Taylor, F. W., 114
Temperino, **130**
Terry, Eli, 114
Thomas Flyer type 35, **80**
Thomas, Parry, 103, 105
Thorne Engine Special, **101**
Thruxton, circuit of, 95
Thunderbolt, **105**
Torricelli, Evangelista, 25
Toyokawa, Masaya, 179
Toyo Kogyo, 239
Toyota, **179**
AB, **179**
Land Cruiser, 191
Trabant, **226**
Tracta Gèphi, **90**
Tremulis, Alex, **221,** 234
Trépardoux, Jean, 51, 52, 58, **58**
Trevithick, Richard, **24,** 28
Trevithick, Vivian, **24**
Triumph, **198**
TR 2, **208**
1800, **198**
Trossi, 87, 88
Tucker, 224, 226
Tucker, Preston, 225, 226, 234
Turrell, 68
Tydol Special, 98
Tyrrell, 77, 86
1971, **97**
Tyrrell, Ken, **97**

# U

Uchiyama, Komanosuke, 178
Unser, Al, 98
Unser, Bob, 98
Ur Banner, 10, 11
Usines Perfecta, 57

# V


Vaccarella, 88
Vacheron, 80
Valturio, Roberto, **14,** 15
Vanderbilt Cup, 85
Vanderbilt, William K., 85, 103, 104
Varzi, Achille, 87, 88, 92
Vauxhall, 76, 235
  Prince Henry, **122**
  1910, **82**
  1914, **83**
Verbiest, Ferdinand, 14, **14**
Vespa 400, **220**
Voisin, 55, 150, 163
  Biscuter, 147
  C 23, 147
Voisin Frères, 147
Voisin, Gabriel, 147
Volkswagen, **188,** 189, 211, 218, 224, 228, **228,** 238, 239
  Beetle, 218, 228
  Scirocco, **202**
  type 166, 188, **188,** 189
  type 82, 188, 189
  1302, **202**
  1600 TL, **235**
Volta, Alessandro, 34, 35
Volvo, 239
  144, **235**
Von Guericke, Otto, 25
Von Liebig, 39


# W


Wagner, 87
Wagonette, 75
Wanderer, 163
Wartburg 1000, **236**
Watt, James, **22,** 25, 26, 28, 34
Welleyes, **72, 73,** 75
Weymann, **127, 147, 148, 153,** 231
Wheeler, Frank, 98
White, 33, **118**
  type 0, **118**
  1912, **121**
White, Lee Strout, 115
White Triplex, **104**
Whitney, 114
Wilkinson, Joseph, 36
Wills-Sainte Claire, 130
Willys, John N., 120
Willys Overland Motor, 184, 190, 191, 194, 207
  Jeepster, **188**
  MA, **185**
  MB, **185**
Wimille, 88, 92
Wimpff and Son, **38**
Winton, 66, **128**
Winton, Alexandre, 66
Wolseley, **67,** 69
  6 HP, **67**
  1904, **78**
  1100, **236**
Woods, **41**
Wright, 147
Wynns's Friction Proofing Special, **101**


# Y


Yoshida, Shintaro, 178


# Z


Zborowski, **103**
Zeppelin, **159,** 163
ZF, 96
Zündapp Janus, 220